HENRY PONSONBY

Margery H. Moorwood

November 1944.

Ri)-

HENRY PONSONBY

QUEEN VICTORIA'S
PRIVATE SECRETARY

His Life from his Letters

BY

HIS SON

ARTHUR PONSONBY

(LORD PONSONBY OF SHULBREDE)

" Don't knock.   Come in."

LONDON

MACMILLAN & CO. LTD

1943

PRINTED IN GREAT BRITAIN
BY R. & R. CLARK LIMITED, EDINBURGH

TO

MY SISTER

AND

MY BROTHER

CONTENTS

ILLUSTRATIONS

INTRODUCTION

MY father's letters and papers were preserved by my mother until her death in 1916. Subsequently additional and more official correspondence was added and eventually the accumulated mass of material came into the possession of my eldest brother (Major-General Sir John Ponsonby) five years ago. He consulted me as to what should be done with such a quantity of original documents : should they be deposited in safe keeping and left for future generations to deal with ? Should some expert biographer be entrusted with them ? Or should a son, who could draw on his memory and understand things which might be obscure to strangers, sift and arrange the papers and perhaps in time put together in book form the life and work of Queen Victoria's Private Secretary ? After much deliberation we decided on the last alternative and the cases were removed to my house.

When they were unpacked I found that they consisted of 117 boxes, each containing 150 to 200 letters, 12 bound books of early letters, not to mention a memorandum book, diaries and a number of packets of unsorted papers. The arrangement of the material in a manageable form alone took some months of the time I could spare. The task I had undertaken appeared far more formidable than I expected. While I knew at once that less than one per cent of the papers would actually be used for quotation or reference, they would all have to be perused and most of them carefully read. I found that my second brother Fritz (Lord Sysonby) had sorted and roughly arranged according to date the more official letters received by my father, some of which are quoted in Chapter XIV, and I was inclined to think that, had he been spared, he himself would have undertaken the task now entrusted to me and would of course have been far better qualified to perform it. I was conscious that my equipment for designing anything in the nature of a biography out of all this material was meagre. On the other hand, as one of a family for years closely associated with the Court, many of the people mentioned were known to me, and I was fortunate in having my sister's and my brother's memories to help me in catching echoes from the past. I myself had had opportunities of contact with the Queen when I was a boy ; and service as Private Secretary to a Prime Minister and a fairly long political experience in both Houses of Parliament came in useful. Political histories and biographies of statesmen could be consulted for episodes of over fifty years ago.

The mass of correspondence shows that my father and mother were keepers and not destroyers of letters. There may be no particular intention or merit in either practice. But posterity is grateful to those who do not destroy their papers because in addition to the few or many documents which may have historical significance, a number of letters describing the day's doings, referring to unknown people or recording trivial events, have the cumulative effect of giving the atmosphere, domestic or professional, and revealing the character, the disposition and even the passing moods of the writer. There emerges from the perusal of the bundles of letters a salient fact which throws light not only on Henry Ponsonby's character but on his career. He was a quite exceptionally punctual correspondent. In the age of telegrams, telephones, typewriters and wireless, the art, as it may well be called, of letter-writing has largely fallen out of fashion. Letters which have special literary merit have been collected from the past and published. But when the writer aspires to no literary merit and just jots down, in almost diary form, impressions and events as they occur, there may be comparatively little to quote ; but there will be a fuller disclosure of personality than can be derived from letters written with an eye to publication.

My father's three chief correspondents were his mother, his brother and his wife. In the two former cases hardly a week passed without their receiving a letter from him until they died. In the last case not a day passed, when they were separated, without a letter, and indeed sometimes two, arriving from husband to wife in the course of the twenty-four hours. This punctuality was not an effort undertaken from a sense of duty, but is constantly referred to as a pleasure. He felt he was talking to her. I have regretfully found that most of the other side of the correspondence is missing. We may be sure he kept every letter she wrote. But during the twenty-one years of her widowhood while carefully preserving his letters she must have destroyed most of her own. In this respect too the greater part of the collection of letters received is one-sided as only occasionally was a rough draft of his letter kept.

Much that was regarded as important in the mid-nineteenth century may seem now in retrospect to be of little consequence and more remote than if measured by years because of the shattering events of the twentieth century. Those who have survived from the earlier period until today may have had their whole perspective dislocated and those who only read of the past may dismiss too readily a time of comparative calm as negligible. But no good historians make the mistake of weighing the importance of one period as compared with another. They may suggest that certain causes led to certain consequences. But they will never blame contemporaries for regarding with concern the events of their own day since the future for them must be a sealed book.

Nevertheless I have had to be on my guard lest interested absorption in so detailed a record of a life and career should distort my sense of proportion. I had in fact to keep in view not what interested me nor even what I thought important, but rather what objectively might be considered a view of a period of history from the inside, hitherto unrecorded yet worth recording, and the personality and career of the recorder.

When I began, interest in Queen Victoria was at its height. Collections of letters, biographies, plays and films were appearing in rapid succession after the centenary of her accession. Could there be anything more to be said ? I noticed however that while the earlier years of her reign were very fully dealt with, the long years of her retirement were very sketchily passed over with the assistance at times of a little fiction. Lytton Strachey indeed admits this in his well-known book : [1]

The first forty-two years of the Queen's life are illuminated by a great and varied quantity of authentic information. With Albert's death a veil descends. Only occasionally, at fitful and disconnected intervals, does it lift for a moment or two ; a few main outlines, a few remarkable details may be discerned ; the rest is all conjecture and ambiguity. Thus though the Queen survived her

---

[1] *Queen Victoria*, by Lytton Strachey (1921).

great bereavement for almost as many years as she had lived before it, the chronicle of those years can bear no proportion to the tale of her earlier life. We must be content in our ignorance with a brief and summary relation.

The concluding six volumes of the Queen's letters have done much to fill this gap and in my possession I found letters and papers giving almost daily details of this period. But with all the new material at my disposal I made up my mind at the outset that anything I might put together should not just be a supplement to the many biographical studies of the Queen but a life of my father, his career, his work and character, and more especially his method and the function he filled which owing to his extreme reticence had only been occasionally recognized in some of the reviews of the later volumes of *The Letters of Queen Victoria*.

I have made no attempt to give a consecutive history of public affairs during the twenty-five years of my father's service as Private Secretary, although the Sovereign and therefore her Private Secretary were naturally concerned officially with every incident, negotiation, legislative proposal and major appointment. A selection has been made of particular occasions on which he was consulted, was the transmitter of messages, the negotiator and adjuster of differences and the unrecognized author of settlements. I have borne in mind that stale politics make unattractive reading and that the conscientiously accurate chronological method in biography, while useful for students, may often miss the more psychological and individual aspects of character which are independent of dates or time. But in writing a life of Henry Ponsonby, the Queen necessarily had to come into the picture. In fact his job had to be fully described. His job was Queen Victoria. Seen by an attendant who for long periods was in daily personal contact with her and was able therefore to appreciate the more intimate and human side of her character, the Queen emerges still further strengthened in the reputation she has now gained in history. While already known characteristics may be no more than further emphasized, a fresher and more authoritative interpretation would seem to be given in cases where she may have been misunderstood.

The book contains no sensational revelations nor disclosures of secrets. Some legends are indeed disposed of ; and if there were any scandals, they were the last thing my father would have committed to writing. When he was puzzled or irritated he says so, when he recovered his spirits he says so and when he was depressed at his enforced separation from his wife he invariably says so. The letters are not composed in well-phrased literary style. They have no pedantic regard even for grammar. They are talk, an epistolary method for which he had a special talent ; pleasant to write and pleasant to read. In fact he followed the precept laid down by Dorothy Osborne who in one of her letters to Sir William Temple wrote : " All letters, methinks, should be free and easy as our discourse, not studied as an oration nor made up of hard words as a charm ". This did not interfere with his masterly command of telling argument in his official letters and reports.

Care has been taken so far as possible not to re-quote documents already published in books, although reference has been made to them when needed to explain the cause or the sequel of incidents incompletely dealt with in the letters. If there are persons connected with the Court or with the public life of the period who are not mentioned or if there are known events to which no reference is made, it must be remembered that my object has been only to use as material my father's collected and preserved correspondence and that I have made no research beyond this into easily available papers and books which might help to fill in every gap.

It is with respectful gratitude that I have received the gracious permission of His Majesty The King to publish some of Queen Victoria's communications to my father.

I must also acknowledge with thanks permission given by the following for the publication of letters or for helpful advice : Lord Bathurst, Lord Bessborough, Miss F. M. Biddulph, Lord Crewe, Lord Cromer, Duke of Devonshire, Lord Dufferin, Major G. Ellis, Lord Esher, Mr. A. C. Gladstone, Lord Granville, Lord Goschen, Lord Halifax, Lord Harcourt, Lord Knollys, Lord Linlithgow, Lord Lytton, Sir Ivor Maxse, Dowager Lady Mayo, Lady Mersey, Lady Oxford, Lady Reid, Lord Rosebery, Sir Odo Russell, Lord Salisbury.

Mr. Owen Morshead, librarian at Windsor Castle, read through the typescript and not only helped me to correct inaccuracies but made valuable suggestions and gave advice on the selection of illustrations. All papers of interest which remain have been handed over to Mr. Morshead for preservation in the royal library.

I am greatly indebted to Miss Nan Willson of Haslemere for her assistance in the somewhat prolonged work of typing and retyping. She has also rendered special help in correcting the proofs.

ARTHUR PONSONBY

Shulbrede Priory, Sussex
1942

Quotations from letters, unless otherwise described, are all from Henry Ponsonby's letters to his wife.

Queen Victoria's communications with many abbreviations and the broad black edge of her notepaper into which parts of some words run, have not always been easy to decipher. Illegible words are marked by dots within round brackets.

CHAPTER I

Henry Ponsonby's Father

IN 1815 on June 18 was fought and won a great decisive battle which changed the history of Europe and sealed the fate of Napoleon Bonaparte — the battle of Waterloo.

At the close of that day amid the débris of abandoned arms, scattered accoutrements, corpses of soldiers and carcases of horses, there lay on the deserted field the prostrate body of a young English Colonel of Dragoons. In him the spark of life was not yet quite extinguished. No more than thirty-three years old, the young officer writhed in mortal agony, seven times wounded and pinned to the ground by a corpse across his legs. Disabled in both his arms and losing his sword in a cavalry charge, he had been felled to the ground by a blow from a sabre ; pierced in the back up to his lungs by an enemy lancer who broke the silence in the scene of desolation with the cry, " *Tu n'es pas mort, coquin ?* " ; turned over, tossed and tumbled by the passage of two squadrons of cavalry over him, plundered by wandering stragglers, yet miraculously he was just alive. Owing to help from a passing officer who placed a knapsack under his head and quenched his burning thirst by a drink from a brandy flask,[1] he survived the night after lying for near eighteen hours prostrate, and was carried to the village of Waterloo in the early morning.

The charge he had led was undertaken entirely on his own initiative. Unable to reach his commanding officer, he decided then and there that there was not an instant to lose ; because he was convinced that if the French column in front of him gained more ground, it would be too late to stop them.

---

[1] On the appearance in the late seventies of a painting of this episode by Philippotaux (the French battle painter) it was discovered that " the passing officer " was Baron de Laussat, a young man at the time, not middle-aged as depicted by the artist.

So exclaiming " They must not be allowed to come further ! "
and with the cry " Come on, 12th ! " he dashed down the
field followed by his men. The charge was successful but the
leader of it fell. For many weeks his recovery was despaired of.

This wounded and shattered young officer, Colonel the
Hon. Frederick Cavendish Ponsonby, survived this fearful
experience and lived for another twenty years to marry and
have six children.

His eldest son, Henry Frederick Ponsonby, the subject of
this memoir, in the vast correspondence his position obliged
him to conduct, punctually dated every paper to which he
put his pen. But on his letters, instead of June 18, he always
wrote " Waterloo Day ". As a soldier himself he was no doubt
pleased thus to commemorate the great battle. But it was
rather as a son that he was legitimately proud to remember
the gallant part his father had played in that historic victory.

The family of Ponsonby [1] dates back to the thirteenth
century in Cumberland, where there is a village of that name.
Colonel Sir John Ponsonby (1609–1678) left Haile Hall where
the family resided, went over to Ireland and raised a regiment
of horse for service under Cromwell. His eldest son and
subsequently his descendants remained at Haile. Sir John
and his children by his second wife took up their residence in
Ireland. His son William was created Viscount Duncannon
and Lord Bessborough. His grandson Brabazon was the 1st
Earl of Bessborough. Frederick, the 3rd Earl, was Brabazon's
grandson and Sir Frederick Ponsonby's father. He married
Henrietta Spencer, daughter of John, 1st Earl Spencer.

Frederick Cavendish Ponsonby was born in 1783 and
brought up at Roehampton where his father, then Viscount
Duncannon, one of the Lords Commissioners of the Admiralty,
lived at that time. He and his elder brother John (afterwards
4th Earl of Bessborough) were educated at Harrow. He
entered the school in 1791 and remained there for seven years.
His mother showed her attention and affection for her sons
by constantly writing to them, specially when on her travels.
Lady Duncannon subsequently as Lady Bessborough is shown
in the published correspondence [2] with Lord Granville to have
been one of the most entertaining and engaging letter-writers

[1] *The Ponsonby Family*, Major-General Sir John Ponsonby.
[2] *Lord Granville Leveson Gower* (Private Correspondence).

of her day. But in these letters she confines herself to describing in the simplest language what may interest and amuse her little sons. A few of the boys' letters have been kept, written in a very large handwriting on ruled lines. In letters written from Harrow when he was about nine Frederick describes a game the boys had with " clay men and guns and swords " ; and he adds later, " the man that sells the soldiers to us thinks we are going to fight France ". " The man that sells the soldiers " was right ; and in less than twenty years little Frederick with a real (not a clay) sword was destined to spend the most arduous years of his life in that fight. Unlike his father and his brothers, Frederick followed the military tradition of the family, which had up to his day supplied at least a dozen members as officers in the army, including Major-General Henry Ponsonby who fought at Dettingen and fell at Fontenoy.

Frederick's military career started with a Cornetcy in the 10th Dragoons in 1800. He went through the various steps of promotion and by August 1807 was a Major in the 23rd Light Dragoons. In 1805 and 1806 he was at home in England. He was elected member for Kilkenny and sat from 1806 till 1826, and subsequently from 1826 to 1830 for Higham Ferrers. Although therefore an M.P. for twenty-four years there is only one reference in a letter to a vague intention to go to the House of Commons : 1810. " I think in December of doing my duty in Parliament " : and there is no record in Hansard of his ever having spoken. In most of these years he was occupied elsewhere. There is a little incident related by his mother Lady Bessborough which shows that Frederick was able to show decision as well as tact and courtesy in small matters. Describing Nelson's funeral she writes : [1]

> St. Paul's was wonderfully fine. Frederick was on guard in Charing Cross and came to great honour for his civility. Woronzow (the Russian Ambassador) has just call'd here saying he had only just discovered who the officer was to whom he and the other Foreign Ministers ow'd the having seen anything and that he empress'd himself to call and thank Cap. P. in all their names for his attention and *Courtoisie*. Think of their having compleatly neglected assigning them any places ! And when they were refused at St. Paul's and came in a body to see the procession they were rudely

---

[1] *Lord Granville Leveson Gower* (Private Correspondence).

stopp'd and Woronzow got into such a passion that had not
F. luckily come up at the moment I believe he would have
declared war in the name of Alexander. F. was shock'd,
said it was impossible his orders could extend to them and
ordered a party of dragoons to escort them ; meanwhile
sent to the D. of York and got them placed in St. P. *Vous
direz que je radotte mais j'ai fini.*[1]

Frederick Ponsonby served throughout the whole of the
Peninsular campaign. Most of the letters he wrote home to
his mother or his sister-in-law have been printed.[2] The
distinguishing feature of his reports of engagements is that
when he takes a prominent part, as he often does, he dismisses
it as if it were of no consequence. His account of the battle
of Talavera in 1809 is meagre as he says " You will have read
quite enough of it ". Fortunately in this case there are two
other accounts which tell us a great deal more.

An historian gives the following account : [3]

> The 23rd, under Colonel Seymour, rode wildly down into
> the hollow, and men and horses fell over each other in
> dreadful confusion. The survivors, still untamed, mounted
> the opposite bank by twos and threes ; Seymour was
> wounded, but Major Frederick Ponsonby, a hardy soldier,
> rallying all who came up, passed through the midst of Vil-
> latte's columns, and, reckless of the musketry from each
> side, fell with inexpressible violence upon a brigade of
> French chasseurs in the rear. The combat was fierce but
> short ; Victor had perceived the first advance of the English,
> and detached his Polish lancers and Westphalian light-
> horse to the support of Villatte, and these fresh troops coming
> up when the 23rd, already overmatched, could scarcely hold
> up against the chasseurs, entirely broke them. Those who
> were not killed or taken made for Bassecour's Spanish
> division, and so escaped, leaving behind 207 men and
> officers, or about half the number that went into action.

An officer of high military rank, who was importantly
engaged in that battle (Talavera), wrote concerning the
conduct of Major Ponsonby on that day :

[1] Ninety-three years later the young Captain's grandson married the Russian
Ambassador's great-great-granddaughter.
[2] *Lady Bessborough and her Family Circle*, edited by the Earl of Bessborough and
A. Aspinall, 1940.
[3] *The Peninsular Campaign, 1807–1814*, by William T. Dobson.

Ponsonby is my greatest comfort. He has behaved most gallantly, and is indeed a most excellent officer. He deserves particular praise for having, with *two* squadrons, kept in check *nine* French squadrons, supported by artillery and riflemen, during six hours.

In the bloody conflict, Major Ponsonby saw Lieutenant Richard Power of his own troop killed when they charged the French infantry. Actuated by the ardent feelings of friendship, he repaired the next day to the field of carnage, attended by almost the only sergeant of his regiment who had not been killed or wounded, to search among the slain for the corpse of his Lieutenant, and with his own hands (assisted only by his sergeant) performed the painful office of committing the body of his young military friend, in the field of battle, to an honourable grave.

Again at Barossa in 1811 he led his dragoons in a charge which though costly stopped the execution of a turning movement on the part of the enemy. He describes it in a letter to his mother written from Cadiz, of which the following is an extract :

I charged with the Cavalry and got a blow on the head and another on the arm, but of no sort of consequence ; indeed no blood was drawn, so that I have not even a claim to a place among the wounded. . . . I lost my horse in the field, not by a wound, but feeling a good deal exhausted by fatigue and the knock on my head, I got off and fell asleep ; when I awoke everything about me was gone. I am in great luck to have been in this business. . . . When I say I was hit, I tell you the simple fact, for I have often suffered more in a cricket match than upon this occasion ; a large pair of Whiskers saved any part of my face from a scar. I believe I can swear to the mark of a sabre and that is all ; and as to my arm, you will perceive it is rather invigorated than otherwise by my writing so much.

Lord Palmerston in a letter to Lady Melbourne wrote : " I am happy to tell you that Fred Ponsonby is safe. You may tell Lady Caroline [Frederick's sister married to William Lamb, later Lord Melbourne] that the charge of the 23rd was one of the most gallant things that ever was done."

In June 1811 Frederick was appointed to the command of the 12th Light Dragoons, having been assistant Adjutant-

General with the Cavalry since 1810. But in August, owing to a recurrence of fever, he was pressed to go home on leave. At first he refused as he looked on asking for leave as a disgrace. Wellington however ordered him home. So he landed in England in September and returned to the Peninsula at the end of December restored to health.

The series of Frederick's letters already published [1] need not be repeated here. They are mostly addressed to his sister-in-law Maria (Lady Duncannon). In them in addition to comments on the military situation he occasionally describes social entertainments, as when at a ball at Joseph Bonaparte's country house, " in waltzing *after* supper I got a tumble by sticking my spurs into a lady's gown and brought half Madrid down with me ". In October 1812 he was wounded again. He refers to it as " a little accident " and hopes his name will not appear in the list of wounded. His cousin Colonel William Ponsonby however, writing to Lord Bessborough, describes it as " a musket shot in the thigh ", but is reassuring in declaring " there is every reason to hope that he will be very shortly on his legs again ".

In 1814 Colonel Ponsonby was sent to communicate the news of the peace to the Marquis of Wellington at Toulouse. Lord Dalhousie wrote : " Colonel Ponsonby has requested to be the bearer of this letter : his activity assures me it will reach you sooner by him than any other person ". He rode the 150 miles in nineteen hours.

On the termination of the Peninsular War Colonel Ponsonby had the distinction of receiving two gold medals : one with two bars on which are inscribed VITTORIA and SALAMANCA ; the other a gold cross on the points of which are inscribed four battles in which he took part, BAROSSA, VITTORIA, SALAMANCA and NIVE.[2]

In March 1815 Frederick Ponsonby was in England and received orders to embark for the Netherlands " in consequence of Bonaparte's arrival in Paris ". He did not attend the Duchess of Richmond's famous ball in Brussels. But having heard that the enemy were advancing he was on the field at six o'clock in the morning.

---

[1] See *Lady Bessborough and her Family Circle*, Lord Bessborough and A. Aspinall (1940).

[2] Now in the possession of his grandson, Major-General Sir John Ponsonby.

The stirring events of military triumph and personal suffering on that day have been described. Lady Bessborough in a letter to Lady Duncannon writes from Brussels on July 18, 1815 :

> Frederick ought to publish his history like Byron's narrative as *Mon agonie de 24 heures*, for I believe so many horrible adventures and wounds never befell one individual in the same space of time, at least none that ever lived to tell it.

His sister, Lady Caroline Lamb, went out early in July and there are letters from her to her eldest brother which show her devoted affection for Frederick. She used to correspond with him during the Peninsular War and when she did not write often enough the reprimand came, " Tell Caro she is shabby ". There is a letter from William Lamb giving a full account of Frederick's condition.

There were other visitors in Brussels who were not sure that Lady Caroline's presence was very helpful to her brother. Lady Georgina Lennox, writing to Lady Georgiana Bathurst (July 3), remarks in the course of her letter :

> Lady Caroline Lamb is arrived to nurse her brother Col. Ponsonby who is doing very well, but she will hurt him I fear. The Surgeon told her the best thing she could do would be to hold her tongue ; in answer to her wishing to know if she had not better read to him all day.

Lady Bessborough accompanied her son home to England, landing at Dover on August 11, 1815.

Six years later in 1821, while he was in Florence with his father, Frederick wrote to his sister Caroline mentioning letters received from her son Augustus and commenting on one of her novels she had sent him :

MY DEAR CARO,
      We are all going on perfectly well here, the weather is very cold. We have this day had a letter from you, I hope you are much better in health, pray write often, you cannot think what a comfort it is to us all to hear from you. Augustus's letters are excellent, they tell us all the news, they are extremely pedantick which makes them more amusing, he speaks of the funds like an old stock jobber and of the state of the world like a worn out Politician.
      I shall give your book to William who we expect every

day, it is really very good, there are some inconsistencies :
the Lady's age must have been at least thirty at the earthquake.   You mention her coming to America before the
time of the taking of Portobello.   You must excuse my very
short letter.   My love to Maria, I do not write to her this
week.   My Father, Barbara and the Children are perfectly
well.

Florence appears to have been the beginning of a long tour
through Italy, of which he kept a very careful diary noting all
the pictures and monuments he saw in various towns right down
to Naples.   The voyage seems to have lasted over two years,
including calls at Tunis and the Morea and ending up with
Malta and Corfu.

There are a number of Sir Frederick's letters and memoranda written with his left hand on account of his wounded
right arm, and not always very legible.   But what seriously
detracts from their interest is that (unlike his son) he very
seldom dated his manuscripts and frequently omitted even the
name of the place he was at when he wrote.   In the case of
this diary however the writing is very neat though small and it
is dated throughout.

To go back to the year after Waterloo.   In August 1816
Colonel Ponsonby had sufficiently recovered from his wounds
to be entrusted by Lord Combermere on the Duke of Wellington's suggestion to conduct an enquiry with two other officers.
A Lieutenant had been beaten by an actor on the stage of a
theatre at Boulogne.   The Duke regarded this as " a disgrace
to the Army " and ordered an enquiry to be held as to whether
there was not ground for bringing the matter before a General
Court Martial.   The outcome of this little episode is not related.

It is not surprising that Frederick Ponsonby should have
been on intimate terms with the Duke of Wellington.   He had
an unbounded admiration for the military genius of the great
general and the Duke regarded with something like affection
the promising and reliable young officer.   It was during the
Peninsular War that an officer in one of the engagements was
guilty of an error for which he was so severely dealt with that
everyone considered it more than he deserved.   No one however dared approach the Duke on the subject till at last it
was suggested that Frederick Ponsonby was the only officer
who might make the attempt.   He did so and got the Duke to

listen. Wellington, or rather Wellesley as he then was, re-considered the case, pardoned the officer and thanked Ponsonby for having drawn his attention to it. In later years Ponsonby wrote out in a little red leather notebook " The Duke's opinions on various military subjects, being the substance of several conversations with him ". In one passage he writes :

> The Duke was always of the same opinion with Bonaparte that the art of war cannot be learnt tho' it may be assisted by studying the campaigns of great Generals and not the numerous theoretical opinions and writings on the subject . . . but when he (Bonaparte) speaks of Waterloo, he establishes theories and Maxims and proves that the Duke ought to have been beat according to the true principles of the art of War. But what is this art of war? Bonaparte says you fought with a *défilé* on your rear but Bonaparte fought the same battle with two in his rear. Bonaparte accuses him of twenty other deviations from the Principles but he, the Duke, won the Battle. What then becomes of the true principles of the art of war ?

Beyond military associations there was a close personal friendship between the two soldiers. We find, after Ponsonby was wounded at Santarem, Wellington insisting on his being moved to his own quarters. While we should like more of their conversations in these days, we get a characteristic glimpse of Wellington when Ponsonby writes :

> He was in the habit of coming into my room every day. He came one morning but did not say a word but continued walking up and down the room. I saw that something was on his mind. At last he went to the door and said on going out : " Poor old Cox was killed last night." He felt his loss very severely.

Frederick Ponsonby inherited from his mother recklessness in expenditure and play. He was not a good man of business. In his early days he ran into debt and on one occasion was helped out of " a great scrape " by Lady Bessborough who paid the bills. The passion for gambling was not uncommon in those days. But he had the rare capacity to cure himself of this weakness. This is shown by letters from the Duke [1] of which relevant extracts may be given. In the first one, dated December 4, 1821, he is writing to Lord Duncannon expressing

---

[1] *Lady Bessborough and her Family Circle*, Lord Bessborough and A. Aspinall.

condolences at Lady Bessborough's death and telling him he
had lately written to her. He then refers to the proposal that
Frederick should be sent to India :

> The subject of my letter to her and my object in writing
> to her was to suggest to her a mode of saving your Brother
> from going to India ; which from having been there myself,
> however lightly I may think of such a destination in the case
> of any other, is in his case a species of banishment, and I was
> anxious to avoid it for him if we could tye him up from Play.
> This last object was at one time effected, and I should think
> we might attain it again. You will be the best judge whether
> anything can be done in this way. If it can, I am perfectly
> ready to co-operate as his friend and old Commander ; and
> I would propose that we should send him either to India or
> elsewhere abroad at a later period when he would be higher
> in the service, and might be enabled from what he could
> receive to repay what might now be advanced for him. I
> have said nothing to him upon any part of this subject, and
> of course shall say nothing to anybody.

The second letter from the Duke, dated March 21, 1822,
is addressed to Frederick himself (although the name of the
recipient is suppressed in Wellington's *Despatches, Correspondence
and Memoranda*, where it is printed) :

> I cannot conclude this letter without urgently entreating
> you to recollect what it is that has obliged you to separate
> yourself from your family and friends and to quit the most
> advantageous and agreeable position that can fall to the
> lot of any man in England. I am afraid you can go to no
> part of the world whether near or distant in which you will
> not find means and opportunities of getting into similar
> scrapes ; and you may rely upon it that their only results
> will be to occasion fresh and increased regret to yourself,
> and sorrow to your family and friends and none more than
> to him who subscribes himself. . . .

In a letter to Wellington less than six months later (July 1822)
Frederick writes :

> With respect to play I am afeared few people would
> believe me when I say I have quite given it up but I feel I
> can speak confidently on the subject and if there is any
> faith in man I promise that your advice shall not be forgotten.

After Waterloo the Duke gave him the silver canteen he

MAJOR-GENERAL SIR FREDERICK PONSONBY K.C.B.

himself had used throughout his campaigns. This is still in the possession of the family. The Duke was godfather to Frederick Ponsonby's second son born in 1827, who was called Arthur after him.

Colonel Ponsonby was knighted as K.C.B., appointed A.D.C. to the King and received several foreign decorations. In 1825, having been promoted Major-General, he was given the command of the troops in the Ionian Islands, which had been placed under the protectorate of Great Britain by the Treaty of Paris, 1815, and in the following year he was appointed Governor of Malta, where he remained for ten years. In March 1825 he married Lady Emily Bathurst, daughter of the 3rd Earl Bathurst.

Passing through Paris on his way home on leave in 1831, he wrote to his brother-in-law, Lt.-Colonel the Hon. Seymour Bathurst, describing a dinner with Louis Philippe who had been elected the year before King of the French :

> Sep. 18, 1831
> We dined yesterday with the King. During dinner there was a charge of Cavalry in the street and after dinner loud cries of " *Mort aux Ministres* " who also dined at the Palace, during this the King and Queen were talking to us most amiably . . . turning round now and then and saying " *Ah ! Voilà encore l'émeute.*" The Riot was serious in some parts of the town and will probably be so again tonight and I cannot suppose it will occasion serious consequences. . . . There never was a King and Government who deserved the affection of the people of France more than the present. But there are several strong parties and the mob of Paris who would be glad to throw everything into confusion, and this state of things is assisted by the great commercial and agricultural distress. For the sake of the whole world we must hope the war fanaticism will be defeated.

Lady Emily writes on the back of this to her brother an amusing account of the fashions :

> *Chales* is the rage now in way of dress for everything, waistcoats, gowns, etc. It is a sort of cashmere with every sort of pattern, they often look like Chintze for furniture . . . the only smart thing that everybody in the streets, up to the Queen, wear are feathers, an old coloured gown with a Bonnet and feathers are constantly to be seen in the streets.

And in a further passage torn by the seal of the letter she discourses on ringlets (" some large ").

During his Governorship at Malta Sir Frederick showed firmness and judgment as an administrator. He devoted much time to effecting economies and in ecclesiastical matters gave just and sympathetic attention to both Roman Catholics and Anglicans. He made several improvements in the fortifications of the Island. There is a passage in a letter to Seymour Bathurst which shows his views on prison reform :

> I am far from thinking a prison should be a comfortable place, everything should be done for the health and reformation of prisoners but the prevention of liberty should be felt and the labour should be severe. Now in fact the Prisoner is as well fed as and does less real labour than the poor inhabitant of the country. . . . I want so far as it is practicable some system of separation to be devised by which the young or those under sentence of a short period, may be kept apart from the old hands.

On the social side we get a first-hand view from two eminent visitors. Henry Edward Fox (4th Lord Holland) writes in his journal :

> April 25, 1829. Gozo. Malta
> The house in which the General lives is extremely small. He and Lady Emily received me very kindly. They are living in great retirement and have carried with them none of the luxuries and very few of the comforts of life. They have only one servant, a Greek. The dinner was very unpretending and simple. We sat some time in the drawing room, the General smoking all the time. He is one of the simplest, most manly, unaffected men I know, with very good sterling sense, a sweet temper, and with the manners and experience of a man that has seen much of the world and has profited by what he has seen. The extreme patient good humour with which he submitted to all his sufferings during the battle of Waterloo and in his very slow recovery afterwards, are said to have been the means of carrying him through. The slightest irritability would have proved fatal. Since that day he has been unable to use the fingers of his right hand and now writes with his left ; but he contrives with singular ingenuity to wield a racket or indeed to clench anything with it. Lady Emily is just as she was before her marriage, very good humoured. The child [Melita] is the image of Lady Caroline Lamb, and bids fair, I think, to be as spoiled and as wilful. . . .

Malta. April 26, 1830

We breakfasted with Lady Emily. The General who had been up for hours remained smoking in the verandah. After breakfast he came and talked with us. He has acquired by his rapid rise no humbug and pomp of office but is just as free and open as I remember him fifteen years ago.

W. Meredith accompanied Disraeli on a visit to Malta later in the same year. He writes :

He [Dizzy] paid a round of visits in his majo jacket, white trousers and a sash of the colours of the rainbow ; in this wonderful costume he paraded all round Valetta, followed by one half of the population of the place, and as he said putting a complete stop to all business. He of course included the Governor and Lady Emily in his round to their no small astonishment. The Governor, a brother of Lady Caroline Lamb, was reputed a very nonchalant personage and exceedingly exclusive in his conduct to his subjects. Disraeli, however, was not dismayed and wrote to his brother as follows :

August 29th, 1830

Yesterday I called on Ponsonby and he was fortunately at home. I flatter myself that he passed through the most extraordinary quarter of an hour of his existence. I gave him no quarter and at last made our own nonchalant Governor roll on the sofa from his risible convulsions. Then I jumped up, remembered that I must be breaking into his morning and was off ; making it a rule always to leave with a good impression. He pressed me not to go. . . .

Ill-health obliged Sir Frederick to resign the Governorship in 1836. He received a letter from Lord Glenelg expressing the King's " entire and unqualified approbation " of his administration. He adds : " Nor can His Majesty forget that the sufferings by which your civil career is thus arrested, are the direct results of that career of Military Service which has given you so distinguished a place among the successful candidates for the approbation of your King and the gratitude of your country ".

In Malta a high stone column was erected to his memory. It was still there when Henry Ponsonby called at Malta on his way to the Crimea. But in a violent storm in 1864 it was unfortunately blown down. The base of the column with the inscription is still preserved.

Sir Frederick Ponsonby died suddenly in January in the following year, 1837. Arthur Ponsonby, his second son, refers to the event in the preface to his journal. It occurred in a wayside inn at Murrell Green (Hants) while the family were returning by travelling-carriage from Canford where they had been staying with Sir Frederick's brother, William Ponsonby (Lord de Mauley) :

> Henry, I and Lilly were the children and were just going to tea in a room up stairs, my Father and Mother being in a room down stairs and just going to Dinner, when we heard a scream and down stairs we ran. I remember it as if it was yesterday. Somebody stopped us at the Door of the Dining Room not before I remember looking in and seeing my Father leaning back in a chair close to the Fire. We were taken away and told our Father was dead. I believe he died of heart complaint, at any rate, it was awfully sudden. A messenger was dispatched to Canford and Lord de Mauley arrived next day to help my Mother in her troubles. The Body was taken to Canford and my Mother and us left next day for London, posting. We were too young to feel the great loss we had. . . . I remember our governess a Miss Edwards telling us not to observe or ask my Mother questions when we saw her with a Widow's Cap on.

The best eulogy of this distinguished soldier may be quoted in conclusion as it comes from an early and intimate companion : [1]

> In former days we lived much together. I have seen him in sickness, in danger, in difficulties, in prosperity, in society, alone, with myself — I may say in every situation in which man can be placed, and I never knew his beautiful disposition vary from that perfect state in which his gentle and noble mind had fixed it. He was without guile or any of the bad passions so common to other men. He was devoid of one particle of selfishness — he was gentle as he was brave, and brave as he was gentle — he blended the two to perfection — he was a proof that modesty is the handmaid of valour — his judgment was sound, his head clear, his heart the best that ever beat — but I shall never end praising him.

Lady Emily Ponsonby survived her husband for forty years. On each successive anniversary of Waterloo a deputa-

[1] *United Service Journal*, April 1837.

tion from the 12th Lancers waited upon her, bringing her a
bouquet of flowers up to the time of her death.

In selecting Henry Ponsonby's father for special mention,
instead of tracing his ancestry in all directions, the object has
been to give fuller recognition to the conspicuous services of
this distinguished soldier whose career is only touched upon
incidentally in military histories.   Account has also been taken
of the close resemblance between father and son, not in career,
but in character.   To pick out only one special characteristic
in both of them : each in his own sphere was constitutionally
incapable of blowing his own trumpet.

HENRY FREDERICK PONSONBY
(1825–1895)

Grandparents	Frederick, 3rd Earl of Bessborough	.	1758–1843
	Lady Henrietta Frances Spencer	.	1760–1821
"	Henry, 3rd Earl Bathurst	. .	1762–1834
	Lady Georgina Lennox .	. .	d. 1841

Parents
- Major-General the Hon. Sir Frederick Cavendish Ponsonby   1783–1837
- Lady Emily Charlotte Bathurst .   .   1798–1877

Uncles
- John William, 4th Earl of Bessborough .   1781–1847
- William Ponsonby, Lord de Mauley .   1787–1855
- Henry, 4th Earl Bathurst   .   .   1790–1866
- William, 5th Earl Bathurst   .   .   1791–1878
- Colonel Thomas Seymour Bathurst .   1793–1834
- The Rev. Charles Bathurst   .   .   1802–1842

Aunts
- Lady Caroline Lamb   .   .   .   1785–1828
- Lady Louisa Georgiana Bathurst   .   1792–1874

Brothers
- Lt.-Colonel Arthur Valette Ponsonby .   1827–1868
- The Rev. Frederick John Ponsonby .   1837–1894

Sisters
- Melita Ponsonby   1830–1895
- Julia Ponsonby   1831–1906
- Barbara Baring   1834–1918

Wife
- Mary Elizabeth Bulteel, d. of John Bulteel and Lady Elizabeth Grey   1832–1916

Daughters
- Alberta Victoria Montgomery   .   .   1862
- Magdalen Ponsonby   .   .   .   1864–1934

Sons
- Major-General Sir John Ponsonby   .   1866
- Lt.-Colonel Sir Frederick Ponsonby (Lord Sysonby)   1867–1935
- Arthur (Lord Ponsonby of Shulbrede) .   1871

CHAPTER II

From Birth to Marriage

HENRY FREDERICK, Sir Frederick Ponsonby's eldest child, was born in Corfu on December 10, 1825, while his father was in command of the troops in the Ionian Islands. His brother Arthur and his three sisters Melita, Julia and Barbara were born in Malta where Sir Frederick was appointed Governor in the following year, 1826. His brother Frederick was born posthumously in England.

Arthur, in some preliminary pages of reminiscence which preface a diary he kept regularly after 1849,[1] says little of his brother in the very early days. We only find that " Henry and I waylaid the dinner going in and coming out " of the dining-room at the Governor's palace. He describes himself as " rather spoilt and very much of a pickle ". On one occasion he " stuck pins into the calves of a consul who came in full dress to a Levée " till at last the visitors to the palace used to keep " a sharp look out " for him.

Some letters from two great-aunts show that Henry at the early age of about eight had begun to develop a practice which became specially characteristic of him for the rest of his life, namely that of being a punctual correspondent. The two old ladies, Lady Catherine and Lady Susannah Bathurst, were much touched by his attention to them, receiving as they did a letter from him " by every packet " from Malta. " You are an excellent correspondent," one of them writes, " and very kind in writing so constantly."

On settling in England after Sir Frederick had resigned the Governorship of Malta, the two boys first stayed with a tutor at Geneva, and were then sent to a school at Coombe Wood, Kingston. Arthur gives some particulars of this establishment, where the boys' studies, superintended by a large staff

[1] *Not published.*

of masters, seem to have been conducted on the intensive system, so that " at the end of the day we were tolerably confused having too many things to learn ". He relates the first parting from his brother :

I remember in 1839 Henry receiving a letter asking him what profession he would choose. We read it, I remember distinctly, under an old horse chestnut tree that stood at the corner of the lawn and the letter from M. [Lady Emily] suggested Sandhurst and a few months afterwards he went there. I remember I was home for the holidays when he was taken to Sandhurst and I cried, it being the first time I was separated from him.

One letter from Henry to his mother written from school remains. It shows that he early discovered how to use what was pleasant in order to avoid the unpleasant, with a frank disclosure of his intention :

To *Lady Emily Ponsonby*

Coombe Wood, May 27, 1839

MY DEAR MAMMA,
I was so very glad when I found that at last you were coming home again and that I was to go to you on Saturday next. You said you would settle about our coming home, may I put a word in for it. That is unless it would be inconvenient to you for us to come early that is I mean our early which is about 7, 8 or 9 o'clock and not your early for you are such very early people ; the reason of this is because I wish to skip a nasty lesson in the morning and I should also like to breakfast with you if I can, all this is if I can.

A letter received by Lady Emily from a friend gives the first description of her son :

April 29, 1840
. . . We were allowed the pleasure of having your dear Boy for two nights with us. He is indeed *very pleasing* and so gentlemanlike in looks and manners, with that " something " so attractive in the Ponsonbys — how shall I describe it ? extreme gentleness united to great manliness.

Henry remained at Sandhurst for about three years and gained a reputation for steadiness and diligence. " You have, my dear Ponsonby," wrote one of the authorities, " from your exemplary conduct, every claim to anything your Captain can

HENRY PONSONBY AS A BOY

grant you." The report in 1840 when he was fifteen ran : " Every one of the Masters speaks of Gentleman Cadet Ponsonby in very favourable terms for his uniformly good conduct, gentlemanlike manners, and general attention to his studies ; there is no doubt of his doing well by perseverance in the same course ".

From now on having left home he allowed very few days to pass without writing to his mother. While they were punctual his letters are of no special merit. He expresses no opinions and ventures on no criticisms. They are a simple recital of facts and events, travel notes and lists of people he meets. Lady Emily's letters also give little more than accounts of family doings. But her repeated and touching expressions of affection, " you are the greatest comfort I have ", " your dear self having been granted to me and been a blessing to me throughout ", show that in addition to her love for her son, she leant on him as a prop and an adviser and she found his reliability an unfailing support throughout her long widowhood.

A little episode when Henry was sixteen on his holidays is worth relating. A Waterloo banquet was held annually on June 15. His grandfather Lord Bathurst, who had been Secretary for War and the Colonies during the Peninsular War, was the only civilian who attended. His aunt, Lady Georgiana Bathurst, took the boy in the afternoon to the room laid out for the banquet. While looking at the decorations which included a bust of the Duke of Wellington, who should walk in but the Duke himself. Seeing Lady Georgiana he came round and spoke to Henry about his father, whom he well remembered.

When in 1844 Henry, who had received his commission as an Ensign in the 49th Regiment, was transferred to the Grenadier Guards, he was officially introduced to the Duke at the Horse Guards by Lord Fitzroy Somerset and " he said civil words to me on joining his regiment ".

There is a note in the volume of correspondence which concerns the time when he was quartered in London and describes his association with Holland House :

> Lady Holland took a fancy to me and frequently asked me to dinner. The company though small generally consisted of some of the leading men of the day : Lord J. Russell, Lord Ponsonby,[1] Colonel Fox, Mr. Luttrell, Mr.

[1] Ambassador at Constantinople and Vienna ; created Viscount 1839.

Macaulay, Lord Brooke, Dr. Babington, etc. One night I
sat between Charles Dickens and one of the Fitzwilliams.
Dickens was very silent in the general conversation but
talked to me quietly about his travels in America. One
night someone blundered about a story I happened to have
read that day. Lord John Russell trying to correct him
also got wrong. I said, " I think that is not exactly the
story." " Tell the story," said Lady Holland. So I told
it : Jerry White, Oliver Cromwell's chaplain, made love to
his daughter Frances. Oliver caught him one day on his
knees before her. Furious, he enquired what this meant.
White replied he was imploring her to soften the heart
of her obdurate waiting woman. Frances pretended this
fiction was true. Cromwell gave his orders and the Rev^d Mr.
White and the lady's maid were married there and then.
The relation of the story gave me a sort of sham literary
reputation. I got bumptious and cut in where I had best
have been silent. They talked of La Fontaine. " Did he
ever write anything besides his fables ? " I enquired. Lady
Holland smiled. The men were silent. Lord Ponsonby
said, " I will endeavour to answer the somewhat indiscreet
question of my kinsman," and proceeded to explain to me
the nature of the *Contes de La Fontaine*.

Henry Ponsonby's services to a succession of Lords-Lieutenant
of Ireland began in 1846 by his appointment as A.D.C. to
his uncle Lord Bessborough. He continued in the same
capacity to Lord Clarendon and was subsequently appointed
joint Private Secretary with the Hon. Gerald Ponsonby in
1850. He was A.D.C. to Lord Eglinton in 1852, Private
Secretary to Lord St. Germans the following year and finally
to Lord Carlisle in 1855. It may well be imagined that his
experiences in these nine years were a useful training for his
eventual work.

There is full correspondence in this period describing his
doings, his work, the political ups and downs, the social entertainments and the plays acted, of which he sometimes was the
author. For a holiday in 1852 he went off for a couple of
months' tour abroad. In Belgium he visited the battlefield of
Waterloo. He travelled on to Switzerland, Germany and
Italy, describing all sights and adventures in letters to his
mother. He kept a very bald diary in Dublin, and there is
also a punctual diary kept by Gerald Ponsonby describing
walks he and his fellow secretary took. The outstanding merit

of this particular diary, however, is the beautiful little drawings of old houses, churches, etc., with which he illustrated his entries both at home and abroad.

From all this a detailed almost daily account of events at the Viceregal Lodge could be constructed. But this would be out of all proportion to the space which must be devoted to the more eventful periods in Henry Ponsonby's later life.

Two testimonials from former chiefs may be quoted when he left Ireland to go to the Crimea. Lord Clarendon in a letter to Lord Panmure wrote :

> I wish to mention for the information of General Simpson that Henry Ponsonby is gone to join his Regiment and that I will answer for his being as good a Workman as any in that Peninsula. He was for 5 years my A.D.C. and assistant Private Secretary. . . . I know of no young man to be compared to him for intelligence, industry and trustworthiness. . . . Simpson may not be aware of what a valuable man he now has at his elbow.

Lord Carlisle in a letter to his wife wrote :

> It is a real misfortune to me that Henry Ponsonby my private Secretary is to go out to the Crimea immediately. He was not only a most delightful inmate of a family, with the most perfect temper and great intelligence, but his experience of affairs and of society during his residence here of 8 years made him invaluable as an adviser.

Before the break with his life in Ireland he was in very close correspondence with his brother Arthur, who had been through the Kaffir war and went out to the Crimea in 1854. The decision came in the following year that Henry should join his regiment and with alacrity he made his preparations and left England in July 1855. In a last letter to his mother expressing his sadness at parting from her he adds : " I have been looking forward to this all my life so am very happy to start on active service ". Interesting as his experiences in civil life had been, his highest ambitions lay in the life of a soldier.

He had had full information in letters from Arthur of the varying fortunes of the war, the hopes of an early victory, the false report of the fall of Sebastopol, the rumours, political changes, criticism of the generals, abuse of the French, mismanagement and delay and also a graphic description of the attack on the Malakoff and the Redan. Writing to Arthur, a few weeks before he himself left, Henry says, " Because we don't get a telegraph of a victory every day people get frightened and think all sorts of nonsense ".

Colonel Ponsonby disembarked in the Crimea on August 13. He was not destined for a clerical job as Lord Clarendon had suggested but joined his regiment, the Grenadiers, and found himself within ten days in command in the trenches. The account of how he passed the night of August 24 may be given in his own words :

The first time I had a command in the Trenches was with a working party in the advanced sap. On receiving the detail in the morning I went over to the Light Division to make arrangements about their parties, and then ordered the Guards working parties to parade at 7 the usual hour when it began to get dark. I posted my party in the 5th parallel where they lay down till it got dark enough for them to go forward and work. I then went to look for the Light Division party which I found. When I returned in an hour my Guards party were at work in the open in front of the Trenches. I joined them. We all spoke low as the Russians in the Redan were not 200 yards off. Ferguson and I urged the men to push on their work. Suddenly the moon came out. Some shots were fired at us and the men left off working. A cloud threw us into darkness again, but there was some little confusion caused by the shot, which had wounded one or two. Suddenly I heard a loud rush near me. Several men were on the ground. All rose again but one. He was killed by a round shot. I ordered the men to carry his body to the Trenches.

But grape now knocked down more. To continue working for the present was impossible and I desired the party to retire to the 5th parallel. An Engineer officer met me here and suggested I should set the men to work to deepen the Trench here which was too small to be useful. It was on limestone and chalk so that to cut through it was difficult, and as the cover was not 3 feet high the men had to work under difficulties. Suddenly I was knocked into a hole. 3 or 4 men fell upon me and a heap of stones and rubbish. For an instant my wind was bagged — and other men came to us and dragged us up — we were not hurt. I suppose a round shot had struck the parapet and had knocked it down upon us. I crept on to where Ferguson was and as I appeared in the moonlight quite white with the chalk he said I looked like the ghost of the Commendatore in *Don Giovanni*.

I now went to report my proceedings at the General's Bunk. Seymour S.F. Gds. was Com^g in our Trenches. He was troubled with the applications of the exhausted men who were waiting to be relieved, but in consequence of the move of the Highlanders were still on duty past midnight.

I had scarcely left Seymour when a shell burst very near me. One of the pieces knocked him down and the officers came to tell me he was killed and asked me for orders about the relief. I found afterwards that Seymour had been carried home stunned. To all applications I could only reply that they must stay where they were till the relief came. Seymour had been wounded on the back of his head. It was fearfully hot in the Trenches — and if one went out to the open one was pretty sure to get knocked over. I was horribly thirsty till a private of the 77th gave me a drink from his bottle. One soon gets accustomed to the sounds of the shot and shell — but the horrible noise of the rockets always startles one. From our right I could see there was a deal of fray in the French Trenches — and I could hear the shouts of the Russians who seemed to be making little sorties. When I returned to Ferguson I found him and Serjeant Hale firing at a form which they maintained was a Russian. But it did not move. I now got a message from a Colonel in the Line that as senior officer he had taken command and that I was to withdraw my working parties to the rear and there await further orders. This I did. While we all laid down near the first parallel I went up to the Gordon Battery which was occupied by sailors. Harry Keppel was here in high spirits. It was just drawing towards daybreak when he always gave the Russians a tremendous fire. This he began to do at once and received several Russian replies which however did no harm while I was in the Battery.

As day began to break I returned to my party and soon received directions to march home. It was the most lovely morning. I rode along with Carrick but he was too sleepy or tired to talk much. We got to Camp about 6 and I turned in for a couple of hours and was awoke by Arthur who had come to see if I was all safe after the night in the Trenches. The Sap we had begun was extended on the following night when the subaltern in command was killed.

There were more attempted attacks, long intervals of wearisome waiting relieved by the organization of games, cricket, rounders and even the performance of theatricals, and of course he was constantly riding about making inspections. In December he took up his quarters in one of the huts which had been sent out from England. In a letter he gives an amusing description of his abode with his tent lining as a canopy for his bed, a canvas ceiling over which he pasted *The Times* to keep out the wind, walls covered with illustrated papers and a chest of drawers without any drawers given him by Arthur from Sebastopol. After the snow and storms, the mud, discomfort and faulty organization during the winter, and the loss of many lives including some of his friends, negotiations for peace began, and towards the end of January the Russians accepted the terms without reserve and peace was concluded.

This is no place to survey the whole history of the war in which so many British lives were unnecessarily sacrificed. It may safely be said that no other campaign in which British troops took part was accompanied, not only at its termination but during the actual conduct of the operations, by so much political and military controversy, recriminations and bickerings as the Crimean War.

Colonel Ponsonby writing in his diary at the end of the year had no illusions as to the " glory " of the war in which he himself had been a participant :

> Out went 1856. When it first came we were at war. But Russia was exhausted and longed for peace. France was getting short of money. Her troops had been gloriously successful and she was for peace, so the Congress at Paris declared for peace. England was dissatisfied ; her last action was the failure at the Redan. She wanted more glory. Sardinia was dissatisfied. Russia tried to evade the terms of the treaty but France held all to their word. Then the English, dissatisfied with the war, began the abuse of their generals : Lucan, Cardigan, Airey, Lord Raglan, Simpson — all got a share. The friends of one general cried down another till at length, if all was true, our generals must have been cowards and traitors but the fault of this proceeding was found out.

He also wrote a memorandum on the command of the British forces :

> Lord Raglan may not have been the most able general, but no man could have been found who would more thoroughly have cemented the Alliance between the two Armies than he did. The French were under orders from home and so frequently attempted to plunge into absurdities that it required a skilful general to keep them straight. After Lord Raglan's death the command devolved on Simpson who was utterly unfitted for it.
>
> The Duke of Newcastle told me that when he went to see him he found Simpson seated at an empty table which only bore an inkstand and a pen, yet he declaimed loudly against the amount

of correspondence forced upon him. " How can I do anything with all these dommed papers I have to write ? "

Steel told me that the day before the attack — 7th Sept. — Pelissier sent to ask Simpson to lend him one or two English Battalions to join the French in their attack on the Malakoff. He did not require their assistance, he did not expect they would have much to do, but it was merely for the sake of being able to say that the English and French fought together. Simpson however declined.

Arthur Hardinge told me he was sent by Simpson after Codrington's men had failed at the Redan to ask Sir Colin Campbell if he would try it with the Highlanders, who were quite fresh, but Sir Colin refused as he thought the slaughter would be so great — and useless since the Russians could not hold it after the Malakoff was taken. Some Highlanders at night crawling over found the Redan empty.

Henry Ponsonby arrived back in England on July 1. On July 3 the brief entry in his diary states : " Went to London. Got some plain clothes. Shaved off my beard. Dined at the Grenadiers' dinner. Prince Albert and D. of Cambridge there."

Just after the Crimean War there are references in the correspondence, specially in Lady Emily's letters, to a proposal that her son should be given a command in India. The precise nature of the command does not appear but the fact that Colonel Ponsonby was a candidate for it is undoubted. A competing applicant was appointed and the incident passed without further comment as just one of the chances in the routine of army promotion. Examined in retrospect however with full knowledge of his subsequent career, the incident has some significance. For it can be seen that had Ponsonby received the appointment, his military ambitions would have been satisfied and his life would have been devoted to the career of a soldier while service at Court would not have come his way. These ambitions were not only inherited but were fostered by his deep admiration for his father's record. As it was in December 1856 Prince Albert, whether or not owing to what he saw and heard of the young A.D.C. during his visit to Ireland with the Queen in 1853 when Lord St. Germans was Lord Lieutenant, appointed Colonel Ponsonby as his Equerry and so Court life began, although he still remained on the active list of the army.

He did not forget to write to his mother as soon as possible when he took up his duties :

To *Lady Emily Ponsonby*

Windsor Castle, Feb. 2, 1857

When I arrived here on Saturday I found that Franco Seymour had gone leaving me word of what was to be done. I found my room a very comfortable one and after a short time had a visit from Mortimer West [1] who was formerly in the Grenadiers who showed me the way to dinner and all I had to do.   Saturday night was a household dinner as the Queen and Prince Albert dined alone. The household dinner consisted of the Duchess of Wellington, Miss Macdonald and Miss Cavendish, Lady Caroline and Miss Barrington, General Grey, Colonel Biddulph and West and Lord Dufferin, most of whom I knew. On Sunday morning we went to Chapel. The Queen gave me a smiling bow. Prince Albert shook hands. Afterwards we skated, the Prince of Wales was there and his tutor Mr. Gibbs. The Prince of Wales is one of the nicest boys I ever saw and very lively and pleasant. We skated after lunch as well and Dudley [2] came and when we came back to the Castle the Prince of Wales asked us to his room — such a comfortable room and very full of ship models.

The Dinner was rather awful considered in a social light tho' excellent considered in the gastronomic light. I found myself at a corner next a young lady in Black who I knew was a foreign princess and on the other side Grey who being deaf and the pauses at dinner long I was unable to ask who she was, whether it was etiquette for me to speak first to her, what I was to call her, and what language she discoursed in. By fish time it was evident she didn't intend to begin so I made a bold attempt in pure British and ended my observation with a " mum ". It succeeded and we got on very well. I afterwards ascertained she was Princess Feodore Hohenlohe. After dinner is very awful. We all stand jammed against a wall and our observations are necessarily few and of an uninteresting nature.

Today we have been skating all day. There was a council. I saw Lord Spencer — and Lord Granville who congratulated me — also Castlerosse [3] — and Lord E. Bruce.

Riding with Prince Albert, accompanying him at functions, on travels abroad and at various royal ceremonies were the

---

[1] Afterwards Lord Sackville.   [2] Colonel, afterwards Lord de Ros.
[3] Afterwards Earl of Kenmare.

ordinary routine of an Equerry and are dull to read about. In
1857 there was the usual commotion over a royal wedding
when the Princess Royal was married to the Crown Prince of
Prussia. Ponsonby dreaded being attached to a German
Prince. " I am getting up the German Princes ", he writes ;
" there are a wonderful number of them " : and later : " I
look after the Prince Consort as usual and shall not have to
lead about the Prince of Sedlitz Stinkinger. I hear H.R.H.'s
trousseau is very splendid but she has some odd things such as
twenty pair of indiarubber clogs and two drawers of sponges."

In May 1859 he notes a little episode which shows that
personal animosities in politics were not deep in those days
even during a general election.

> May 14, 1859
> Last night there was a concert at the Palace and it was very
> amusing to see Lord Derby who was in the highest spirits
> chaffing Lord Palmerston, Lord Clarendon and a number
> of other Whigs into the midst of which he had got and who
> were all roaring at his jokes.

And later, at the time of the excitement over the volunteer
movement and the reviews held for them, he relates :

> " What an interesting sight," said Palmerston to the
> Queen at the volunteer Levée as the full-bodied volunteers
> rushed heatedly up into the presence of their sovereign.
> " Very much so," answered the Queen, " but don't you
> think there is rather a——" Here the Queen put her hand-
> kerchief to her nose. " Oh," said the Premier, " that is
> what we call *esprit de corps*."

During the visit of the Queen with the Prince Consort to
Coburg in September 1860 a rather serious accident occurred
in which the Prince was involved. While arriving in his
carriage the horses ran away and as he saw them heading for
the gates of a level crossing he jumped out before the crash
came. He fell on his face and was cut on the head, while the
coachman was badly hurt. His Equerry arrived on the spot
and was commissioned to go at once and tell the Queen but
" on no account to alarm her ". As he himself was rather
alarmed this was no easy task, but he managed to minimize
the effects of the accident.

The one slightly amusing action on the part of the Prince

related in the letters, occurred at Frogmore where the Duchess of Kent lived, in the grounds of Windsor. The Duchess objected to the pheasants and other game being shot. Prince Albert and a party were shooting there one day when they saw her carriage coming. The Prince ordered everyone to hide behind the palings, but her carriage came unexpectedly close and " she was inexpressibly surprised " to see the Prince and a dozen others crouching in their hiding-place.

We may doubt if the Prince laughed at his mother-in-law's surprise. Humour was not his strong point. In fact in later years Ponsonby (in reminiscence of his time as Equerry to " the great and the good ") says he had " unmistakable marks of the Snark ".[1]

Although the correspondence shows that Ponsonby was interested in the political questions of the day there is no mention of the Prince's views or work in that connection. The duties of an Equerry were confined to purely formal attendance on the Prince.

In a very brief diary (1857–1861) there are references to Mary Elizabeth Bulteel coming into waiting as Maid of Honour in London or Windsor, and in September 1860 during the visit of the Queen and the Prince to Coburg. She was the daughter of John Bulteel of Flete, in Devonshire, and Lady Elizabeth, daughter of Charles, Earl Grey, the Prime Minister. Colonel Ponsonby's regimental duties as commanding the 1st Battalion of the Grenadier Guards at Windsor gave him opportunities of meeting the Maid of Honour when she was in waiting and also when he himself was discharging his duties as Equerry. But as might be expected in the case of so reticent a man, there is no word in notes, diary or correspondence of the growth of the intimacy between them. It seems their meeting-place was the cloisters of St. George's. In January 1861 they were engaged to be married. He wrote to his mother (January 29, 1861) : " The Queen last night as she went to bed called me and having warmly congratulated me, said, ' I highly approve of your choice but you have taken from me the best

---

[1] It will be remembered in the enumeration of the Snark's characteristics :

> The third is its slowness in taking a jest.
> Should you happen to venture on one
> It will sigh like a thing that is deeply distressed
> And it always looks grave at a pun.

of my household.' " He took his bride to see his mother at Hampton Court and there is a letter from Lady Emily written immediately they had left :

> I quite wanted to sit down and tell you (what I trust I showed) my very great pleasure at your visit. Yes, my very dearest, you have indeed chosen one to make you happy, and her manner to me is *so* charming. I don't know how to say enough but that as long as I live shall I try to show *how* pleased I am with your choice.

The last entry in the diary is the bare statement : " Tuesday, April 30, 1861, at St. Paul's Church, Wilton Street, London, I married Mary Elizabeth Bulteel ". They rented a house in the Cloisters at Windsor. In a letter to his mother-in-law in November he tells her of a visit paid to them :

To Lady Elizabeth Bulteel

Windsor, November 7, 1861

Although we are infinitely superior to those people who are delighted with a glimpse of royalty, we cannot deny (don't mention it, please, in the parish) that we were very much grattered and flattified by a visit from Victoria by the Grace of God, etc. We went out for a walk on Tuesday and pending our absence, Her Majesty, the Prince Consort and Princess Alice came in with the baker's boy at our back door, but being met by the watchful Ayling [the maid], were sent round to the front door and told we were out. Our baffled Sovereign retired to Mrs. Biddulph's from which place of security she beheld our return and came with us here. They all seemed very much pleased with our house and the things in it, though the view from its being a bad day was not effective. She asked where Lady Elizabeth was to be when she came here, and at the same time the Prince asked where Lady Emily was to be, and we showed them the Guest room but whether they thought it was impossible that one Mother should ever inhabit a room the other had slept in, or that a confusion arose as to who was which's Mother, I don't know, but we got into a difficulty between Lady Elizabeth and Lady Emily and vice versa, double yer all round sort of thing that we left the discussion in an entanglement. What they most admired, though I say it as shouldn't, was that valuable wardrobe from Pamflete contemptuously treated by Mary and spurned by Ayling which has become the chief feature of my room and one of the seven wonders of the house. Our noses have been slightly

turned up since this visit, and we are only just beginning
to associate with other folk.

We have had an unusual influx of visitors since the
return of the Court. To some of these Mary is gracious and
gives tea ; to others she puts on her bonnet and behaves
with severe politeness. She has also been much occupied
by the running for the Minor Canon Trial Stakes which
takes place this week. There are ten candidates for the
place, each of which has a turn at the service in St. George's
and the best is to get it. Mary returns from the Chapel with
a more facetious than reverent account of the style of these
Ecclesiastical Competitors and what with her and Mrs.
Wellesley [the Dean's wife], the Chapter have a heavy
weight of female influence brought to bear on their decision.

In the very next month occurred the illness and death of
the Prince Consort. In a series of letters to his mother Colonel
Ponsonby describes the last days and specially emphasizes
the suddenness and unexpectedness with which the turn for
the worse had come. So much has been written already on this
calamity in various appreciations of the Prince's services and
character that quotations from letters are in this case unnecessary. The Queen subsequently appointed the Prince's
Equerries as extra Equerries to herself.

In 1862 Colonel Ponsonby was ordered to accompany a
battalion of Grenadier Guards to Canada and military work
for a time absorbed him. The baby Alberta Victoria born
in May was entrusted to the care of Lady Elizabeth Bulteel,
and husband and wife sailed in July. The military precau-
tion of sending a small force to Canada was taken on account
of the strained relations between England and America during
the Civil War. Colonel Stevenson was in command at Montreal,
Colonel Ponsonby second in command. After two years all
question of danger had passed and the Guards were recalled.

The fullness of the correspondence in these two years,
which included a tour in America, is sufficient to give a detailed
account of their doings, their abodes, their friends, military
and social occupations and opinions with regard to the progress
of the Civil War and indeed makes a finished picture. But
again here the designed proportions of this book must limit us to
no more than passing glances. Generally speaking the Canadian
visit was of particular value to the recently married couple. It
afforded them an opportunity, surrounded as they were for

MARY PONSONBY

IN CANADA

COLONEL PONSONBY

the most part by strangers, of falling back on one another's
company, learning to adjust their dispositions to one another
and so laying the foundations of the sympathetic and enduring
companionship, based on deep mutual affection, which lasted
without a break through all the vicissitudes of thirty-four years
of married life.

A few of the sidelights on their domestic life may be quoted :

To his Mother-in-law, *Lady Elizabeth Bulteel*

Montreal, August 31, 1862

. . . I should like to tell you how our excellent dinners at
home are prepared.   About ten at night a single knock comes
at the door and Mary disappears.   This is Bridget Murphy,
the cook, come for her orders as to the marketing at 6 the
next morning and to listen to a lecture on cooking.   I hear
through the door : " Will I put the pittyatee with the jam ? "
" No, no, the potatoes come up as usual.   But to make the
pudding take four spoonfuls of the best strawberry jam,
etc."   This is a case of reading from Francatelli, then a
great deal more conversation, and the result is I get an
excellent dinner the next day.

To his Mother, *Lady Emily Ponsonby*

Montreal, February 6, 1863

Our sleigh drive last Saturday was to a place on a neighbouring island where we walked on snowshoes and had luncheon.
We drove home at a sharpish pace and at a corner in the
road I galloped round, not allowing for the slewing or swing-
ing round of the sleigh, which it did and quietly overturned
us in the snow.   Half a dozen fellows came to help us out
again and we were quickly in our places and so home.
Mary never said a word as we went over but quietly plunged
into the snow over me.

To *Lady Emily Ponsonby*

Chambley, June 5, 1863

We have rains and cold weather here which, however,
Mary does not object to, as she has been at our garden and
the weather is propitious for cultivation.   I am working at
sowing and weeding, while Dumphy, like soldier gardeners,
is digging and delving.   She walks about with an enormous
knife as if she was going to stick us if we didn't work, and
with sticks and paper and seeds in her red bag and in excellent working costume, full of orders and directions, with

an occasional eye on Gill planting the tomatoes and a look at the poultry in the back yard. In the midst of this voices are heard and visitors announced in the drawing-room, so she goes in in her grubby dress which is far better than Mme. Levilly's moiré antique piqué de mousseline de laine, and there receives the visitors who are dressed as duchesses. After which she returns furious at the follies of visiting in the country and Dumphy and I catch it accordingly.

The correspondence of course touches fully on politics, the progress of the American war, regimental news and gossip about officers, residents and visitors.

After their return to England the Ponsonbys settled again at 6 Cloisters, Windsor, where three more children were born, Magdalen, John and Frederick. Visits to one another's families and other expeditions are noted. Henry presented his father-in-law with a book of autographs (which he himself had compiled with his own pen) accompanied by a letter drawing attention to its extraordinary value. The book has been handed down and is still in existence, bound in red velvet. It contains amongst others the autographs of Julius Caesar, Dante, Queen Elizabeth, Cardinal Wolsey, the Man with the Iron Mask (Je suis — signature indecipherable), Sir Isaac Newton, Sir Christopher Wren (with his first design of St. Paul's) and a blot made by Shakespeare !

Owing to Colonel Ponsonby's absences in these years as Colonel in the Grenadiers in London and at Beggars Bush Barracks in Dublin, and his waitings as Equerry, he began in the intervals the habit of writing a daily letter to his wife. But one of his most regular correspondences ceased. In 1868 a great blow came to Henry in the death of his brother Arthur at the age of only forty-one. They had been inseparable as children, had been together in the Crimean War and again in Dublin where Arthur, who had exchanged from the Grenadiers into the 12th (the Suffolk) Regiment, was quartered for some time. When apart their full and detailed correspondence shows their unsentimental but very genuine devotion to one another. Arthur was an unconventional and very enterprising soldier, full of original ideas and with even less regard for appearances than his brother. Socially his company was sought by all for the reliability of his friendship and for the amusement derived from his habits and his inventions, such as

" the Society for promoting indigestion and gambling in foreign parts " which he started in India where he was quartered as Colonel of one of the battalions of his regiment. It was at Jubbulpore that the cholera broke out to which after forty hours' struggle he succumbed.

Henry Ponsonby's final abandonment of military life came when in 1870 he was appointed Private Secretary to the Queen.

CHAPTER III

The Private Secretary and the Household

THE chronological sequence, observed up to this point, must now be abandoned in order to deal effectively with Henry Ponsonby's twenty-five years of close attendance on Queen Victoria. To recite in order of date the incidents connected with foreign, imperial and domestic politics and with the royal family would mean relating in detail the whole history of England.

The post of Private Secretary to the Sovereign is a comparatively modern creation. Before the reign of George III the constitutional theory held that the Home Secretary was the King's Private Secretary and that it was undesirable and irregular that anyone who was not a Privy Councillor should be admitted to Cabinet secrets. At first George III not only wrote but kept copies of his letters. But in 1805, when the King had become practically blind, Lt.-General Sir Herbert Taylor was appointed Private Secretary in defiance of the tradition. He was a man of considerable experience, having held a military command and been Private Secretary to the Duke of York. Taylor retained the office until George III's final attack of insanity in 1811. He was then appointed Private Secretary to Queen Charlotte. He sat as M.P. for Windsor (1820–1823) and was Master General of the Ordnance in 1828.

As Regent, George IV had no Private Secretary. But gradually he employed the Keeper of the Privy Purse in that capacity. Sir William Knighton, an eminent physician, held that office and proved to be a remarkably good adviser, not only politically but in the management of the huge debts and chaotic financial affairs of George IV after he came to the throne. In 1830 William IV reappointed Sir Herbert Taylor who, after serving as Ambassador in Berlin, had been admitted

34

to the Privy Council and was in retirement. In the Reform agitation Taylor's patience and diplomatic tact were generally recognized.

No Private Secretary was appointed when Queen Victoria ascended the throne. Mr. George Anson occupied the post of Keeper of the Privy Purse. In the earlier days Baron Stockmar acted in the capacity of Private Secretary although he was not so called. The Prince Consort owing to his lively interest in public affairs was the Queen's chief adviser. General Charles Grey, a son of Earl Grey, the Prime Minister, after serving as Private Secretary to Prince Albert from 1849 to 1861, became Private Secretary to the Queen and held the office till he died in 1870.

When therefore Colonel Ponsonby was appointed to succeed General Grey in 1870, the office had become regularized and officially accepted, although he was not sworn a member of the Privy Council till 1880.

In a memorandum recording his appointment Ponsonby writes :

> On the 31st March 1870 Biddulph [1] told me that the Queen intended to offer me the appointment of Private Secretary and on the 8th of April I was gazetted to the office and at the same time placed on Half Pay of the Grenadier Guards in accordance with arrangements I had made some time previously.
>
> My selection for the place had not been made without considerable opposition. The Duke of Cambridge was foremost in expressing a regret that one who was known to have such extreme radical tendencies on military and other matters should be placed in such a position and the Duchess of Cambridge made no secret of her son's dislike to me for my political views and told my mother at the meeting at the Cambridge Asylum that although she congratulated her and considered that in many ways I would make a good Secretary, she would not disguise from her that the Duke believed the appointment a bad one from a political point of view. Prince Christian was also opposed to my appointment for similar reasons and added that he knew my wife's views were very extreme. Franco Seymour [2] told me that he himself was hoping against me and that he had heard officers of the Guards denounce me with this reservation

---

[1] Sir Thomas Biddulph, Privy Purse.
[2] Major-General F. H. G. Seymour, afterwards 5th Marquis of Hertford.

that in military matters they knew I was not a destructive.

The Queen disregarded the remonstrances and was pleased to appoint me sending me at the same time a hint through the Dean of Windsor that I was to be cautious in expressing my opinions and not to permit my wife to compromise me in her conversation, which she assured me she had no intention of doing or of being herself compromised by being supposed to agree for an instant with the opinions of Court officials.

During his waitings as Equerry Henry Ponsonby had opportunities of learning the customs, habits and inner workings of Court life. More than this, he was able from time to time in conversation and consultation to get the benefit of the experience of General Charles Grey, his predecessor as Private Secretary, and to assist him occasionally in his work. Grey being Mary Ponsonby's uncle, was known to them both as " Uncle Charles ". Their intimacy therefore enabled Ponsonby not only to get an insight into the work but to learn the best methods of helping and guiding the Queen and the sort of approach to her which might inspire confidence. General Grey had had to deal with the first shock of the Queen's bereavement and knew what advice would be listened to and what advances would be rebuffed. The Queen had among some of her more difficult habits that of leaning on her Private Secretary to make the necessary adjustments on delicate and personal social points. As for instance when a young Lady-in-Waiting appeared (for those days) rather heavily made up. " Dear General Grey," said the Queen, " will tell her." When the message was conveyed to him he was heard to murmur : " Dear General Grey will do nothing of the kind." In graver matters he sometimes was unable to conceal his exasperation but not in her presence. Towards the end he was handicapped in his work by his deafness. However the Queen certainly appreciated his services and on his death wrote : " Good, excellent General Grey, his discretion, sense and courage made him invaluable ".

While the qualifications necessary for the position of Private Secretary to a sovereign might be generally defined, any definition of the necessary qualifications for the position of Private Secretary to Queen Victoria would be much more difficult to make. Ponsonby's nine years in Dublin under

GERALD WELLESLEY
Dean of Windsor 1854-1882

GENERAL CHARLES GREY
Private Secretary 1854-1870

successive Lords Lieutenant gave him useful experience of the workings of a Household on a small scale. His punctuality and conscientiousness as a correspondent and his knowledge of men made him obviously well suited for such a post. Practice from early youth made his pen his chief medium of expression. By writing he conducted his work. But by writing too he found his relaxation from official business. From the early days of their marriage he and his wife contributed many articles to the *Pall Mall Gazette* and other periodicals. Very often the *nom de plume* " Sebastian " which he adopted might be found in the correspondence columns, generally discussing some military question of the moment. There were articles or letters of his on more miscellaneous subjects such as " Shooting for a Bag " (showing up the vulgarity and unsportsmanlike methods of those whose sole object was " to kill the greatest number of pheasants in the shortest space of time ") ; others on " The Tower Ghost ", " The Absurdity of a Spiritualist Séance ", refutation of the legend that the kilt was of ancient origin and correcting Lord Randolph Churchill who had said that Marlborough was created a Duke after Blenheim whereas it was two years earlier in 1702.

To the *Naval and Military Gazette* from 1869 onwards he contributed a series of entertaining articles (under the name of Major Quill) which purported to describe the discussions between officers in a club which he called The Smokantauk. He adopted a sort of sham official phraseology beginning " Lord Hotspur took the chair and lit his cigar at 4 o'clock ", and the opinions of all types of officers, General Drinkwater, Captain Smart, Lieutenant Ranker, etc., were given on the military questions of the time. As late as 1890 he published a series of articles on Culloden in *Scottish Notes and Queries,* and the fiction which had grown round the battle of Hastings was another historical subject which engaged his attention. He liked ferreting out strange facts and exposing false traditions, and he was also fond of genealogical puzzles.

Among his papers are a number of notebooks many of which contain notes on historical episodes from the military point of view. Most of them refer to American history and would seem to be jottings from his studies when he was in Canada. A very carefully written foolscap manuscript of some fifty pages contains a summary of the history of North America from the early days of its discovery. In it he gives special prominence to the military side, with full detailed lists of the naval and military forces employed and the names of the ships and regiments and their commanding officers. It is not carried further than the year 1759. His overwhelming work in later years must have prevented him from continuing the manuscript which was obviously intended for publication as a book.

In his numberless private letters superimposed on his daily official correspondence all written in his own bold clear hand, often with copies kept, Henry Ponsonby must have written tens of thousands of letters. They were not notable productions of literary value. They would not stand being collected in printed volumes. Affectation or elaboration of style was as alien to him in writing as it was in speech. Pedantry and pomposity in others he always met with ridicule or some disarming joke, because it was unintelligible to him that anyone should adopt that style. Mentally he put a mark against them.

His letters to Ministers or officials while dealing briefly and clearly with the business in hand were often relieved by a sentence or postscript of intensely amusing comment. In writing to Cecil Spring-Rice, at the time Chargé d'Affaires at Dresden, he adds at the end of the letter : " The Queen would be grateful if you would request her Chargé d'Affaires at Dresden to take a less humorous view of Royal funerals ". In a letter to Randall Davidson, Dean of Windsor, on December 6, 1884, he writes : " Do we officially believe in Purgatory ? Canon Luckock of Ely wrote a book about the future state. He apparently knows all about it. He states that the Queen nas expressed herself warmly in favour of his book (??). And so wants to send another . . ." [1]

But in letters and memoranda on delicate or perplexing problems and disputes he had a genius for setting down quite simply and with an almost judicial balance arguments persuasive in their lucidity which would make a reader say " It could not be better put." As Gladstone's Private Secretary wrote : " Mr. G. thought nothing could be better or more clearly expressed than your letters. He is a great admirer of your letter-writing powers."

Ponsonby had no pretensions whatever as a scholar.

---

[1] *Randall Davidson, Archbishop of Canterbury,* by Dr. G. K. A. Bell (Bishop of Chichester).

Having for the greater part of his life to wade through official documents not cursorily but thoroughly, making himself sufficiently accurately acquainted with their contents as to be in a position to explain or advise, little time was left to him for literature, although he often makes comments on the books of the day. But he liked best exploring by-paths and specially in military matters indulging in his rare leisure moments in research.

He was by no means an accomplished linguist. But in his early youth he had learned Italian. His working knowledge of French enabled him to converse and, more difficult, to write complimentary letters when occasion demanded ·on the visits abroad. Of German he knew less. This did not matter as a German Secretary was generally in residence to deal with the not inconsiderable amount of German correspondence. But his dismay may be imagined when during his waiting in 1867 at Osborne the Queen lent him the Crown Prince's journal not printed but written in German. He often refers in a humorous way to his ability to start a foreigner in his own language and then receive the resultant prolonged monologue with sufficiently appropriate interjections to put Monsieur, Herr or Signor at his ease.

In early days (1852), writing to his mother from Milan, he relates :

> Between us sat a sombre-looking man in black. After some time I addressed him in German but he shook his head ; then French but it wouldn't do. Then English which he understood but answered in Italian. I worked up what I remembered of it and to my surprise, though I could say but little, I found I soon understood him pretty well and then he rattled away at all rates . . . an hour and a half was enough of him, but I suppose I must have been a good listener for he shook me warmly by the hand when we parted.

There are several chaffing references to his French compositions in his letters to his wife who was an accomplished French scholar. Writing from Biarritz in 1889 he says :

> The Queen complained of the lies in the newspapers. So I wrote a French article for her. *Que voulez-vous ?* Read the enclosed and say if Voltaire or Racine could have written better.

The Queen was a good linguist, and what with German and French governesses always at hand the foreign correspondence could be adequately attended to.

Poetry was not a necessary part of a Private Secretary's equipment. Henry Ponsonby had a liking for it, could recite lines from memory (specially from Tom Moore) and occasionally indulged in rhyming himself. When General Du Plat, one of the Equerries, was lodged, as some of the courtiers were, at Barton Manor, a beautiful old manor-house in the grounds of Osborne, he declared that as he lay in the four-poster bed there he had reached the height of his ambition, he wanted nothing and envied no man. He received the following lines :

LINES FOUND IN A FOUR-POST BED, BARTON, FEB. 4, '84

Princes and Kings your distance keep
And here let me contented sleep
I do not envy things like you
I want no ribbons red or blue
I want no silver notes nor gold
I want no acres broad and cold
I want no room for more expansion
I want no proud palatial mansion
I want no papers pamphlets books
I want no grand expensive cooks
I want no curious sumptuous wines
I want no forests rivers mines
I want no horses dogs or coaches
I want no lockets pins or brooches
I want no yacht to cross the ocean
I do not sigh for more promotion
I want no change in my condition
I've reached the height of my ambition.

But in the high and responsible office to which Ponsonby found himself appointed in 1870, intellectual talents of any high order not only would not have been appreciated but would have distracted him and so hindered rather than helped him. What was wanted was a certain amount of worldly wisdom in the best sense, and more especially a good knowledge of human nature, a sense of proportion which involves a sense of humour and infinite patience in dealing with what was often trivial and sometimes even absurd.

On taking up his office he began by keeping a memorandum book in which he set out the various public questions of interest which occupied attention and the Queen's attitude to

them. The Franco-Prussian War was the public event which
overshadowed all else. The Queen's sympathies were naturally
for Germany, with which she was so closely connected through
many of her relations. Newspapers which were pro-French
suggested that she interfered, just as newspapers which were
pro-German accused Lord Granville, the Foreign Secretary,
of being too French.

Although the Queen was on the side of Germany in the war,
she seems to have retained a sentimental appreciation of
Napoleon III which is expressed in the letter she wrote to
Colonel Ponsonby at the time of the Emperor's death :

From *The Queen*

Osborne, June 14, 1873

. . . The Queen feels the poor Emperor's death very much
& she rejoices to see the feeling of regret & sympathy felt
in England. He had many faults no doubt but he did an
immense deal for France that everyone must admit & his
once strong hand is terribly wanted now in the state of
anarchy in which France is. He was a most faithful ally
to this country, much attached to it & most hospitable to
the English & to those who trusted him most loveable
charming & amiable. The Queen can never forget that, &
these qualities are shown most in the real overwhelming
grief of all his attendants. *The Daily Telegraph* has very nice
articles but not so *The Times* who used to bow to Napoleon III
when he was all powerful. It ought to be the reverse.

Her Private Secretary was certainly, but no doubt tacitly, far
from being in agreement with these sentiments. He had
suspected the charlatan, a type he detested. This is shown by
a passage in a letter written to his mother, Lady Emily Ponsonby,
from Balmoral after the surrender at Sedan, dated September
9, 1870 :

The Prince of Wales dined and I had a hot and noisy
but not angry discussion with him about the Emperor whom
he rather pities. I see nothing to pity. He has dragged
down his nation to ruin, plunged them into an awful war,
when it was his duty to have known they were unfit for it,
taken command when he knew he could do nothing and
finally in the midst of a starving disorganized army, sur-
rendered himself prisoner *before them* and drove out in the
smartest carriage with splendid footmen, equerries, etc., to
live at ease in a beautiful castle, while France is at its last

gasp. I can't conceive who can say a word for him. He has shown himself to be an impostor and a coward and the country which he made dependent on his will is in a hopeless state. I pity the French but they have brought it on themselves and must suffer. . . . One thing is evident. The Bonapartes are at an end in France.

When after the *débâcle* it was secretly suggested that the Queen might intervene to stop the civil war, Thiers, who would have no dealings with the Commune, seemed ready to consider the idea. But the Queen strongly objected. " The Central Government of Paris one day might not be the same the next." There was no stability. So the matter was dropped.

In August 1871 the Queen's illness at Balmoral was more serious than was publicly known. The swelling under her arm alarmed Dr. Jenner and Dr. Marshall, and Dr. Joseph Lister (afterwards Lord Lister) was sent for from Edinburgh. It took some weeks before she was restored to health. It would be impossible to recite all the comments in the letters made on the public and even domestic matters which arose month by month. The published correspondence of the Queen deals with most of them, and in subsequent chapters of this book the major episodes will be dealt with where more light can be thrown on the Queen's attitude and her Private Secretary's interventions.

But one or two less known minor events are worth mentioning. In 1875 there was an incident culminating in a fatal accident which occupied at the time a good deal of public attention. But because it had no political or public significance it was soon forgotten and naturally hardly a word of reference to it appears in any histories. The inside view which can be gathered from Henry Ponsonby's letters and papers need not be elaborated as it only corroborates the details given in the extract from the Queen's Journal.[1]

The bare facts were that while the *Alberta*, the royal yacht commanded by Captain Welch, was carrying the Queen, two of her children and her household across the Solent on August 18 from the Isle of Wight, a privately owned yacht, a schooner, the *Mistletoe*, approached so close that she was run down by the *Alberta* and the yacht was sunk, three lives being lost. Henry Ponsonby, in the train proceeding from Gosport

[1] *Letters of Queen Victoria*, Second Series, vol. ii, p. 417.

to London, wrote immediately to his wife a first-hand account which ends : " I ran down at once to the Queen who came forward pale and caught tight hold of my arm — and then I saw the masts toppling and going down. It must have been over in less than two minutes." It may well be imagined that the calm of Balmoral was greatly disturbed for many weeks on end, while the inquest was held and adjourned. There were daily discussions on the details of the accident with the usual discrepancies which appeared even on the part of eye-witnesses. Sides were taken ; the press took it up and strong pro-*Mistletoe* and equally strong pro-*Alberta* opinions were formed.

The Queen's attitude was never for a moment one of complaint that she had been placed in a position of danger. From the beginning her first thoughts were about the lost lives and the damage done. But naturally her hope was that blame would not fall on her officers. When Ponsonby in one of many talks assured her that in any case she was in no way implicated, she did not agree and brought forward a purely theoretical argument. " I am not a mere passenger on board the *Alberta*. I am in command, my flag is flying and I give orders from it."

The verdict on September 10 was one of accidental death, with an opinion that Captain Welch was in error of judgment. The Queen accepted this without protest, but the controversy continued. There was on one side the question of the direction in which Welch steered the royal yacht when he saw the danger, the pace at which she was going, and so the possibility of the collision having been avoided. On the other hand the *Mistletoe*'s direct approach and its owner's subsequent claims and contradictory statements damaged his case.

The Queen's Private Secretary was drawn into the discussion in a way he would gladly have avoided. He was induced by the Queen and others to write a letter to Lord Exeter, the Commodore of the Royal Yacht Squadron, commenting on the practice which yachts had of sailing up close to the royal yacht in order to get a view of the Queen. The letter was written long before any verdict was reached. But most unfortunately the letter was published without date after the verdict was given and so appeared to be an adverse opinion from high quarters given in defence of the *Alberta*. Public comments on this letter were made and were a great source of vexation to Ponsonby. With his judicial mind he quite saw the force of several of the charges brought against Welch, an attitude strongly adopted by Lord Alfred Paget, much to the Queen's annoyance. An injudicious invitation to Welch from the Prince of Wales to come and stay at Abergeldie was fortunately stopped. Although the owner of the yacht, distracted by the loss of his sister-in-law and two of his men, as well as his yacht, was inclined, in spite of having originally said it was not Welch's fault, to claim high damages, the matter at last passed away into oblivion, but not till after the publication of the papers which included a reprimand on Captain Welch. The Queen had hoped that publication might be avoided. Disraeli said he would see what could be done. "Every effort will be made to fulfil your Majesty's wishes." But he did nothing. Publication was inevitable.

Parliament was not sitting at the time of the occurrence but there was a debate on April 10 of the following year. By this time the incident was past history, and though sides were taken and recriminations continued, no further public interest was taken in the accident.

In 1882 a rather disagreeable case which was tried in the Central Criminal Court before Mr. Justice Lopez necessitated the presence in the witness-box of Sir Henry Ponsonby. A junior clerk (Young by name) was charged with sending the Queen's Private Secretary a letter threatening to murder the Queen and Prince Leopold and demanding with menaces certain money. The letter was sent to the Home Office and proceedings were instituted, the Attorney-General prosecuting. Preposterous as the letter was and evidence of handwriting having been given, nevertheless the young clerk had a good record and was only seventeen years old. It looked rather as if he had been made the dupe of some unscrupulous scoundrels. The jury however returned a verdict of guilty and the judge passed the heavy sentence on him of ten years' penal servitude. The Queen wrote :

> The Queen is very glad to see the severe punishment given this man who sent a threatening letter & that the judge has acted so properly. It is indeed high time that this system of threatening & trying to frighten people sh^d be checked.

There was question of a memorial for the remission of the

sentence. But the Queen wrote to Ponsonby, May 31, 1882 :
" The Queen trusts that no one will think of yielding to an
agitation for a remission of Young's sentence & thinks it
monstrous to suggest it at *this* moment ". The youth was not
released on licence until March 1890, after he had served
nearly eight years of his sentence.

It is not at all surprising that the routine work of the office
of Private Secretary, combined as it was later on in Henry
Ponsonby's case with that of Privy Purse, should cover a very
wide range. This it always must do with every Sovereign's
Private Secretary. But up till 1878 he had to deal with it
single-handed. The particular practice the Queen insisted on
involved the writing in manuscript by the Private Secretary
not only of important political papers but of notes on numberless seemingly unimportant matters. In the nineties when her
eyesight was beginning to fail he had a sort of little spirit
stove on which he laid his letters for the Queen so that the ink,
which if blotted might be made faint, could be dried jet black.

There is an amusing instance of the Queen's severity
about handwriting in 1881. A letter arrived from Lord
Carmarthen [1] (aged nineteen) who was acting as an assistant
secretary at the Colonial Office. He forwarded an address
from Khama, the Bechuanaland Chief. The letter and the
address were sent in to the Queen. She wrote :

> The Queen cannot help drawing Sir Henry's attention
> to this atrocious & disgraceful writing for a young nobleman.
> Sir Henry sh^d write to someone saying the Queen thinks he
> sh^d . . . improve his writing to become distinct. It is too
> dreadful. What would Lord Palmerston have said !

As a matter of fact the writing though childish was quite easily
legible, whereas the Queen's minute took a quarter of an hour
to decipher. Indeed, what with abbreviations, underlinings
and the very broad black-edged notepaper she always used to
the end of her life and into which the end of some words disappear, the deciphering of many of Her Majesty's letters has
been very puzzling.

Typewriting, which was beginning to be adopted in Government offices in the nineties, she strongly objected to, in spite of
Lord Rosebery's pleadings for it. So it was that half a dozen

---

[1] Afterwards Duke of Leeds.

small points which could be disposed of in ten minutes' conversation had each of them to be submitted in writing on a separate sheet and sent to her upstairs in a locked despatch-box. It can be noted however that the Queen never suffered in her life from a moment's indecision : when Sir Theodore Martin suggested that a man should come to lecture to her on Shakespeare, she simply wrote : " The Queen dislikes lectures ". She wasted few words in her comments and marked what was obvious with " App^d ". But her approval or consent could never be taken for granted. Moreover at any moment she might take up some obscure question, as in 1872 when she became indignant about " the Regents Park Canal being so dirty ". Out of the packet of the submissions a few typical samples may be detached.

1879. A submission of a list of preachers for Osborne, suggested by the Dean of Windsor.

Name	*Queen's remarks*
The Dean of Westminster.	*Too long.*
The Dean of Christchurch.	Sermons are like lectures.
Dr. Bradley.	Excellent man but tiresome preacher.
Mr. Roberts.	X
Mr. Birch.	X
Mr. Tarver.	X
Mr. Rowsell.	

The Queen's Minute.—The Queen likes none of these for the House. The last of all is the *only good* Preacher excepting Dean Stanley & he is too long. Mr. Rowsell unfortunately reads very disagreeably but those crossed are most disagreeable Preachers and the Queen *wonders* the Dean c^d mention them. . . .

1885. Letter received complaining that the Queen in her *Leaves from the Highlands* had called Tomintoul " a dirty town ". Sir Henry Ponsonby suggests that Dr. Profeit (the Balmoral factor) should be asked if he knows anything of the writer of the letter.

The Queen's Minute.—Yes — but the Queen only stated the exact truth & everyone knows it — " a Tomintouler " is a bye word & she will *not change it.*

Windsor Castle
December 1 1881

General Sir Henry Ponsonby
presents his humble
Duty to Your Majesty
He believes that Mr
Sendall's appointment
is to be withdrawn.

This is a triumph

FASCIMILE OF NOTE BY PONSONBY WITH THE QUEEN'S COMMENT

1885.   Canon T— S— writes about some confusion with regard to the proofs of a book of his having been seen by the Queen.

The Queen's Minute.—He is a rather meddling & officious man, as we know.

A test of the Queen's memory occurs in 1881.   A correspondent asked whether a bust of the mother of George III in biscuit (china) which had been handed to Colnaghi for presentation to the Queen in 1842 had in fact been presented as there was some doubt on the subject.   " Sir Henry Ponsonby does not suppose Your Majesty can remember anything about it."

The Queen's Minute.—The Queen remembers it perfectly & thinks it is in the China room at Windsor.

There is another test which reaches still further back.

1892.   A man writes about an anecdote of the Queen when she was seventeen.   Visiting Lord Fitzwilliam's garden, the gardener warned Princess Victoria to be careful as it was very " slape ".   The Princess asked what that meant and at the same moment slipped down but was unhurt.   " There," said Lord Fitzwilliam, " Your Royal Highness has soon found out what ' slape ' means."   Sir Henry suggests that the Queen cannot be expected to remember small events of this sort.

The Queen's Minute.—*Entirely* true in every word.   I remember it very well.

In 1881 there was a proposal to appoint Mr. Walter Sendall Lieutenant-Governor of Natal.   He was strongly recommended in high quarters, and Lord Kimberley, then Colonial Secretary, supported the appointment although he admitted there was opposition and wrote of " the outcry in the colony which is very unfortunate ".   The Queen appears from the first to have opposed the appointment ; so that when Sir Henry Ponsonby sent in a minute (December 1, 1881) informing her that " Mr. Sendall's appointment is to be withdrawn ", she wrote : " This is a *triumph* to the Queen & shows how right she was in at 1st *not* approving it ".

1886. Sir Frederick Leighton asked leave to have copied a picture of the Queen by Sir Martin Archer Shee.

The Queen's Minute.—It is a monstrous thing no more like me than anything in the world.

1887. It was submitted that a sergeant who had been convicted of embezzlement should be deprived of his Victoria Cross.

The Queen's Minute.—The Queen cannot bring herself to sign this. It seems too cruel. She pleads for mercy for the brave man.

1892. A well-known lady asks if her daughter may write an article on the Royal Mews and Kennels.

The Queen's Minute.—This is a dreadful & dangerous woman. She better take the facts from the other papers.

1893. Letter asking if " The Giant's Child " which was being recited in various places was, as said, by the Prince Consort.

The Queen's Minute.—Utterly untrue & utterly without foundation.

1893. A painter asks leave to engrave one of the pictures he painted for the Queen.

The Queen's Minute.—Certainly not. They are not good and he is very pushing.

1889. The Clerk of the Privy Council submitted through the Private Secretary that as the Queen's speech was never read actually at a Council but after a Council, no Council need be held and the speech could be submitted by one or two Ministers without any Council. Lord Cranbrook was of the same opinion.

The Queen's Minute.—*No.* I do *not* agree. I wish it sh^d continue as heretofore as it is *The Queen's speech.*

Vivisection was a practice to which the Queen was violently opposed. There are two submissions dealing with it. In 1879

Mr. Lyon Playfair asked whether the New Medical School Buildings at Edinburgh might be called the Victoria College.

The Queen's Minute.—Yes, on *one condition* viz : that *no* rooms for vivisection are included in it.

In 1882 there is a submission for the presentation by a lady of a book against vivisection. Sir Henry Ponsonby says he " is always a little afraid of Lady enthusiasts ".

*The Queen's Minute.—*The Queen will readily accept it. The subject causes her *whole nature* to boil over ag^st these " Butchers " (Doctors & *Surgeons*).

The Queen was very fond of dogs and had statuettes put up to them in the castle grounds when they died. Against the muzzling orders she vehemently protested in letters.

There are a number of other submissions on such subjects as false press reports, a drunken coachman, keys for certain servants, permissions for dedications of books and for copying pictures and innumerable applications for apartments at Hampton Court, Kensington Palace, etc. etc.

Messages had sometimes to be conveyed by the Private Secretary on matters he himself had not initiated. This for Canon Dalton (who had been tutor to Prince Albert Victor and Prince George) :

From *The Queen*

Windsor Castle, December, 1885

As Tutor Mr. Dalton never said " Grace " but as Canon he does & she hears has done so in Latin. Pray tell him it must be in English and only *one.*

Dalton's reply was that he should never have dreamed of varying the grace he repeated at the Queen's table.

At the time of the 1887 Jubilee numbers of authors sent presentation copies of their books to the Queen. On one of them which contained anecdotes of her life she comments : " People sh^d send their books to the Queen *before* & not *after* they are published with *endless mistakes* ". She refers to certain passages as " quite wrong ", " stupid story repeatedly contradicted ", " all total myths ", " a complete invention ", " a complete fable ", " quite untrue ", " never threw her arms round her uncle's neck & sobbed ", " the fullest of inventions & untruths "

of any of the " Lives she had seen ".   " Sir Henry must tell
this man how erroneous his anecdotes are." [1]

In 1888 a letter was submitted from Princess Victoria Mary
of Teck [2] asking that her mother, Princess Mary, Duchess of
Teck, might have a carriage to take her from the station at
Windsor to see the Fourth of June celebrations at Eton.

Message from the Queen (through Miss Stopford).—The Duchess
of Teck may have a carriage tomorrow but Sir Henry must
make it very clear that it is not to be asked for again.

In the same year there is an instance of the Queen, who was
strongly Protestant, holding politically tolerant views on the
subject of her Roman Catholic subjects.   Sir Henry Ponsonby
submitted a " respectfully worded protest against the mission
of the Duke of Norfolk " (probably in conveying to the Pope
the Queen's thanks for his Jubilee congratulations).   Sir
Henry adds " other protests have been made but much more
violent ".

The Queen's Minute.—It is very properly worded, but they
entirely forget how many 1000 Catholic subjects the Queen
has who cannot be ignored — And it is grievous to think
that what w^d be so good for the peace of Ireland will probably
be prevented by these well meaning but fanatical Protestants.

Also in 1888 Oscar Wilde wrote asking for leave " to copy
some of the poetry written by the Queen when young ".

The Queen's Minute.—Really what will people not say & invent.
Never c^d the Queen in her whole life write *one line of poetry*
serious or comic or make a Rhyme even.   This is therefore
all *invention* & a *myth*.

At Osborne in 1892 Sir Henry submitted that Miss Low was
writing a book on dolls and " asks if she can be informed
whether Your Majesty as a child liked dolls ".

The Queen's Minute (in blue chalk, difficult to read).—The
Queen has no hesitation in saying that she was quite devoted
to dolls & played with them till she was 14.   Her favourites

---

[1] Compare the Queen's many corrections on Agnes Strickland's *Queen Victoria
—from her Birth to her Bridal (1840)* fully described in *Agnes Strickland* by Una Pope-
Hennessy (Chatto & Windus, 1940).
[2] Afterwards Queen Mary.

were small ones & small wooden ones which c^d be dressed as she liked & had a House. None of her children loved them as she did — but then *she* was an *only* child & except occasional visits of other children lived always *alone*, without companions. Once a week one child (Miss Victoria . . . Mrs. Harrison) came & occasionally other (? young cousins) came (. . .) but the Queen *really* LIVED alone *as a child*.

In 1884 the original statue of the Duke of Wellington had been erected on the arch at Hyde Park Corner (the Office of Works was the department concerned).

The Queen's Minute.—The D. of W.'s statue is *a perfect disgrace*. Pray say it ought to be covered over & hidden from sight. [On the suggestion of the Prince of Wales it was eventually removed to Aldershot.]

In 1893 the question of a successor to Mr. McA., the chaplain at Hampton Court Palace, was raised by the Lord Chamberlain's department. Ill-health prevented him from continuing his duties. It was urged that Mr. McA. had for some years given satisfaction.

The Queen's Minute.—This is a mistake. He *never* gave satisfaction & was most interfering & disagreeable.

There can be no question that according to more modern ideas an extra burden of work fell on the Private Secretary which should have been delegated to other officials ; and it was work of the most tiresome character such as details of Court functions, dates of Drawing-Rooms, marriages, funerals, reception of foreign royalties, etc. etc. Considering what Ponsonby's real work was, these interruptions, which required much attention in order that the arrangements might work smoothly, were vexatious in the extreme ; nor need recurring references to them be recited. But perhaps Ponsonby's note on a curiously awkward reception of a foreign royalty may be given :

The Empress of Austria came to England to hunt in March 1876 and sent to say she would call on the Queen at Buckingham Palace or Windsor on her way through. The Queen replied she was busy holding a Court but would see her another day. The Empress sent to say she would come on the following Sunday for luncheon. The Queen did not like receiving her Sunday but could not refuse. All was arranged for her coming to Windsor at 1.30. At 12.15 when we were all in church she telegraphed to say she would come at 1. Service was hurried over and she was received at 1.15 — and left at 1.30. She was blocked up by the snow at Slough and did not get back to London till 4.

Henry Ponsonby was fortunate in his colleagues in the royal Household all through the changes which were inevitable in his long service. The trust and regard amounting to affection which they extended to him helped him in his work. The loyalty they all felt for the Queen bound them together in the peculiar Victorian Court atmosphere. They were sympathetic to one another's perplexities caused sometimes by the unaccountable caprices and idiosyncrasies of their royal mistress. Advice or caution was accepted from Ponsonby, and even members of the subordinate domestic staff would lay their grievances before him. There are references to many members of the Household in his letters, notes of appreciation or amusement about the newly appointed Maids of Honour, the habits of the Ladies-in-Waiting and the topics of conversation at dinner. He never attempted to assert any authority, to administer any reprimand or to criticize unduly. So his advice was sought and followed except in one or two negligible cases.

It will be appropriate here to say a word or two about his chief colleagues.

Sir Thomas Biddulph like Henry Ponsonby was a soldier, having served in the Life Guards. He was Master of the Household for fifteen years and was appointed Privy Purse in 1867. So Ponsonby as an Equerry had already known him and when he became Private Secretary they were close colleagues for eight years. Whenever they were apart, for often the Privy Purse work had to be conducted in London, they kept up a regular correspondence. Ponsonby soon learned much from him for Biddulph realized better perhaps than anyone the difficulties which the Queen's impetuosity and also her inconsiderateness might produce. " The fact is," writes Sir Thomas, " the Queen sitting in the garden at Balmoral issues arbitrary orders with what eagerness she determines to unsettle them again." He could not conceal his annoyance at " the unceremonious and inconvenient manner " in which she sometimes treated the wives of her officials. Referring to her he uses the expression

SIR HENRY PONSONBY AND COLONEL BIGGE

SIR THOMAS BIDDULPH
Privy Purse, 1867-1878

" upstairs " as if the Household were just domestic servants downstairs to be ordered about as she wished. On many subjects Sir Thomas would not compromise. He was very firm although always courteous, and he gained confidence in his position because his advice was invariably sound. The relationship between the two men was further fortified by the close intimacy between their two families who lived as neighbours in Windsor Castle, the Biddulphs at Henry III Tower, the Ponsonbys at the Norman Tower. Their daughters were brought up as sisters with the enduring affection which lasts a lifetime, and Ponsonby's eldest son John at the age of about six drew up a list of his friends in which the " Biffufs " rank next after his own family. When Sir Thomas died in 1878 Ponsonby felt his loss very severely because there was no one else who understood the ins and outs and ups and downs so fully. In a letter to his wife he writes :

> I am not surprised at the universal feeling for poor Biddulph for I really don't think he ever had an enemy — at any rate he had a number of friends ; and people like the Duke of Cambridge used to look on him as a bulwark against the radicalism I might instil into the Queen's mind. So his advice, always good, was well taken by them and when they saw how right he usually was, they felt grateful ; and I think so many people really liked him for his own sake.

The Queen, whose habit it was to try and make amends in a post-mortem eulogy, wrote " of the most grievous loss " : " Dear excellent Sir Thomas Biddulph was one of the best & kindest of men, & so straightforward sensible & true. The Queen is g^{tly} upset by it."

The Master of the Household, Sir John Cowell, was another courtier of long standing. He was an officer of the Royal Engineers and had been governor to Prince Alfred and also to Prince Leopold. He was appointed Master of the Household in 1866 and remained in that position till he died in 1894. A more ungrateful post can hardly be imagined, especially at Balmoral, where there were several who were attempting to be Masters of some part of the establishment and no doubt had more rapid access to the Queen. Often when he took the initiative his orders were countermanded or messages reached him through some intermediary, perhaps one of the ladies or governesses.

I don't think [says Ponsonby] he much minded messages coming through me as he could always reply and have it out with me, but when it came through various women, he disliked it. But it is the way of the Royal family. I remember Biddulph was a little hurt and told me I ought to be hurt when we were informed of Lord Derby's resignation by Mlle. Norèle [the French governess]. But I satisfied him that one Tory more or less was of such minor consequence that it was fitly a matter for the French governess.

With Cowell Ponsonby had many brisk arguments and much chaff. The Master of the Household besides being a theologian had a store of specialized scientific knowledge. He was a great believer in Jenkins's prophetic weather charts and in 1889 a storm was promised for the crossing of the royal yacht to Cherbourg. On arriving after a particularly fine and smooth crossing Ponsonby telegraphed to Cowell, "Fine passage — Jenkins". To Henry Ponsonby's amusement one of his sons believed that Sir John Cowell *was* Jenkins.

On the death of Sir Thomas Biddulph it was suggested in some quarters that Cowell should be promoted to the office of Privy Purse. There is among the papers a long, charmingly confiding and modest letter from Sir John to his old friend and colleague saying quite emphatically that he felt himself " utterly unsuited for such a position ".

When Sir Henry in 1878 was appointed Privy Purse in addition to the office he held of Private Secretary it was obvious that he must have assistance. Two assistant Secretaries were therefore to be appointed. The Queen wished one of them to be Major Arthur F. Pickard, an officer in the Royal Artillery who had won the V.C. in wars in New Zealand in the sixties and was Equerry to Prince Arthur. He knew his way about, was tactful and clever. " He was in full favour at dinner [with the Queen] and managed his talk very well touching only on light subjects." Unfortunately there was one serious drawback. He suffered from bad health and had to go abroad in the winter. In 1880 he died at Cannes on what was to have been his wedding day. He was to have married the Hon. Ena MacNeil, who was an Extra Woman of the Bedchamber to the Queen and subsequently became the third wife of the Duke of Argyll.

Fleetwood Edwards, a captain in the Royal Engineers,

was appointed assistant in 1878. He had accompanied General
Sir John Lintorn Simmons to the Congress of Berlin. He was
very efficient and businesslike. His regard for his chief is
expressed by Edwards in a letter written in 1882 when the C.B.
had been conferred on him :

> I can take the opportunity of saying in writing what I
> might find it difficult to say in person — viz. that I am very
> grateful to you as my chief for the very kind and friendly
> consideration you have *uniformly* shown me and which
> has rendered my work pleasanter and easier than it would
> *often* otherwise have been. Perhaps I have not shown my
> appreciation of it — but I feel it.

He eventually succeeded Sir Henry as Privy Purse, became a
trusted and intimate adviser of the Queen and was one of the
executors of her will. In the new reign he was appointed
Serjeant-at-Arms in the House of Lords.

The second assistant appointed in 1880 was Lieutenant
Arthur Bigge, a Royal Artillery officer who had served in the
Zulu War and been A.D.C. to Sir Evelyn Wood. The extracts
below are from two letters of Ponsonby to his wife and explain
how Bigge came to be brought to the royal notice at Balmoral
and are otherwise not without interest :

> Balmoral, October 21, 1879
>
> As the Queen has gone up to the Glassalt we are left here
> in peace. I walked to Abergeldie with Miss Cadogan and
> Lieut. Bigge. He was the Prince Imperial's intimate friend
> at Woolwich and in the Artillery so his presence at Aber-
> geldie is of great comfort to the Empress. He says the Prince
> was a clever fellow certainly and devoted himself to any
> work he had to do. He has many of his letters here chiefly
> discussing military affairs. A long memo on the improve-
> ments desirable in Artillery. Bigge says he may be right or
> wrong but he knows very few Artillery officers who at 20
> could have written such a paper. His examination at Wool-
> wich was perfectly fair and he passed nearly at the top of the
> list. He was not first in French. He was most eager and
> attentive in any matters he took up. He very seldom talked
> much of his prospects in France and when he did it was
> usually in chaff. Still it was evident that he always hoped
> to return there. Whether he ever believed he would, Bigge
> cannot say. Bigge upholds Frere's policy. He admitted
> after much argument that the invasion might have been

postponed but insists that war would eventually have come
and that the state of alarm of the border colonies justified
action.   He believes in S. African confederation and indeed
sees no other possible future for them short of anarchy.
The Empress talks a good deal to him. . . . It is whispered
that she intends next spring to go to Zululand and visit the
spot at Helyetozi.

Balmoral, October 22, 1879

. . . Bigge told me she [the Empress Eugénie] had begun to
speak to him of other subjects now and that they had got
her to amuse herself a little and got her to peep out, as if by
accident, at her French servants who had put on kilts to try
them — and this made her laugh.   So every effort is made to
distract her attention and they were delighted when I said
she had not dwelt on the Prince or Carey.   When I came
down to the tea room Bassano was there with Bigge —
Mlle. Larminat, and Mme. d'Arcos — besides Miss Cadogan
who I think prefers their converse which is decidedly very
flowing — to Miss Pitt's.   Uhlman the servant was then
sent in with the picture I had asked to see, the Queen having
told me of it.   By Protais.   The Prince's body in his Artillery
uniform lying dead on the ground at Helyetozi — his sword
in his hand — the likeness perfect.   A dark night and sense
of utter desolation.   But a gleam in the clouds sends out
faint rays in which you can detect Notre Dame and the Towers
and Domes of Paris — as his last dream.   It is a beautiful
picture.   Small and well finished — Uhlman explained it
to me.   Bigge is a very nice fellow and has much to say on
every subject.   I believe he was a good adviser to the Prince
when he was a young boy just joining the Artillery.

When Ponsonby was in London busy with negotiations,
he had a sort of code in telegraphing to Bigge at Balmoral.
There is a draft of one telegram recommending different sorts
of wines and brandy obviously referring to certain Ministers.

Ponsonby's first impression of the officer who was to be his
assistant Private Secretary for fifteen years proved to be rapidly
and fully justified.   Bigge soon learned the hang of things and,
combined with assiduous diligence and good judgment, he had
a talent for distinguishing between the mole-heaps and the
mountains as well as an appreciation of the lighter side of a
Court life out of which on occasions a good deal of amusement
could be derived.   These were qualities which appealed
strongly to his chief, and a friendship far stronger than that
which might be occasioned by mere co-operation in official

work grew up between them. His final tribute to the Queen's Private Secretary and the debt he owed him are recorded elsewhere.[1]

When Queen Victoria died Sir Arthur Bigge was appointed Private Secretary to the Prince of Wales, and when the Prince succeeded to the throne as George V, he rendered very conspicuous service as Private Secretary to the sovereign and was created Lord Stamfordham.

In the Privy Purse office in London Mr. D. Courtenay Bell, selected originally by the Prince Consort as an assistant, held the position of Permanent Secretary from 1876 to 1888. He was an F.S.A. and author of historical books on London. His experience had given him a fund of information. He was succeeded in 1888 by Mr. Walter M. Gibson.

Among the ladies of the Household there were several who to some extent encroached on the work of the Private Secretary by being, as ladies, in closer touch with the Queen and therefore entrusted with some of her correspondence. The widow of the 3rd Marquess of Ely served the Queen in a very intimate capacity for many years. Lady Ely, a Woman of the Bedchamber, had neither specialized knowledge nor particular discretion for so important a role. Owing to defective articulation and a habit of whispering, her " messages " to other members of the Household were often misunderstood, and when understood were sometimes lacking in tact. Judging by some of her letters (in the packets of letters received) it would seem that she also lacked any clarity of expression in writing. But the mistake was more in the Queen's practice of sending messages than in the shortcomings of the messenger, who at any rate was devoted and conscientious. Ponsonby refers to her " mysterious whispering " and on some occasions did not " strain his ears to hear her ". But the matter was more serious when telegrams and letters were sent to the Prime Minister without the Private Secretary being informed. But poor Lady Ely was worked too hard. This is shown by a passage in a letter to Ponsonby from Sir Thomas Biddulph, dated London, September 25, 1876 :

> I saw Lady Ely today. She is pretty well, but not strong. She had not seen much of any political people, and was principally taken up with her own health and

[1] See p. 402.

waiting. She says she cannot go on as it is, that it is killing her, and asked what to do. I said write plainly to the Queen what you can do, and make it clear that if H.M. cannot agree to your terms, you must resign. I think this would bring the Queen to reason, if firmly done. She says six weeks at a time is the utmost possible, and that all the Doctors urge her to do less. She says what is true, that she never sees a creature there, and the Queen will not allow Ely [her son] to come and see her. He was in the house and she asked me to see him. I said yes, with pleasure. Then she said, " Oh no, perhaps the Queen would not like it." However I saw him and he is anxious about her waiting, and I must say spoke very kindly. But it shows her absurd fear of the Queen, suggesting that the Queen would be angry with me for seeing him !

In a subsequent letter Sir Thomas writes : " I called on Lady Ely today but missed her. I had hoped to hear the last Beaconsfield news as I fancy he humbugs Lady Ely much as he does the Queen."

A prominent Lady of the Bedchamber who is constantly mentioned is Jane Lady Churchill, wife of the 2nd Baron Churchill. She was of an entirely different type from Lady Ely. She never interfered in politics nor was she the conveyor of messages. But she was vigilant and helpful and had great common sense. She put the Queen's interests first and foremost and had the courage on more than one occasion to override strong influences from other quarters to which the Queen was inclined reluctantly to submit. Later the Hon. Horatia Stopford, also a Woman of the Bedchamber, became what may be described as the Queen's messenger. Judging by one of her letters conveying what amounted to a reprimand there could be no doubt about its clear expression, but it is a matter of surprise that Ponsonby should have tolerated this method of conveying admonitions. He would have readily accepted a friendly word of caution from the Queen herself. The last who held this position of intermediary was the Hon. Harriet Phipps, daughter of a previous Keeper of the Privy Purse. She was efficient, simple and businesslike and rendered admirable service in the concluding years of the Queen's reign.

The German correspondence was conducted by Mr. Herman Sahl for many years and he was succeeded by Mr. Muther. Sahl was rather a character, clever in his way but absurdly touchy, always looking out for slights or what he thought were insults and sometimes absenting himself from meals in a huff. It took some time for him to overcome his sense of injury over a dispute as to who should be allowed to ride the ponies. But subsequently he had a high regard for Ponsonby and continued correspondence with him from Darmstadt after he had retired from the post of German Secretary.

Doctors played a formidable part in the royal Household wherever it was resident. This was not because the Queen was nervous about her health. Far from it. She was indeed hardy and seldom even in winter did she miss her drive in an open carriage. But members of the royal family, officials of the Household and domestic servants were more susceptible to illness. There was the Queen's resident physician and the local doctor. At Windsor there were several. One of them Ponsonby refers to as " a very good man, a very great bore and a very bad doctor, is a great gossip and wearies my life out with grievances and quarrels. . . ." There was the eminent doctor called in on special occasions and doctors attached to other members of the royal family. When two of them did not agree it provided food for discussion, specially at Balmoral. Dr. Morell Mackenzie does not come into the picture personally but it may be imagined that after the death of the Emperor Frederick the public discussion about him became almost a question of international politics, and of course reached into the Victorian Court where there was fuller knowledge of the facts of the case.

Sir William Jenner, the famous President of the College of Physicians, is constantly referred to in the letters, more especially from Balmoral. There was considerable doubt whether the Queen influenced Jenner more than Jenner influenced the Queen. She could quote him when she did not want to leave Balmoral. But it was noticed that at the time of political controversy the violence of the Queen's views and the expressions she used seemed to suggest that it was not only medicine which he prescribed in his intimate talks with Her Majesty. Jenner, with what is described in his biography as " his robust Common Sense ", was the most virulent Tory. He flung down his challenges with such gusto at Household dinners that Ponsonby on occasions found it difficult to restrain himself in his replies. Nevertheless the Private Secretary enjoyed Jenner's presence and was always sorry when he went away. He stirred the stagnant waters into a stream, sometimes a turbulent stream. Here is a typical reference to him :

> Osborne, April 22, 1883
>
> Jenner has been here in very high spirits and chaffed me immensely. Du Plat and I were down on him, but he is good at repartee and in roars at his success, he is a great addition here especially when in such a lively humour and so violent also in his abuse of the government and the medical Bill for the government of Doctors in the United Kingdom. He roundly abused Carlingford and Lord Cairns because they could not understand him. I refuted an argument of his which he said he did not use. " Why," I exclaimed, " you said so just now." His eyes disappeared and in a calm voice he said, " I strongly advise you to consult an aurist, the first aurist in London, there is something extraordinarily wrong about your ears."

Sir Douglas Powell was occasionally favoured by an invitation. After dinner one night during the interminably long wait when everyone had to stand, Douglas Powell fell down in a faint. He was carried out and the Queen asked what had happened. When she was told, all she said was, " And a doctor too ! "

Dr. James Reid was appointed resident physician in 1881. In addition to his high qualifications as a doctor, the fact that he was a Scot and a German scholar attracted the Queen's attention to him. On arrival he was informed that he would not dine with the Household. He was quite content with this arrangement which the Queen herself had laid down because, although she was fond of doctors, she still believed in the old convention that they should be put " below the salt ". Very soon however members of the Household, on some occasions when the Household dinner was likely to be dull, found their way in to dine with Dr. Reid where they would be sure of pleasant entertainment. The Queen of course heard of this : " I hear Dr. Reid has dinner parties ! " So the restrictions on the resident physician broke down to the benefit of the Household dinner. Reid's home in Scotland, Ellon, Aberdeenshire, was near Lord Errol's place. He used to relate how Lord Errol read prayers every day sometimes with com-

BALMORAL 1878

Lord Cross, Miss Phipps, Sir H. Ponsonby, Lord Bridport, Sir Thomas Biddulph,
Lady Ely, Sir William Jenner, Miss Lascelles, Alick Yorke

ments as if he were thinking. One day he read in the lessons, " It is easier for a camel to go through the eye of a needle than for a rich man, etc.", on which he exclaimed " Oh, that's damned nonsense. Let us pray." In 1882 Ponsonby came in close contact with Dr. Reid and wrote : " He gives excellent sound opinions on questions when they come within his bearings ". Soon there developed between the two men an intimacy and friendship which lasted till the end. Ponsonby liked someone who could detect what was serious and take it seriously and never take the trifling or ridiculous out of proportion. Moreover Reid's opinion was well worth listening to. Although he never obtruded his interference beyond his own professional sphere, that sphere grew as time went on and his advice was accepted not only by the Private Secretary but by the Queen herself even when it reached beyond questions of health. With his perhaps over-acute sense of humour Ponsonby knew he could get a response from Reid and that he would share with him the very occasional relaxations. When in London for a few days he writes to Reid : " Throw Physic to the dogs and come and see Barnum. I have got a box." At Balmoral when Dr. Royle was in charge in Reid's absence and Von Herff, a German visitor, was staying there, Ponsonby writes to Reid :

Herff went to call on Mackenzie at Glenmuick with Royle. The latter having no card, turned Herff's over and wrote his name on it. Herff in the evening astonished the company by saying : " I left my card at Glenmuick and Dr. Royle wrote his name on my backside."

Dr. Reid received a baronetcy in 1897 and in 1899 married the Hon. Susan Baring, Lady Ponsonby's niece. She was a daughter of the 1st Lord Revelstoke, and had formerly been a Maid of Honour. Sir James Reid was not indeed just one of a long series of doctors but a counsellor as well as a physician. His services, more especially in the concluding years of the reign when the Queen's advancing age was added to occasional ill-health, although known to very few, deserve special recognition.

Gerald Wellesley, Dean of Windsor, although not strictly speaking a member of the royal Household, was regarded by the Queen as a most reliable adviser, and to him she confided not only social and political matters when she was in doubt

but also family affairs. He was kind, cautious and judicious
and ever ready to serve her, although he did not always relish
the role of intermediary which was forced on him, sometimes even, as will be shown, between the Queen and her
Private Secretary. She came to regard the position of Dean of
Windsor as her own nomination, a view not entirely shared by
the ecclesiastical and political authorities. On Dean Wellesley's
death in 1882 she wrote to her Private Secretary :

> Balmoral Castle, Sep. 18, 1882
>
> The Queen thanks Sir Henry Ponsonby for his letter of
> sympathy on a *universal* & *irreparable* loss, which is crushing
> to her ! *Irreparable !* The last of her valued *old* friends &
> the *most* intimate of all. The dear Dean was with her for
> *33 years* — knew our children from their earliest childhood
> & 3 from their births — shared any joy & sorrow as well as
> any trouble & anxiety ; was large minded c^d understand
> anything so well — made allowances for everything & was
> such a wise, excellent adviser, the Queen thinks with g^t
> knowledge of the *world* & Windsor without him will be
> strange & dreadful.

And on September 26, 1882 :

> The Queen thanks Sir Henry Ponsonby for his two
> letters. The bare thought of replacing or rather filling up
> the beloved Dean of Windsor's place (for he cannot be
> replaced) is very painful to the Queen but she fears it must
> be faced. The Queen is glad that Mr. Gladstone sees that
> the appointment of Dean of Windsor is a personal & not
> a political appointment ; she will therefore *not* expect Mr.
> Gladstone to suggest names to her. For obvious reasons
> & after much reflection on the subject, the Queen thinks
> that it w^d be best to associate the office of Domestic Chaplain
> with that of Dean of Windsor. It is therefore of more
> importance that the future Dean sh^d be a person with whom
> she is pretty well acquainted & whom she can confide in,
> than that he should be a distinguished Churchman or a
> brilliant scholar. There is one of the Canons, Canon
> Anson whom the Queen w^d have liked to appoint had it
> not been that his health obliges him to reside abroad for at
> least 6 months in the year & just at the time she is most at
> Windsor.
>
> What the Queen wants is a tolerant, liberal minded,
> broad church clergyman who at the same time is pleasant
> socially & is popular with all Members & classes of her

Household,— who understands her feelings not only in ecclesiastical but also in social matters — a good kind man without pride.

The Queen after much thought & consideration has thought of Canon Connor who unites the different qualifications which the Queen has enumerated. She only regrets he is not of higher social & ecclesiastical rank. But he is of a good family & is a thorough gentleman & universally respected. He is an Honorary Canon of Winchester & father-in-law of the Bishop of Newcastle & has been for some years Chaplain to the Queen.

. . . The Queen knowing how well Sir Henry understood the peculiar position in w^h the dear late Dean stood with respect to her & the Royal family, feels sure that he will also see at once all the difficulties of the new appointment & how her comfort & feelings are in this case of paramount consideration.

The Queen has not the slightest idea whether Canon Connor w^d accept it.

Canon Connor (Vicar of Newport, Isle of Wight) was appointed. He died within a year and was succeeded by Randall Davidson (later Archbishop of Canterbury), in whom the Queen was again fortunate in finding an admirable adviser.

A close intimacy grew up between Davidson and Ponsonby. Dr. G. K. A. Bell, Bishop of Chichester, in his *Life of Archbishop Davidson* (1935) writes :

Ponsonby was about sixty when Davidson became Dean and throughout his tenure of the Deanery they were on terms of the closest friendship. Every day when the Court was at Windsor after Service in the private chapel at 9 A.M. Davidson and Ponsonby used to pace up and down in the Castle walks discussing most things in the Castle and out of it. Nor is there much doubt that while the Dean learnt much from his intercourse with Sir Henry, the latter came to rely more and more on the younger man's shrewd judgement for help in all manner of political and general problems. Ponsonby was a man of great charm, a letter writer of considerable wit and skill and considerable insight. To quote Davidson, " Ponsonby, I think, showed great capacity in all political matters, advising the Queen admirably and communicating with her Ministers in exactly the right sort of way. . . ."

Equerries and Grooms who changed according to their periods of waiting, the Lord Chamberlain, the Lord Steward, the Master of the Horse and the Lords in Waiting who were political officials who changed with the Government seem all to have been on friendly terms with the Private Secretary. The Lords in Waiting were resident and it was not always easy to find appropriate persons to fill the post. " Life would be happy but for Lords in Waiting " ; and again : " Blow the Lords in Waiting. Every one I suggest is objectionable. One has corns, another is dull, another is a bore. By the exhaustive process we are nearing the oppressed."

These are sentences from letters to Sir Spencer Ponsonby-Fane who for long held the office of Controller in the Lord Chamberlain's Department. They were first cousins, and the correspondence between the two on a multitude of subjects in which the Lord Chamberlain's department was concerned was voluminous. It was seldom carried on in correct official language. The scribbled notes (most of them kept, on both sides) were sometimes perhaps slightly flippant and certainly might have shocked the higher authorities. But it saved much time to be able to cut out all formalities. For instance this is Ponsonby's epitome of correspondence on fixing the date of a Drawing-Room in 1890, written on a telegram sent to Aix-les-Bains (where the Queen was staying) reporting, " Drawing-Room is gazetted for Thursday 15 May " :

> You say Consult Prince.
> We say This will delay but all right we will.
> You say Why this delay ?
> We say *Tu l'as voulu, Georges Dandin.*
> Prince says Any day 14 or 15.
> We say 15.
> You say Impossible.
> We say Very well 16.
> You say Oh no 15.
> There is no pleasing you any way.   H. P.

On the occasion of another Drawing-Room in 1892 :

Henry Ponsonby to *Spencer Ponsonby-Fane*

Princess B. seems to think it possible that H.M. wd. go to one Drawing Room. But H.M. in sad and mournful tones said to me she was damned if she would.

The copying of pictures in the royal collection was another subject of frequent exchanges of letters. One of the pictures

Ponsonby describes as " the picture of the Tower of London at midnight in a fog ".

Several letters were exchanged with Spencer on the ghost at Hampton Court. It was just the sort of absurdity which ordinarily made Ponsonby impatient. Moreover he knew all about the tradition, having often stayed with his mother in the apartment allotted to her in the Palace. But as Princess Frederica and her husband Baron von Pawel-Rammingen had complained of being disturbed by it, he wrote fully with slightly exaggerated solemnity which Spencer no doubt understood.

Some subject would crop up which for various quite unimportant reasons became magnified and occupied far too much of Ponsonby's valuable time. " The interference of the Princesses did not make things easier." The installation of a lift at Buckingham Palace was discussed for weeks. But perhaps latterly the controversy over the Queen's band lasted longer than any other. Indeed the full correspondence, the history, the personalities of the Masters of Music, the legal tangles and the Queen's comments would fill a fair-sized volume. One of the Queen's protests is quoted by Ponsonby :

H.M. says, " I pay £3000 a year and when I ask 8 or 10 of my band to come here they say ' No, contract prevents it.' When I ask my band to play during dinner at Windsor, ' No, contract prevents it,' and when I say show me the contract, ' No ' ".

The conveyance of the crown from the Tower to the House of Lords for the opening of Parliament was one of Spencer Ponsonby-Fane's duties. In 1886 he complained that all the protection he had in the royal carriage was " two puffing Beefeaters " who walked on either side as fast as they could manage it. This, going through the dense crowds, he thought insufficient, and asked for an escort of Life Guards. He argued that if it was known what was in the carriage " half a dozen determined men could make short work of it and carry off the whole thing before my friends recovered their wind ". The Queen agreed to the cavalry escort.

On one previous occasion it fell to Ponsonby to fetch the crown from the Tower. He went in a four-wheeler and put the crown in an ordinary band-box — the safest way of all.

F

But too much space must not be devoted to Household anecdotes : a collection of them, it may well be imagined, in over quarter of a century, taking into account the eccentricities of some of the courtiers, although entertaining, would be excessive.

Henry Ponsonby's dislike of honours and decorations was instinctive. It was in keeping with his hatred of publicity, ostentation and not always well-merited distinctions. He liked to do his work quietly and if he received gratitude or commendation from his royal mistress that was sufficient, and he appreciated it fully. The time had not yet come when decorations were to be cheapened. New orders with some thousands of members had not yet been instituted and the acceptance of foreign decorations was strictly regulated. So that, apart from well-earned war medals, officers in the services, courtiers and Ambassadors wore very few stars or medals. Ponsonby was content to wear his two Crimean medals and the order of the Medijieh which officers who fought in that war had been allowed to accept.

In 1872 the Queen wished to confer on him a C.B. (civil division). This placed him in a dilemma. He had no doubt in his own mind that he did not wish to have it. But the wording of a refusal was no easy matter. Considerable correspondence ensued and the Queen consented to withdraw the offer. In a letter to the Queen (August 29, 1872) he wrote :

> As Your Majesty is graciously pleased to say he may still decline the offer, he throws himself on Your Majesty's goodness and most humbly asks permission to do so. The feeling that he is doing his duty to Your Majesty and earning Your Majesty's approbation without expecting honourable decoration (to which he is indeed not entitled) would be far more grateful to him and would if possible increase the desire he has to serve Your Majesty to the best of his ability. Your Majesty's great kindness has always made his duty a pleasure to him and he earnestly trusts he may be permitted to continue to serve Your Majesty as he has done and to earn Your Majesty's most gracious approval.

From *The Queen*

. . . She knows that his motives for declining the honour are most creditable to him. The Queen will therefore now leave the matter alone.

But it was inevitable that the question should sooner or later be raised again. In January 1879 the Queen, no doubt fearing another rebuff, went to the trouble of making her approach through two intermediaries. Lady Ely wrote to Dean Wellesley informing him of the Queen's wish that General Ponsonby should be awarded a K.C.B. The Prince of Wales was anxious for it but " the Queen is afraid he will not accept ". Then followed a correspondence between the Dean of Windsor and General Ponsonby. The Dean, as the most trusted adviser of the Queen, especially on confidential and personal matters, urged him to accept the honour with every argument he could think of. Ponsonby's reply gives his last protest before inevitable defeat :

Osborne, January 8, 1879

As Lady Ely refers to Mrs. Ponsonby who of course must be consulted, it is possible she thinks that my wife was the cause of my refusing the C.B. — which is not the case, for I was bitterly opposed to being daubed with that blotch before I spoke to her about it.

I now write before I have shown her your letter so that you should know what I alone think about a proposition which hurts me much, since at the conclusion of the last discussion I was told it would not be offered again till I left the Queen's service. Is this a hint ?

You refer to my predecessor, the opinion of my friends, and the effect on my successor. I never heard much reference made to Grey's refusal — and I do not take my views from anything he said or did about it. He declined and there was an end of it.

The opinion of my friends when I was advised to ask it — when I last refused — was almost unanimous that I should not take it. Biddulph said however that I was wrong. That as long as I held the position I did I was bound to accept unrepiningly whatever punishment was inflicted. . . .

. . . At present my position in the Household is high. You want to place me below Cowell and Elphinstone — very well — but don't expect me to hold any influence over them. I shall be below them. If the Queen had such a title to give as " Moderator of the Dissenting Chapel in Peascod Street " how would you like to have it ? Would you not struggle against it as long as you could ?

Remember your object is to raise me in my office and to make me hold up my head — which I do — you then cover it with abominations and still expect me to be proud of myself !

The matter ended by the Dean writing to Lady Ely that Ponsonby " would not refuse the gracious offer if made ".

The G.C.B. naturally followed in 1887. The Queen wrote : " She intends conferring the G.C.B. on Sir H. Ponsonby for his long faithful & valuable services ".

When the Prime Minister's private secretary, Monty Corry, was raised to the peerage as Lord Rowton the Queen suggested that Sir Henry should be approached for a similar honour. His refusal of this was to be expected. He was probably with his wife at the time as there is no reference to it in the correspondence.

CHAPTER IV

Queen Victoria's Position

QUEEN VICTORIA ascended the throne at the age of eighteen. In the first few days Greville remarked, " Nothing can be more favourable than the impression she has made and nothing can promise better than her manner and her conduct." As the time passed she became, so to speak, saturated with an instinctive, rather than a deliberately assumed, consciousness of the supremacy of her position. So that to the end of her life the habit of dominating with a certain imperiousness but with complete assurance and self-confidence, and always with dignity, her relations, her household and her domestic servants, far from being relaxed seemed to grow stronger and had a disconcerting effect even on the most well informed and opinionated of her Ministers.

When Ponsonby was appointed her Private Secretary in 1870 she was fifty-one. She had reigned thirty-four years. The security of her position was unassailable and she was well aware of it. The Prince Consort had been dead ten years. It might be supposed that after the most acute period of her loss had passed, her interest in public affairs would have been at its height and that after a few years it might have slackened and she might have begun to be content, on becoming an old lady, merely to sign documents and approve decisions. Precisely the opposite was the case.

Having recovered from the first shock of her husband's death, she began to show an increasingly lively interest in public affairs accompanied by an increasing desire to interfere. She had an accurate memory and on occasions showed a businesslike capacity. Her almost childish excuse of incomprehension was merely a form of the intense obstinacy she had inherited from her grandfather George III. She was a woman and could be very capricious, as was shown, for instance, in the occasional and unaccountable relaxations in her usually rigid moral outlook. Far from assuming a consistently ingratiating manner or a stereotyped and smiling amiability, she was incapable of any pretence or of attempting to conceal the severity or disapproval which her facial expression often very clearly betrayed. Yet her latent charm and friendliness broke through with equal naturalness and at once evoked not only the loyalty but the affection which inspired those who came into close contact with her. She disliked being thwarted and those who tried to argue her out of her attitude were never given a second opportunity. She was impetuous in her rapid decisions but never did she yield to the vice of indifference. Her originality probably came from having in her childhood, as she remembered, " lived always alone, without companions ".

Queen Victoria did not belong to any conceivable category of monarchs or of women. She bore no resemblance to an aristocratic English lady, she bore no resemblance to a wealthy middle-class Englishwoman, nor to any typical princess of a German court. She was not in the least like the three queens regnant (omitting Mary Stuart who was just the wife of William III), her predecessors. Mary Tudor was a fanatic, Queen Elizabeth was an autocrat and Queen Anne in her harassed and ramshackle way was occupied in coping with the intrigues around her. Victoria in religion was an orthodox Protestant with Presbyterian leanings, she had had no Roger Ascham to give her a scholastic education and she did not spend her leisure moments like Queen Anne in playing Bach. Moreover she reigned longer than all the three other queens put together. Never in her life could she be confused with anyone else, nor will she be in history. Such expressions as " people like Queen Victoria " or " that sort of woman " could not be used about her. Her simple domesticity appealed to a vast number of her subjects ; she was intensely human, but the unique nature of her personality and position claimed special attention and often awe from those who reached her presence.

There might be princesses and duchesses, there might be women distinguished in many spheres, there might be empresses, there might be queen this, that or the other in history, but for over sixty years she was simply without prefix or suffix " The Queen ".

Her interest in public affairs was stimulated rather than

QUEEN VICTORIA
circ. 1858

mitigated by her personal isolation and residential retirement the conditions and nature of which are described in another chapter. But by 1871 it was beginning to be strongly felt that the strictness of what had become a habitual withdrawal from public life should be relaxed. Something therefore must be said with regard to the comments, criticisms, protests, not to say attacks in conversation, letters and press paragraphs which were occurring with greater frequency in the opening years of Ponsonby's Private Secretaryship and which he at first regarded with some considerable apprehension.

He noticed the anti-monarchical feeling was growing. Ministers were inclined not to consider her. The best form of government, said Goschen, was a Queen who always lived in Scotland and never troubled her Ministers. Her withdrawal from public life and the Prince of Wales's unpopularity, based on exaggerated rumours, might encourage still further the emergence of a republican movement. " If therefore ", Ponsonby writes, " she is neither the head of the Executive nor the fountain of honour, nor the centre of display, the royal dignity will sink to nothing at all." He and Sir Thomas Biddulph, the Keeper of the Privy Purse, were in complete agreement in their misgivings. " The Queen will talk ", said Sir Thomas, " as if she were Mrs. Jones and might live just where she liked," and Ponsonby writes : " Both bemoaned the present state of affairs here [at Balmoral] because we think she is getting to like to be still more alone and to see no one at all, governing the country by means of messages through footmen to us ". Some of the Princesses were anxious about it but had no influence. " Very serious talk with Princess Alice who takes the gloomiest possible view of all the talk, even abroad, about the Queen's retirement and not even seeing much of or talking to her children."

The press took up the question of her " hoarding " (that is to say putting by for private use the allowance provided by the Civil List for ceremonial purposes) ; and when the matter of her retirement came to a head in 1871 there were many press paragraphs. At that time the newspapers were often openly critical of the Court. Not only the less responsible papers but the more authoritative organs felt no obligation to submit to any uniform restraint in their comments on royal proceedings. False gossip could on occasions be refuted. But in this case the facts were publicly recognized and the inferences were therefore legitimate. Curiously enough this freedom of the press had no effect whatever in weakening the monarchy. One newspaper said, " Here we are on the very eve of a grave political crisis with a possible ministerial resignation and a probable dissolution and yet with the nonchalance of a Queen of Saturn or Jupiter, her Gracious Majesty will start in a day or two for Balmoral where she will be just about six hundred miles from the seat of Government ". In another the matter was seriously argued, with the concluding sentence : " It seems however that there is nobody to tell her that she is causing pain to the loyal and enabling the enemies of the Throne to rejoice ".

Lord Halifax,[1] a favoured Minister, although a Liberal, wrote several letters to the Private Secretary on the subject. In one of these he says : " But it is impossible to deny that H.M. is drawing too heavily on the credit of her former popularity and that Crowned Heads as well as other people must do much which was not necessary in former days to meet the altered circumstances and altered tone of modern times ". The following is from another of his letters, dated August 28, 1871 :

> I don't much care for the papers alone but one cannot meet anybody who does not tell the same story and one finds from this that the papers do express the common feeling and opinion.
>
> It matters less what Society thinks in London though even what *they* say does harm but the mass of the people expect a King or a Queen to look and play the part. They want to see a Crown and a Sceptre and all that sort of thing. They want the gilding for their money. It is not wise to let them think that for all the Queen *apparently to them* does, there is more than paid and that they could do without a sovereign who lives at Osborne and Balmoral as any private lady might do.
>
> Neither Kings, Lords, Ministers and soldier officers or anybody else can succeed now-a-days without doing a good deal more than they used to do.

Ponsonby in his memorandum book gives a detailed account of the proceedings in 1871 which is worth quoting in full :

[1] 1st Viscount Halifax, Lord Privy Seal.

QUEEN'S SECLUSION

Helps [1] and I agreed that there did not appear to be any necessity for troubling the Queen now upon what would be expected of her next year, but that in the circumstances it was of great importance she should not go to Balmoral till after the Prorogation. Lady Ely asked me about this and told me she told the Queen what my opinion was as above. This also was Biddulph's. It was necessary at once to take some steps on the subject but the Ministers did not seem to do anything at first and left it to the last moment. The Queen knowing my opinion did not enter into the matter any further with me, but communicated her views through Helps — a proceeding which some of the Ministers resented as he was an unauthorized channel. But they took advantage of this to express more freely their views. The Queen would not listen to much. The Lord Chancellor [2] came and had a long interview. What he said to her I do not know. He told me that he earnestly wished she would stay till the 21st the day of — or the day before the Prorogation. But she had made up her mind to go on the 15th and she said she would delay till the 18th if that were of use, otherwise she would go as settled originally. The Queen afterwards wrote to the Chancellor a repetition of what she had said to him in which she observed that she had seen from long experience that the more she yielded to pressure and alarm whenever it is not for an important political object it only encourages further demands and that she is then teased into doing what is bad for her health.

If any important question were to be decided she would not hesitate in sacrificing her convenience though she might not be able to do so on account of her health but when it is merely to gratify a fancy of the troublesome House of Commons, especially when it is their fault, she must say she thinks it unreasonable. After dwelling on her health and inability to do more now, she went on to find fault with the questions asked in Parliament which should be met with a high tone of reproof, and the Minister ought boldly to say she cannot do more than hold out hopes of her doing so. She has failed in none of her regal duties. It is abominable that a woman and a Queen laden with care and with public and domestic anxieties which are daily increasing should not be able to make people understand that there is a limit to her powers. Referring to the Prince who was killed by work and to Bright and Childers who were made ill by work she asked if this was what was desired of her. Unless her Ministers support her she must give up her burden to younger hands. Perhaps then these

---

Sir Arthur Helps, Clerk of the Council.   [2] Lord Cairns.

discontented people may regret they have broken her down while she yet might be of some use — Did the Chancellor ever reply to this ? Did he tell her it was not a trifling fancy of the Ministers but a matter of great importance that she should do more ? I cannot tell. But it is evident she still thinks she is asked to do things merely to support a political party. In the mean time the children were much distressed and wanted to get her to do more. They asked Sir W. Jenner but he said his care was her health and not her actions. He therefore positively refused the Crown Princess, Princess Louise and Prince Arthur's entreaties, saying he could be of no use. Mr. Candleish asked in the H. of Commons whether she were going before Prorogation and Gladstone replied he could not say but there was a postponement and that there would be no delay in business. He then wrote to the Queen to say he had learnt of her decision of going North so soon with the deepest regret as did all the Cabinet. I was at once sent for by Jenner who said the Queen was quite upset by this letter and very ill from the heat and worry. I was directed to telegraph to Mr. Gladstone that the Queen was very unwell and could not postpone her journey — and I then wrote to say that the Queen had fully explained it all to the Lord Chancellor and must go. The Council would be at Balmoral and there would be no delay in the Prorogation. The Queen observed also that he had not replied to her letter to the Lord Chancellor. Jenner then spoke to me in a very earnest manner on it. Said he had charge of her health and would do his duty. If the Ministers did not believe him as they evidently did not he could do nothing more. But he would not advise her to do things against her health for a political object. "But," I said, "you could ask her to try — perhaps it would not do her harm. Besides which it is not for the good of the Government but the existence of the Queen." No, he would not hear of that. It was entirely for their good and it was outrageous to worry her while she was unwell. The consequences might be most serious. But I said : "People ask how can she attend Gillies' Balls at Balmoral and not stand a little of the London balls." He said (which is very true) that at Gillies' Balls she speaks to none but at London balls she would be expected to speak to many. "But why shouldn't she live more in town and drive about there ? " "Because it makes her head ache." "Well, if she is ill now how can it be good for her to travel so far ? " "Of course it is. When people are ill they are often ordered off to a distance at once." In the afternoon Gladstone telegraphed to say if she could stay till 19th Saturday Parliament might be prorogued that day and moreover she could hold a Council early and go off in the middle of the day. This the Queen would not do and I replied, "A Council on the 19th necessitates a postponement of the journey till the 21st because of Sunday. This has been decided against already. The Queen is feeling far from well and could not postpone the journey."

Gladstone telegraphed again later but I could only give him the same answer — which I did with regret. All this time the communications from the Queen had been made through Helps or to me from Jenner who told me she was without anyone to help her. I told Jenner that without changing my opinion — that she ought to wait for the prorogation — I was of course her servant, I need not thrust unasked my views upon her — but I would of course punctually obey her commands. In the evening I received a note from the Queen saying she was unwell, that I was to write to Lord Granville and ask if he could prevent any more irritating letters from being sent to her. This gave me an opportunity of writing a few words as mildly as possible for Jenner declared that anything would make her ill and I therefore expressed my great regret at her having been worried by this question which " he fully believes has only been submitted to Your Majesty as a matter for calm deliberation without the remotest intention of being annoying. The Government have probably found themselves compelled to bring the matter before Your Majesty in consequence of the attacks to which they are exposed from those who complain they keep Your Majesty in the dark, or from those who maintain they desire to secure for themselves uncontrolled power. This no doubt made them submit the question for Your Majesty's consideration but they never had the remotest intention of annoying Your Majesty." Still from what the Queen afterwards wrote, what Jenner said and from what even Brown said in bringing the message I was convinced the Queen thought the Ministers were urging this for their own purposes. I therefore in thanking Mr. Gladstone for a letter he wrote to me told him he should be careful in expressing himself to the Queen to make it clear that what he urged was for her good and not for the advantage of his party. He thanked me — lamenting bitterly the whole affair. " A meaner cause for the decay of thrones cannot be conceived. It is like the worm which bores the bark of a noble oak tree and so breaks the channels of its life." He explained to the Queen that he had not answered her letter to the Chancellor for fear of troubling her further and it is true that being repeatedly told not to irritate her further it was difficult to know what to do. But as in her second letter to the Chancellor she said " the result of years of experience has taught her that to yield to mere idle clamour and fancy when NO real important object is at stake only entails further demands " — I think they should have answered that it was an important point. Finally we left Osborne the Queen very unwell and worse at Windsor. But we came North and arrived at Balmoral where she was very unwell for some days. The Council was held there. Lord Granville and Sir Wm. Jenner had some sharp discussions on the question. And finally the paragraph in the *Lancet* declared that the Queen was unable to do more than she does do.

After we got to Balmoral the Queen really was very unwell and an abscess formed under her arm which Lister of Edinburgh was sent for to operate on.

It will be seen that in this case the Queen's ill-health was a serious argument on her side. The accusations against her for hoarding were easily disposed of by the explanation that savings in the Civil List went back to the Exchequer not to the Privy Purse.

But having triumphed on this occasion, her decision that nothing should interfere with her retirement to Balmoral became still more determined.

In 1872 her health had recovered, she was taking a close interest in public questions and had " a complete knowledge of the political position ", but absolutely refused to go to Windsor or London.

In 1873 Ponsonby again became apprehensive. In November Cardwell [1] wrote a letter from the War Office conveying approval and congratulations to the troops after an engagement but in his own name, not mentioning the Queen. This was just the sort of thing that enraged her.

> This I thought [writes Ponsonby] gave me an opportunity for giving her a hint, how power was slipping out of her hands and for frightening her against the growing assumption of her ministers. I mean that they seem to care less and less what they submit to her. I don't blame them as she persists in living up here [Balmoral] and seeing them so seldom. But it gave me an opportunity for a gentle observation. She took no notice of it but altered my letter to Cardwell making it stronger.

Further he says, " The public are not fools enough to suppose that the Queen living up here alone without Ministers can be governing ". He feared the waning power of the monarchy, noticed that Ministers preferred to be out of the way and " were not telling her anything of subjects of importance ". Her differences which recurred with Cardwell

[1] Secretary of State for War.

might have been overcome if she had seen and talked to him. All the time she seemed ready for work, initiated the Inquiry into Railway Accidents and was able to influence Ministers when she saw them. The dilemma was seldom absent from Ponsonby's mind.

The Queen's decision in 1876 to be present in person at the state opening of Parliament was received in all quarters with great satisfaction. There was however fear that there might be some hostile demonstration against a sovereign who was so seldom seen. The following reassuring letter is from Disraeli's Private Secretary, Montagu Corry (afterwards Lord Rowton) :

> January 25, 1876
> The repeated confidential reports of the Police to the Home Secretary induce him to believe that the opening of Parliament by the Queen, in person, will be very popular, and is looked forward to by the masses, entirely, with gratification. Nor is there, in what reaches him, the slightest reason for apprehending the occurrence of an unseemly act, nor any but a becoming welcome to Her Majesty.
> Mr. Secretary Cross, in addition, feels bound to mention that a widespread desire is reported to exist among " the people " that Her Majesty should be graciously pleased to go to Westminster, on the 8th of February, in full state.

If however any people supposed that this single emergence of Her Majesty signified the abandonment on her part of her habits of seclusion they were entirely mistaken. She made no change whatever. As time passed the Queen's set purpose ceased to be a matter of dispute and all concerned in the Government of Great Britain had to accept Balmoral as just as much part of the seat of Government as Downing Street.

For a moment in 1878 Ponsonby wondered if possibly the uneventful stagnant atmosphere of Balmoral itself might not help to move the Queen more frequently from it.

> For the last two days [he writes in 1878] the Queen's dinners have been appallingly dull. I really have nothing to say nor has anyone else, and I rather prefer that this dulness " pounds of it " should be felt — and I believe it is felt. That is to say the Queen lamented the general dulness yesterday to Lady Ely. But whose fault is it ? She contrasts all that her daughter is doing in London and is sour with the comparison and by no means pleased at Prince and

Princess Christian going to Buckingham Palace for a week. And Biddulph has got some pleasant message that he is to hint to them they are not to do it again.

Later in 1881 a letter from Sir Francis Knollys shows that the avoidance of London was still a subject of discussion at Marlborough House. The Queen had refused to hold a levée.

> She remained at a ball at Balmoral last autumn from 10 till 2 and danced at it repeatedly. I should have imagined that this would have been a greater effort for her and a greater strain on her delicate constitution than holding a levée.

Even early in 1886 a strong article appeared on her continued retirement. The following letter from the Queen illustrates her indignation :

> Windsor Castle, Feb. 26, 1886
>
> . . . The Queen has been very much hurt by an article in the *St. James's* imputing to her the bad state of Society & making out there had been no Courts for 20 years ! ! Whereas excepting Balls & parties & going to Theatres & living in Town the Queen *neglected nothing* & it is most disheartening & ungrateful to almost threaten her if she does not do much more, when morally & physically she is doing much more than she can bear with her overwhelming work. It is very wrong. She never went out into general Society before 61 & never w^d have done it.
>
> Since her illness in 71 — these attacks had ceased but now when she is older & far less fit to do things, they have begun again.
>
> The Queen has been twice before to the Albert Hall since 71 & went today to hear Gounod's splendid music & Albani's glorious singing. . . .

Courtiers might grumble among themselves, Ministers might protest, and the press might attack her, the Queen's decision hardened and was unalterable. But so little was known of how she occupied herself for weeks and months that the strange life at Balmoral became something of a mystery, never satisfactorily fathomed by visitors who had no more than a passing glance at her highland retreat.

No wonder she was wanted at functions and Drawing-Rooms. No substitute among the Princes and Princesses could fill her place. The Duchesses and the débutantes, the Ministers and the crowd wanted to see the Queen. Not only had she the historical background of a long line of monarchs, she had also her own background of the popular young Queen in what was becoming a remote and romantic past.

On the occasion of the official opening of the Exhibition connected with the recently erected Imperial Institute in 1886, Lord Rosebery urged that the Queen should come in full state with a crown in order to impress the imagination of the Colonial representatives who would all be present. " The symbol ", he wrote to Ponsonby, " that unites this vast Empire is a Crown not a bonnet." It is doubtful whether the Private Secretary even conveyed this suggestion to the Queen. He knew far better than Rosebery her hatred of any personal spectacular display. The modestly dressed widow had really become for the people the symbol of their sovereign whose intimate homeliness endeared her to her subjects more than ever at this date. Crowns and pageantry may have been necessary conventions for other monarchs. To her they were of no significance, and in this her point of view was quite original. So the bonnet triumphed. She wore it at both her jubilees. However at Drawing-Rooms and other indoor state functions she did wear a little diamond crown and displayed the Koh-i-noor diamond and her Garter ribbon. In spite of the smallness of her stature and absence of beauty, she managed always by her wonderful carriage and deportment, which had characterized her from her early youth, to present unaccountably a figure of such dignity and distinction as to arrest the attention of the most unobservant spectator who at once decided that no one else in the assembly mattered.

It must be admitted that there were some who disliked the Queen and thought her dowdy and disagreeable. They consisted chiefly of those who expected and longed for her smile and had received only what was known as the drill eye of critical disapproval.

The Queen's strict retirement was primarily based on her over-indulgence in what may be called the luxury of woe. Balmoral reminded her more than any other place of the Prince Consort. She cherished his memory, had an annual service at his tomb at Frogmore, collected relics of him, never altered her attire of deep mourning and her characteristic widow's cap, and even retained over half an inch of black edge on her notepaper till the end. Deaths and anniversaries of deaths drew from her repeated expressions of grief sometimes in rather exaggerated terms as if to make up for not having paid much attention to the deceased when they were alive. Mixed with her genuine sorrow one cannot help detecting on occasions a note of resentment if not anger at the loss, so that one almost expects to find some direction in her best style of political indignation instructing her Private Secretary to address some remonstrance to the Almighty.

However the Private Secretary would have found his own position quite intolerable had his duties merely consisted of dancing attendance on an obstinate middle-aged lady who knew little of what was going on and cared less. But he soon gained a high opinion of her powers and was constantly amazed at her industry. " I really do think ", he sums up his opinion in the early years, " she has very clear good sense and sees things in an honest way." In looking through the papers one might be disposed to agree with Lord Granville who in 1882 said, " it was impossible to treat the Queen as a great states-man because she was such a child, but equally impossible to treat her as a child because she had the *aperçus* of a great statesman in some things ". But " the child " had caught Lord Granville out on an earlier occasion. It was on the question of a jointure being voted for the Grand Duchess Marie of Russia on her marriage to the Duke of Edinburgh. At a Council held at Osborne in July 1873 Lord Granville came with a scrap of paper from Gladstone to Colonel Ponsonby :

" Palmerston's settlement," he said, " is the only one we can stand by. Surely when that was made with the Queen's consent you can scarcely expect we shall now go back to old precedents of the Duke of York. No. We must stand by that and the Queen is sure to see that it is fair." Granville twiddled the paper of Gladstone's, gave it to me to read and merely said, " You see we can't well set aside the agreement of Palmerston's." I had no opportunity of asking what this was. But later I saw the Queen who was in wrath at the idea of our refusing a jointure to the Grand Duchess, England being too poor ! I told her about the Palmerston agree-ment. Off she went to a box, opened it and began to read. It was very much what she said. It promised jointures to all the wives of princes ! Therefore as Ministers had so vehemently said they would stick by this, she hoped they would. This very much took Granville aback when I showed it to him and he proceeds to see Gladstone with it today — I must say I think the Queen is in some things an excellent woman of business.

This is a good instance of the Queen's remarkable memory, and she would talk sometimes of the very early years of her reign.

Ponsonby asked her one day whether it was true as stated in a magazine that the Duchess of Montrose and Lady Sarah Ingestre hissed her at Ascot. She said : " Quite true. I did not know that ever had been published. They sent to let me know privately they didn't hiss me. They hissed Lord Melbourne.[1] He was an excellent man but too much a party man and made me a party Queen. He admitted this himself afterwards."

The Queen had a success in 1880 in carrying her way against her Minister. The Government desired to make Sir Garnet Wolseley a peer while he retained the post of Quarter-Master-General so that he might speak in the House of Lords on behalf of the War Office. The Queen emphatically turned down this suggestion and the following comment is made by the biographers of Lord Wolseley : [2]

Gladstone tried again and again to alter the Queen's decision but found her adamant and in the end he had to give way because he was wrong and the Queen right.

It is not true to say that the Queen never listened to a case being argued which was in opposition to her own view. But it depended how it was done and who did it. She was a keen critic of personality and would allow things to be said by one person which she would not tolerate from another. Strict propriety in stories and anecdotes was the general rule but there were certain people who might amuse her in their infringement of that rule. So also in serious matters, if a case were put with sincerity and knowledge she might listen, provided of course she had no preconceived prejudice against the person who had the courage to do it. After the Afghan War, for instance, she was strongly opposed to the withdrawal of British troops from Kandahar. Ponsonby in a letter from Balmoral, June 18, 1881, wrote :

[1] *Greville Memoirs.* Edited by Lytton Strachey and Roger Fulford (Macmillan, 1938). Vol. iv, June 24, 1839.
[2] *Life of Lord Wolseley*, by Major-General Sir F. Maurice and Sir George Arthur.

G

. . . Very few people can go against her, because she pays them off by never speaking on the subject again but she also respects strong convictions. The officers who were for retiring from Kandahar gave their reasons in a hesitating way seeing they were unpalatable and Macpherson began by saying it would be cheaper to give it up — she listened to nothing more. But when [Colonel] Sir Neville Chamberlain spoke it was with fire and energy : " Oh Ma'm, never let anyone persuade you to make such a fatal mistake as to keep Kandahar — a hateful, useless, abominable hole which it is dishonourable to stay at one instant longer than we can. I implore you to come away." She listened to Chamberlain and said he had moved her. . . .

In early years the Queen had amused and enjoyed herself at parties, balls, concerts, the opera and plays. While in the initial period of her strict mourning she cut all such entertainments out of her programme, natural it was that the inclination to enjoy a little fun and amusement should re-emerge if only to relieve the monotony of the routine which even she herself at times felt to be dull.

She would not go about London of course in quest of entertainment. She commanded the entertainment to come to her. Gradually actors were summoned to Windsor where a stage could be erected in the Waterloo gallery, famous singers came and indeed entertainments became a feature of Court life. Even to the inmates of Balmoral some relief came in the same way. George Grossmith was ordered there. He heard there was only an ancient Erard in the castle. So he asked to bring his own Brinsmead which he took about with him. In March 1893 Irving was commanded to give a performance of *Becket* at Windsor Castle. Some of the correspondence which passed on this occasion is worth quoting.

Sir Henry Ponsonby (March 2) wrote to say that all arrangements had been made and Irving's manager was quite satisfied about the size of the stage. On this letter the Queen wrote :

The Queen is rather alarmed at hearing from the P^{ce} of Wales & P^{ce} George that there is some very strong language (disagreeable & coarse rather) in *Becket* w^{h} must be somewhat changed for performance *here* so close. Pr^{ss} Louise says that some *scenes* or perhaps *one* are very *awkward*. What *can* be done ?

The P^r of Wales thought Sir Henry sh^d see & speak to Irving.

The Queen hates anything of that sort.

To *The Queen*

March 6, 1893

Sir Henry Ponsonby with his humble duty is glad Your Majesty does not see anything very objectionable in *Becket* and he certainly thinks that no fault can well be found with it, though the language is sometimes strong — as is natural. He has written to Lord Tennyson as desired by Your Majesty.

From *The Queen*

If it *were possible* to curtail or modify some few things in the scenes between Rosamund & Queen Eleanor & Fitzurse it w^d be more agreeable but perhaps it c^d not be. Sir Henry & Mary sh^d just look at it. The whole piece is curtailed for as it was written & printed it is very long.

Besides writing to Tennyson Sir Henry asked Irving to come and talk it over, and the matter was adjusted.

There is an almost pathetic plea for a little jaunt in 1892. Writing from Windsor, the Queen asks :

Does Sir Henry Ponsonby think it possible for her to go *privately* to see *Venice* ? She hears it is really admirably done. P^{ss} Beatrice is delighted & it is a real success. In the day of course & it is not a theatre or a play & it will be 5 months & $\frac{1}{2}$ after her dear grandson's death & $3\frac{1}{2}$ after her dear son-in-law's & she w^d very much like to see it.

We may be sure Ponsonby gave his sanction without consulting anyone else.

The Queen inaugurated as well amateur theatricals both at Balmoral and Osborne. In two of her Grooms-in-Waiting, the Hon. Alec Yorke and Colonel Arthur Collins, she had two excellent actors and competent stage managers. What she enjoyed most of all was superintending the rehearsals, altering to her liking the script of the plays (as she did with *Becket*) and criticizing the performances of the Princesses and courtiers who were the actors. In the autumn of 1889 when Ponsonby was away, he received an account of the theatricals from his Assistant Secretary Arthur Bigge who himself played a part.

The play was a translation of a French piece called *L'Homme*

Blasé. When the cast was made up but before they knew their parts the Queen bade them perform before her. She was amused ; but finding that Princess Beatrice who had a good part in the first act did not come on again, she ordered Colonel Collins to re-write the last act so that she might reappear. On this point Major Bigge writes : " I think Collins ought to have added to the printed description in the Programme : ' The return and reconciliation to her first husband of Mrs. Iron-brace is by command ' ". To begin with, the marriages in the acted version were an insertion. In the French original there were none ! This much amused the Empress Eugénie who was present.

> The result of the rehearsal [Bigge writes] is that H.M. thinks I better not call her daughter " a degraded woman " and I agree ! But wasn't it a funny situation — there in the Queen's room, so apostrophizing H.R.H. ! Also she is *not* to say to Sir C. in describing her wooing to Clutterbuck, " I had nothing to offer as dowry but my virtue," to which C. replies, " Ah, little enough ! "

After the actual performance he writes :

> Everyone seems much pleased, but none more so than H.M., who has extracted the maximum amount of fun and interest out of the fortnight's preparation.

Amateur theatricals which superseded *tableaux vivants* became almost an annual event. One more may be mentioned, in January 1893 when *She Stoops to Conquer* was performed, admirably produced by Colonel Collins in the Council Room at Osborne. Sir Henry himself had a small part and three of his children also performed. The chief ladies' parts were taken by Princess Louise and Princess Beatrice. It was rather an ambitious attempt. But any failure of memory on the part of the performers was tactfully concealed by a claque of footmen at the back of the audience.

It was in the direction of music and the drama that the Queen showed her special interest and desire for entertainment. To the sister art of painting she paid little attention except by sitting for her own portrait. " I don't think she cares for pictures," writes Ponsonby, " and she abominates a gallery or an exhibition." Literature did not occupy the Queen's time very much. Sometimes she spoke to Ponsonby

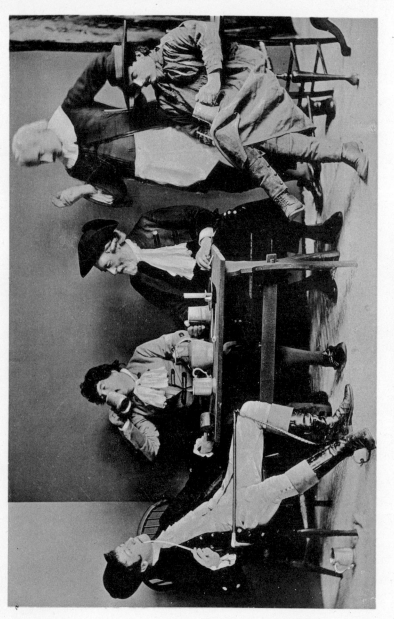

SHE STOOPS TO CONQUER, Osborne 1893
Tony Lumpkin (Arthur Ponsonby), Tom Tickle (Lord Lorne),
Jack Slang (Sir H. Ponsonby), Stingo (Major Legge), Twist
(A. Cowell)

of books of the day which were being talked about and asked what Mary Ponsonby thought of such-and-such a book. The Duchess of Roxburghe recommended the novels of Marie Corelli. She began one of them. But on Ponsonby courteously informing her it was " bosh " she seems not to have proceeded any further.

Any early description of Queen Victoria which omitted some of her nine children with whom she was constantly surrounded would not be a faithful picture of her. She was devotedly attached to all children and remained so all her life. But she loved them generically not individually. That is to say that while she might prefer some to others, her feelings towards them all underwent a change when they grew up. This attitude of a mother towards her children is by no means uncommon. In a letter [1] addressed to Augusta, Queen of Prussia and afterwards Empress of Germany, she makes an honest confession of this change of feeling, on the occasion of the engagement of the Princess Royal, her eldest child, to the Crown Prince :

Balmoral, Oct. 6, 1856

. . . I see the children much less & even here, where Albert is often away all day long, I find no especial pleasure or compensation in the company of the elder children. You will remember that I told you this at Osborne. Usually they go out with me in the afternoon (Vicky mostly, & the others also sometimes), or occasionally in the mornings when I drive or walk or ride, accompanied by my lady-in-waiting, & only very occasionally do I find the rather intimate intercourse with them either agreeable or easy. You will not understand this, but it is caused by various factors. Firstly, I only feel properly *à mon aise* & quite happy when Albert is with me ; secondly, I am used to carrying on my many affairs quite alone ; & then I have grown up all alone, accustomed to the society of adult (& never with younger) people — lastly, I still cannot get used to the fact that Vicky is almost grown up. To me she still seems the same child, who had to be kept in order & therefore must not become too intimate. Here are my sincere feelings in contrast to yours.

In the period under review her children were all fully grown up ; some were married, others were about to marry, and the general impression gained is that their presence at her

[1] *Further Letters of Queen Victoria*, ed. by Hector Bolitho, 1938.

Court, sometimes several together, gave her little pleasure and led on occasions to differences which were not helpful and were liable to produce rather than prevent " rows ".

In spite of what she wrote to the Queen of Prussia, circumstances eventually culminating in tragedy drew Queen Victoria into very close and affectionate contact with her eldest daughter, the Crown Princess. But in the earlier years attempts to induce the Queen to appear more in public were resented as much from her daughter as from anyone else. Moreover the Crown Princess lacked tact and, being by far the most intellectual of the family, on account of the training she had received from her father, was for some time regarded with suspicion. On the other hand her often too openly expressed preference for the country of her birth, although it caused offence in Germany, was naturally appreciated in the British Court. She never ceased to keep in touch with all that was going on in England. One night at dinner she told Henry Ponsonby that she took in and read regularly the *Quarterly*, the *Edinburgh*, the *Fortnightly*, the *Saturday* and the *Journal of Mining and Metallurgy*. In one of the letters written from Osborne, when he was in waiting the year before he was appointed Private Secretary (January 8, 1869), Ponsonby describes a conversation with Lord Clarendon (then Foreign Secretary) :

> He spoke to me on the Princess Royal, was full of admiration for her talents, but says she throws everything away by the heedlessness of the common courtesies of life. That she is unpopular in Prussia not nearly so much for her opinions, which if she behaved civilly she might get people to listen to. At Paris where she went to see the Exhibition, I believe, said Lord Clarendon, she passed her time in studying surgical instruments and never gave a glance at the grand things the Parisians were so proud of. No doubt this was excellent for her education, but it did not please.

When the Emperor Frederick died the serious controversy over Dr. Morell Mackenzie, one of the doctors who attended him, was closely watched by the Queen. At that time and till her own death the Empress Frederick was in constant correspondence with Sir Henry's wife, with whom she had always been on the friendliest terms.[1]

Prince Alfred, afterwards Duke of Edinburgh, was un-

[1] See *Mary Ponsonby*, ed. by Magdalen Ponsonby, 1927.

fortunate in being the member of the family who came in for the most criticism and around whom hot disputes arose. He lacked the charm of his brothers and Ponsonby cannot help remarking on the look in his eyes which did not inspire trust. As to his musical accomplishments, there was an inclination to overrate them. His own Equerry declared, " Few people had a more natural gift for music and few people played more execrably on the fiddle ". After a dinner one night with the Prince of Wales at Abergeldie in 1871 Ponsonby writes :

> After dinner we played whist. Gladstone and I against Wales and Brasseur.[1] We played rather well. But Alfred went off to the pianoforte, which Zichy played, while Alfred accompanied on the fiddle. Anything more execrable I never heard. They did not keep time. They or perhaps the fiddle was out of tune and the noise abominable. Even Wales once or twice broke out, " I don't think you're quite right." This for an hour. I quite agreed with G. that it was a relief when we got away from that appalling din.

Prince Alfred's social gifts in company did not appear to attract people to him. Later, in 1889, Ponsonby writes :

> Fortunately for me I don't go to the smoking room. I gave that up long ago and positively refuse. Now the Duke of Edinburgh occupies the chair and talks about himself by the hour. Those who go are quite exhausted. Prince Henry has given up smoking in consequence.

After his marriage to the Grand Duchess Marie of Russia and his establishment at Clarence House there was some fear at Marlborough House that if he interested himself in art and music he might become a sort of rival to the Prince of Wales.

It would be possible in quoting letters and memoranda to give a full account of the complications over his marriage, the difference of religion, the suspicion that Russia's policy in connection with the expedition of Khiva was mixed up with it, the secrecy maintained, the Prince of Wales not being told of it, etc. etc. But although there were some fairly acrimonious paragraphs in the press it was not a matter of any real importance, and eventually the Duchess of Edinburgh found favour with Queen Victoria.

[1] The Prince's former French tutor.

Prince Arthur was the favourite son. Yet in 1867, when he was about seventeen and coming to Osborne to see his mother after a long absence, Ponsonby, who was then Equerry-in-Waiting, notes :

> The Queen is an odd woman. I believe she is as fond of her children as anyone. Yet she was going out driving and started at 3.25. Just as she was getting in up comes the advance Groom to say Arthur had arrived and was following, yet she wouldn't wait for one minute to receive him, and drove off.

Prince Arthur practised very strictly the habit of never confronting the Queen direct but approaching Ponsonby as an intermediary.

She was not enthusiastic about his engagement to Princess Margaret, daughter of Prince Frederick Charles of Prussia, in 1878. She wrote to her Private Secretary :

> May 2, '78. Windsor
> She cannot deny that she does not rejoice so much at the event — she thinks that so few marriages are really happy now & they are such a lottery. Besides Arthur is so dear a son to her that she dreads *any* alteration.
> But it is entirely his *own* doing and as she, the Pr^{ss}, is so much praised & said to be so good, unassuming & unspoilt, *serious minded* & *very* English we must hope for *the best* & that one so good as he is being very happy.

In later years she cherished the idea of his succeeding the Duke of Cambridge as Commander-in-Chief and she was therefore strongly opposed to his having an Indian Command in 1885. The visits Ponsonby received from the Duke of Connaught in those days were frequent. The Indian appointment was turned down by the Cabinet for military as well as political reasons.

In 1881 Ponsonby describes what cannot have been a very hilarious family party :

> We had at dinner the Dukes of Edinburgh, Connaught and Albany and their two Duchesses which with Princess Beatrice makes a large element of Royalty. But the Queen keeps the conversation entirely under her control and does not allow any of them to talk too much. Lady Ely, Bridport, Carlingford and I formed the inferior gallery.

In the case of her youngest son Prince Leopold there was an element of tragedy. He had inherited the disease known as haemophilia or bleeding, so that the slightest little accident, slip or bruise prostrated him for some time. He was generally intelligent but had no particular talents. The Queen's attitude towards him was one of apparent solicitude in his constant ever-recurring illnesses, combined with thwarting and interfering with him when he was well. In 1877 when there was special anxiety about his health she was sympathetic so long as it gave her an excuse for remaining at Balmoral. But when the delay she considered had been long enough then she said : " He must be well enough to travel." The question continually cropped up as to what he should do. The Queen wrote to her Private Secretary from Osborne, February 21, 1877 :

> Prince Leopold has been working very steadily. The Queen will send boxes down & Gen¹ Ponsonby will select what is of interest for Leopold to read & make abstracts of. He is getting much quicker at it.

He took an intelligent interest in foreign affairs but was unfortunate and indeed became mischievous in some of his interferences in politics. So when the Queen told Ponsonby to give him work, he really did not know what to do because the Prince had no powers of concentration or of mastering any subject. But when Leopold wanted to do something himself he was often prevented. The Queen stopped him from being a captain of Volunteers in 1872 although the Prince of Wales was in favour of it. When in 1875 he agreed to receive the Freedom of the City, she wrote at once to the Lord Mayor to cancel the invitation. In 1883 the question arose as to whether Prince Leopold's desire to go to Canada should be acceded to. Lord Granville wrote expressing doubt but asking what the Queen's view was. Ponsonby telegraphed back : " At first surprised and dead against it somewhat more softened now but by no means advocating it and stands entirely aloof ". Even in his private affairs, when the Prince wanted to shoot or to go about socially and have some fun, the Queen's supervision stopped it. Sir Thomas Biddulph's assistance was enlisted to lecture him. To this Sir Thomas very much objected. In June 1878 Ponsonby writes :

It is awkward talking to Leopold in the sense the Queen wishes as I do not in the least agree with her. She has laid down absolute rules for what he is to do, coming such a day and going such a day — never to dine out or to go to a club — to come to Osborne in July and leave it the day the Regatta begins and all in that strain. I cannot support such a system and for one thing know it is useless to try it on. Will the Queen never find out that she will have ten times more influence on her children by treating them with kindness and not trying to rule them like a despot?

That Leopold chafed under this treatment is not to be wondered at. He must have cursed the illness which tied him by a chain to his mother.

In 1882 as Duke of Albany he married Princess Helen of Waldeck and Pyrmont, a sister of the Queen of Holland. She is the single instance quoted in the letters of a member of the family who refused to write to the Queen when there was any trouble, refused to send messages through an intermediary and insisted on confronting her " face to face ". In one quoted instance the interview must have been lively as after it the Duchess of Albany did not appear at the Queen's table but dined alone with her husband.

When the Duke of Albany died in 1884 there was a great outpouring of grief and lamentation, in which can be detected the note of resentment at having another of her children taken from her.

Mourning was strict. It was suggested by the Prince of Wales that the Queen might take just one Drawing-Room. Upon which Ponsonby received the following message through Miss Stopford :

Balmoral Castle, June 7, 1884

The Queen has just received your note concerning the Drawingrooms, and I am desired to tell you that H.M. " will not *hear* of any being held this year — that even if there was ONE the Queen would not allow either Princess Christian or Princess Beatrice to attend, and that the Princess of Wales could not be *alone* — that a Drawingroom held this Season would have to be in very deep mourning, which would be undesirable, in short the Queen will not hear of it, and begs that nothing more may be said to her about it. People have no right to expect Drawingrooms for their own convenience of going abroad. That no Court Balls or Concerts would be given, which is the chief reason for many being presented. That *Levées* are quite different ! "

Except for an injunction that Princess Christian ought not to have stayed at Buckingham Palace and must not do so again, and an indignant protest that she had taken one of the Queen's ladies as her Lady-in-Waiting at Cumberland Lodge in Windsor Park during Ascot week, Princess Helena, the Queen's third daughter, is only mentioned incidentally in the papers.

Princess Alice, who was supposed to have been the favourite of the Prince Consort, does not seem to have had her way with the Queen, judging by a small incident Ponsonby relates in 1875 :

> I told you that Princess Alice at Osborne had talked very loudly at dinner about a horse she wanted, quiet enough for herself and strong enough for a charger for Louis, but the Queen changed the discourse pretty smartly to the beef and cutlets. It seems however that Alice has got round Colonel Maude. The Queen promised to give two ponies to the children and Maude writes to suggest that instead of these ponies the Queen should give a horse now at Hampton Court, quiet enough for the Princess to ride and strong enough for Prince Louis ; but the Queen is awake and has desired that her original intention of giving the ponies shall not be altered.

Princess Louise's engagement to Lord Lorne in 1870 occupied a great deal of attention. The Queen approved but there was some opposition in other quarters. Ponsonby in congratulating the Queen inadvertently referred to Lord Lorne as an Englishman. He was at once corrected. " Colonel Ponsonby speaks of his being a young Englishman, but he is *not*, he is a Scotchman and a Highlander." Princess Louise however found no more favour with her mother than any of the others and her rather Bohemian habits were watched and disapproved of. On her making some suggestion with regard to the heating of the new room at Osborne the Queen wrote : " Yes. But she must not interfere too much. She is not practical." So far as Ponsonby himself was concerned, he repeatedly refers to the liveliness of Princess Louise's conversation at the Queen's dinner and the relief this gave to the too frequent dullness amounting sometimes to gloom.

Princess Beatrice, the Queen's youngest child, became as time passed her mother's devoted and constant companion and was fondly regarded by the public who habitually saw her sitting with the Queen in her carriage drives. She was also entrusted with the more intimate correspondence. After her marriage to Prince Henry of Battenberg in 1884 she continued to occupy the same position. Prince Henry, a pleasant and genial man, might well have been envious of the important careers of his two brothers, Alexander of Bulgaria and Louis who served in the British Navy. As the Queen's son-in-law he had higher rank. But his ambition was to serve his newly adopted country in some active way. He therefore volunteered for the post of military secretary to Colonel Sir F. Scott who commanded the expedition to Ashanti in 1895. But most unfortunately he contracted the fever which claimed many victims and he died on his journey home.

The Duke of Cambridge was the Queen's first cousin. Personally she had a great affection for him. It was noticeable at a Drawing-Room when she came into the Ante-room where the royalties were assembled, she would single him out for a word of conversation before turning round and proceeding to the Throne Room. But frankly, judging by the many papers reciting events with which he was closely concerned — the Duke must have been a great nuisance. At a time when army reform was under discussion he was not just conservative but hopelessly reactionary and not only opposed change but quarrelled with those who proposed it. At the same time he took the liveliest interest in the welfare of the soldier and was generally popular in the army among all ranks.

It would be wearisome to recite his views, recorded elsewhere, on Cardwell's reforms, on the policy of Childers, on linked battalions, on the appointment as Adjutant-General of Wolseley, whom he detested as a reformer and feared as a rival, on the recommendation of the Hartington Commission that the post of Commander-in-Chief should be abolished and on his own retirement. The Queen was reluctant to take up his strong objections because it would then be clear that he had been complaining to her. Some of the royal family took his side and supported the idea that he should stay on as Commander-in-Chief, a position he had held since 1856, so that he might be succeeded by the Duke of Connaught.

The following letter shows the Duke had warm supporters inside the Office :

From *Lt.-General G. B. Harman*

Horse Guards, War Office, S.W.
26th Jany., 1888

I was exceedingly glad to receive your views on the subject of the Commander-in-Chief being succeeded by a " Board ", I most entirely agree that it would be an abomination and I believe the greatest misfortune that could befall the Army. I devoutly hope that the Queen will never assent to such a proposal should it ever be made to Her Majesty. I am fully aware that there exists a strong party who advocate placing Army administration under a Board but I fear they are actuated in their own personal interests, which is alas ! too often the case in the present day. The Duke is the best friend the Army has, and knows its requirements better than any living man, and were it not for what many are pleased to call " his obstruction " to the reforms that are so constantly being advanced, the Service instead of being the popular profession it now is would soon become quite the reverse.

I hope our C. in C. may long be spared to hold his Office and eventually be succeeded by another Royal Duke.

But the difficulty was that the Duke himself kept on changing his mind. Ponsonby's method with him, as shown by the draft of a letter in the correspondence, was to praise the Duke's views but point out the difficulty of pressing them, then " it appears to me that there is no alternative but to adopt the new ideas ", and finally " Your Royal Highness should place yourself at the head of the movement and guide it ". Sometimes he would even say " As your Royal Highness so rightly suggested " and then put his own ideas in the mouth of the Duke, who was quite pleased.

In the crisis over Wolseley's appointment as Adjutant-General the Duke received a good deal of support from outside. An indiscreet and facetious courtier (not in the Queen's Household) wrote to Ponsonby : " The R. family would like to burn at the stake — Childers, J. Adye, Buller and G. Wolseley ".

Among Ponsonby's letters to his wife during September to

December 1881, chiefly from Balmoral, there are several which
give in the fullest detail an account of the deadlock caused
by the Duke's refusal to accept Wolseley as Adjutant-General.
The details, intrigues and changes took up many hours of his
time.   But in retrospect the affair cannot be considered oı
sufficient importance to occupy more than a few lines in these
pages.

The adjustment reached in the quarrel, in which personal
antipathy formed such a large part, it can be seen was largely
due to Ponsonby's judicial handling of the elements of discord.
The Queen had to be restrained so that her interference
might never be suspected.   She disliked the Secretary of State,
Childers, and Mr. Gladstone behind him.   A deaf ear had to
be turned to the Prince of Wales' constant and violent protests
and his dislike of Wolseley.   The old Duchess of Cambridge
had to be ignored and full advantage had to be taken of
the Duke's occasionally more reasonable moods.   Eventually
Ponsonby's suggestion, that Wolseley should be appointed and
the Duke induced not to resign anyhow for six months, was
adopted.   Indeed it was not till 1895 that the Duke resigned
the post of Commander-in-Chief and was succeeded by his
rival Sir Garnet Wolseley.

It would be impossible to relate how much the time of the
Queen and her Private Secretary was taken up by the grievances,
complaints, poverty, debts and more especially desires for
rank and promotion of the many minor royalties who hovered
at a distance round the Court.   The Queen disliked most of
them and was always ready to check their pretensions.   When
a dispute arose in 1878 about the exact precedence of three of
the minor royal relations, Ponsonby, estimating the relative
importance of such a question, quotes Dr. Johnson : " Tell
me first which goes in first, a louse or a flea ? "   When one
Highness, distracted by his own and his wife's debts, declared
he would go abroad and offer his sword to some foreign nation,
Ponsonby only writes, " I cannot imagine what nation would
accept his sword ".   When told that the possible engagement
of a young princess of the English royal family to a German
princeling would not be permitted, Ponsonby asked why.
He was informed that the young man could not dance the
Fackel Tanz (a dance with torches).   Unacquainted with the
regulation that only princes above a certain rank could be

allowed to join in this particular dance, Ponsonby simply enquired : " Why don't he learn it ? "

The Queen used to refer in her letters to " the feeling abroad " on the question of the moment. She was able to do this from the correspondence she kept up with various European courts with which she had direct links. To mention only a few : she had contact with Germany through her daughter the Princess Royal, who eventually became Empress, and through her grandson the Kaiser William II, as well as her daughter-in-law the Duchess of Connaught. Her son the Duke of Edinburgh married the daughter of the Czar Alexander II and he subsequently succeeded as Duke of Saxe-Coburg-Gotha. Her daughter Princess Alice married the Grand Duke of Hesse. Her daughter-in-law the Princess of Wales was a daughter of the King of Denmark. Her daughter-in-law the Duchess of Albany was a sister of the Queen of Holland. Leopold King of the Belgians was her first cousin. Her granddaughter married the Crown Prince of Roumania.

There is also ample evidence to show that as time went on she was regarded with veneration and respect by the rulers of the nations. So that there was some excuse for her impatience on occasions at not being able owing to her constitutional position to interfere on her own initiative. On the other hand there were also times when her Ministers considered that a personal letter from her to another sovereign might lead to good results.

In a study of Queen Victoria's political influence it is suggested that the passing of the Reform Bill in 1832 is the decisive date at which the Crown, ceasing to be powerful, becomes influential. But the author, commenting later on the episode of the Queen's telegram *en clair* to Gladstone on Gordon's fate,[1] remarks that this " opened out the very distinct possibility of a Government resigning, not because it no longer possessed the confidence of the House of Commons, but because it no longer possessed the Crown's confidence. That so late as 1885 there should have been this possibility is a most striking piece of evidence of its continued political power." [2]

The above-mentioned telegram was not by any means the

---

[1] See p. 230.
[2] *Political Influence of Queen Victoria*, by Frank Hardie, 1935.

only instance in which the dividing line between influence and interference was perhaps not intentionally but certainly overstepped. The general public, however, at the time was not cognizant of any instances of either influence or interference on the part of the sovereign ; nor did she for a moment wish that they should be.

CHAPTER V

The Queen and the Prince of Wales

IF in recording comments and criticisms made by the Queen on her children and relations, her attitude to her eldest son, the Prince of Wales, has been omitted it is because it was the most important and has been the subject of much discussion and some controversy, and therefore deserves a separate chapter. Not only was it governed by the confession above quoted [1] which she made in her letter to the Queen of Prussia, but it must be borne in mind that strained relations amounting in some cases to open opposition have often existed between the sovereign and the heir to the throne. Many instances can be found in past English history and they were destined to occur again in later years. Curiously enough however there was not any sort of opposition of a political nature between the Queen and her son. They were both Conservative Imperialists. There is hardly an instance of controversy on any major domestic, foreign or imperial political question. The Prince's wife too seems to have met with the Queen's entire approval. It would indeed have been difficult for anyone to have quarrelled with the Princess of Wales. Yet with the Prince, disapproval, rows and, it must be acknowledged, bickering reached a more acute pitch than with any of her other children.

The Prince Consort with his professorial methods of intensive education had been more or less successful with his eldest daughter. But his eldest son, instead of submitting to, reacted against this system and only retained a competent knowledge of German and French. From early days he was disinclined for study of any kind. As time passed, the nature and habit of life of mother and son became very strongly contrasted. An elderly lady living in almost austere retire-

[1] Chapter IV, p. 85.

ment in what amounted to a backwater, and a young man who by his position naturally became the centre of smart society, could not possibly see things through the same spectacles. As the dowdy simplicity of the Court if anything increased, the gaiety and frivolity of the Prince's *entourage* became more exuberant. While his manner to his mother when they met was studiously courtly and deferential, never would he approach her and talk over with her face to face even the smallest dispute which might arise. Before his severe illness in 1872 his general conduct came in for a good deal of public criticism, and rumours about his debts were magnified out of all proportion. During his illness, which was a very severe attack of typhoid contracted at Londesborough Lodge, near Scarborough, the Queen showed the greatest solicitude. She went to Sandringham for a day on November 29, and returned there on December 18, staying eleven days. There are daily letters from Ponsonby, who accompanied her, describing the crisis of the illness, the anxious watching and the conversations and comments of other members of the royal family who were present in the house. The arrival at Sandringham of so large a number of the family, considering too that they were by no means all on good terms with one another, made the arrangements far from easy. Then there were their Household attendants and of course the doctors. The Queen however was completely master of the situation. Not only did she guard the sick man's door as sentry to prevent a Princess from entering but she herself decided who should leave Sandringham and when they should go. In one of his letters Ponsonby writes :

> Yesterday Haig and I went out towards the garden by a side door when we were suddenly nearly carried away by a stampede of royalties, headed by the Duke of Cambridge and brought up by Leopold, going as fast as they could. We thought it was a mad bull. But they cried out : " The Queen, the Queen," and we all dashed into the house again and waited behind the door till the road was clear. When Haig and I were alone we laughed immensely. This is that " one-ness " we hear of.

Quotations from two of his graphic letters may be given, written when the Prince's condition was improving, because they describe the general atmosphere in the house, and comic relief is provided by an episode in which the Duke of Cambridge took a prominent part :

Sandringham, Dec. 14, 1871

There seems to be a determination with some people to make the worst of everything. . . . Stephy [1] turns up her eyes and tells me wondrous horrors ending up by saying the Queen was by no means happy. " Dear me," I said, " you surprise me, as I have just had a message as to whether Princess Beatrice and even some of the others might go tomorrow." Stephy considerably taken aback went to bed. Lady Macclesfield [2] was worse for she announced that all bad symptoms have increased, dwelling specially on delirium. The men disappear much after dinner so the women are not harassed in the little drawing room. When I went in I saw Aunt C.,[3] Lady M. and Stephy whispering violently — A. Ellis [4] and his sister whispering and Haig [5] sitting close gazing with astonishment. It was too much. I burst out laughing. So did he and we left the room followed by Mrs. H. also laughing immoderately. Cambridge has been full of talk but old Knollys [6] says he utterly refuses to discuss military matters and converses on nothing but drains. He had carried Knollys off to half a dozen rooms where he thought there was a smell and Princess Louise's room has been proclaimed uninhabitable which in the present crowded state of the house is inconvenient. This afternoon the Duke thought there was a bad smell in the library where we were sitting and when F. Knollys came in and said he smelt it, the Duke jumped up and said " By George, I won't sit here," and went about smelling in all the corners — A. Ellis and I roaring. . . . There may be a bad smell though I don't perceive it. But if you have a room hermetically closed and 5 or 6 people sitting in it all day long, it must have a fusty smell. But the Duke is wild on the subject and is examining all the drains of the house. . . .

Sandringham, Dec. 15, 1871

. . . Natural enough while the Prince was ill, to stand in the hall waiting for news, but now this is a mere waste of time. The Duke of Cambridge is one of the busy ones and writes in one library while I write in the other. The gas pipe man came to see about the supposed smell — said he smelt nothing. I went and told the Duke. He rushed in

---

[1] The Duchess of Roxburghe.   [2] In attendance on the Princess of Wales.
[3] Mrs. Charles Grey.   [4] Of the Princess of Wales' household.
[5] Equerry to the Duke of Edinburgh.
[6] Sir W. Knollys (father of Francis Knollys).

at once, caught hold of the gas pipe man, "My dear fellow come here — don't you smell it? Well come here," till the man at last said he did to save himself from being pulled about the room. On this admission Jenner spoke to him seriously and the Duke violently. The man however had nothing to do with the drain pipes but was only the gas man and tried to say so once or twice but no one would listen and he was finally dragged upstairs where the stink, they say, was suffocating. Luckily however the gas man was the right man for it turned out after much rummaging that the smell was an escape of gas and on his doing something to his pipes the smell has entirely ceased. The Queen certainly takes things into her own hands freely. She clears the house tomorrow by sending away Alfred, Arthur, Leopold and Beatrice. . . . The Duke of Cambridge stays on till Monday as the Princess particularly wishes it.

Arrangements for the service of thanksgiving for the Prince's recovery which was held in St. Paul's produced many difficulties and an immense amount of correspondence, most of it exhibiting differences of opinion between mother and son. After the ceremony the Queen wrote to Colonel Ponsonby :

Feb. 27, 1872

. . . She is feeling very tired — but she was so deeply gratified & touched by the wonderful enthusiasm & loyalty shown that she does not care much for that.

It was really a glorious sight. St. Pauls itself is a *most* dreary, dingy, melancholy & undevotional Church & the service except the last Hymn devoid of any *elevating* effect.

The question which occupied most attention from 1871 and in subsequent years was how could the Prince of Wales be properly employed. Ponsonby after consultations and talks with the Queen drew up a memorandum based on the following suggestions of possible fields of activity : (1) Philanthropy, (2) Arts and Science, (3) Army, (4) Foreign Affairs, (5) India. He was in close correspondence with Francis Knollys, the Prince's Private Secretary, with Lord Halifax and Lord Granville as well as with Gladstone. Doubts were expressed from all quarters. In a letter to his wife he writes :

Nothing can be more genial and pleasant than he [the Prince] is for a few minutes. But he does not endure. He cannot keep up the interest for any length of time and I don't think he will ever settle down to business.

And again :

> To get the P. of W. to enter into a subject or decide on it is most difficult. They have to catch snap answers from him as he goes out shooting, etc. Then he runs off on his lark to Trouville where of course business is impossible. . . .

The Queen asking Ponsonby to come and talk to her about it writes : " Ireland & Army matters won't do but Foreign Affairs perhaps might & art to a certain extent — tho' not science ". The wiser heads at Court like Sir Thomas Biddulph were very doubtful as to whether he could be given any responsible duties and were apprehensive of the sort of company he would choose to be associated with him.

Letters on the subject from three leading statesmen may be quoted.

From *Mr. Gladstone*

Dec. 22, '71

I have read with extreme interest your short memorandum stating the case as to the Prince of Wales, and Mr. Knollys's letter in which he treats it at length, but in a succinct and very business like manner. I should much wish Lord Granville to see these papers, if you think proper to send them : if you please, as at my suggestion.

With most of what Mr. Knollys has said, I concur. It is hardly possible for the Prince to make a worthy pursuit out of philanthropy ; I do not mean one worthy in itself, but of adequate magnitude. What we want is not to supply him with the means of filling a certain number of hours : we should seek to give him a central aim and purpose, which may though without absorbing all his time gradually mould his mind, and colour his life. It must be worthy not only of a man, but of *the* man who is Prince of Wales, and heir to the British Throne. Few men could do what Shaftesbury has done in the matter of philanthropy. But Shaftesbury himself could not have done it, had he not had the means by a seat first in the Commons and afterwards in the Lords of giving a practical turn to his efforts, and impressing them with a character of responsibility which has so to speak bridled them, and checked a tendency to excess rarely separated, in the imperfection of human nature, from genuine enthusiasm. But I will not follow the details of the subject. I may say however that a sixth head might conceivably be

added to your five.   It is the social head.   I am convinced
that society has suffered fearfully in moral tone from the
absence of a pure Court.   It was like Arthur's Round Table
in its moral effect.   It did not directly influence many,
but it influenced the highest — those who most need it —
their influence acted upon others, and so onwards in widen-
ing circles.   It is a great and important question whether
and how this want can be supplied.

From *Lord Granville* (the Foreign Secretary)

Dec. 26, '71

Many thanks for lending me these papers.   The question is
of urgent importance, the solution most difficult.   The
Queen desired me to put the Prince on Committees in the
Lords.   I had him named on one of a non-political character.

He attended the first day.   He then came to me to ask
whether the Committee could not be adjourned for ten
days.   He had some engagements, and so on.

I am afraid the Foreign Affairs question would be treated
in the same way.   If the Queen really desired his opinion,
sent for him and consulted him he would probably get
amused and interested.   But if he only gets a few bones after
they have been to the Prime Minister, and the Queen, and
finds nothing but despatches telling him only what he has
skimmed a week before in the paper, he will cease reading
them.   If all the drafts are to be submitted to him, the delay
will be intolerable.

If he makes a suggestion on them, it will probably be
snubbed by the Queen, or necessarily argued against by me,
and he will make no more.   And as to really confidential
matters, will they remain secret?   He asked me to keep him
informed during the war.   One evening I got 4 messages
from different friends, telling me to be careful.   One of my
first notes to him had been handed round a dinner party.

All this will not prevent my doing anything in my power
to cooperate.   But unless you can give him something to do,
which must be done, I doubt anything coming of it.

From *Lord Halifax* (Lord Privy Seal)

Sep. 6, 1872

. . . The question as to Ireland will not be disposed of till
Gladstone is satisfied that it won't do.   He has taken up the
question warmly and he must have it out with the Queen.   I,
myself, think that the P.'s going to Ireland is the only
practicable mode of providing him with regular employ-

ment, and if the objections to his going to Ireland, the force
of which I fully admit, are insuperable I am afraid that all
the good intentions and good resolutions of last autumn will
vanish into empty air.   I think *the Offices* may be tried but
I very much doubt their providing regular employment.
The India office offers the greatest facilities, and if that
scheme is to be tried, I would begin there.

But do you suppose that the Prince wd. not pretty generally find some good reason for not going to the office in a
morning, when in London?   If not where is the regular
work?   He might not have the same temptations in Ireland ;
and there wd. be more feeling of the obligation to do something there.   I believe it to be Ireland or nothing : unless
he takes so well to business *here* as to be encouraged to go
there.

At the end of 1872 Francis Knollys introduced the subject again
in a letter :

8 Decr., 1872

I should have written to you directly after Mr. Gladstone
had left here, had anything as regards the question of employment resulted from his visit.   But he did not even
mention the subject to the Prince, and the latter said nothing
to him.   G. will never again have so good an opportunity,
and the whole thing is too disheartening.

G. was evidently very much pleased at having been
asked, particularly for the Princess' Birthday, and was I
suppose reluctant, while stopping in the House, to do or
say anything in any way as he thought distasteful to H.R.H.
The Prince was however quite ready and prepared for the
subject, and as G. made himself very agreeable and pleasant,
H.R.H. would have been more influenced by him then than
on ordinary occasions.

. . . The one who made the greatest impression upon
everybody here (Prince and Princess included) was Mr.
Forster who particularly pleased the Prince in every way.

The first political party here was I think altogether a
great success and I hope it will induce H.R.H. to continue
to ask the leading men on both sides to Sandringham.

Ireland for a few months to entertain there was turned down.
India was favoured by Ponsonby but the Prince did not like it.
Art, science and philanthropy were all no use.   His " perpetual
search for amusement " is referred to, and it was " impossible
he should see state papers and criticize and object ".   The
Queen would not stand it, because she was jealous lest he

should interfere in important matters. For years this continued to be a grievance and puzzled successive heads of the Foreign Office. The Prince protested, not because he was really interested but because he objected to being ignorant of important affairs which might be discussed in his hearing. In 1873 he complained of not having received any boxes from the Foreign Office for two months, and again in 1877 he received a telegram when he was at Naples, saying things abroad were very critical although he had not received one word on the course of events. Disraeli explained to the Queen that he could not be given confidential papers as " he lets them out and talks to his friends about them ". The Queen gave instructions that some papers might be sent to him but not the confidential ones. The Foreign Office found it difficult to know where to draw the line, as the following letter shows :

From *Sir Julian Pauncefote* (the Permanent Under-Secretary at the Foreign Office)

25 Jan., 1887

I am sorry to find from your note to Barrington [returning the Italian Draft] that the Queen disapproved of its being sent to the Prince of Wales as it is marked " Very Confidential ". I have of course directed that the Draft should not go to His Royal Highness, but I should be extremely obliged if you could *privately* and without troubling Her Majesty on the subject, give me some indication as to where to draw the line in selecting the Documents to be sent to the Prince. I was greatly pleased to think that, when you last wrote on the subject, I was authorized to use a free hand in the matter and I have accordingly sent to him all despatches of real interest whether marked " Secret " or not. I hope I may continue to do so as I think it most important at this critical juncture that he should see what cards are in the hands of the players in the great European game which is going on, and how they are being played.

Note of *Sir Henry Ponsonby's* Reply

Quite right to let H.R.H. know what is going on — but as the direction of affairs is not in his hands it does not appear to be necessary to submit confidential drafts for his consideration before they take effect.

But there were cases in which the Prince's complaints

would appear to have been justified ; more especially when Disraeli never consulted or informed him with regard to the Royal Title Bill, in which he was certainly closely concerned. He never heard from the Queen about the Duke of Connaught's engagement to be married, and was hurt when Lord Granville informed him of it telling him " to be discreet ", as that implied he was not.

In 1873 the Queen prevented him from accepting the Colonelcy of a Russian regiment. He took this very badly because he dearly loved uniforms. Of course it was on the advice of her Ministers who (the message came) " thwart him in every single wish he expresses ".

In 1874 the Prince, exasperated by the recurring regulations, restrictions and fuss about the shooting in Scotland, refused to go to Abergeldie. John Brown and Grant, the head keeper, were involved. Ponsonby without mentioning Brown or Grant managed to smooth down this trouble.

There was a dispute over the voyage arranged for the two young Princes, Albert Victor and George ; the Admiralty and Dalton, their tutor, took different views. The Queen backed Dalton, the Prince the Admiralty. Occasionally Ponsonby, in order to clarify a situation for his own guidance, wrote down headings showing the confusion of opinions. This controversy is best epitomized by such a memorandum :

I am much perplexed about this *Bacchante.*
1. Plan proposed to the Queen who did not at all like it.
2. Dalton sent by the Prince of Wales to urge it. Queen's objections not pressed.
3. Unanimous condemnation by the Cabinet of the plan.
4. Indignation of the Queen and Prince at their interference.
5. Cabinet said they didn't. Plan adopted.
6. Controversies on the selection of the officers. The Queen supporting what she believed to be the Prince of Wales' choice. Sometimes it appears he wished for others. Final agreement on the officers.
7. The *Bacchante* announced to be the ship. Who chose her, when and where I don't know.
8. Chorus of approbation.
9. Strong whispers against her. No stability. The Queen doubtful. The Prince of Wales doubtful. Dalton very doubtful — prefers *Newcastle.*
10. Smith [First Lord] furious, outwardly calm. Offers to turn

over crew to *Newcastle* — an old ship full of bilge water. Sends reports in favour of *Bacchante*.

11. Scott ordered to cruise in search of a storm so as to see if she will capsize.
12. Scott returns, says she won't. Dalton not satisfied. Wants to separate Princes.
13. Queen says this is what she first thought of but Dalton said it was impossible. Let him consult Prince and Princess of Wales.
14. Queen mentions doubts to Lord Beaconsfield.
15. B. observes he has been already snubbed — but if his advice is wanted he will give it.
16. Knollys says Dalton is wrong.

It was finally decided that both Princes should go together on the *Bacchante*.

In 1881 the Prince of Wales had a great success at a civic reception at Liverpool. He asked Ponsonby why the Queen did not take more interest in it. Ponsonby writes to his wife :

> The fact is that these functions are for the moment delightful but the relation of them very tedious and H.M. don't like being bored and after the first account was over had had enough of it.

Dean Stanley of Westminster died in July 1881. The Queen was much upset at his loss. When she found that a ball had been arranged at Marlborough House to take place just before the funeral, her indignation knew no bounds. She dispatched a telegram from Osborne to Sir Henry Ponsonby who was in London, as well as one to the Prince of Wales, pointing out the " extreme impropriety " of such a thing and saying how shocked she was. The message was conveyed to the Prince who said he was distressed but he had had to attend other public functions, the Dean was not a member of the Government, and as the invitations had gone out, he could not postpone an entirely " official reception and ball ". The Queen wrote again :

> If the Prince of Wales can only say he is hurt & distressed at my remarks I am more so. Public functions like Brighton are different. There is only one Dean of Westminster. The feeling will be great except among the heartless Society.

In July 1882 the Prince resolved to go out with the Guards expeditionary force under Wolseley to Egypt. The Queen refused to allow this and the Government supported her veto. At the same time she appreciated his desire to help in a national emergency. This is shown by the following letter to the Prince from Sir Henry Ponsonby (July 31, 1882) :

Y.R.H.'s gallant offer of joining the expedition to Egypt has greatly troubled the Queen. H.M. agreed with Y.R.H.'s desire to be of use, and warmly appreciated the gallant wish to see service. But the imperative demands of public duty compelled H.M. to point out the grave difficulties and inconveniences of such a proceeding, and having been advised by the Government as well as several leaders of the Opposition that it would be inexpedient and most unwise, considering Y.R.H.'s rank and position, to join the expedition as a spectator and impossible for Y.R.H. to be attached to it on duty, the Queen finally and conclusively decided that it was necessary to ask Y.R.H. to abandon the idea. But H.M. was so pleased at the proposal having been made and so convinced that it would be heartily appreciated by everyone, that I think that the Queen would be glad if it were made generally known.

On the intended publication of *More Leaves* in 1884 the Prince wrote expressing doubts as to whether the Queen's private life should not be kept private, considered sacred and not exposed. The Queen sent down to Sir Henry the letter,

which she thinks he will think strange considering how much talk & want of reticence there is in his Home & how little he keeps anything to himself & how continually he lives in Society. . . . It is very strange that objection sh^d come from that quarter where gr^t strictness as to conduct is not generally much cared for.

When Lord Randolph Churchill resigned the Chancellorship of the Exchequer in 1886 the Prince sent the Queen a letter he had received from him.

From *The Queen*

The Queen thought the proceeding so strange of the P. of W. to send her this most objectionable & incorrect letter from Lord Randolph. . . . It is most undesirable & even dangerous for the P. of W. to be in communication [with him].

Even when the Prince recommended that his admirable Private Secretary Francis Knollys should receive a K.C.B. the Queen raised many objections. So it went on : his suggestions on minor matters were either disregarded or rejected. On a recommendation for some appointment the Prince wrote to Ponsonby : " I have written to suggest it and hope I shall not receive a severe snub for doing so ". As late as 1892 Sir Francis Knollys says in a letter to Ponsonby :

> The P. of W. writes to me that there is not much use his remaining on at Cowes as he is not of the slightest use to the Queen ; that everything he says or suggests is pooh-poohed and that his sisters and brother are much more listened to than he is. All this is a pity and not very encouraging.

The baccarat scandal at Tranby Croft naturally produced a great deal of correspondence owing to the Prince being called into the witness-box when Sir William Gordon-Cumming's case came on. So much has been written about this that it will be unnecessary to say anything more. The Queen's feelings may be imagined. One of her messages about gambling, as usual sent in a roundabout way, did not reach its destination. The Duke of Cambridge was charged to deliver the message direct to the Prince of Wales at Sandringham. But his courage failed him and he tried to get Sir Francis Knollys to convey it. But Sir Francis declined. There were several other even more serious society dilemmas, to put it mildly, of which all records were no doubt destroyed.

All these instances of controversy demonstrate the broadening difference of outlook between the Queen and her heir. They were indications of the dawn of different standards of social conduct which by reaction were to divide still further as time passed mid-nineteenth-century respectability with its rigid and perhaps inconsistent codes from the license and disregard of all restriction as the twentieth century advanced.

The altercations between the Queen and the Prince could be multiplied but the instances given here are sufficient to show the awkward relations between the two. Although not directly associated with any political policy, the Prince's social courtesy and civility to Gladstone and for a time his friendship with Sir Charles Dilke did not improve his relations with the Queen.

The very friendly association between the two Private

Secretaries, Sir Henry Ponsonby and Sir Francis Knollys, allowed messages to be edited and unnecessary disputes nipped in the bud. In the strained relations which grew up between the sovereign and the heir to the throne there were faults on both sides. If only they had had habitually friendly talks together, like many mothers and sons, all would have been well. But even in small matters, as for instance hunting at Osborne on which the Prince had strong views, when Ponsonby suggested his talking to the Queen about it he immediately let the matter drop.

On the more serious side with regard to public questions, the reading of confidential papers and responsible official work being found for the Prince, the Queen was undoubtedly justified. She had measured his capacities and inclinations and knew that nothing could be expected from him in this direction.

The Prince of Wales' charm of manner is very often alluded to. It would be quite impossible to overestimate what amounted to genius. It is not too much to say that in spite of drawbacks, faults and failures, it *made* him. With a dignified presence, a fine profile (as his coins show) and a courtly manner, he never missed saying a word to the humblest visitor, attendant or obscure official. He would enter a room and, with the skill of an accomplished billiard player, look forward several strokes ahead, so that no one was left out. The appropriate remark, the telling serious phrase and the amusing joke, accompanied by a gurgling laugh to the close friend, made all delighted even to watch him. Although he never mastered a state paper he had a wonderful talent for picking up tags gathered from people in the know, as Sir Charles Dilke, who was intimate with him, noticed. So that foreign Ambassadors, Ministers of the Crown, representatives of the services and eminent men in all walks of life regarded him as the most accomplished Prince and later the best-informed monarch that ever reigned. But it was all *façade*, the most engaging, decorative but quite misleading *façade*. There was practically nothing behind. His wonderful social tact could not always be a sufficient screen for his official ignorance. When he died, the chorus of exaggerated praise engineered by those who had been deluded by his friendly charm, turned criticism for a while against the Queen for not having enlisted his services more. But in her day Queen Victoria knew better.

The misunderstanding which arose in 1889 between the Prince of Wales and the German Emperor is fully related in the published *Letters of Queen Victoria* (3rd Series, Vol. I). But it may be noted as a case of some serious importance in which the Queen took the side of her son as against her grandson. A letter from the Prince of Wales' Equerry gives a good survey of the whole situation :

From *Major-General Sir Arthur Ellis*

19 April, 1889

I did not know that P. of W. had asked the Queen the question " if Herbert Bismarck wishes to see me, shall I see him ? " If he did this it entirely alters the situation, and the question not unnaturally provoked the opinion held, in the cipher telegrams, holding the views the Queen does. I contend that her mind has been perverted by the Empress Frederick who is too violent, and only sees the Bismarck action from her point of view, and not from a Prussian national point of view.

The quarrels are no doubt *two*, but each depends on the other. The P. of W. was on good terms with the Chancellor, and had made his son in England a petted friend, which flattered the old man and was as far as it went useful. At *old* William's funeral (when I went with him) all was smooth, all parted friends. Personally I was disgusted with the greedy haste *young* W. showed to succeed, illustrations of which I could easily prove.

On Emperor Frederick's death the P. of W. to my certain knowledge went to Berlin imbued with the greatest anxiety to keep well with his nephew, with the Chancellor *e tutti quanti* (I was *not* with him). The first 24 hours all was smooth but the Empress Frederick succeeded in inflaming him with her own personal animosity that very likely the P. of W. said more to Herbert Bismarck and to the Chancellor than was prudent. We must make every allowance for the Empress Frederick's state of mind, considering what she lost all round. But the Germans make no allowance for the P. of W.'s brotherly feeling for his sister's sake. He not only made the pot boil over there, but stayed on longer than desirable and it went on boiling over. *All* his personal remarks went to the Chancellor's private ear.

Bismarck is great, but *very* vindictive. His son is a caricature of the father. He had too the additional misfortune of having been once the petted friend of P. of W. There is no such enemy as the discarded friend. This sounds like copy book morality but it is nevertheless true.

Every mistake the Empress Frederick made — she probably made about two big ones every day — was credited to the English influence of her brother's late visit. *Les absents ont toujours tort* and he was the scapegoat against which all Berlin hurled themselves. I know this from many sources.

On H.R.H.'s return he avoided Talleyrand's proverb — that " the tongue was given one to conceal one's thoughts " — and he was very open-mouthed. All this again went back to Berlin and the Chancellor's private ear. Old Bismarck was helpless against P. of W., but like Mary " *he pondered* " and retaliated thro' the nephew, the new master, like fresh wax in his hands. The system of espionage, which is one of the pillars of continental government, gave him handles to turn. Lies no doubt — but here and there an impudent remark *true*. The conversation with Grand Duke Vladimir at luncheon, so twisted as to assume another meaning, seemed to obtain greater value by some questions once put without further intention by P. of W. to Bismarck as to whether in his lifetime the Emperor Frederick had seen a possible peaceful solution of the great vexed political question between Germany and France by some give and take rectification of frontier ?

Here was the opportunity ! ! They poisoned the young W.'s mind (already nauseated by having *English* theories crammed by his mother down his throat) and declared that P. of W. had insulted the Emperor Frederick's memory — by recommending a cession of all Alsace-Lorraine, which on the face of it, is absurd and untrue. Then came the Frankfurt speech which young W. delivered " as a reply to my uncle Bertie ", as he himself says.

. . . The two quarrels are linked one into the other. No English gentleman would behave like either Emperor W. to his uncle or like Bismarck father and son. But we must not forget that they happen none of them to be *English gentlemen*, and we must take them as we find them — pure Prussians. Every German and Austrian knows what *that* means. . . .

A little judicious lying all round will probably heal the outer surface, but the under matter will still fester. All *cordiality*, real friendship in Berlin is gone for ever. The real beginning and cause for this *is the Empress Frederick !* — whose champion in Berlin the P. of W. is regarded to be. I am quite sure that no one in England can realize the universal feeling of dislike (combined with pity perhaps) with which she is regarded everywhere — in Germany and even in Austria — where Bismarck is *not* beloved.

Had the P. of W. seen Herbert Bismarck he would at least have been in a position to retail to his father and his monkey master the real condition of the P. of W.'s feelings towards them all. He is a rough brute, but an intelligent one, and he would have seen where their weak points bristle out. . . .

Whether everyone is always judicious or not is another matter — certainly in the treatment of his belief of what P. of W. said the Emperor was to the last degree ill-advised and misbehaved, according to *our* standard.

This is my view of the situation. Take it for what it is worth. I try not to be influenced by my personal affection for P. of W. but I *do* see the foreign side having all my life some knowledge and experience of what Englishmen call " damned foreigners ".

Except for a twopenny-halfpenny dispute at Balmoral with regard to some message sent by a footman to Abergeldie, the Prince's relations with Ponsonby were very friendly from the earliest days. More than that, the Prince knew that Ponsonby's interventions on his behalf had not infrequently prevented trouble. He was eternally grateful and showed it when he chose Sir Henry's second son (Fritz), one of the Queen's Equerries, to be his assistant Private Secretary when he ascended the throne.

Without embarking on any notes about the Queen and her grandchildren, to whom as children she was as much devoted as they were to her, there was a romantic episode, hidden at the time but common knowledge in subsequent years, which can just be mentioned because, difficult and controversial as the circumstances were, it forms one of the instances in which the Queen and the Prince were in complete accord. In spite of the Prince having developed the traditional unsympathetic severity with his heir, the suggested engagement of Prince Eddy, the Duke of Clarence, to Princess Hélène of Orleans was at first favoured by him and led as may be imagined to an immense amount of correspondence. More than six months later, in June 1891, Prince Eddy was still endeavouring to get the Queen to intervene on his behalf with Princess Hélène, but of course she could not and the whole project was bound to be turned down.

In a full correspondence Henry Ponsonby and Spencer Ponsonby-Fane discuss in detail the marriage (which was to take place in 1892) of the Duke of Clarence to the Princess to whom he was subsequently betrothed.   There is something sadly dramatic in finding with hardly a break in the sequence of letters that the arrangements under discussion for Prince Eddy's marriage change to those for his funeral.

CHAPTER VI

Balmoral

AS Henry Ponsonby's wife and family only came up to Scotland on one occasion the series of his letters from Balmoral is the most complete of any. His attendance on the Queen there was hardly interrupted for over twenty-five years for he was there as Equerry-in-Waiting before 1870. It was intimated indirectly to him that were his family resident in a neighbouring house such as Abergeldie Mains he would probably be with them instead of in the castle when the Queen wanted him. Moreover his leave of absence was fragmentary, and seldom did Her Majesty grant him more than a week or two's respite from attendance at Balmoral when she was in residence. The result of this is that these daily letters present a picture of life at Balmoral in a way that cannot be furnished by any other letters or reports in that period.

There have been monarchs who for a time have lived in seclusion. There have been monarchs of eccentric tendencies who have devised fantastic surroundings. But the life lived by Queen Victoria and her Court in her Highland home resembles nothing handed down to us by historians.

Windsor Castle, by its very nature as one of the world's greatest royal residences and its proximity to London, involved ceremonies, royal visits and a certain amount of pageantry and display indispensable and fitting to the life of a sovereign. Osborne was inconveniently accessible. It retained in its routine a Court atmosphere in which ceremonies and receptions were bound to occur, more especially since Cowes, as a yachting centre, at the foot of the hill, attracted every year a number of distinguished visitors including foreign royalties. Even the journey to Cowes from London, which meant crossing the Solent to the Isle of Wight, led to delays which fretted the tempers of Cabinet Ministers. On the change of Government

in 1884 Ponsonby writes to Horace Seymour, one of the Private
Secretaries at 10 Downing Street :

> The Solent is covered with steamers carrying Ministers
> hither and luncheons are prepared in various rooms for such
> as must go at 2, at 2.30 and at 3.   The Queen's yacht *Elfin*
> has gone to look for some of them at Portsmouth.   The
> Queen's launch *Louise* is searching about Cowes Harbour
> for others.   The Queen's yacht *Alberta* has gone to South-
> ampton for the Duchess of Edinburgh.   So our Navy is
> well employed.

But Balmoral six hundred miles from London was quite
another matter.   This Highland retreat kept alive the memory
of the happy days the Queen had spent there with Prince
Albert after they had purchased it.   It was charged with
associations with the past and was eminently suited for the
seclusion and retirement which she needed and on which she
insisted.   She would hardly alter by a single day the date she
had fixed for her departure to the North or her return to the
South.   Kings and Emperors might desire to pay a visit to
this country, Ministers might plead for her presence in London,
overworked officials might deplore the long journey required
in order to reach her, disparaging comments might appear
in the press.   It made not the slightest difference.   Both of
her chief Prime Ministers complained bitterly but privately.
Disraeli wrote from Balmoral : " Carrying on the Government of a country six hundred miles from the Metropolis
doubles the Labour " ; and Gladstone confided to Lord Rosebery " The Queen alone is enough to kill any man ".

Apart from its architecture and peculiar tartan decoration
the castle had no homely comforts.   In atmosphere and indeed
in actual temperature it was cold.   The Queen hated fires.
Warned one day at Osborne that the Queen was coming to
pay a visit, the Ponsonby family set to work to remove the
drawing-room fire in a bucket of water, quickly opening all
the windows to get rid of the stench.   Describing a conversation at dinner at Balmoral, Ponsonby writes :

> We had a fierce discussion headed on each side by the
> Queen and Princess Beatrice as to whether if you were con-
> demned to one or the other you would rather live at the
> Equator or the North Pole. Princess Beatrice was for

the Equator but the Queen fierce for the North Pole. "All doctors say that heat is unwholesome but cold wholesome."

So in rooms and corridors in the castle her preference for the North Pole was noticeable.

In 1884 Ponsonby heard some opinions of Balmoral Castle. Gladstone and Mrs. Gladstone had come over as they were staying near by. She was shown the Minister's Room.

> "There," said Gladstone, "is the room where I have been very comfortable. It is not such a hole as Harcourt describes it " — from which I gathered that the Home Secretary had not been complimentary when at Invercauld about Balmoral. With them was Lady Dalhousie, looking lovely. I said I hoped she thought the house pretty. "A frank question requires a frank answer and I will tell you I never saw anything more uncomfortable or that I coveted less." Lady Mandeville, who called later blue with cold, was equally sour in her remarks on our Highland Palace.

Balmoral had nothing of the delightful holiday atmosphere of an English or Scottish country house with a hostess devoting herself to the entertainment of her guests. On his return to Balmoral after paying some visits Ponsonby writes : " Every private house strikes me as so comfortable after the severe dreariness of our palatial rooms here ". Neither had the castle the freedom for individuals to be found in a large hotel. It had a curious resemblance to a school. But as a matter of fact it was quite unique. In what known establishment do persons in the same building communicate with one another by letter ? This habit of the Queen's, which accounts for the enormous number of written communications from her, would seem to have arisen from her disinclination to talk over matters, great or small, for fear of opposition, controversy or criticism. But she infected her Court with the same method of intercourse, so that when there was what Ponsonby frequently alludes to as " a row " on, they communicated with one another in similar fashion. The Queen further complicated the epistolary tangle by writing through an intermediary to her own children.

Anyone who thought that life at Balmoral meant a relaxation from Court etiquette, where an easy-going informality might be enjoyed, made a great mistake. Discipline was very strict. The presence of the Queen, who sometimes for days was

BALMORAL 1886

(standing) Major Edwards, Sir H. Ponsonby, Lord Bridport, Dr. Laking, Dr. J. Reid, Lord Cranbrook

(seated) Lady Erroll, Hon. Rosa Hood, Miss Bauer

unseen except by her dressers and perhaps a Lady-in-Waiting, was felt in the remotest recesses of the castle. No one was allowed to go out till the Queen had gone out. Neglect of this regulation brought a sharp reprimand. On one occasion the Private Secretary and his assistant happened to be out a few minutes before the Queen left the castle. The severe tone of the four-page letter he received resembled that of a head-master to a naughty boy :

From *The Queen*

Osborne, July 12, '85

The Queen *must* ask that both Sir Henry & Major Edwards sh^d *not* be out on Sunday M^{rg} or any other *at the same time*. Not 5 minutes after the service in the Chapel was over she sent to say she wished to see Sir Henry in a $\frac{1}{4}$ of an hour but was told he was gone to church. She then sent for Major Edwards & was then told he was out too.

This is extemely inconvenient. *Here* the Queen is always within reach till $\frac{1}{4}$ to . . . She goes in & must rest till 2. She must ask Sir Henry to take care that this does not happen again & that by 12 one or other of the gentlemen (Sir Henry or his Assistant P. P. & P. S.) sh^d be *at hand*.

There is now especially so much of a public & private nature wanting arrangement & *constant* attention [she] *must* have the necessary assistance she requires, being quite done up with *all* her work and anxieties for the last 6 or 7 weeks.

The Pr^{ss} too is getting in need of rest & quiet. She is quite done up by all she had to do at Windsor.

Sir Henry can send the Queen questions about anything thro' Miss Phipps who is very clear quick & discreet & is quite able to do what Lady Ely & Miss Stopford do.

There are several such communications, notably a very sharp one on her Private Secretary having allowed his assistant to open a confidential letter :

From *The Queen*

Osborne, Dec. 22, '86

. . . The Queen has been *much* annoyed at Sir Henry again letting Mr. Dering's[1] very *private* & confidential letter ab^t Alfred's & the Duke of Coburg's differences come here & be opened by Major Bigge as a common letter . . . the Queen *strongly* remonstrates at *private* communications being

---

[1] Chargé d'Affaires in Coburg.

treated as if 3 instead of one in g*ᵗ confidence* were interested with them. It must *not* happen again — Sir Henry should have given Mr. Dering his direction.

She usually went out late in the afternoon, but sometimes earlier : " The Queen has gone out for the day with her luncheon in a basket — so I'm off also ". The date of the arrival and departure of each member of the household was decided by her. The four dinners (the Queen's, the Household, the upper servants, the lower servants) were supervised by her. The Equerry was not allowed to give orders to the stables or to the Highlanders. The Maid of Honour was not allowed to go out with the gentlemen without a chaperon. The room in which the Household might sit after dinner was fixed by her. The eighteen ponies were strictly divided into five categories, each one apportioned to particular people. Anyone not fitting precisely into one of the categories had to ask special permission. This led to a prolonged " row " when Canon Duckworth, Boehm (the sculptor) and Herman Sahl (the German Secretary) protested. Ponsonby in order to shield the Queen had to pretend it was his order.

Attendance at church was obligatory. But when Ponsonby was asked whether he would partake of the Sacrament in the Scottish Kirk as the Queen had decided to do so, he said no ; not because he felt it wrong or illegal but because he objected to being ordered or even asked to a sacred ceremony, " the essence of which was the discretion and freedom of the individual ". The Queen needless to say carried out her own decision, in spite of warnings and even objections from the Archbishop of Canterbury, the Dean of Westminster and the Dean of Windsor. No report of it was allowed in the Court Circular but the ecclesiastical and legal side of the question produced a mass of correspondence with which her Private Secretary was very much bored.

The Queen, as already shown, was particular and critical about sermons. They had to be orthodox, short and interesting. But they did not always fulfil all these qualifications. One Sunday the minister, Mr. MacGregor, preached on the devil. Afterwards he asked Princess Louise whether the Queen liked his sermon. " She said she had not heard but that she should think not, as the Queen did not altogether believe in the devil. MacGregor looked with a pitying eye and only said ' puir body '."

Conversation at the Queen's dinner, to which the Private Secretary was of course constantly invited, depended entirely on the Queen's mood, which was naturally sometimes governed by her health. Here is a dinner in 1872 which was not hilarious :

> Queen's dinner was painfully flat partly I think because she had a cold, partly because she sat between Leopold who never uttered and Gainsborough who is deaf and partly I suspect because she is nervous about Alice's movements as it appears she has not gone yet. We all dined, the three women, Du Plat and I, and there were prolonged silences broken by the Queen, Leopold and C.'s respectable coughs, Cowley's deep cough, S.'s gouty cough and all the servants dropping plates and making a clatteration of noises.

Generally speaking public affairs could not be discussed at dinner, more especially if they were absorbing the Queen's attention. A Lady-in-Waiting who mentioned a political subject was told such subjects must not be spoken of at dinner. Visiting Cabinet Ministers had to be warned of this. One night in the earlier years, Ponsonby, who was sitting next to Princess Beatrice, announced that someone they all knew was engaged to be married. There was a silence. He received a message afterwards that the question of marriage must never be mentioned in Princess Beatrice's presence. An unpleasantly loud voice or the opening of a subject of conversation by anyone other than the Queen herself was frowned on. But she knew how to divert the conversation if embarrassment were created by an indiscreet question. An example may be given (without any clue to the indiscretion, which will only be recognized by those few who have retained recollections of the intimate gossip of the late seventies). It was at dinner :

> One only difficulty. The Queen asked me and Pickard if we knew Capt. Clarke, the Prince of Wales' Equerry. " His wife was I believe a Miss Rose." I believed she was. Whereon Beatrice asked if Sir J. Rose had any other daughters. I became absorbed in my beef. Pickard quietly said, " Yes and also three sons," whom he expatiated on, and the Queen asked me whether I did not think Lady Cunynghame so like the late Lord Hardinge.

It would be a mistake to suppose that the Queen was

always gloomily severe. Far from it. Comments not infrequently occur such as : " Last night the Queen seemed prepared for prattle and talked away on minor topics." She liked
relating reminiscences of the past : how once she took up a
fork at a ball supper in mistake for her fan and walked into the
ballroom with it : " Not so bad as poor dear Mama [the
Duchess of Kent] who took the snuffers for her pocket handkerchief and went out walking with them ". Years before
when she was returning in the State Barge from seeing the
Thames Tunnel " they were nearly run over by a steamer.
What she chiefly remembered about this incident was the
curious variety of Lord Byron's oaths as he hulloaed from the
barge to the steamer." He was Lord-in-Waiting.[1] On
another occasion she said " she remembered seeing George
III's statue going down Long Walk to Snow Hill in 1829 and
asked me why there was no inscription. I said, yes there was,
in Latin ' To the Best of Fathers ' by George IV. The Queen
laughed. ' The Best of Fathers ! Why, they never spoke ! ' "
She went on to complain that Greville had written a great
deal that was untrue and she would like to correct " gross
errors ".

In the spring of 1880 a little frivolity was allowed to be
introduced by the Queen herself " taking up a sporting line.
She talks of Hartington's horse and the Duke of Westminster's
horses for the Derby as if she were on Epsom Downs. By her
suggestion we have got up a Derby lottery. She has taken two
tickets and the Princesses a number of others." (They all
hoped the Queen would win. But it was Ponsonby who drew
Bend Or.)

Visiting Ministers or foreign royalties seldom added to the
gaiety. But one evening Prince John of Glücksburg (brother
of the King of Denmark), whose English was not perfect,
heard from a lady, who came down late and sat next to him,
that she had locked her door and could not open it for some
time. He repeated this loudly across the table : " So you see
she was confined before dinner." On another occasion he
said : " I am agreeable to see the Queen dances like a pot "
(meaning top).

The Household dinner varied according to the particular
members of the Household who were in waiting. Some were

---

[1] Admiral, cousin and successor of the poet.

lively, others were not. Their relations to one another were
not those of chosen friends but of fortuitous acquaintances,
although in the course of time some became lasting friends.
At Windsor or Osborne there were often visitors, military or
naval officers, and there were incidents, London gossip or
anecdotes from the Club of the Royal Yacht Squadron to
enliven the conversation. But on most days at Balmoral
nothing happened. Stagnation dulled everyone's wits.
Ponsonby, who of course was more often present than anyone
else, used to start arguments and refute statements merely to
provoke discussion. In his letters he sometimes enlarges on
the idiosyncrasies of some of his colleagues both male and
female and he always welcomed the visits of Cabinet Ministers.
But for reasons mentioned elsewhere he had to be rather
careful when touching on politics which, at the Household
dinner at any rate, was not taboo and sometimes led to hot
controversy.

He never welcomed the presence of large numbers of the
royal family at Balmoral and it is doubtful whether the Queen
did either. " Some bother crops up," he writes, " and then I
am made a buffer."

The chief sport at Balmoral was deer-stalking which on
great occasions ended in the evening with a torchlight dance
round the carcases " while the gillies absorb whiskey and sing
songs ". Ponsonby considered stalking deplorable waste of
time and made every excuse possible to get out of it. But he
could not always do so. He would stuff literature into his
pockets for the wearisome long waits. One day the *Fortnightly
Review* and the *Daily News* " fell out when I was walking with
the Princes, to their astonishment ". He was quite a good
shot and killed his share, but without enthusiasm. Drinking
to the memory of Prince Albert round the cairn erected to him
was an annual function which also involved the consumption
of a great deal of whisky. The Braemar Gathering for Highland
Games was another annual event which the Queen generally
attended with a far from enthusiastic Household.

But the gillies' ball stood out as the recurring entertainment to which the Queen herself was specially devoted. She
loved dancing and danced very well. As years passed Ponsonby
became doubtful not only of the necessity but of the desirability
of her indulging with such zeal in dancing reels. Yet as late

as 1891 when she was seventy-two, at an informal dance in the
Castle drawing-room, he is obliged to admit : " The Queen
danced with Prince Henry [of Battenburg] ; light airy steps
in the old courtly fashion ; no limp or stick but every figure
carefully and prettily danced ". But the usual gillies' ball was
a rough-and-tumble affair with a great deal of shouting and
she never missed it. John Brown organized them and was
usually her partner once or twice in the evening. Even on the
death of the Grand Duke of Hesse it was only postponed for
three days. When the Balmoral factor died there was " much
low spirits in the household at the announcement of another
gillies' ball. It was not put off because the Queen does not
regard it as a gaiety and in this the household heartily concurs."
One of the many times when she refused to go south we find
this comment : " Innumerable difficulties from the Queen
staying on here ; and I can't conceive for what purpose,
except for the gillies' ball on the 9th ". Sometimes Ponsonby
slipped away for part of the time on the plea of deciphering
telegrams or other work. But this was not always accepted :
" I didn't get back [to the ball] till 11.30 when I found some
asperity at my absence. Explanations ensued, culminating
in my dancing a Hooligan [1] with the Queen."

Even the seclusion of Balmoral was insufficient. From
time to time the Queen disappeared for a few days to the
Glassalt, a lodge she had built in 1868 amid pines beyond the
Linn of Muick.[2] While she was away, alone with perhaps a
Lady-in-Waiting, she was quite inaccessible. No decisions
on business were possible. In the midst of the criticisms on the
Queen's refusal to entertain the King of Denmark (1875)
Ponsonby writes : " But who can speak ? No one. She has
gone to the Glassalt and there is an end to all arguments."
The truth was that she was a most industrious hard worker
and needed " complete rest from the continued grind. . . ."
" She always returns the better and the livelier for it ", he
adds.

There were very occasional excursions away from Balmoral.
A visit in 1872 to Dunrobin produced an awkward situation.
The Duke of Sutherland had purposely, but without warning,

---

[1] Hoolachan, a noisy form of reel.

[2] The house-warming, including the consumption of a great deal of whisky,
is fully described in *More Leaves from the Highlands*.

invited H. M. Stanley, the explorer, in order that he might
be presented to the Queen. There happened to be at the time
a considerable controversy about Stanley's reliability owing to
his practice of self-advertisement and sides were hotly taken in
public. Lord Granville who was in attendance and Ponsonby,
and indeed the Queen herself, were greatly annoyed at being
trapped into a recognition of and consequently conferring
an honour on Stanley. The Duke refused to yield. When it
was found there was no way out, it culminated in Stanley being
presented and receiving a gold snuff-box with brilliants.

In 1875 she went to Inveraray. Even here the usual set of
four dinners was insisted on. Strangely enough the Duke and
Duchess of Argyll, her host and hostess, were not always invited
to the royal dinner in their own house ! The proceedings do
not appear to have been very lively :

> Inverary, Sep. 25, 1875
> Our evening here consists in the Queen coming in to the
> drawing room for ten minutes or so and then we sit about
> and talk. McCallum More [1] (Lord Lorne) in his kilt and his
> belt studded with boars' heads, the skiff of Lorne etc., and
> adorned with the thistle ribbon, talks to the strangers ;
> the Duchess presides at the tea table with Lady Dufferin,
> Lady Churchill and a daughter. Louise gets a Presbyterian
> Minister on a sofa near her ; another Minister sings songs.
> Campbell of Islay wanders about, joining in the song, or
> sipping his tea, and I sit with an enormous book of the Argyll
> letters since 1660 which Lorne lumps into my lap.

There were also quite informal expeditions such as the trip
to Lochmaree in 1877. Having a picnic luncheon, sketch-
ing, talking to old women in cottages and making purchases
in the village shops, the Queen thoroughly enjoyed herself.
She genuinely liked associating with humble people in the
villages. This led to many stories which were pure fabrications.

But the periods of stagnation at Balmoral were only very
rarely relieved by a visit or an expedition. Year by year for
four, five or even six months the heavy and disciplined dullness of the life became on occasions almost unendurable unless
Ponsonby was fully occupied with his political or international
work, which fortunately he very often was. He refers to it

---

[1] More correctly MacCailein Mor, a thirteenth-century chieftain who was slain
by the Lord of Lorne (*Burke's Peerage*).

specially in his letters to his wife on his return to Scotland after
a brief holiday. " The veriest trifles become important and
rows are almost watched for ", and again, " drizzling work
with plenty of rows ". Apropos of a case in the newspapers,
Lady Waterpark remarked that some people when even
temporarily unhappy would kill themselves. H. P. : " In that
case suicide might be common here ".

Cabinet Ministers tried to find excuses. Lord Hartington
pleaded a party for Newmarket and the Queen was annoyed
that he should think that more amusing than coming to
Balmoral. Lord Carlingford said he felt his return to waiting
like a prisoner getting back into his cell again. Lord John
Manners declared : " Yes, this is a very curious place and more
curious things go on here than I should have dreamt of ".
And Lord Salisbury unlike some other ministers did not
" attempt to conceal his disgust with the place " and was
" heartily glad " when the time came for him to get away.
Campbell Bannerman in a letter to his wife wrote : " It is the
funniest life conceivable : like a convent. We meet at meals
and when we are finished, each is off to his cell."

But up to the end the Queen triumphed completely, even
in the face of all the efforts used to break down her regulated
and rigid retirement. The publication of *Leaves from the
Highlands* and *More Leaves* which had an enormous circulation
was of great assistance to her, not that there was the smallest
deliberate intention on her part to delude the public. Whatever
the merits or demerits of these volumes may be, they present
an innocent and rather sentimental picture of purely domestic
events, expeditions, family goings and comings, little ceremonies, country scenes and deaths, births and marriages.
It would not require much research, however, to pick out a
date recording some colourless, unimportant incident and to
find in her correspondence on the same day some letter to the
Prime Minister or the Private Secretary expressing in her most
vehement language her desire to interfere in high matters of
national importance. But this was all excluded from the
volumes and the general public, including radicals and even
republicans for a short time, were satisfied there could be no
harm whatever in a monarch who spent all her days so innocently in her Scottish retreat.

Her *entourage* knew better. But one and all were discretion itself. There they were : the Lady-in-Waiting, the Maid of Honour, the Minister in Attendance, the minister of the kirk, the resident physician, the Lord-in-Waiting, the Equerry, the gillies, the governesses, the Private Secretary, the Privy Purse and even the Royal Highnesses with or without their wives or husbands, none of them knowing when they might be wanted or what they might be wanted for, but all of them nervous lest they might not be on the spot when the summons came.

Yet in spite of the dullness and even gloom, unattractive entertainments and closely supervised sport, they submitted, not only because protest was futile and even political pressure was useless, but partly because, even in such an atmosphere and in spite of her caprices, they became eager to serve a sovereign who by her demeanour showed such reassuring self-confidence, and also and by no means least because she was able by her charm, fitfully exercised as it might be, to inspire affection and even devotion.

Although the name of John Brown is closely associated with Balmoral, the inclination to omit all mention of him was very strong owing to the absurd gossip and fanciful rumours which accompanied any reference to him in those days. Nevertheless in the Balmoral routine Brown stood out as a feature. He started life as a stable-boy in the employment of Sir Robert Gordon, the owner of Balmoral. The Queen and Prince Albert rented the house in 1848, purchased the whole property in 1852 and re-built the castle, which was completed in 1855. John Brown was taken on by them as a gillie. Subsequently he became personal attendant to the Queen and remained in her service wherever she went until he died at Windsor in 1883. Nothing indeed that John Brown said or did was of the smallest consequence except perhaps his seizure of the mad youth who pointed an unloaded revolver at the Queen when she was passing in her carriage in London in 1872.

Brown was a commonplace rather coarse type of man with little of the shrewdness and humour usually found in the Scottish character in the humbler classes, although on occasions he showed good sense. His head was naturally turned by the attention the Queen paid him and by her employment of him in a peculiarly privileged position. To his rudeness, his overbearing manner and his contributions to quarrels and altercations in the Household there are several references in the correspondence.

Historical parallels could easily be found of monarchs who have made favourites of their lackeys, and indeed many elderly ladies have come to be dominated by a domestic servant. One can imagine the relief and relaxation, amidst obsequious bowings and the guarded language imposed by Court etiquette, of being talked to quite naturally, even rudely as an equal. Court jesters in centuries past were allowed this privilege. That Brown should have taken full advantage of the Queen's infatuation is not in the least surprising. But it did come as a surprise to strangers. Lord Cairns, the Lord Chancellor, staying at Balmoral in the autumn of 1874, had of course to go to a gillies' ball, entirely organized and managed by John Brown. " What a coarse animal that Brown is," he remarked : " Oh yes, I know the ball could not go on without him. But I did not conceive it possible that anyone could behave so roughly as he does to the Queen."

Brown understood the Queen. But even he could not always have his way or satisfy her whims and fancies. One winter when she was angry because her sleigh stuck in the snow he told Ponsonby that it did not matter what sleigh you had, six large people must weigh heavily and " ye canna go like lightning as she wants to do ".

Hearing the Queen was going out and seeing John Brown with a basket, one of the Maids of Honour asked if it was tea he was taking out. " Wall, no," he replied, " she don't much like tea. We tak oot biscuits and sperruts."

In conveying messages he never had recourse to any softening civilities. When the Mayor of Portsmouth came to ask the Queen to go to a Volunteer review, the Private Secretary sent in the request to her and hoped to get the reply privately that he might convey it civilly to the Mayor. As they both sat in the Equerry's room waiting, Brown put his head in and only said, " The Queen says saretenly not." " So there was an end of the matter and the Mayor went away much crestfallen."

In matters of sport he was allowed practically a free hand. A royal son-in-law on going out to shoot one of the coverts at Osborne found Brown had been there before him and there were no birds left. Protest was of course impossible. As to the fishing at Balmoral :

> At 6 in the morning he sends up to find out how the fish are. If he hears a bad report he does not go out and the Queen offers it to Dr. Marshall, and there are always jokes about his never catching anything.

A quarrel with Brown Ponsonby soon learned was out of the question. In the earlier years, owing to some altercation with regard to the gillies' ball, Prince Alfred (the Duke of Edinburgh) took offence at Brown's excessive rudeness and refused to speak to him, greet him or answer him. Strained relations lasted for some days. Ponsonby prevented it coming to the Queen's ear as he knew quite well that Prince Alfred, who was not entirely free from blame, could not possibly come well out of it and it might develop into a major " row ". He knew wisely that in quarrels an apology on either side can seldom be expected. So after a little private conversation with each of the parties he brought them together quite naturally, and casual ordinary greetings were exchanged and peace was restored.

Clearly Ponsonby's calm, judicial and friendly method gave Brown confidence in him and respect for him. But there were occasions when the situation required action as well as words. The Queen was going out for her afternoon drive and, having got into the carriage, was waiting for Brown to take his usual place on the box. She was kept waiting. Ponsonby who was at the door, suspecting what the trouble was, went upstairs and sure enough found Brown on his bed not in a fit state to go out. Having turned the key in the lock he went down to the entrance and, without a word to the Queen, himself mounted the box and they drove off. The Queen knew what it was and knew that he knew. But on this as on other occasions she turned a blind eye.

Occasionally John Brown in expansive moments ejaculated some of his crude political views. In 1872 he wanted the Government to be turned out : " A good thing too, the sooner they go the better. That Gladstone's half a Roman and the others had better be gone. We canna have a worse lot." Then in 1878 : " I asked J. B. today if he wanted war. He exclaimed most vehemently ' Damn it no — I beg your pardon — but

I think it would be awful ; dreadful deal of fighting and at the end no one would be better and a' would be worse for it '."

The Queen's marked and sustained infatuation for Brown accounted very naturally for his arrogant manner and demeanour. By so often giving offence he contributed to his general unpopularity. The gillies were jealous of him ; the servants, although he made favourites among them, feared him ; all the Household disliked him and several of the royal family including the Prince of Wales detested him. Ponsonby throughout remained neutral, balancing obligations as well as watching lest a storm in a teacup, of which there were many, might develop into something more serious if not quickly adjusted. He knew there was no danger whatever in Brown's relations with the Queen and neither publicly nor domestically was the Highland attendant of any real consequence. He realized that the Queen's devotion to him dated back to the happy days before her widowhood and had from that an almost sacred foundation. He might be a nuisance and often was. But personal irritation, exasperation or loss of temper with him must never be magnified so as to endanger the smooth working of much more important matters. Further than this he recognized Brown's value. This appears from a letter written from Balmoral a few weeks after John Brown's death in 1883 :

> The Deeside looks very pretty with the light green birches and the sun was bright if not warm while the hills have patches of snow upon them. It was a day that one could easily understand would make the Queen low and she was low. She had been to Brown's grave. We also went there. There is no stone up yet. But it is next to his father's which has a most elaborate tombstone with the history of the whole family upon it. Wreaths from Princesses, Empresses and Ladies in Waiting are lying on Brown's grave. He was the only person who could fight and make the Queen do what she did not wish. He did not always succeed nor was his advice always the best. But I believe he was honest, and with all his want of education, his roughness, his prejudices and other faults he was undoubtedly a most excellent servant to her.

The Queen's grief at the loss of one on whom she depended for daily and almost hourly attendance it may well be imagined was very deep. References to it occur in several letters. The first one only need be quoted, written a few days after Brown's death :

> The Queen is trying hard to occupy herself but she is utterly crushed & her life has again sustained one of those shocks like in 61 when every link has been shaken & torn & at every turn & every moment the loss of the strong arm & wise advice, warm heart & cheery original way of saying things & the sympathy in any large & small circumstances — is most cruelly missed. She hopes to see Sir Henry for a moment this even^g but he must be prepared to find her very nervous & very much shaken.
>
> The Queen can't walk the least & the shock she has sustained has made her very weak — so that she can't stand.

Ponsonby received a framed and enamelled photograph with " a touching inscription on the back ".

Sir Francis Knollys [1] wrote from Sandringham and said in the course of his letter on Brown's death :

> I have for a long time been one of those who have thought that if anything happened to him worse might happen — I mean in this way that his successor might do a great deal more harm than Brown, who after all I suppose of late years confined his interference chiefly to the stables, shooting and the servants — quite enough perhaps. But if he had been an ambitious man, there is no doubt, I suppose, he might have meddled in more important matters. I presume all the Family will rejoice at his death, but I think very probably they are shortsighted. . . .

After Brown's death there had necessarily to be a reorganization of that part of the Household over which he had completely dominated. The Highlanders demanded that their orders should come only from the Queen direct. Ponsonby at once vetoed this idea and set to work on other plans for submission to the Queen. " Like the Abbé Sieyès I am continually producing new constitutions ", he writes.

In the next reign most of the cairns, monuments, memorials, inscriptions, seats, etc., commemorative of John Brown in the grounds of the royal residences were removed.

Sir Francis Knollys' apprehensions were by no means wide of the mark. He was right in saying that Brown was no public danger. Not only had he no temptation in that direction

---

[1] Afterwards Viscount Knollys, Private Secretary to King Edward.

but he had not the necessary education or intelligence for the role of a spy. Subsequently however a successor arose but of a very different type, and again Ponsonby's talents as a negotiator and adjuster of differences were called for, but in more difficult circumstances as the Queen's second infatuation grew.

The dominant position acquired by the Munshi Abdul Karim can be related briefly. It was at Balmoral in 1887 that the Queen first engaged some Indian servants. Major-General Dennehy, who had been political agent in Rajputana and subsequently appointed Extra Groom-in-Waiting, was placed in charge of them. At first the Queen was merely excited about them as a child would be with a new toy. Their attendance in their picturesque costumes gave a ceremonial reminder that she was Empress of India. Tutors were engaged, wives invited and, writes Ponsonby, " she has given me a Hindu vocabulary to study ". Rapidly towards the end of the year two were singled out for special favour, Abdul Karim and Mahomet. Dennehy was useless.

From *The Queen*

Balmoral, Sep. 12, 1887
Sir Henry will see what he [Lord Dufferin] says about Indian servants. It is just what the Queen feels & she cannot say what a comfort she finds *hers*. Abdul is most handy in helping when she *signs* by drying the signatures. He learns with extraordinary assiduity & Mahomet is wonderfully quick & intelligent & understands everything.

After increases in salary which Ponsonby as Privy Purse was told to grant, Abdul Karim was relieved from domestic service. He declared he did not belong to the servant class. At a theatrical entertainment in 1889 he refused to sit in the row with the dressers behind the guests, so retired to his room. After this not only did he always stand apart from the servants but he was told to join the Household in the billiard-room and sometimes at meals. This caused a commotion especially among those of the Queen's Household who had served in India and knew that his pretensions were groundless. The Private Secretary had some difficulty in rounding this corner and persuading the Household to say good-morning to him. The Munshi also began boasting of the number of clerks he had under him and Arthur Bigge wrote : " Don't you think

THE QUEEN
With John Brown and the Keeper

THE QUEEN
With Indian Servant

it well to resist these moves upwards ? " At the Braemar games in 1890 on the Queen's instruction he stood, " a very conspicuous figure, among the gentry ".

    The Duke of Connaught was angry and spoke to me about it. I replied that Abdul stood where he was by the Queen's order and that if it was wrong, as I did not understand Indian Etiquette and H.R.H. did, would it not be better for him to mention it to the Queen. This entirely shut him up.

This was one of the usual attempts on the part of her sons or daughters to get Ponsonby to act as an intermediary with their mother as they dared not approach the Queen direct.

    At last Abdul Karim became the Munshi Hafiz Abdul Karim, the Queen's Indian Secretary, and all photographs of him handing dishes to the Queen were destroyed. His name appeared in the Court Circular and in the official ceremonial at public functions. A bungalow was built for him at Osborne, fully appointed with furniture and linen, " his aunts " and a mysterious friend stayed with him, and rumours were circulated, but Ponsonby was powerless. " As long as it was English or European work I got on fairly. But these Injuns are too much for me." Abdul Karim now did a good deal more than dry the Queen's signatures so handily. The Duke of Connaught was by no means alone in his objections ; the Prince of Wales, other members of the royal family and at last Ministers of the Crown became suspicious of leakages through certain contacts the Munshi had with India, and by 1894 published attacks on him began to appear. On one of these occasions there is a communication from the Queen to Ponsonby in which she says :

Florence, Ap. 10, 1894

The Queen wrote rather in a hurry when she mentioned to him the stupid illnatured article or rather letter about the poor good Munshi & she w^d wish to observe that to make out that he is so *low* is really *outrageous* & in a country like England quite out of place as anyone can [see] this. She has known 2 Archbishops who were the sons respectively of a Butcher & a Grocer, a Chancellor whose father was a poor sort of Scotch Minister, Sir D. Stewart & Ld Mount Stephen both who ran about barefoot as children & whose parents were very humble & the tradesmen M. &

J. P. were made Baronets ! Abdul's father saw good and honourable service as a Dr & he [Abdul] feels cut to the heart at being thus spoken of.

It probably comes from some low jealous Indians or Anglo-Indians, & N . . . Ahmed is fond of writing & writes well but the thing is *he* is *fond* of putting himself forward in Print w^h the Queen warned ag^st not that much will ever come out of this nonsense. The Queen hopes & is sure Sir Henry will *not* allow it in any way to *influence* him or the Queen's action but it sh^d *stop him*. The Queen is so sorry for the poor Munshi's sensitive feelings.

Nothing however was done and the Munshi remained till he was disposed of in the new reign.

It would be an interesting speculation to imagine what would have happened if John Brown had been alive. But we do not even hear what the Highlanders thought of the oriental invasion. We can only see that no greater contrast could possibly exist between two servants who gained such conspicuous and favourable attention from the Queen than there was between the gruff, rude, direct and devoted Highlander and the bland, smiling, furtive and scheming Indian.

The Indian episode was by no means just one of the " twopenny-halfpenny " affairs over which the Private Secretary had so often to waste his time. It certainly made a break in the monotonous routine of Balmoral.

The lovely scenery of the Deeside and the surpassing beauty of the hills in all seasons are often noted by Henry Ponsonby, who was a great walker. He could not refrain from commenting in his letters to his wife on the beauties of nature round Balmoral in which at times he seems to have found some consolation. It was the annual forced separation from his wife for weeks and months, year after year, which he never ceased to resent. At Windsor or Osborne he had his home close by. He could relax amid his family in the evenings and steal an hour or two during the day. At Balmoral his daily letter to his wife was his pleasure because he could imagine he was talking to her ; and in receiving news from her which was read and re-read, he could feel for a moment that he was at home.

CHAPTER VII

Ponsonby's Method

A PRIME MINISTER has to direct his attention to subjects covering a very wide range. Even eighty years ago and more the business of Government had developed in complexity and detail both in the foreign field, owing to the electric telegraph, and more still in home affairs, owing to the increase in domestic legislation ; and although it had by no means reached the still wider range which more frequent correspondence and rapidity of communication have brought about to-day, it was placing a heavy burden on the head of the Government. But the Prime Minister had his colleagues as departmental chiefs to whom all technical questions could be referred and he had his Cabinet for arriving at final decisions.

Henry Ponsonby's department was the Sovereign, and the sovereign was Queen Victoria. Every Government decision on policy had to be submitted to her. Every departmental decision of any importance came before her. Every one of the higher appointments had to receive her sanction. There was nothing automatic about this. There was no rubber stamp.

He soon understood that while his work involved much correspondence, the drafting of reports and abstracts, the mastery of parliamentary Bills, the framing of submissions, the reading of Foreign Office dispatches, conveying messages, conducting interviews and, later, when he became Keeper of the Privy Purse as well, a certain amount of administration, organization, accounts and purchases, there was a factor governing much of his work which required something more than diligence and punctuality. The interests of the sovereign must of course always be borne in mind. That went without saying. But the personality of Queen Victoria must never be left out of account. That required vigilance, discretion and special perception. There could be no official regulations laid

down for it. She had established a routine to which he had
to fit in. She laid down certain instructions which had to be
obeyed. Her technique and the often bewildering consequences of her injunctions had to be mastered. Her pre-
dilections and her character had to be studied.

Tact and civility in serving a sovereign might be easy
enough. Serving Queen Victoria was by no means plain sailing. Here was a problem in adaptation, guidance, restraint
or encouragement which could hardly be absent from his
mind whenever he put pen to paper. He had learned something
from his predecessor. But after he had got into the saddle
the pace increased and dilemmas, deadlocks and dangerous
corners became more frequent. He framed no settled Machia-
vellian plan. He felt his way gradually. On General Grey's
death he wrote deploring his loss and added : " It is quite
true she seldom saw him of late but he always boldly wrote
what he thought and, tho' it irritated her, it sunk in and did
good. I know the Ministers thought he might have done
more, but I believe he knew how far he could go and, owing
to this, his advice was never altogether disregarded ". This
was the keynote of Ponsonby's method : never to risk completely losing influence. In the early years of his private
secretaryship he was obliged to talk over with the Queen the
gossip, rumours and grossly exaggerated reports on the subject
of her seclusion. " Of course," he writes, " if I had been a
brave able clever man, I might have read her a lecture on her
duties. But of course I did nothing of the sort. Had I done
so, I suppose I should never have the subject approached
again." In his otherwise cordial eulogy of the Queen's Private
Secretary,[1] Archbishop Davidson criticizes him for lack of
courage and not " standing up bravely to oppose the Queen ".
This comes curiously from the Archbishop who, close as his
relationship was with Her Majesty, himself never behaved
thus. He knew as well as Henry Ponsonby that anyone who
did this only did it once.

So on any ticklish question Ponsonby never opened with
a direct negative or contradiction. He noticed how the
contrary method in the case of one of his colleagues was fatal :

When she insists that 2 and 2 make 5 I say that I cannot
help thinking they make 4. She replies there may be some

[1] See p. 63.

truth in what I say, but she knows they make 5. Thereupon
I drop the discussion. It is of no consequence and I leave
it there, knowing the fact. But X—— goes on with it,
brings proofs, arguments and former sayings of her own.
No one likes this. No one can stand admitting they are
wrong, women especially ; and the Queen can't abide it.
Consequently she won't give in, says X—— is unkind and
there is trouble.

Ponsonby trusted in fact to her good sense, of which he had
quite a high opinion, eventually straightening things out.
But she must not be bullied into a confession of error. Passing
mood and health had always to be taken into account. As
years passed her vigour was sustained and indeed seemed to
increase. In 1873 he writes : " Yesterday the Queen was on
the rampage ", and twenty years later in 1893 : " The Queen
is full of business and sending ticklers all round, as much as to
say ' I'm back, so look out ! ' "

On certain occasions Henry Ponsonby was entrusted with
negotiations, social as well as political. That he was successful in these cases can be shown. He was no doubt aided
by being in a commanding position owing to the power and
authority behind him. But he also fulfilled the function of an
interpreter, one might almost say translator, adapting the
sense without mistranslation of opinion impetuously expressed,
sometimes with considerable violence. Here there might have
been a temptation to startle by literal quotation or to eliminate
all character in his translations by a not inaccurate but bald
version of his message. He managed to avoid either extreme.
His letter generally had to be submitted and he invariably
made it reflect the Queen's mood and state her opinions without any of the harsh emphasis which might give offence. But
the Queen's insistence on written rather than verbal communication with the officers of her Household (who were in the
same building) made it on some occasions necessary for him to
correct mistakes and even reject decisions by means of a letter.
In this he excelled, and we can find wrapped in the orthodox
courtier's phraseology the happy sentence expressing doubt
followed by the bolder rejection of views in language which
while uncompromising could not offend.

With regard to the bestowal of Honours, a question which
naturally came up periodically for discussion, Ponsonby did

not gain a very elevated opinion of human nature when he received so many requests from highly placed as well as from humble people for titles, decorations or rewards for themselves. That the fountain of honour should be indirectly approached is not surprising. But he was able on occasions to prevent some applications reaching the Queen. He had the legitimate and constitutional excuse that recommendations could only come through the Prime Minister. He himself was never inclined, indeed he always peremptorily refused, to exert the influence his office gave him to obtain an appointment, promotion or any professional advantage for a friend or member of his family.

Little trivial details about functions were whenever possible kept away from the Queen. " Quite absurd to bother her on these twopenny details ", Ponsonby writes. " I have taken a deal on myself and if things go wrong may get toko. But someone must decide something. There is a deal too much talk."

One thing he learned quite early was the undesirability of taking offence at the Queen's methods of expression. He knew that if angry she might speak or write in exaggerated terms, and although she was unlikely openly to retract, the matter might be allowed to drop. Fuller knowledge of the facts would convince her because she was not fundamentally unreasonable. An instance of the wrong method was brought to his notice in 1872.

The resident physician Dr. Marshall was not supposed to dine or to be invited to dine with the Household. Lord Charles Fitzroy, an Equerry, said he had dined frequently. The Queen said he had never dined. Lord Charles insisted that he had (which was the case). Three messages came through Lady Ely that Dr. Marshall had not dined. Lord Charles took offence, felt his word was doubted and laid the matter before his brother the Duke of Grafton. He sent a letter to Lady Ely with a list of the times Marshall had dined. The Queen avoided the point by writing on the subject of whose fault it was that Marshall was invited. Ponsonby intervened supporting Fitzroy. But the only effect of this was to make him unreasonably indignant with Ponsonby, who therefore suffered, as those who try to intervene in a quarrel often do. The trouble was not disposed of for six months.

Ponsonby's memorandum on it ends : " Row concluded. Biddulph advised me to shake hands. I did so. May 1873. Ended."

Scattered through the papers may be found several examples of how Ponsonby steered his course between the rocks in difficult circumstances. These collected together illustrate what may be called his method. It will be seen that while taking into full account the particular circumstances of each case he never omitted careful consideration of the relationships and the personalities of the individuals involved. But he admits himself : " The fact is that any advice I give to H.M. must be given in a most gingerly way ". Some of the cases may be related in more or less chronological order.

In August 1873 when arrangements were being made for the Queen's holiday trip from Balmoral to Lochmaree, the minutest details of the journey had to be submitted to her. In the list of those who were to accompany her she would not allow more than *one* housemaid. There was a protest. The domestic servants (like the Princesses) never hesitated to make Ponsonby their intermediary. He was asked to object. This is the way he did it. He sent in (abbreviated in his own words) : " Of course quite right that only one housemaid should go for the smaller work. I would send to hire a girl from the Hotel. Stray girls were not always very honest. So I hoped the Queen would not leave things about to tempt her. I got an answer that another housemaid should go from here."

In preparation for the Prince of Wales' visit to India in 1875 a serious difference of opinion as to the staff and friends who should accompany him arose between Balmoral and Marlborough House. The Prince of Wales' selections were strongly objected to by the Queen. Ponsonby saw at once that altercations on this subject between mother and son would be most undesirable. The proceedings are best told in his own words :

> I told you that I had eagerly urged that everything should go through the government and not direct between this and Marlborough House and I had refused to submit Knollys' somewhat crisp letter. Now I have to prevent the Queen doing the same though I had not much difficulty so far. Dizzy called on the Prince of Wales for list of friends

going.   The Queen having objected to some, the Prince of Wales drew up the list in his own hand, and saw Dizzy who seems to have given way which I am not surprised at, Dizzy is not Gladstone.   He says now with the deepest humility that he hopes the Queen will not object to the list and says the Cabinet think on the whole the list will do.   Whereupon Lady Ely rushes with this box to me and says the Queen wants me at once to write to Knollys.   I refused flat and wrote to the Queen to say why, and advised her to take Dizzy's advice.   She had put the matter in his hands and should abide by it.   He said he was convinced the Prince would not give way and further objections would lead to embarrassments, but if wished he would caution C. and B. against larks.   It was evident that any further opposition was useless, nor was it in my belief reasonable as I believe these two are sharp enough to behave themselves. . . .

[Later.]   The Queen has agreed in my observations far more than I expected but maintains she should express her dislike of those going as she cannot truthfully approve.   I have suggested that instead of saying anything against these, she might regret that he had not selected more distinguished men more eminently qualified to act as guides to him in India.

Ponsonby was on strong ground here in supporting her Prime Minister's advice, which the Queen was not always willing to take even when Disraeli held that position.

Again on the Royal Titles Bill in 1876 (conferring on the Queen the title of Empress of India) he advocated, when opposition arose, that she should follow Disraeli's advice although Ponsonby himself considered the Prime Minister had handled the whole matter very clumsily and in a way that gave rise to unfounded rumours.   When he was urged to tell the Queen that public opinion was against the Bill, he writes : " How can I put my opinion against the Ministers' ? . . . Ought I to make her distrust her Prime Minister ?   My duty is to make her rely on him " ; and again, writing from Baden where the Queen was staying : " I feel convinced that Dizzy has so mismanaged it, first by keeping it purposely or accidentally a secret from the opposition and then by making it a series of mysteries, that the excitement is due to him.   But I cannot attack him to her.   I am bound to support him and further must continually advise her to follow his advice."

There was opposition in the Lords as well as in the Commons

and *The Times* was critical.   An account in the memorandum
book tells the whole story.

ROYAL TITLE 1876

Lord Granville wrote to the Queen to apologize for intruding
but as she had consulted him he now (March 13) thought it right
to tell her there would be the greatest opposition to the Bill.   He
regretted but could not prevent it — and asked was the measure
necessary — if necessary is it desirable to force it in the teeth
of an opposition ?   Would it not be better to adjourn ?   Hartington will move for adjournment if necessary.   The Queen told me
she could not think of withdrawing it.   All England had thought
she was Empress of India.   This Bill only affirmed the popular
impression.   To withdraw the Bill would be to assume she was rebuffed, when no such desire existed.   To adjourn would only
be to prolong an unpleasant discussion.   She sent me up to see
Disraeli.   He read Granville's letter.   He said there was no popular
feeling against the measure.   The papers were all connected with
the Liberal party who were civil to the editors.   " You meet at
a gentleman's table a dirty man who shocks your feelings by eating
with his knife — gradually you discover that the dirty man is an
agreeable and clever fellow and you find that he is one of the
editors of a London paper who treated on a social equality by
a great statesman becomes his devoted friend and writes up his
party.   We Tories (possibly from a mistaken view) have not
taken up editors and so have no newspapers to write us up.
You are a Liberal, I am a Tory — but we both agree in our
wish to serve the Queen therefore you must allow me to speak
out frankly and to say that this is a regular party move.   The
Opposition think they see an opportunity of damaging me and
they forget that in this instance they also attack the Queen.   But
I do not want to bring her name in.   The Bill is ours entirely and
we take the whole responsibility.   We are certain to carry it.   If
by any chance I am defeated I resign.   I cannot and will not
think of withdrawing the measure.   The country are either in
favour of it — or not against it.   To adjourn would simply be to
give time for getting up agitation against it."

I returned to Windsor and saw the Queen at 11.30 and gave
her this message.   She was pleased with it.   I replied to Granville : " By Disraeli's desire I am commanded by the Queen
to thank you for your letter tho' she regrets to learn the contents.
She does not wish you in any way to urge Hartington to press for
adjournment.   I do not clearly understand why the Liberal party
should object to the Queen calling herself by a title, by which
she was called by a Liberal Secretary of State when late Govt.

were in office?" I added privately from myself that she was very hot about it — angry with Liberal party and I was in black books as she seemed to hold me responsible for them. Lord Granville wrote later to say that Hartington had proposed his amendment so as to prevent Anderson's more unpleasant motion. I replied by telling him I had given his letter to the Queen — who was as anxious as ever in favour of the measure. I ventured at the same time to observe to H.M. that I was quite convinced that with the exception of the Ultras the desire of all Liberals was to prevent any annoyance being caused to H.M. and that they were as anxious as any to preserve the grace and dignity of her great position. H.M. did not make any reply. The Queen sent me Theodore Martin's letter saying the conduct of the opposition was disgraceful,[1] and Princess Louise's letter saying it was absurd to suppose the royal family wished to take title of Imperial.—I replied " The opposition arises from different causes. 1. Anderson, Cowen and other avowed republicans to whom the title of Queen is equally abhorrent with that of Empress. They hope to damage Monarchy. 2. Gladstone and friends really are frightened by the idea that ' Empress ' is to supplant ' Queen '. 3. Some politicians who do not much care for the question itself see an opportunity for attacking the Govt. 4. Forster and others honestly think that Disraeli has not sufficiently explained that it is not Y.M.'s intention to adopt title of Empress of England and that the people look on the bill with suspicion and it will make Y.M. unpopular. 5. Lords Granville, Hartington and others are truly anxious to serve Y.M. but have difficulty in keeping Ultras in order. They would wish any bill of this sort to pass unanimously but finding there was opposition, Lord Granville considered it his duty to let Y.M. know. I feel sure that the large majority of Liberals all desire to be of real service to Y.M. especially those who have served you. You must however abide by Disraeli's advice. He has introduced measure in the way he thinks most judicious and he must advise Y.M. how to go thro' with it."

The Queen however said that there was much excitement about it and when Lorne told her he had been whipped up for Monday 20 — she was anxious that Disraeli should clearly say she never intended to be Empress of England nor did the Princes intend to be Imperial. She telegraphed up and wrote to this effect and Disraeli sent down a draft of words he proposed to use — beginning with : " I am commanded to say ". The Queen showed them to me. I doubted whether it was right to bring in her name with a message of this sort. I asked Biddulph, he

[1] *Letters of Queen Victoria*, Second Series, vol. ii, p. 450, Queen's letter to Theodore Martin.

was quite against it. I went up to London and saw Disraeli. He said the Chancellor saw no harm but perhaps the form might be altered. He would consult the Speaker. Also would see Hartington. Finally he gave the assertion as from himself. A letter written by the Queen to me in 1873 says enclosing an address as Empress of India : " These words make the Queen again think of her wish & indeed determination to take the additional title of Empress of India. Not to *raise her* rank but to add to the higher title." On the 25th of Feb. I told the Queen that the excitement against the Bill arose because people thought she would call herself Empress of England and the Princesses Imperial Highness. She replied " It is just because we consider Queen as good as Empress that the idea is to add Empress *after* Queen of Great Britain & Ireland — and Imperial Highness is not dreamt of. The Queen must insist on *Empress* of India as she has certainly been styled so — and it suits oriental ideas." I asked if I might give her permission to Disraeli to state this and she said certainly. I wrote to Disraeli to say so — and saw him — but left him perfect freedom to do what he thought best. He would not give the style to Parliament — and in my opinion increased the storm against it. Disraeli wrote to the Queen at Baden that the so-called agitation against the Bill is artificial — there is no sound feeling on the subject. It will not do to concede anything. The utmost firmness is required. The opposition think they have unexpectedly a chance and will hesitate at nothing.

I think Disraeli is rather too much afraid of imaginary bogies at Marlborough House and too anxious to get the Queen's name in it. The Prince of Wales I found afterwards was sore at Disraeli never having told him of his intention to bring in the Royal Titles Bill. He wrote a remonstrance. Disraeli's answer was that he did not know his address ! Lord Granville afterwards said he thought Disraeli's mismanagement of the affair had caused the chief trouble — though it must be remembered Lord Granville objected to the word Empress throughout. He thought the Queen had not acted constitutionally in trying to influence votes — but he attributed it all to Disraeli.

The Bill was eventually passed by a large majority in the Commons.

Nothing was more difficult than to guide the Queen when she was anxious to give public expression to her natural and justifiable emotions and her deep compassion. This was the case when the tragic news of the Prince Imperial's death in Zululand reached her. He and his companions in a reconnaissance party were surprised by a body of Zulus. Others escaped but Prince Louis Napoleon was killed. On July 14, 1879, the Queen wrote :

> The Queen rec^d these most painful & distressing details. They are terrible evidence of want of right feeling & decency & of lamentable want of firmness or even of comprehension of their duty on the part of Lord Chelmsford & others ! The Queen feels as if she sh^d never get over this dreadful thought.
>
> The poor manservant said with tears in his eyes he felt he " w^d have died 100 times to save his life ". The Duke of Cambridge is in despair & considers all " tells very ill for all concerned ".

As may be imagined there were articles in the press both here and in France and Ponsonby received a mound of correspondence. Captain Carey who was in command of the reconnaissance party wrote self-vindicating letters which were unfortunately published, and feeling ran very high. There was a Court-Martial and Mrs. Carey wrote a letter to Sir Henry Ponsonby enclosing a letter which she asked him to transmit to the Queen. His reply was firm but not unsympathetic :

> Osborne, August 1, 1879
>
> Lt.-General Sir Henry Ponsonby presents his compliments to Mrs. Carey.
>
> He need scarcely assure her how deeply he feels for her in the most painful circumstances in which she is placed. But he is compelled with great regret to explain to her that he has no power to bring her letter to the notice of the Queen. Her Majesty's decision on the proceedings of the Court Martial can only be arrived at after consultation with her responsible ministers and Sir Henry Ponsonby is precluded from submitting to the Queen the points connected with Captain Carey which Mrs. Carey has brought forward in her letter.

Ponsonby disagreed with those who were inclined to blame the higher military officers in command of the troops in Zululand. Heroic the Prince Imperial's conduct may have been, but his insistence on serving in such a war he considered foolhardy and unnecessary. The Queen's attitude had to be watched. The unfortunate tragedy had so deeply moved the military authorities that it would be a mistake for the Queen personally to add fuel to the flames. " The Queen says ", Ponsonby writes, " that she feels the Prince Imperial was our guest and

lost by the carelessness of her officers and it is her duty to
protect the Empress. A fine feeling, perhaps. But I tell her
she had better leave it alone, and this she don't like." In what
way he conveyed this to her does not appear, probably it was
verbally. But a consequential controversy arose after the
funeral at Chislehurst, which was attended by members of the
royal family, and this split public opinion into two rival factions.
The sentimental emotionalism produced violent opposition
when it was proposed that a statue of the Prince Imperial
should be erected in Westminster Abbey. The unfortunate
Dean of Westminster (Arthur Stanley), the authority for sanc-
tioning such a proposal, rather precipitately gave his consent
and was therefore subjected to violent attack in part of the
press. A Memorial Committee was appointed in July 1879,
on which the Prince of Wales, the Duke of Edinburgh and
Prince Leopold sat. Lord Sydney the Lord Steward was also
a member and wrote to Ponsonby describing the strong differences of opinion, amounting to a threat of retirement on the
part of the two elder Princes :

> It would indeed be a disgrace if the matter broke down
> from a Royal personal Row with the Editor of the *Morning
> Post* [Borthwick was in favour of Westminster Abbey] or a
> quarrel between the two Elder Brethren with the youngest
> of the Royal Family [Prince Leopold] ; but I do not acquit
> the journalist of having been much too presumptuous.

Later he reported having heard that the Queen had written
privately to the Government.

The situation thus produced is best described in a letter from
the Dean of Westminster, Ponsonby's reply, and an extract of
a letter from Dean Wellesley of Windsor :

From *The Dean of Westminster*

July 29, 1879

What do *you* think should be done about the Prince Imperial's
monument ? I granted the request at once, as it was made
to me in the full belief that it was just the thing which would
gratify the public feeling of the country — and also with the
conviction that it would add to the interest of the Abbey. So
far from its being pressed upon me by the Queen or the
Princes I believe that the Princes were rather averse to it
and the Queen (whose permission as being in a royal Chapel

I felt bound to ask) evidently in her reply had doubts on the subject. The sudden change (if so be) in the public interest took me by surprise. I wrote immediately a note to Sir Stafford Northcote offering to withdraw the permission if the Government thought it contrary to the public interest, or else if they wished to take no part in the question to undertake the whole responsibility. I sent to him also the memorandum of which copies appeared in the newspapers. The result you know. It appears to me that the Government having declined to interfere I have no alternative but to proceed *unless* the Queen should be pleased to say that in as much as the grace of the proposal is much impaired by the unexpected division of public feeling, it is undesirable to continue a project which was adopted in consequence of a unanimity which has ceased to exist. The remonstrances I receive are very violent, chiefly anonymous, but some have come from highly respectable persons and conservatives.

The newspapers are divided. *The Times* and *Morning Post* approving and the *D. News* and *Echo* and *Pall Mall Gazette* against. It is a very curious phenomenon and it is possible that I was precipitate in giving my assent, but I had not a shadow of doubt at the time. Of course if the Queen decided that it should be stopped and yet did not wish her name to appear in the matter I could then undertake the refusal. But I could not recede without having privately or publicly the full authority of the Crown or the Government behind me unless the remonstrances took a more serious and formal tone than they have yet assumed.

To *The Dean of Westminster*

Osborne, August 1, 1879

Your relation of the circumstances as far as the Queen is concerned is I think pretty correct. She did not quite like the idea of the monument in the Abbey at first but when decided on she warmly adopted it and thinks it would be ungracious in the extreme to go back. This at any rate was her opinion a few days ago, but I will speak again to her and let you know.

The point you now raise is whether the controversy which now rages does not rob the act of its grace, and whether in these circumstances it is not wiser to retire. At first it was assumed that you alone had uncontrolled power over the Abbey. In that case the responsibility was yours and you were free to act as you thought best. But the Queen's name has now been introduced into the discussion and her power of approval or veto acknowledged. Whatever she does must

be done — even in the Abbey — by the advice and consent
of her Ministers who are bound to defend her acts in Parliament. I therefore think that in this matter she should consult the Government before she expresses any opinion upon
what has now swelled itself into a burning question.

Dated the same day there is a rough draft of a note from
Ponsonby to the Dean of Westminster. " The Queen is by no
means willing to abandon the idea of Westminster Abbey. . . .
She considers that to give it up now because a few persons
object would be a mistake."

From *Dean Wellesley* (of Windsor)

I agree with the Queen and yourself as to the weakness
now of a retreat. It must be fought out. There were no
sufficient grounds for the statue in Westminster Abbey to
set out with. The defence of it was yet more unfortunate.
But to recede from the proposal now would be the worst
folly of all. St. George's never occurred to me. Next to
a statue on Chislehurst Common it would have been the very
best thing because (as at the Funeral) it would have shown
the personal and private affection of the Royal Family
towards him, while at the same time it would have been a
sufficiently distinguished spot. For after all here is the very
thing. Stanley was obliged to draw a distinction in his
letter between Henry VII Chapel (as exceptionally for
Royalty) and the great Abbey itself in order to justify his
permission for the statue to be in the Abbey at all — a
distinction without a difference in the public eye.

But Westminster Abbey once offered and announced,
we must make the best of it and any change would be most
painful to the Empress and family and be regarded as a
defeat by the public. The little Dean, besides, had far too
much pluck for this.

The press reported that the French Government for political
reasons was strongly against the proposal for a statue in Westminster Abbey.

The upshot of the controversy was that Westminster Abbey
was abandoned and a recumbent statue of the Prince Imperial
was placed in St. George's at Windsor in the Bray Chapel.
Dean Wellesley and Ponsonby may have found it a delicate
and difficult matter but they had strong backing, and the
compromise of St. George's was undoubtedly the right solution.

L

A small instance of Ponsonby's " gingerly way " is shown in this brief passage from a letter in June 1880 :

> The Queen asked me who could represent her [at the funeral of the Empress of Russia]. I said, the Duke of Edinburgh. The Queen said " No, of course he couldn't." I said " Of course he couldn't." But as I did not know why, I got back to him in the course of conversation and said it was a pity he couldn't. So she telegraphed to ask him if he could and he said he would.

Certainly the most delicate and difficult of Ponsonby's interventions occurred between July 1883 and March 1884. Delicate, because the Queen's deepest emotions were in question, and difficult, because he quite decidedly made up his mind from the outset that a project she had conceived must at all costs be turned down. In connection with the publication of *More Leaves from the Highlands*, which was to be dedicated " to the memory of my devoted personal attendant and faithful friend ", she expressed her intention of herself writing a memoir of John Brown. When asked to write a Life of John Brown, Sir Theodore Martin had got out of it by some very lame excuse about his wife's health. A Miss Macgregor was employed to put the Queen's language in some sort of literary shape. Sir Henry Ponsonby began by suggesting that he should refer the manuscript to one or two others who had more knowledge of literary forms than he had. The Queen sent it to him in February 1884, accompanied by the further proposal that Brown's private diary should be printed. The matter having now occupied the Queen's attention for several months and Sir Henry being more than ever persuaded that publication would be quite impossible, he proceeded to write to the Queen at some length. He begins by an appreciation of what the Queen herself had written, he criticizes some of Miss Macgregor's alterations, he refers to Brown's private journal, and after hinting that people outside the Court might not understand some of the references, he lets himself go :

> But as Sir Henry proceeds he becomes more bold and asks the Queen's forgiveness if he expresses a doubt whether this record of Your Majesty's innermost and most sacred feelings should be made public to the world. There are passages which will be misunderstood if read by strangers and there are expressions which will attract remarks of an unfavour-

able nature towards those who are praised ; and Sir Henry cannot help fearing that the feeling created by such a publication would become most distressing and painful to the Queen.

The Queen took this surprisingly well, excusing herself by saying she had only intended it for private circulation. But this letter killed the project and the papers were destroyed.

There are many instances of free translations of the Queen's letters of instructions. But a notable example may be given of the conveyance of a royal admonition in a letter of warm appreciation. It will be seen that the appreciation was never suggested by the Queen. But had it been omitted or had the Queen's letter been conveyed verbatim it would certainly have given serious offence.

The occasion was the receipt of a long letter from Pretoria written by Sir Garnet Wolseley to Henry Ponsonby in December 1879, giving a graphic account of the completely successful engagement against the chief Sikukuni which terminated the troubles in Zululand. In it Wolseley paid a warm tribute to both officers and men who took part in the capture of the chief's stronghold. Towards the end of his letter Sir Garnet wrote about Army Reform and, although with full eulogies, he unfortunately referred to the views of the Prince Consort, adding : " I often recount to myself the many important changes which were made during his lifetime, changes which we have only lately learnt emanated from His Royal Highness. Were he but alive now we should have real reforms and not the sham substitutes which we have often given to us under that name."

Ponsonby sent the letter in to the Queen. She wrote (January 26, 1880) :

> This is a shameless & shameful letter. Pray take advantage of what he says ab^t the P^{ce} whose name he takes in vain to say that you know that *many* of the changes made w^d have been most highly disapproved of by him & that the short service was almost universally admitted to be ruin to the efficiency of the army. Col. Stanley w^d be shocked at this Letter w^h is intolerable in its tone & so w^d Sir E. Wood, his friend.

Not a word of congratulation or commendation. Here is

Ponsonby's translation (as the letter was addressed to him the reply had not to be submitted before being dispatched) :

> I have to return you many thanks for your letter which contained so many references to subjects of importance that I considered myself at liberty to show it to the Queen who read it with very great interest. The Queen was sincerely glad when she received some time ago the news of your successful operations against Sikukuni's fort, and your account of the operations on that occasion and of the conduct of the troops gave her very great pleasure indeed.
>
> The war against the natives is now practically at an end and if you can induce the Boers to consolidate the Union they have themselves concluded with us, you may be proud of the success of your mission to S. Africa.
>
> Nothing is being done about Army reform as we are all waiting for the report of the Commission. But I think I ought to let you know that the allusions in your letter to short service, implying that the Prince Consort was favourable to that system, did not meet with the Queen's entire approbation. For H.M. maintains that the Prince was opposed to it, and all his opinions lead her to the conviction that he would have objected to the serious reduction of the term of a soldier's service. It is however impossible to define accurately the probable opinion of those who were influenced by totally different circumstances to such as now surround us.
>
> But facts are always valuable and the testimony you give of the steady conduct of young troops under fire is more important than any amount of argument.

It will be seen that in spite of the instruction " say that you know " he avoids fathering the Queen's opinions and quite correctly translates them as her own.

Of course there were occasions on which Ponsonby had to do what he was told against his better judgment :

Osborne, April 23rd, 1883

After the lapse of a fortnight, the Queen has taken up the unearned increment speech of Chamberlain. I suspect from her utterances which are so like Jenner's that that eminent physician has given her a dose of his anti-Chamberlain views for he poured his vials of wrath at me about Chamberlain and possibly incensed the Queen. I don't think Chamberlain's was a good speech, but I cannot see that it means all that is attributed to it, and I don't see any good in stirring

up the row. However as H.M. insisted on my writing to
Gladstone about it, I suppose I must write.

A major instance of difference of opinion is given in the
next chapter. But it would be a mistake to give an impression
that the Queen and her Private Secretary were often at sixes
and sevens. This was very far from the case, as can be shown
by numberless occasions when her reliance on his judgment
and his indefatigable determination to serve her interests and
strengthen her position brought them in close co-operation in
various crises.

As early as the third year of his private secretaryship a
political deadlock occurred in which the sovereign was constitutionally involved. The defeat of the Liberal Government
on the Irish University Bill at the beginning of 1873 led to
Gladstone's resignation. But Disraeli, the leader of the Opposition, refused to take office. The dilemma lasted almost a
fortnight. It necessitated constant interviews by Ponsonby
with the two leaders separately, both of whom at the outset
were in a very obstinate mood. The Queen only had her
Private Secretary to advise her and he had only been a short
time in his office so was more or less on his trial. She maintained the strictest impartiality and the dilemma was overcome.

In reply to Colonel Ponsonby's congratulations on the
termination of the crisis the Queen wrote :

> It is for the Queen much more to thank Colonel Ponsonby
> for the great help he afforded her & for the great judgement,
> tact & zeal he showed during those trying days — & she was
> specially touched by the anxiety he showed that she should
> in no way be misrepresented.

The deadlock over the Franchise Bill in 1884 was a far more
serious matter as it involved a conflict between the Commons
and the Lords. The complicated negotiations lasted from
February until November. There was need for a good deal
of translation or adaptation by Ponsonby of the Queen's views
indignantly expressed when she found the House of Lords being
attacked, and many interviews had to be held with the chief
actors. The details of this deadlock as well as those of the
Irish University Bill above mentioned have been fully set out
and published. It is therefore unnecessary again to recite the
stages in the prolonged controversy but the acknowledgment

by the Prime Minister of Ponsonby's share in bringing about the eventual agreement may well be quoted :

From *Mr. Gladstone*

December 1, 1884

In writing to acknowledge the important aid so " timeously " given by the Queen, I thought that my thanks to her should stand alone. But having allowed now a decent interval, I fulfil my intention and desire to record my sense of the tact, discernment and constancy with which you have promoted the attainment of an accord, and thus made an important contribution to political power where its preservation was of so much importance.

To which may be added a letter from the Prime Minister's Private Secretary :

From *Sir Edward Hamilton*

December 2, 1884

I can assure you that Mr. Gladstone felt what he wrote to you. You have secured a very high place in Mr. Gladstone's estimation ; and I often have the pleasure of hearing him sing your praises. The burden of his song is loudly re-echoed by those who work for him ; and we all in Downing Street join in the chorus.

There was also a tribute paid to the part the Queen's Private Secretary had played in June of the following year by Lord Granville in the House of Lords.

In the foregoing pages it can be readily seen that the Queen had reason to place full reliance on a man who could have easy access to her Ministers, with whom he was on terms of friendship, and that the guidance he gave her had the effect of enhancing her position. Indeed many expressions of her appreciation of and gratitude for his services could be quoted. A few will suffice. In 1877 she mentions " his indefatigable help and work " and expresses the hope that " he will rest a little ". Unfortunately she rarely provided opportunities for this. In February of the same year she actually drops the third person when she writes to him on the death of his mother, Lady Emily Ponsonby, to whom she well knew he was very specially devoted : " I cannot write formally in the 3rd person to you at this moment of overwhelming grief . . . ", and she

adds many touching expressions of sympathy at the loss which
she knew he felt deeply.

In a letter to his wife on July 5, 1878, Henry Ponsonby
records an amusing case of harmony between him and the
Queen :

> The Queen and I at the present moment live rather in a
> mutual admiration society for she writes a letter saying the
> Duke of Cumberland is a fool and I say it is perfect, and then
> I write a letter saying he is a damned fool and she says it is
> admirable. In fact we are all trembling at the proclama-
> tion he intends to issue for if he comes out as a real claimant
> to Hanover there will be an end of the whole business.

Letters were exchanged between them on every New
Year's Day. One of these may be quoted :

From *The Queen*

Osborne, January 1, 1882

> The Queen thanks Sir H. Ponsonby very much for his kind
> letter of good wishes & in wishing him & Mary & his children
> a very happy New Year, she wishes to express her sincere
> thanks for his unwearying devotion which she knows how to
> appreciate.
> The past year has indeed been a terrible one. She lost
> two of her dearest & most valued friends . . . a dear rela-
> tion & other friends & acquaintances & the horrible murder
> of the poor Emperor Alexander II & of President Garfield
> were amongst the worst features of the eventful year of 81.
> May 82 be happier & brighter.

On January 1, 1891, she "asks him to accept the expression of
her sincere gratitude for his constant valuable services ", and
in 1893 when he was beginning to show signs of the strain, she
writes :

> She wishes to thank him for his kind zealous & invaluable
> services w^h she trusts he may long be able to continue but
> she *trusts* he will not work quite so hard & let himself be more
> helped.

It may be fairly said that the harmony established between
the Queen and her Private Secretary was creditable to both.
Through the political differences she recognized his constancy
and fidelity. Behind her obstinacy and caprices he saw her
honesty and sincerity. His method was successful. Smooth

running was not always to be expected. If his patience was sometimes almost exhausted and his temper sorely tried, it was not against the Queen that he ever showed or indeed felt the smallest resentment. It was on occasions the attitude of the Court, the visitors or some of the royalties which taught him, an argumentative man himself, the need of constant restraint which he was enabled to exercise, confident as he became of his capacity to steer a steady course between the rocks.

This chapter may fittingly be concluded by a quotation of a passage from a memorandum [1] found among Mary Ponsonby's papers, describing her husband's work :

> It is difficult to say anything about the spirit in which he worked without being led into speaking generally of his character. Upon this point I feel strongly how painful it would be to say what I should feel afterwards fell short of the truth, perhaps still more painful to speak openly in appreciation and praise of what is in my eyes too precious to allow others to share with me, that is the knowledge of the simplicity and force and at the same time of the shrewdness and gentleness which went to make up that strong, generous and loveable character. I may, without running the risk of falling into either mistake, say there is one supreme note which appears to me to strike one throughout the whole correspondence and which corresponds with the dominant impression in my mind with regard to him. That note is self-effacement. It is not only that the absence of egotism and vanity was simply a second nature, it was above all the absence of effort and the unconsciousness with which he put himself always last which was astonishing. The remarkable thing was that in this self-effacement he put as much will and concentrated energy in his work as another man would do who wished to see the result of his personal effort, and have the satisfaction of having his exertions recognised and his claims in success acknowledged.

[1] See *Mary Ponsonby*, edited by Magdalen Ponsonby (1927), p. 189.

CHAPTER VIII

Political Differences

WRITERS and reviewers have paid as full a tribute to Ponsonby's skill and tact as the published documents enabled them to do. But the difficulties and obstacles he had constantly to overcome can now be shown as not only consisting in sometimes re-drafting or toning down the Queen's first impetuous expressions of opinion, in fact, to use a modern metaphor, acting as a shock-absorber, but in actually reaching her, in penetrating the atmosphere which surrounded her, in threading his way through the official tangles, in counteracting what he deemed to be objectionable influences and in preventing her seclusion becoming an excuse for forcing her into a backwater. Further it can be noticed that in the longer political communications, while the Queen's general style is skilfully retained, the arguments, the protests and the queries are set out with a clarity and sequence of thought of which, unaided, she would have been quite incapable. The pepper and mustard are retained as light seasoning but not obtruded as potent ingredients.

Descriptions of Henry Ponsonby's tact and anxiety not to ruffle the Queen might easily be taken to mean that he completely subordinated his private convictions and political opinions and became a mere echo of the sovereign's views. He had been brought up in the Whig tradition, but unlike his brother Arthur he had never stood as a candidate for Parliament. He had followed political changes very closely and his sympathies were with the Liberals. But he was in no sense a party man and in spite of his personal admiration for and friendship with Gladstone, he was often critical of Liberal policy and Liberal methods. However, he was not going to pretend that he approved the denunciations of Liberal men and measures or that he was ready to abandon his political faith.

As shown by his memorandum on his appointment [1] there was opposition to his selection as Private Secretary for this very reason, and a caution was given him at the outset. His wife, who also had Liberal views and was a great reader of advanced literature, inadvertently aggravated the suspicions. She was considered " clever ", a very undesirable quality in Court circles. But the suspicion did not stop with his appointment. It continued from time to time to crop up and cause him embarrassment and annoyance. The politically unsympathetic tone of his surroundings in this respect had the effect very naturally not of mitigating but of accentuating his political attitude, which he found it difficult to disguise.

Osborne, April 23, 1873

There seems to be a general Tory atmospheric disturbance. Whether it be that when the pot is boiling the scum comes to the top, or that they are doing their best to discredit the Government, or that here we are enveloped in Tory density, I don't know. But not a day passes without some crime being attributed to the Government — some sneer uttered about them or some *dénigré*ing remark most of which go to the Queen and set her against the Ministers. Perhaps now it does not really matter whether the Queen dislikes them or not, but I think Sir R. Peel was right in insisting that the ladies of the bedchamber should change with the Government. Incessant sneers or conversation against a policy always damages. I must say the Queen says as little as possible but one can't help seeing that she is impressed by it.

Balmoral, Nov. 1876

The Queen has got some strange idea that you are in frequent communication with the radical leaders and when I repeat a sentiment I have read in the papers or even quote some Liberal expression of Derby's when out of office or of Carnarvon's she thinks I get it from you. In a sort of way therefore she makes me responsible for the speeches of the Radicals and thinks she can send them messages through me — by which she means through you.

The following selection of letters at the time of the Eastern Question (1876-1879) shows that the difference of opinion between the Queen and her Private Secretary became at times serious. While the Queen was never tired of inveighing against the speeches and attitude of the Opposition and expressing her

[1] See p. 35.

detestation of Russia, Henry Ponsonby could not conceal that he favoured Gladstone's policy.

A skeleton outline of dates will remind the reader of the sequence of events :

Abdul Hamid succeeded as Sultan in 1876. Russia's declaration of war, April 1877. Surrender of Plevna, December 1877. Armistice and peace preliminaries, January 1878. Treaty of S. Stefano, March 1878. Great Britain neutral. Turkish atrocities in Bulgaria taken up by Liberal opposition, which became anti-Turk. War continued. Russians approached Constantinople. Reserves called out. Fleet sent to Bosphorus. Russia agreed to revision of Treaty of S. Stefano. Great Britain agreed to defend Asiatic Turkey if Sultan would accept reforms. Congress of Berlin, June 1878. Treaty signed, July 1878.

In August 1876 Ponsonby told his wife that the affairs in the East were occupying close attention. On hearing of the atrocities by the Turks in Bulgaria the Queen had said some responsible Minister ought to make a protest. Ponsonby thinking he was on safe ground wrote to Gladstone (September 7, 1876) on the receipt of his pamphlet : [1]

I received your pamphlet which you have been kind enough to send me, at an early hour this morning, and knowing how very much interested the Queen is in the question and has been since the end of June when the first rumours of the atrocities reached her, I read it at once and sent it in to H.M. without loss of time.

I ought not to say more, but I can't help remarking that the Queen has not ceased expressing her horror at what she heard (at first only in hints in the despatches) ever since the end of June. Your views seem to my own mind to be excellent, and while encouraging the just indignation of all classes, give a lead which I imagine will be followed.

A letter of Disraeli's had treated the matter flippantly. The Queen excused this on the ground that he had not yet received full reports, and before long she was attacking Gladstone for making so much of the incidents in Bulgaria.

Memorandum

September 1876

The Queen thought the conduct of the Opposition very unpatriotic, but I could scarcely allow that they had no

---

[1] *Bulgarian Horrors, and the Question of the East.*

grounds for their arguments which were much the same as some used by the Queen. I did not think it was right to convert the opportunity into one for a party truce and I pointed out that in some respects the Government action, now, was the same as that advocated by the Opposition.

The Queen was especially angry with Mr. Gladstone and the Duke of Argyll.

When at Windsor at the end of October, the Dean told me that the Queen had been pained at my taking Mr. Gladstone's part and he hinted to me that it was desirable I should be silent. I therefore avoided the subject as much as possible on my return to Balmoral — till the Queen began it. Then the Queen told me that she thought the object of this country should be to prevent Russia from constantly threatening the position of Europe and it seemed to her the best way would be to unite the Principalities (freed from Turkish rule) into one country under a Christian Prince. (This was going much further than Gladstone.) But soon after this Lady Ely told me that the Queen lamented my obstinacy in opposition to the views of the Government (? what were their views?) and wished I would more heartily support Lord Beaconsfield's policy.

At Windsor my wife learned first from Mrs. Wellesley [the Dean's wife] that the Queen objected to our " advanced views " and later Lady Ely told her from the Queen that Her Majesty was distressed at my taking the part of the Liberals in the controversy — and feared that she (my wife) urged me on. Mrs. Ponsonby replied with some indignation that she did not influence me and that she was sure I never acted against the Government, though I told the Queen sometimes what I thought. Lady Ely apologised. Later Lord Beaconsfield said to me " I know you don't agree with me, but I know you convey my messages accurately to the Queen ".

To *The Queen*

Balmoral, Sept. 25th, 1876

General Ponsonby with his humble duty begs leave to enclose a cutting as to what the Duke of Argyll would have done — " what Lord Derby is now doing ".

Mr. Gladstone in his speech today earnestly hopes the Government will adopt the policy of the country (anti-Turk). If so, the movement ceases to be a political one and he will rejoice at it. If not, the movement becomes one directed against the Government.

Mr. Gladstone implied last week and the Duke of Argyll

boldly says, that the refusal to join in the Berlin note was an error.

It certainly looks now as if this separation from other powers was a mistake — though the country supported the Government at the time and the Duke of Argyll found no fault while Parliament was sitting.

But General Ponsonby cannot help remembering that Your Majesty by no means approved of this " isolation " at the time and said so. Sending up General Ponsonby to remonstrate — and afterwards when Your Majesy gave in to Mr. Disraeli's arguments Your Majesty expressed a very strong opinion and desire, that this separation should not be given out to mean that we took part with the Turks, and that they should be made to understand we were not supporting them.

Unfortunately this advice of Your Majesty's was not followed. It is true the Government did not support the Turks — but they allowed it to be supposed they were doing so. This is now one of the main points of attack made by the leaders of the Opposition. They say that they know nothing of the policy of the Government. That Lord Beaconsfield hinted it was not in accordance with the popular feeling, and therefore that they ask for the meeting of Parliament in order to elicit from the Government an explanation of their policy.

From *The Queen*

Balmoral, October 10th, 1876

. . . The Queen is sorry that General Ponsonby should *not see* how culpable the agitation of several former Ministers has been as well as the very serious results it has produced abroad, as well as how it increased the Government's difficulties, for from *all* sides & *all* colours of politicians there is but one feeling. The Liberal members do their party harm by the line they have repeatedly taken of *violent hostility* towards the Queen's Government, the Queen *sincerely regrets*.

To *The Queen*

Balmoral, October 11th, 1876

General Ponsonby presents his humble duty to Your Majesty, and quite agrees that some very outrageous speeches have been made at public meetings.

His own remarks had reference to the generally expressed feeling throughout the country of horror against the atrocities and desire to cease supporting Turkey. This national feeling was of the greatest use to Lord Derby and to use the words of a Cabinet Minister nothing could strengthen the hands of the Foreign Secretary more than this burst of indignation which has gone through the length and breadth of the land, and it has enabled the country to do — what no other country has done — to express its just indignation at the atrocities and to speak in the name of the Queen, of the Ministers and of the people. It is this union which gives such force to Lord Derby's remonstrance.

When the speakers at public meetings pass from this theme to their own schemes and the condemnation of those of others, harmony becomes discordance. Many are beyond consideration — others may assist the public to form ideas, while some so entirely accord with Lord Derby's as to be in reality aids to his policy.

To *The Queen*

General Ponsonby most humbly and respectfully thinks that Your Majesty is quite right in saying that some Liberals have done much harm to their party by their views, but many have discarded all desire to act as a party in this matter and have spoken independently.

To *The Dean of Windsor*

Balmoral, November 6th, 1876

I was thinking of inflicting upon you the correspondence I had with the Queen about Bulgarianism, but spare you. Throughout, I extolled her wisdom. I pointed out how she had declaimed against these horrors long before the public and how just she was. She was pleased. But pitched into Gladstone and the noisy Liberals. I stuck up for Gladstone, not as a friend, but because I thought he was right. And I was pleased that she should, contrary to her usual plan of banishing a controversial subject, talk freely and let me talk freely on this, but it now turns out she objected, and complained to you of my want of sympathy. How impossible it becomes then to discuss any matter with her.

I have been sympathetic since I returned. Because really I do think Gladstone is making a mistake now, and I see no necessity for his becoming the champion of Russia. So the sympathetic chord between us is again attuned. She is deeply interested in the East. Sends orders and telegrams incessantly. Talks eagerly over those which come. Yet tomorrow she goes for 3 days to the inaccessible Glassalt !

To *The Queen*

Balmoral, November 6th, 1876

General Ponsonby presents his humble duty to Your Majesty.

He was much struck with what Your Majesty said this afternoon on the necessity of giving as much independence as possible to the Turkish principalities, and to form a barrier of free States against Russian aggression. This would involve the establishment of independent States in Bosnia.

Such a zone could not fail in due time to restore tranquillity in Eastern Europe if protected by the Powers and it would relieve the Turks of the charge of a rebellious population.

It is to be hoped that Your Majesty's representatives at the Conference will therefore attend, free to act, and unfettered by promises of maintaining the present state of affairs. These Christian States and neighbouring provinces must eventually become independent.

If Your Majesty's views were carried into effect and England took the lead in obtaining as much independence as is at present practicable for these provinces, the populations would look up to England as their friend. But if we oppose every such proposal, the Russians will carry it against us, we shall be looked on as the enemy of these growing countries who will therefore throw themselves into the arms of Russia. No doubt the difficulties are enormous, but so they are to every solution.

The one, however, indicated by Your Majesty would seem to be by far the best calculated to produce a lasting settlement.

To *The Queen*

November 7th, 1876

General Ponsonby with humble duty returns Your Majesty's excellent letter. The Plenipotentiaries should be unfettered and prepared to discuss other proposals besides our schemes. This letter points out forcibly the necessity of coming to a settlement which shall be lasting. But the conflicting claims of the Princes of Roumania, of Servia and of Montenegro make the solution at present difficult. The freeing of Bosnia and North Bulgaria from Turkish rule would strengthen the Principalities and eventually lead to a practical arrangement.

From *The Dean of Windsor*

Nov. 8th, 1876

The Queen sent you no message either directly or indirectly through me — for this I have always declined to convey.

It places all parties in an awkward position. But in my correspondence with her I gave her to understand that I would tell you what I gathered from her letters, viz. that she wished that you sympathised more with her in your views upon the Eastern question. So far therefore she would grasp that I had spoken to you before your return to Scotland. But you are not in any way committed by this to acquiesce in any line of speech you don't like — but women are easily managed in these things by a little humouring and caution without any departure from truthfulness. . . .

To *The Queen*

Balmoral, November 12th, 1876

General Ponsonby presents his humble duty to Your Majesty and begs leave to thank Your Majesty for allowing him to read Lord Beaconsfield's interesting and able arguments of the suggestions put forward by Your Majesty. These were that the question of the Northern Provinces of Turkey being placed under a Christian Prince should be reconsidered.

Lord Beaconsfield goes further by saying that what he desires is that all European Turkey should be placed under a Christian Prince. But he thinks that the time has not yet arrived for such a change. He therefore does not dissent from Your Majesty's proposal, but thinks it is one for the next generation to consider.

Memorandum

The Queen again complained of my want of sympathy with the Ministers — or rather Lord Beaconsfield — and feared my views were very advanced — and that my wife had made me worse. I was warned that I must not uphold the St. James's [Hall] Conference. There was no particular harm in the Conference, but I thought it inopportune so I could safely say so. It seemed also to have fallen a little flat.

Memorandum by *The Queen*

Windsor Castle

These [papers] are very important. The Ministers who were here (Duke of Northumberland, Lord Chancellor & Mr. Cross) were all most annoying & so is the Government. Lord Salisbury should have liberty of action & not be tied to his instructions. It is the F.O. who are the cause of its being done, & the Queen feels *everything* depends on the settlement being made soon. Would General Ponsonby see Lord Beaconsfield (whose answer she encloses) & say that she therefore urged a Cabinet & does *now* again to *enable* Lord Salisbury to *act* as *he* thinks best. He will never lose sight of important instructions.

The Queen has never made any secret of her disapproval & indignation at Mr. Gladstone's conduct & that of his followers & General Ponsonby may repeat it to anyone — as it is totally different to Home affairs & thus future interests of this country are imperilled by his conduct.

From *The Queen*

Windsor Castle, Dec. 10th, 1876

The meeting in St. James's Hall & the frantic declamations of Mr. Gladstone are grievous as are exhibitions of wrong-headedness of people here, which does us *at this moment fearful harm abroad.* Fortunately no other Minister compromised himself, but the precedent is one which is very mischievous & totally unconstitutional.

The Sovereign is apparently a nonentity to be utterly disregarded at this moment. Foreign affairs *never* were interfered with in this way before. That the Duke of Westminster should have lent himself to such a proceeding is unaccountable.

From *The Queen*

Windsor Castle, Dec. 11th, 1876

The Queen thanks General Ponsonby for his letter received last night. The harm those of the Liberal party who have followed Mr. Gladstone have done themselves — as well as the totally unprecedented line taken will do the great *interests* of this country abroad & among the Queen's Moslem subjects, cause the Queen the *very greatest anxiety* & she wishes it were possible for General Ponsonby to see Lord Halifax some day, or anyone possessing his sound sense & knowledge of what is honourable & right, to see if they cannot prevent further agitation & mischief, or at any rate show that *they can* & will not countenance such very dangerous proceedings. The harm done already is enormous. The Queen cannot *resign* or *retire* as a *Government* does. Though she hopes & thinks that there is no danger of anything of what they know now. In all the unjust & shameful accusations against the Government it should be remembered that many things wished to be done by Lord Beaconsfield were resisted by the red tape influence of the Foreign Office over Lord Derby which have been the cause of endless delays.

M

Fearing some expression of opinion from the Queen against public demonstrations such as the St. James's Hall meeting, Ponsonby adds in one of his letters to the Queen that the Opposition

> are very tenacious of their right to express their opinions and maintain they are justified by Lord Derby's speech when he said he wished to have the opinion of the English people.
>
> It would therefore be dangerous to say anything that might be misconstrued into the remotest hint that the expressions of opinion were displeasing to Your Majesty. But in talking to them (or others) he might confidentially hear what they think.

To his wife he wrote :

May 2, 1877

In April Lady Ely told me the Queen was pained at my anti-Turk feelings and my friendship for the Opposition and that I did not like this Government.   I replied that I had said and written nothing which could give rise to this idea. Later she told me the Queen was satisfied.   But on going to Buckingham Palace it began again and the Dean was telegraphed for from Windsor.   He came.   He did not see the Queen but saw Lady Ely and then told me that the Queen was dissatisfied with my Russian proclivities, my support of Gladstone and especially my want of sympathy for her. He advised me to write to her.   But could give me no idea of what I had said or done.   As he knew nothing and was hurt at having to come up on such an errand.   At first I felt inclined to write rather strongly as I had been very careful in what I had said.   I asked who it was had told the Queen.   If Beaconsfield — of course I ought to resign. Lady Ely said no not him but Prince Leopold.   I wrote one letter, toned it down on the Dean's advice and again toned the second down on Lady Ely's request who said it would alarm the Queen.   So it ended rather weakly.   Of course there is some truth as I can't back up the Turks as many do here — and I do think Harty [Lord Hartington] and Granville are doing well.   But I have been most cautious to say nothing.

To *The Queen*

Buckingham Palace, May 2, 1877

General Ponsonby presents his humble duty to Your Majesty.   He is much distressed at hearing from the Dean of Windsor that Your Majesty thinks he has strong Russian feelings, that he supports Mr. Gladstone's views, and that he has no sympathy with Your Majesty.

General Ponsonby is at a loss to conceive what can have given rise to these misconceptions. He cannot recall to his mind any expression of his which could lead to the belief he upheld the proceedings of the Russians. And in all the communications he has had the honor of holding with Your Majesty he has invariably maintained an opinion antagonistic to Mr. Gladstone's conduct.

He fears that some report from persons imperfectly informed must have reached Your Majesty. But what pains him most is that Your Majesty should think for a moment he was wanting in sympathy with Your Majesty at any time, and especially at present when the fearful responsibilities and anxieties which weigh upon Your Majesty and which Your Majesty so conscientiously feels, are doubled. He knows how much Your Majesty has at heart the honor and the welfare of the Nation and at this crisis when any day may bring forth new and terrible events it would indeed be strange if he did not entertain the deepest and sincerest sympathy, which he most earnestly begs Your Majesty to believe he most truly and heartily feels.

From *The Queen*

Buckingham Palace, May 2, 1877

The Queen hastens to answer General Ponsonby's kind letter & to tell him that it is not from anyone that she has heard anything relative to his opinions at all. But she can't deny she has thought his *tone* of *late* inclined towards *letting* Russia go on — & *not* for *England* to hold that language which she feels ought to have been held *long* ago if we had not been so dreadfully hampered by the strange & (. . .) language about the East of late adopted by many of the Opposition. However she may, feeling so very strongly as she does, have misunderstood this & *she* is glad to find that he does not *feel* as she rather feared. As for his sympathy in her trials that she never doubted. . . .

From *The Dean of Windsor*

4th May

I return the epistle, which I hope will prove an emollient. It is at all costs better to take any opportunity of speaking for yourself and not through a third party. As Balaam was ordered to go — and yet incurred anger "because he went" — so she who sent for me to Town will probably be displeased with my going to Town, as she had no reason for sending for me.

In the first two of the following letters Ponsonby gives a very fair summary of the Queen's attitude. She may often have been impetuous but she hated vacillation even on the part of a Conservative Government :

Osborne, August 16, 1877

We have been rather suspicious of what Germany is doing and I imagine they will try and make peace. So the Queen has endeavoured to ascertain their intentions through Odo [Russell] who says they don't like the Turk in Germany. " I tried in the course of quite a private conversation to awaken Bismarck's sympathies for the Turks — he replied that as far as he was concerned he did not care how soon the d —— d Sultan and his cursed Government went to hell." When the Queen read it she seemed rather amused and laughed at it. So I maintain she is anti-Russian but not pro-Turk. Though Hobhouse, when I said this about someone yesterday observed he could not measure the various depths of folly. Wellesley [1] came here and consulted me confidentially. He said he was taking a private message back — which he had not yet seen — but he was also going to take the still more secret message from the Queen and Lord Beaconsfield to the effect that if there was a second campaign we should join — but not on the Russian side. He said Lord Derby did not know of this. How could he, Lord Derby's servant, take a message of such immense importance without his orders, even without his knowledge ? It was not loyal to do so — and further — the Emperor of course would tell Gortchakoff — he Schouvaloff — he Lady Derby — she Lord Derby and then a row — I spoke to the Queen and she saw Wellesley. I asked her why not tell Lord Derby. She said how can we — he tells Lady D. — and she tells all to Schouvaloff. This certainly was a tremendous fix. I can't believe it — but Wellesley does. Of course the only advice I could give was to consult Beaconsfield, but thought perhaps it might go — not as a message — but that Wellesley should say he knew Lord Beaconsfield's opinions.

Wellesley saw the Queen before and after dinner. He said to me afterwards " I hear you are a strong Russian." (Still !) But said he thought the Queen knew as much as Lord Beaconsfield and had far more defined and clear ideas of her views than Lords Beaconsfield and Derby, and that he agreed in very much she said. She certainly looked forward to the possibility of war. But he could not say that was impossible. But it would be no small war. Russia

---

[1] Colonel the Hon. F. A. Wellesley, Military Attaché at St. Petersburg.

would put forward every man for it would be almost a struggle for existence. I said "Don't tell me — but tell the Queen." He said he had — and he had told Lord Beacons- field who said if it was forced upon us we must accept it. At any rate we could send out a hundred thousand men. . . . Wellesley looked enquiringly at me. Yes we could — a great strain but we could, it is a question of money. But how could we keep up the supply in an unpopular war ? Un- popular ? he asked. I thought it would be popular. Well every war is popular at first. But at the first reverse the row would be great. He trusts and believes in the Emperor. He disbelieves in Russian atrocities because he does not think that cruelty is their characteristic. That women and children have been killed and wounded in conflicts he thinks most probable — but every Englishman he has seen (and many very anti-Russian) deny any deliberate atrocities. He says the Russians are liars. Still there are some things which they cannot lie about without something transpiring. They hate the English. Every evening at dinner Adlerberg or someone reads out the telegrams. Those about England are listened to with breathless anxiety. But they always contain something unpleasant said in England by Ministers or by someone against Russia. Wellesley was most agree- able, talked to me till late and went away early this morning.

Balmoral, August 30, 1877

Some people say the Queen has no real power — but look at this — small though it is. She is very indignant about the atrocities and implies they are far worse on the Russian side than the Turkish and that the Emperors of Germany and Austria only hear one side. It is not her fault if the Emperor of Germany only hears one side for she sends dollops of reports of Cossack, Bulgarian and Russian atrocities to the Crown Princess for him. However Germany and Austria have protested against the Turks violating the Geneva Convention and asked us to join, which Derby at once did. This made the Queen indignant. She refused her approval unless we also remonstrated with the Russians : Derby and Beaconsfield pointed out that the Grand Vizir himself ad- mitted that some of his roughs may have done so — and promised to teach them manners. So we had this to go upon besides the official reports. But we had no report as to the Russians doing so. The Queen sent for me, read me out a paragraph from Consul Blunt's despatch in which he says he heard the Russian artillery had fired on Ambulances (rather vague) and at once tackled her ministers on this.

I could not help expressing my surprise at her having discovered this in such masses of papers, and she told me Leopold had found it. Whereupon I transmitted her stiff remarks to Beaconsfield and Derby who replied they had not observed the paragraph. The former said he would at once remonstrate — the latter that he saw no objection. So we remonstrate. This is entirely the Queen's doing. Also about Servia going to war. She insisted on our calling on all the powers to urge Servia to keep quiet. We had saved her from destruction last year and had a right to speak. Derby said he had spoken to Austria and didn't think it of use saying anything more — but the result of telegrams is that he is going to ask the others. Of course they will do nothing but the Queen has had her way.

Taken from her point of view she is more determined and energetic than her Ministers.

May 31, 1877

The Dean [Wellesley] writes to me very confidentially that it wasn't Lord Beaconsfield who said anything to the Queen of my pro-Russian and Gladstonian proclivities but the Prince of Wales. Some letters I wrote to him. I have only written one this year and that was about A. Ellis. Last year I wrote one or two which the Queen who was then anti-Turk seasoned before I sent with some anti-Turk spice. Possibly it may be inconvenient to remember this now and so it may be put down to my account. But as all this was ancient history I scarcely see how it accounts for the Dean being telegraphed for to correct my opposition proclivities. Of course as I did to a great extent hold these opinions I can't complain — but I don't think I spoke 'em out.

He explains further that he constantly restrains himself from expressing his opinions even at household meals when pro-Turkish views are loudly expressed.

Balmoral, November 18, 1877

. . . At the present moment I am rather rejoicing at the accusations which were made — and I believe still are hinted against me of being pro-Russian. The Queen evidently distrusts me in that particular and shows me only parts of her discussions with Beaconsfield. This of course is quite right, but what I might be hurt about, would be that she employs Lady Ely to write to Monty Corry. Not only however am I not hurt, but I consider myself very fortunate in being spared this. For the Queen's sentiments are strong Turk. . . . If therefore I wrote to Corry I must

adopt these arguments which it would be difficult to do —
Corry answers as if from himself, but clearly in the Beaconsfield sense. While this skirmishing is going on the Queen
brings her artillery to bear on Beaconsfield himself. This
fire has been a little too much for him and he has slightly
resented it. He will not declare a positive policy on possible
events and will not declare that war shall be made if the
Russians approach Constantinople. He implies that his
opinions lean that way but protests against binding the
Government to any fixed line beforehand. The Queen's
arguments are : if you have no fixed policy cut and dried —
the moment will come and you will then be debating instead
of acting. She looks on the struggle as one for supremacy
between herself and the Czar. Beaconsfield has brought
her to this view, and has told her so more than once — and
I am not quite sure that the conduct of the Government has
not brought it almost to this pass. But Northcote clearly is
not of the Turkish party. And I gather that the Queen
would have far preferred to have had John Manners here
with his enthusiasm for Carlists, Legitimists and Turks than
the steady Northcote who will not be forced and argues his
points with her. To get back to Lady Ely's correspondence
I was going to say that not only am I well out of it, but with
my supposed Russian proclivities Beaconsfield cannot think
I am urging the Queen forward in that direction.

At the same time I confess I am much disturbed at the
state of affairs. Had we from the first openly sided with the
Turks we possibly might have prevented the Russians going
to war — I only say possibly. But what was impossible I
think was that we could have fought on the side of the Turks.
Even Corry in his letter expresses a doubt whether the
Country was prepared for it. Or we might have taken the
Russian side. As Gladstone and you would have done.
But I doubt also whether the Country was prepared for this
either. Or we might have been absolutely neutral. Lord
Derby's despatch proclaimed our neutrality and that ought
to have been absolute. But it wasn't — we made the Turks
think we sympathised with them — we thus encouraged
them to go to war. Layard's discourses to the Sultan are
more than friendly — we have dozens of Military Attachés
with the Armies in the field who must naturally become pro-
Turkish and who encourage the idea of English sympathy
with Turkey, and Beaconsfield's speeches complete the idea.
But we do nothing for them ! . . . It seems to me therefore
that the result of our policy has been to place our prestige
in charge of the Turks — and that while we cry out to the
world that their defeat will be our disgrace we take no

further steps about it. That they will be beaten no one can doubt — and that we shall be supposed by the world to suffer thereby seems to me inevitable. And that we should go to war for the Turks in any way I believe to be impossible.

To *The Queen*

Windsor Castle, December 18, 1877

General Ponsonby humbly begs leave to say he has sent the box to Lord Beaconsfield.

Germany seems anxious to let Russia settle matters direct with Turkey. Is this because she is sore at our having declined her proffered alliance with us ? Or because she thinks that this will more speedily end the war at the expense of Turkey ?

Note added by the Queen.—Neither — but to *humiliate England* wᵸ so many people in this Country shut their eyes to & are (no doubt unintentionally) helping in ! !

It makes the Queen's very blood boil !

Memorandum

January 1878

In sending me the Sultan's appeal to her the Queen said she wished to communicate it to Russia. I replied " The Sultan has somewhat weakened the effect of his personal appeal by alluding to conditions upon which he hopes peace may be established. If Y.M. desired to communicate with Emperor of Russia it would perhaps be better to avoid all mention of conditions. Lord Beaconsfield might find it useful at this moment before proceeding further to try the effect of a personal appeal from Y.M., but if the Cabinet have actually decided on serious action Y.M.'s Government might think the time for such appeal is past. An enquiry from Y.M. and Lord Beaconsfield would settle this. I submit form of words. ' I have received direct appeal from Sultan which I cannot disregard. Knowing your sincere desire for peace, I do not hesitate to communicate this fact to you, in hope that you may be willing to accelerate conclusion of armistice which may lead to honourable peace.' " Lord Beaconsfield replied it was excellent in conception and expression. As he announced intention of sending Fleet up Dardanelles I asked if it would not be better to delay sending message — but he urged its being sent. So it was sent. Reply came. Much what might have been expected. But the Queen thought it bad. Asked Lord Beaconsfield if he did not think it insolent ? He replied not only insolent but vulgar !

Memorandum

Lady Ely told me the Queen was much alarmed and feared the attack of the opposition, could I not write to Lord Halifax. I said I did not see the use. Lady Ely said I must as the Queen was in such a state and I must say that I knew what the Queen's views were. I said if I asked Lord Halifax not to oppose the policy of the Government I must tell him what that policy was — and that I did not know. Lady Ely simply replied she hoped I would do what the Queen wished. I sketched the following letter. The Queen said it was quite right and I sent it. "Jan. 9, 1878. Dear Lord Halifax. You can well understand that in the present crisis, the Queen, whose whole desire is to uphold the honor and welfare of the Country, is deeply pained by any expressions which may weaken her Government in their policy of maintaining the high position which our nation holds in the world. H.M.'s earnest desire is to secure peace, but in order to effect this her Government must be empowered to speak with force, and she is convinced that supported by an undivided people they will secure a lasting settlement of the Eastern question which will be advantageous to England and as satisfactory as in the circumstances can be expected to the Belligerents and other Powers of Europe. So long however as the Government are assailed by party tactics and find themselves foiled in their earnest endeavours to restore harmony by the declarations of powerful opponents their efforts are vain and England presents the spectacle of indecision and weakness which lowers her in the esteem of the world. Would it be possible for you in any way to put this clearly before those who take the lead on this question and who with the best intentions do not sufficiently consider the course they are pursuing which in their mistaken zeal may lead to the most lamentable consequences?" The Queen added "this is not an actual message to others but as the result of what he knows to be the Queen's strong and earnest feeling".

At the end of one of his subsequent letters to Ponsonby Lord Halifax writes : "I feel very much for you in the very difficult and disagreeable position in which you sometimes must be placed."

Osborne, April 7, 1878

Since the Dean gave me another hint last week that my language was too Russian I avoid the subject with every one. And am — as I have long been — very strictly reserved on these matters with the Queen. The other day she cyphered to the Ministers her indignation at Gortchakoff's language. The only telegram I had seen was the one — now published — about his speech to Prince Ghika. Bad certainly but I didn't see what we could then say. I presumed of course she had some other which I hadn't seen. The Ministers replied puzzled — and she found out it was her mistake. She had read it as being addressed to us. And blew me up for not preventing her from sending the cypher. I said of course I supposed it was in answer to some letter from Lord Beaconsfield which I knew nothing of. The affair ended — but it gave me an opportunity of showing that I cannot be of use if she only shows me half of what is going on. However I must say I see all the F.O. papers only I never know whether Beaconsfield doesn't tell her other things.

Osborne, April 8, 1878

Today I have completed 8 years of being Private Secretary. At first when you were generally with me I liked it well enough, and then when I talked freely to Ministers there was an interest in it, but now it is such awful dullness and the Ministers so seldom speak on anything interesting that it becomes a bore. I dare say they are told to distrust my opinions but it seems to me that they distrust their own still more, for they very seldom let out an opinion of their own, and when they do it is diametrically opposite to what the Queen says she knows from Beaconsfield is the opinion of the Government. Derby and Carnarvon were always ready to speak out openly to me.

Balmoral, October 20, 1879

. . . I had my political conversation with the Queen — repeating what Granville said and alluding to Harcourt, I said they would lay down no fixed programme but would of course attack the Government in their speeches. She asked " But why should the Opposition attack the Government ? " I replied that the duty of the Opposition was to oppose. H.M. exclaimed " Exactly so. They don't care whether the Government is right or wrong but they oppose it simply for party reasons." (This was good.) I rejoined " But they disagree with the Government." She said " The Government have made England feared and respected — therefore do they mean that they wish England neither to be feared nor respected ? I can't believe that of them although the opinion of England went sadly down when they were in office. No — Lord Granville and the Whigs believe, what the Whigs have always been pleased to believe, that they alone can govern and that they have a just cause of grievance if any other party but their own is in office." I cut in " They maintain that the policy of the Government has produced alarm and wars all over the world." " It could not be avoided." I observed " They think that the war in Zulu-land might have been avoided and that the war in Afghanistan was produced by the action of the Government." The Queen replied " Yes — we might have had peace in India certainly by retiring before the Russians — if that is the peace the Whigs desire, I am sure the country will not go with them." We then talked of whether Gladstone intended to return to office and then changed the subject. The Queen looks at foreign affairs always as a struggle for supremacy against Russia and upholds her opinion by quotations from the Diplomatic reports which undoubtedly say that Russia is only waiting her opportunity to attack us. She has suffered a great defeat in Asia and attributes it to our en-couragement of the Turcomans. Lord Salisbury's speech was very Anti-Russia and there is evidently no love lost between our two Governments. The Emperor is at Livadia — concocting plans which are obviously intended to be unpleasant for us. But the Empress won't go there because Princess Dolgorouki is there on the eve of presenting the Emperor with a fourth child.

Among the papers there is a rough memorandum dated April 23, 1880, on the advent of the Liberal Government :

Miss Stopford's message was that the Queen feared I rejoiced too greatly at the change of Government — and that I did not sympathise with her. That I should write and console her.

Draft of his letter to the Queen :

" Sorry she should think he was personally rejoicing — which he is not. He has thought it his duty to Y.M. always to place before Y.M. the state of affairs with the sole object of making Y.M. acquainted as he knew Y.M. would use the best judgment thereon. But he is more grieved that Y.M. should think him wanting in sympathy and he assures Y.M. that he sympathises most deeply in this crisis which gave him the greatest cause for anxiety and he only regrets that he c^d not be of more use than his humble efforts enable him to be."

The Queen's antipathy for Russia continued after the assassination of Alexander II in 1881. The following note by her to Ponsonby shows she had no love for the succeeding Czar Alexander III. It is undated and difficult to read because she wrote in blue chalk (which she resorted to sometimes lest pen and ink might cramp the first ebullition of her fury). It would seem to have been written about 1885 when the Emperor was calling at some port and the question was whether any message should be given to him or to the Empress from the Queen :

> The Queen says *no* to both questions. She has not seen Sir A. Paget or sent any message thro' him — & she cannot have any personal communication with a sovereign whom she does not look upon *as a gentleman*.
> He & the Empress sent a Tel : to the Queen for the New Year w^h she answered so nothing more is required. And as he only stops a few hours he better not (. . .).

The above papers taken as a whole illustrate a major instance of difference of political opinion between the Queen and her Private Secretary. But it did not stop there and the Queen continued from time to time to use such expressions as " your friends ". In 1882 after a complaint against the Government for not giving consideration to her views, she ends up, " Sir Henry should speak very strongly to the Government, to those he sees & knows best & *ought* to be *able* to do so the *more* for belonging to that side. Unfortunately the Government are *not liberal* but radical to the extreme."

To give one more instance : in July 1884 after protesting against a speech delivered by Herbert Gladstone she adds : " Mr. Gladstone is answerable for those under him & his son *is* in the Government. Sir Henry always finds an excuse for Mr. Gladstone's Govt. & their misdeeds."

However aggravating these gibes may have been to him, Ponsonby never took them out of proportion or considered she really mistrusted him. But his refusal to recant politically had, it will be readily seen, a valuable effect. It quite definitely prevented a real conflict between the Queen and her Liberal Governments which undoubtedly might have taken place if her animosity had not been occasionally curbed. Unrestrained, with a Private Secretary who encouraged her in her expression of indignation, she might have found herself confronted with resignations, full reasons being given for them, and a first-class constitutional crisis would certainly have arisen.

Ponsonby's capacity for exercising calm judgment was recognized from the first or he would not have been promoted to so important a post as Private Secretary. Both General Grey whom he had helped and Sir Thomas Biddulph whose opinion counted, detected his value. In political matters he made it his practice to master the facts by correspondence and talks and so elicit the best case on either side before weighing them. Consequently he was trusted by both sides because they knew he was not judging their case by any extravagant utterances of extremists. On the other hand the Queen was apt to allow her prejudices to weigh down the balance on the side of the party she favoured apart from the merits of the dispute in question.

In retrospect one can only be amused at the violence of the Queen's written expressions of opinion, of which more instances will be given in later chapters. But it can well be imagined that at the time it was far from amusing but often anxious work to temper, soften and even eliminate words and phrases which might give pain and offence to prominent Ministers. They after all were more directly responsible for the government of the country than the Queen constitutionally could ever be allowed to be.

CHAPTER IX

Public Affairs

1873–1885

IN dealing with public affairs, which of course mean chiefly political affairs, there can be no question of covering more than a fraction even of the subjects referred to in the collected papers. The illustrations of the Queen's attitude on certain occasions and crises and her Private Secretary's assistance, although hitherto unpublished, disclose no new revelations but are merely supplementary to the correspondence already published, into which they should be dovetailed in order to present in greater detail the full story. The Queen's vocabulary may have been limited in many directions but it was fairly well stocked with epithets of scorn and denunciation. Her notes often show the first violent reactions of the human being which Ponsonby, as her intermediary, had to translate into the cautious disapproval of the sovereign. In addition to the Queen's well-known emphasis by underlining, she had another form of emphasis in addressing her Private Secretary which was reiteration. The second or third letter expressing the same directions, the same objections or the same complaints are not included. The Queen was very anxious that Ponsonby should not misunderstand or have any doubt about what she thought. He never did.

In order to appreciate properly the underlying motive in Queen Victoria's attitude, as shown by the comments written by her to her Private Secretary on political changes and other public questions during the period under review, some interpretation of her guiding principle in politics is necessary. To begin with, while she may very naturally have had her personal likes and dislikes of Ministers and politicians, it may safely be said that personal animosity was not the prime and fundamental cause for her decided and even bitter expressions of opinion. To put it more explicitly, she did not dislike Liberal Ministers and parliamentarians because she thought them personally objectionable (except in a few cases). She grew to dislike them because they represented liberalism which she feared and mistrusted, closely allied as it came to be with radicalism. Socialism had not as yet raised its head. It was merely an abusive term for some ill-defined but catastrophic culmination and the word " democracy " meant pretty much the same thing. Generally speaking she was a conservative Imperialist. But first and foremost she believed herself to be entrusted with the guardianship of a monarchical system rooted in a long tradition. She felt it therefore her first duty to hand on to her successors the monarchy unimpaired and if possible strengthened.

Viscount Gladstone in *After Thirty Years*, written before the publication of the third series of *Queen Victoria's Letters*, rightly points out that up to about 1876 the relations between the Queen and Gladstone were perfectly friendly. He attributes the change, which unfortunately lasted till the end of Gladstone's life, to the influence of Disraeli. If this means that Disraeli deliberately disparaged his opponent to the Queen so as to create a strong personal prejudice against him, this seems unlikely, and a perusal of Ponsonby's correspondence contains no evidence to support such an assumption. On the other hand it exposes clearly enough the causes of the Queen's animosity because the Minister could not be dissociated from his measures. So fear and dislike of Liberal measures and Liberal policy produced similar feelings towards the man chiefly responsible for them.

At first the Queen was disposed to regard her Ministers merely as a continuation of the series she had known previously. Then Disraeli appeared on the scene. Whether her exaggerated devotion for him was to her credit is an arguable point. At any rate it was curious. Whatever may be said of the obsequious flattery and almost absurd servility of his manner and method, Disraeli managed to devise means of enlisting the complete sympathy and the support for himself of one who otherwise, owing to her position, might be an awkward element if not an actual obstacle in the furtherance of his plans and policies. He saw with his subtle discernment how this might succeed, just as he knew that the most effective way of treating his great political opponent lay not in striving in competition with him but by inventing a completely different parliamentary technique. Perhaps his cleverness was shown most of all in the astutely wise forms he adopted for establishing unobstructed contact with the sovereign. Gradually he contrived to reach the Queen by direct correspondence, often avoiding the filter of the Private Secretary, with whom he was on the best of terms, for whom indeed he had great respect, but in whom he recognized Liberal tendencies which might be hampering. Apart from the oriental absurdities which adorned his speech and his letters, he spoke to the Queen in basic English and his memoranda were in the same language. So, whatever the question might be, the Queen was led to believe she knew all about it. But the foundation of Disraeli's success lay deeper than his dependence on the Queen's infatuation for him. She had found the increasing complexity and technicalities of politics difficult to follow. But she scented danger and fell back on the profound conviction which she tenaciously held, namely that the monarchy must be preserved intact. This amounted to a deep religious creed, and she believed she could rely on the unfailing support of Disraeli. The beginning of the rise of democracy, the increasing power of the people and the policies of drastic change she hardly understood but greatly feared. All Liberal measures were suspect in her eyes as attempts to weaken the power and position of the monarch. The republican movement, radical speeches, attacks on the House of Lords, Home Rule, etc., all fortified her determination to thwart a Government that tolerated any of these. Here Disraeli found his course easy. Here Gladstone was at a permanent and increasing disadvantage. The weakness of Liberal foreign policy and the ineptitude, it must be acknowledged, with which Imperialist wars were carried on, further enraged her. Gladstone's personal approach was clumsy compared to that of his opponent. He was the personification of these undesirable tendencies in the new politics. His power over the people was obvious ; his endurance was terrific. She was genuinely frightened of him and she regarded his colleagues with mistrust. That the foundation of all this was political rather than personal is shown by the fact that, after Gladstone resigned, in spite of the Queen's special liking for Lord Rosebery, her language, so far as we see it in her communications to her Private Secretary, was as violent as ever.

Gladstone was incapable of pretence and repelled by insincere flattery. It never occurred to him to adopt different language to his sovereign from what he would ordinarily use. Consequently he entirely failed to gain her ear, not only because she would seldom allow him to approach controversial subjects in his audiences but because the principles of his policy were not of a kind to be easily or simply explained.

The two earliest letters in the following selection give the Queen's views on the English Church and Protestantism. They are so to speak preliminary notes to the letter she finally wrote to Dean Stanley : [1]

From *The Queen*

Glassalt Shiel, Nov. 5, 1873

. . . Speaking of the struggle with the Catholics which the Queen thinks (as so does the Crown Princess) is a movement *all over Europe* as exhibited lately by the *Irish R. Catholic* Bishops in Ireland & which must be firmly resisted by ALL *Protestant Churches.* The Crown P^{ss} says " The only feeling I have in the contest between Catholic & Protestant is one of regret. I do not think it belongs to our age." This may be so but *all* the *Protestant Churches* sh^d keep strongly together & make a strong phalanx forgetting *small differences* of form in *the one great cause* of *Protestantism* & this is what the Queen tries to do. But what do they do in England ? Despise & back down on all but *Episcopalians* & strive to imitate as nearly as we can ALL the Romish forms & try to join with the *Greek Church* & are even often ashamed to be called Protestants. This is the real danger of the *English* Church & depend upon it, it will *not* stand if they do change entirely.

From *The Queen*

Balmoral, Nov. 12, 1873

The Queen thinks there may be much truth in what Lord Granville says, but she would wish General Ponsonby to say that as regards the Higher Classes especially in England there is not that Protestant feeling he thinks & that the want of this in the fashionable circles & near approach to Romanizing views & to Catholic forms which *are* a sure stepping stone to going [? further] is the great weakness we have to contend with in the *English* Church & the great danger in

[1] See *Letters of Queen Victoria*, Second Series, vol. ii, p. 290.

N

which she stands of Disestablishment. With regard to the observation which General Ponsonby made about the cry for Disestablishment she would wish to say that she does not advocate it but is *most anxious* for a *very sweeping* Reformation of the English Church. If we had been in England reformed as every other Protestant Church has been we should never have run the great risk we are running now and if Edward VI or James I's eldest son Prince Henry had lived this would have been the case. We are *in fact in form* NOT Protestants though we are in doctrine ; but form is unfortunately everything with many people. If this Reformation does not take place then the Queen fears there will be no alternative but Disestablishment & that is a bad thing in many ways especially politically. . . .

Memorandum by *Ponsonby*

CHANGE OF GOVERNMENT IN 1874

February 17, 1874.

We came from Osborne to Windsor Castle in the morning and at 2 o'clock Mr. Gladstone came by appointment and saw the Queen after luncheon, when he resigned. He had proposed a large number of honors which the Queen thought too great a number tho' she scarcely objected to any particular individual. Lord Granville wrote to me in fear of H.M.'s refusing them and hinted that such a refusal might cause a delay in resigning. This was almost too much like a threat for me to tell the Queen but I mentioned that if H.M. was ready to approve them she might tell Mr. Gladstone so when she saw him instead of waiting till tomorrow. She did tell him and he said he would be glad to announce them and put an end to further applications with which he was worried. She also offered him the Garter or any other reward he might choose but he declined saying the verdict of the country was against him and he could take no public rewards. I saw him when he came out. He was rather more silent and absent than usual and I enquired " Have you resigned ? " He replied : " Yes, and nothing could be kinder than the Queen. I had feared from her letter that all might not go smooth, but she really was so natural about her regret at parting that I was quite touched." I then expressed my regret at his going and thanked him for the free manner he had allowed me to correspond with him. He assured me that he had been often much obliged to me — and so we said goodbye. I was immediately after sent for by the Queen who gave me a letter for Mr. Disraeli and some messages. I went at once to town and found him in Whitehall Gardens. . . . Mr. Disraeli was very different from what he was last year. Much more open lively and joyous. He did not conceal his delight at the astonishing majority. . . . He read the Queen's letter — wrote an answer and promised to obey the Queen's commands to Windsor. . . .

(There was a Discussion on individual appointments to some of which the Queen objected.)

. . . I afterwards called on Gladstone. Mrs. G. very unhappy at loss of office. Told me that Gladstone when badgered and low received a letter from the Queen. Here he hoped would be some kind words. But no it was harsh and unkind complaining of his not resigning at once because of the inconveniences the delay would occasion for the Duke and Duchess of Edinburgh's arrival. But his interview with the Queen had entirely pleased him again. I then saw Gladstone who was in good spirits, laughed and talked of how I had found him dressing for dinner this time as I had last year. I said the Queen wished to see him on Friday — as she could then see him more quietly than if he came on Saturday with the rest. He said : " But am I to give up the Exchequer Seals then ? " I promised to ask the Queen who decided that he should. On Friday Disraeli came at 3, looking very keen and bright. . . . Gladstone came at 5. He was low and seemed provoked at having to come alone as he thought it would be more seemly if he came with his colleagues. He seemed angry with extreme Liberals — and talked of retiring from politics.

On the following day the two Cabinets came down to resign and to assume office. Duplat [1] and Cowell [2] took care to make proper arrangements that they should not meet. The Queen seemed satisfied with Mr. Disraeli's proposed Cabinet. " What about Sir J. Pakington ? " she asked. " Providence has interposed," replied Disraeli thankfully. (He was thrown out of Parliament.) But he is to be made a Peer. Mr. Bright told me his health would not allow him to fight much. Lord Granville seemed ill. Lord Halifax made the Queen angry, and was doubting Disraeli's honesty. I had a friendly parting with Cardwell who has done so much for the Army and has been so unjustly abused. Lord Granville said it was a mistake for the party his going to the House of Lords. Mr. Lowe was very lively. " I have achieved the drainage of Windsor and I die happy." Argyll sat moodily alone. He generally does. At 3 the new ones came but I did not see any except Derby who hoped I would correspond freely with him. He introduced me to Mr. Cross. Torrington asked Lord Malmesbury if Mr. Cross was married. " I haven't an idea — I never saw the man before." And so the Government was changed.

---

[1] Equerry-in-Waiting.   [2] Master of the Household.

From *The Queen*

Windsor, Dec. 10, 1878

The Queen must say that she does consider the conduct of the Opposition on the Eastern Question which is closely allied to the Indian one, (as indeed all but one of the leading papers do) for the last two years most *unpatriotic* ; & to see old friends & not violent party people, like Ld Halifax join in a party move — at a moment when the honour & dignity of her great Empire are at stake — to *condemn* the policy of the Government which *their* former conduct has rendered necessary — is a cause of deep annoyance pain & *anxiety for the future* to the Queen.

As the Queen can't separate herself from those interests she *does* consider it *very wanting* in *regard* for *her comfort, peace of mind & well being* to act as they are doing & the sooner they are undeceived about *her feelings* the better.

Extracts from letters from *Lord Halifax*

Dec. 20, 1878

I told the printer to send you a copy of my speech in the H. of Lords. I think you will see that there is not in it a single word which breathes of party spirit. Indeed the subject is far too important to admit of party feeling. The Govt. have misstated and misrepresented to an extent I never remember before, but I never alluded to it, and I think that even H.M. herself w^d agree it was not a party attack. It is absurd to say that any disapproval of the policy pursued by a Govt. must necessarily proceed from party motives.

. . . So little did I act in a *party* spirit that I wrote to Lord Cranbrook in September what I have now said in my speech on the conduct TO BE *pursued* and the reasons for it. I c^d say nothing of what they HAD *done* for we did not know it. I think that I did my duty as deeply interested in all Indian questions, but I c^d hardly give a better proof of not being actuated by party.

Jan. 1, 1879

. . . I am much obliged to you for your letter, and glad that you and I are not to be engaged in a controversy.

I see however, that I have much to learn, even in my old age, as to patriotism.

The ground on which you say that I am supposed to be un-English and un-patriotic, is that my motion was " an attempt to parry a blow which England was about to deliver ". That it could not be, for as the war had already commenced, the blow had been delivered. My motion whilst it condemned the course of policy which had brought us into war, expressed our readiness to provide the means for bringing it to a safe and honourable conclusion.

I hardly think that *formerly* the disapproval of such policy would have been thought unpatriotic even by those who thought the disapproval was a mistake.

Silence may be the most prudent, but I confess I am grieved that the Queen sh^d consider my conduct as unpatriotic, and as directed against Her, and I cannot refrain from saying thus much for myself.

On September 2, 1879, after the Zulu War, Henry Ponsonby writes in a letter to his wife :

Beaconsfield can't bear either Frere or Chelmsford and won't see the latter which the Queen says is unfair as he does not hear both sides. B. says he does not accuse Chelmsford of urging on this unhappily precipitate Zulu War the evil causes of which to this country have been incalculable. But he does accuse him of ignorance of the foe, hesitation and dilatoriness. If he had not been furtively apprized of Wolseley's appointment, he would never have advanced on Ulundi which by a crowning error he immediately evacuated.

He goes on to say that Chelmsford criticizes no one but is unconvincing in his answers to questions. The Queen very much favoured him and gave him the G.C.B. Later Evelyn Wood and Buller came to Balmoral and talked over the whole campaign, " which no one appeared to think a very creditable episode to us ".

From *The Queen*

The Queen sends this Mem^m which she feels it a *great necessity* to have conveyed in an indirect way to the Liberal Party for the sake of the *Country* & the *Monarchy* for both which she is *seriously alarmed*.

Prospects of a Liberal Government

Buckingham Palace, March 12, 1880

The Queen is anxious to write once more & more decidedly her very strong objections — indeed her determination *not* to accept Sir C. Dilke as a minister of any future Liberal Govt. It is well known that he is a democrat — a disguised republican, who is in communication with the extreme French republicans. He has been personally most offensive

in his language respecting the Court — the expenses, etc. —
& to place him in the Govt. not to speak of the Cabinet
would be a sign to the whole world that England was sliding
down into democracy and a republic. If the Liberals (so
called for who can be liberals who would play into Russia's
hands & lower the position of Great Britain which has been
with such difficulty restored from its nonentity in w^h it had
fallen in Mr. Gladstone's Government) intend to lean to
the extreme radicals, they can never expect any support
from the Queen. Any reduction of the Army & Navy —
when we may at any time be called to assert England's
position in Europe & in defending her power in India —
the Queen w^d *strongly resist.* She knows that her son shares
her views quite as strongly as she does, & at her age she must
look to the future & to the safety of the country & of those
to whom she hands down her crown.

The army has suffered most severely from the changes
made by Lord Cardwell & its efficiency will be restored with
great difficulty. These are dangerous times & any attempt
to make our institutions Democratic will be *most* disastrous
— Improvements & progress in a right direction & with
prudence will ever meet with the Queen's support but not
constant Change for change's sake.

The Queen will not either accept people who have been
personally offensive to her, like Mr. Lowe, Mr. Ayrton, etc.
She was unaware at the time Mr. Gladstone proposed him
to her that he was the person who had held disgraceful
language towards her or she w^ld never have taken him. A
person (an Englishman) just coming from Russia, was told
by a Russian of high position " It will be a great misfortune
for England if the liberals come in but it will be *a great thing
for us.*" Of course the Russian was told they were mistaken,
as *no* liberal Govt. or any Govt. c^d hold different language
to Russia.

But it is this which alarms all Europe & the distrust felt
by all the Powers abroad — thanks to the violent abuse of
the foreign policy of the Govt. by the Opposition (tho' many
old Liberals & Whigs do not join in it) ought to be warning
to the Opposition to think of the good of their country &
of Europe in general rather than to try merely to drive out
the Govt.

To *The Queen*

Buckingham Palace, March 13, 1880

Lt.-General Sir Henry Ponsonby humbly begs leave to thank
Your Majesty for the Memorandum of which he returns
a copy.

He would like to take an opportunity of showing it in confidence to one or two of the leaders of the opposition he knows well — but to them only as they would repeat the substance of it. Whereas some of the others might misunderstand it — and make mischief.

He asks leave to say a few words in defence of Lord Cardwell's plan. It was based on proposals urged by General Grey — which Sir Henry Ponsonby understood at the time were those of the Prince (but not so thorough).

Even in its modified form it has been generally accepted. Lord Cranbrook did not reverse it. Lord Beaconsfield announced his approval of its principles and Colonel Stanley supported it.

It has not been fairly carried into effect — still it has enabled Your Majesty to carry on two considerable wars with an army on a peace footing.

Whether the strain was not too great for this — or whether the system itself is faulty was the question put before the Committee who have not yet reported.

From *The Queen*

Buckingham Palace, March 13, 1880

The Queen has no objection (. . .) to Sir Henry Ponsonby's showing her Mem^m to one or 2 of the Leaders of the Opposition.

There is *nothing* she fears to be done with *Mr. Forster* who went against every *wish* expressed indirectly by the Queen to him & who *wont* believe or *understand* any of the *dangers* with regard to Foreign matters, India, etc. His original connection with the Quakers has warped his judgment on many questions.

With regard to the Army question the Queen *knows* that the Prince entirely disapproved of General Grey's Army views tho' he was very anxious for improvement in many things & complained to the Queen often about Genl Grey's being so opposed to what HE thought *right*.

The Queen is *no* partizan & *never has* been since the 1st 3 or 4 years of her reign when she *was* so from her inexperience & g^t friendship with Ld Melbourne. But she has, in common with many sound Liberals or Whigs, most *deeply* grieved over & been *indignant* at the *blind* & *destructive* course pursued by the *Opposition* w^h w^d *ruin* the country & her great anxiety is to *warn* them not to go on committing themselves to such a very dangerous & reckless course.

Memorandum

March 17, 1880

It was not desirable to show the Memo.

I told the Queen that my observations could be taken as hints but that her Memo would be looked on as a message and would create a row.

Granville and Hartington would be perplexed by it. It might induce them to abandon their posts as they could both do without office — and the persons named might resent this as interference.

Dilke dislikes Lord Granville and was received by the Prince of Wales (H.M. hoped not) and this might give rise to complications.

From *The Queen*

Baden Baden, Ap. 4, 1880

The Queen sends the letter from Lord Beaconsfield which both Sir Henry & Ld Bridport may like to see.

The gr^t alarm in the country is Mr. Gladstone, the Queen perceives, & she will sooner *abdicate* than send for or have any *communication* with *that half-mad fire-brand* who w^d soon ruin everything & be a *Dictator*.

Others but herself *may submit* to his democratic rule, but *not the Queen.*

She thinks he himself don't wish for or expect it.

Baden Baden, April 5, 1880

For many reasons it is perhaps unfortunate that we are here at this moment but on the other hand I am not sorry that some of the language used, falls on Lady Churchill, Bridport and me. The suddenness of the reverse has made it bitter and the loss of those who have certainly been most attentive to her wishes and even when opposing them, did so with tact and judgment is enough to cause her sorrow and it is a real sorrow. Granville on the other hand who she formerly liked is her aversion. Some incident has taken place to cause this and I think his speech on the Imperial Title Bill had much to do with it. But her indignation is directed, not perhaps so much against Gladstone himself, for she scarcely thinks him responsible for his words — but against those who wish to place him in the first place. Bridport and I pointed out that the natural successor to the present Prime Minister would be the recognised leader of the Opposition and that she should place her confidence when the moment came in Granville and Hartington.

I must say she listened very attentively and agreed with

me when I urged that she should not throw difficulties in their path but support them well even though they suggested some Radical Members of their Government.

I told her that Dilke had met the Prince of Wales at Lord Fife's at dinner, that the Republican had drunk in the honeyed words of Royalty, had written his name down at Marlborough House and had enquired when the next Levée was to take place. To accept him would be politic, to reject him would be to convert him into an enemy, and an able one.

The Queen did not disagree, but said she supposed he would only be suggested for a small place at first. Lowe, she declares, made a gross personal attack on her. To propose him as a Minister would be an insult to her. After some discussion she agreed to accept and support the Whigs, I mean the chiefs of the Cabinet of 68–70, *if* the present Ministry went out pure and simple. The meaning was that the German papers announce a Coalition. But H.M. does not believe in it. She spoke so well, so much to the point and listened so patiently that I was very much taken with the belief that she is determined to carry out the Constitutional principles most conscientiously.

That is I believe her present feeling. But when preyed upon by other influences I cannot of course say what they may do. I have only Bridport to talk these matters over with here. But he has excellent solid sense and though a Tory sees the weakness of his Ministers and fully agrees in the necessity of supporting the Whigs.

I do not envy the coming Ministry. The united Tory opposition will be a considerable one but they will not suffer from them as much as from those who sit on their side, so many of whom have their various ideas and quips. The Home Rulers — Republican Bradlaugh — Labouchere, etc. — and the luke warm men like Lord Stafford who speak against Cardwell and others.

Baden Baden, April 11, 1880

Like you I do not think that Gladstone will wish to come into office, but I am not sure and I agree with the article in *The Daily News* of Friday that this should be clearly ascertained. I have again hinted this — very gently — because as I am under the accusation of being favorable to him there would be a danger of my being considered a partizan and only listened to in that sense whereas I really only wish that the state of feeling in England should be considered and I must say I think it would be wise to be at least civil to him. But the Queen replies as if the question of his coming into office was as improbable as if she were to send for the Archbishop of Strassbourg. And she tells me that the Dean [of Windsor] has told her that Gladstone will not take office and therefore that point is settled. Leopold hints that Lord Beaconsfield will advise her to send for Lord Granville. But as she herself says she may or may not take the outgoing Minister's advice. This is quite true. She will act perfectly within the Constitution if she rejects all advice and sends for any one she pleases. But the moment is a critical one. Shielded by Beaconsfield, people may abuse him for selecting one man over another. But if she throws that shield aside and chooses any one but the popular candidate, popular abuse will be turned direct at her.

My belief is that Beaconsfield will suggest Granville and that will end the matter so far.

In the mean while I urge that we should say nothing here. Nothing is decided as to whether Ministers will meet Parliament or not. Till then it is far better not to commit herself to any opinion whatever.

Baden Baden, April 12, 1880

Almost all the newspapers confirm my opinion today that Gladstone must have the refusal of the Premiership. The more I think of it the more imperative it seems to me to be that he must be sent for. And I also think that it is very desirable he should accept the office. An enormous amount of extreme but undefined Liberalism has come to the top, which recognizes no leader but Gladstone. Him they will follow and be controlled by, but if rejected he may become their leader in a sense that many will not like. Still as far as I can make out the idea of his being thought of at all has not entered the Queen's mind. As I said yesterday she would as soon think of sending for the Archbishop of Strassbourg. When I wrote that — it was a *façon de parler* — yet it nearly came about — for she did send to know who the Ecclesiastic was who was staying in our Hotel — and I was surprised to find that he was the Bishop of Strassbourg. A venerable nice looking old man. I look on this as a good augury, for as we came near this apparent impossibility, the other, i.e. sending for Gladstone, may also come to pass. Beach never or " hardly ever " touches on politics but in walking today I alluded to Gladstone as to the probability of another contest in Mid-Lothian if he took office — and at his name alone Beach broke out into furious abuse. It is extraordinary what bitterness they show towards him and it is this of course which has so exasperated the Queen against him. Also that Gladstone never was sympathetic, never gave in to her ways and though I firmly believe a far truer friend yet he certainly did not comply with her wishes as they have been complied with in the last 6 years. Imperial Title, Public Worship Bill and other matters were originated by her and forced through by Beaconsfield on her behalf — though he himself verily I believe disliked them. The change from this to Gladstone would be most trying to her and in fact she says she will not have him. What this fully means one cannot say but she has declared she would abdicate rather than submit to dictation. Gladstone once told me that this threat of abdication was the greatest power the Sovereign possessed — nothing could stand against it, for the position of a Minister who forced it on would be untenable. True. But on the other hand what a terrible victory it would be for her. It would be almost ruin. And I earnestly hope that these mutterings may not go beyond me. I am really very sorry for the Queen for it is a most painful and trying moment. If she takes either Granville or Hartington she will believe and not without reason that they will be influenced by Gladstone so that unless he is made a friend of I foresee a time of trouble and anxiety.

To *The Queen*

Baden Baden, April 15, 1880

Lt.-General Sir Henry Ponsonby presents his humble duty to Your Majesty.

In reply to Your Majesty's enquiry he believes that the Liberal leaders find it nearly impossible to form a Government unless it is publicly known that Mr. Gladstone declines office. And that if Your Majesty sends for either Lord Granville or Lord Hartington they will be obliged to ask leave to consult him.

Sir Henry Ponsonby looks forward with some anxiety to the future. He must confess he would prefer to see Mr. Gladstone in the Cabinet rather than out of it. In the Cabinet he would be invested with responsibility, advised by his colleagues and influenced by Your Majesty. He is loyal and devoted to the Queen who can control him. He would be a strong barrier against the movements of factious men and can and will keep the Liberal party in order.

Out of the Cabinet, he would have power without responsibility, he would exercise an undue influence over Ministers and he would be thrown into the arms of designing men who would make him unconsciously and unwillingly their leader.

Sir Henry Ponsonby humbly asks pardon for making these remarks which are founded on only a limited knowledge of what is going on in England. Your Majesty will shortly receive better advice from those who have better means of knowing the state of affairs and he feels confident that Your Majesty's excellent wisdom and judgment will decide for the best.

From *The Queen*

(On board *Victoria & Albert*) Ap. 16, 1880

The Queen rec^d Sir Henry Ponsonby's letter yesterday & w^d not have replied to it — as of course there must be so many conjectures which are unanswerable except the one that the *Queen cannot* send for Mr. Gladstone — but she *cannot* leave 2 expressions of his without *a remark*.

He says " Mr. Gladstone is *loyal & devoted to the Queen* " ! ! !

He is *neither* ; for *no one* CAN be, who spares no means — contrary to anything the Queen & she thinks her Predecessors ever witnessed or experienced — to *vilify — attack —* accuse of *every* species of iniquity a Minister who had most difficult times & questions to deal with — & who showed a most unpardonable & disgraceful spite & personal hatred to Lord Beaconsfield who has restored England to the position she had lost under Mr. Gladstone's Govt.

Is this *patriotism* & devotion to the *sovereign*? And what has he brought upon the Queen & country?

Such conduct is *unheard of* & the *only* excuse is — that he is not quite *sane*.

Note by *Ponsonby*

On the 23 [April] Hartington arrived again and anxious to support his advice that Gladstone should be summoned brought Granville to my house. They asked me if the Queen could see him. I said I thought she would — but as she had now deputed Prince Leopold to carry on communications perhaps Granville would only see him.

Hartington said " Oh I am shy of the Queen — but I don't care for Leopold."

In reply I said I thought they would find it difficult to persuade the Queen to take Gladstone. Hartington said his interview yesterday showed that. But they must both try. Hartington saw Prince Leopold and then the Queen. I went to their room afterwards in some anxiety. Granville kissed his hand with a smile like a ballet girl receiving applause. And Hartington threw himself into a chair with " Ha ! Ha ! " Granville exclaimed — " No difficulty at all — all smooth ! "

They returned to London and sent Mr. Gladstone down. He went first to the Deanery and walked up from there. Magdalen and I met him and walked with him to the Castle.

Balmoral, May 23, 1880

Herein is my difficulty. If I am silent I am condemned as unsympathetic. If I agree with the Queen I am scarcely honest and if I support Granville I am condemned. He naturally praises his own side and laughs at the Opposition finding fault with their tactics and quoting from the Prince about the violence of all Oppositions. The Queen dislikes quotations from the Prince's lips which are opposed to her views and declares that for the Whigs to talk of violence in opposition is ridiculous. So far I rather agree and said so. I found that H.M. had read the debate, better than I had, even to O'Donnell's speech. O'Donnell now sits on the Tory side so he is not hated as he used to be by the late Government. I really do think that Granville need not have been hurt at George Hamilton's violence of language, and this was sufficient for my present argument. But of course he must say that Kimberley and Argyll are splendid orators and crushed Salisbury — just as we used to hear that Salisbury crushed Argyll. Still this sort of controversial letter naturally makes H.M. smile at both sides.

From *Lord Granville*

18, Carlton House Terrace, Nov. 29, 1880

I am very glad to hear of the Queen's gracious invitation to Gladstone. I have written to H.M. on the subject. I trust not injudiciously. What happened on Saturday? Forster is supposed to have scratched his head a good deal on the journey home.

From *The Queen*

Windsor, Nov. 1880

Please return both Ld Granville's letters. What annoys the Queen is that Ld Granville makes a great event of the Queen's inviting Mr. Gladstone (which as in May [1] he did not *accept*) — whereas the Queen *naturally* sh^d ask her Prime Minister as soon as she c^d.

Tho' *never personally* liking Mr. Gladstone *that* is NOT the feeling which is uppermost in her mind. It is the feeling of gr^t *displeasure* for the gr^t harm he did *when out* of office w^h told against the late Gov^t & brought all the present difficulties upon us : and this feeling must be lasting. Ld G. does *no* good by *praising* the Queen for being *civil* which she w^d be sure to be on acc^t of Mr. G.'s *position* as it is her duty to be so. Sir Henry c^d perhaps give Ld Granville a hint *as from himself entirely* about this.

[1] The Government was formed in April but neither in Gladstone's *Life* nor elsewhere is there any record of this previous invitation.

The Queen omitted this — she sends another & she thinks unnecessary letter fʳ Lᵈ Granville. She does not want to be particularly agreeable to Mr. Gladstone tho' she will always be civil while he must be her Minister.[1]

From *The Queen*

Osborne, Jan. 1, 1881

. . . Would Sir Henry prepare a letter for her to write to Mr. Gladstone. She *does* expect him to warn both Mr. Bright & Mr. Chamberlain *not* to attack the H. of Lords — for they cannot remain in the Cabinet if they do that again.

Buckingham Palace, March 28, 1881

When I arrived in town I went to see Gladstone to make an appointment for him to come here — and to tell him not to talk of the Wolseley affair. He agreed. . . . He went on to say " My day is drawing to a close and when a man gets worn out he gets gloomy. Formerly I saw no reason why Monarchy should not have gone on here for hundreds of years, but I confess that the way in which Monarchy has been brought to the front in political and foreign affairs by the late Government has shaken my confidence and I dread any shock that may weaken the power of the Crown with the rising mass of politicians. Some — and those you live with probably accuse me of being a radical. I am not. But I believe I have the confidence — possibly far more than I deserve of those who are extreme radicals — but who as long as I am here pay me that respect of following me in most of what I do — even tho' they do not think I am advanced enough."

From *The Queen*

Osborne, Aug. 13, 1881

. . . The Queen sends the letters she recᵈ this evenᵍ and is very anxious at the state of affairs. The H. of Lords cannot be totally set aside or a republic with *one* House had better be proposed. Mr. Gladstone is dragged along by his dreadful Radical following & is ruining the country. If the H. of Lᵈˢ refuses what is to happen ? The Queen believes no moderate people like the Bill[2] tho' they have not the courage to support amendments to improve it.

The Queen thinks it wᵈ be well if Sir Henry cᵈ go up to town tomorrow & see some of the leading people & hear

---

[1] Gladstone on his visit : " She seemed to me if I may say so natural under effort " (Morley's *Life*, vol. ii, p. 628).

[2] Irish Land Bill. See *Letters of Queen Victoria*, Second Series, vol. iii.

what is expected to happen & c^d point out the danger of resisting the H. of L^{ds} *entirely.* The Queen will *not* try to make *them* submit nor will she interfere beyond pointing out the danger of forcing down their throats what they cannot agree to without gr^t danger to the Empire.

If the L^{ds} make a stand & Mr. Gladstone also what is to happen ? It w^d be well if Sir Henry went up tomorrow afternoon so as to *hear* & *see* people on Monday m^g returning on Monday Ev^g. He c^d cypher to the Queen so as to prepare her for what course is to be pursued.

Mr. Goschen made a very *strange* speech.

After the murder of Lord Frederick Cavendish in May 1882 Lord Granville received a letter from the Queen (*Queen Victoria's Letters,* vol. iii, p. 284). His comment on it occurs in a letter to her Private Secretary :

It is quite natural that the Queen should feel strongly on this ghastly tragedy, but some sentences in her letter are such as would almost require our resignation if I were to show the letter to my colleagues.

From *The Queen*

Balmoral, May 21, 1882

The Q. thought Mr. Sexton's language very untruthful threatening & violent — but Mr. Gladstone is determined to trust in these rebels. . . . His retirement & that of his evil genius Mr. Chamberlain w^d make a g^t difference & be a g^t blessing to the country.

From *The Queen*

Balmoral, May 27, 1882

. . . She feels the state of Ireland & the impossibility of getting the Bill [the Crimes Bill] thro' quickly weigh heavily on her & depress her very much. The Queen must complain bitterly of the want of respect & consideration of her views (w^h with her experience of *45* years *might* & ought to be regarded on the part of the Gov^t) especially Ld Granville who she has known *so long* & who also lately *ignores* all her remarks ! She feels *hurt* & *indignant,* as he is the *only* friend (tho' he has never *really* proved to be that) or at least the only *person* she has been in the habit of speaking out to in the Cabinet.

Sir Henry she fears (being so much inclined to the Liberal party himself) may not express strongly *enough* her views &

fears. He sh^d defend her as much as he can. Instead of resisting & trying to stem the downward & alarming course of *radicalism* & indeed but thinly veiled *republicanism*, the Cabinet *weakly yields* to Mr. Gladstone & Mr. Chamberlain who *head* & *lead* this dangerous policy instead of trying as they perfectly could to check it & rally all the good Whigs & moderate liberals whom they have entirely alienated toward them.

From *The Queen*

Balmoral, May 31, 1882

. . . With respect to Ireland & the Ministers, the Queen regrets to see, that she has *no one* real *independent* friend in the Cabinet, never hearing exactly what passes, & finding that *no one* will see the danger of going so much ahead with the radicals. The truth is, that, like so many people, Lord Granville has not the courage of his opinions & therefore is of not the slightest use to the Queen. She thinks him besides very much shaken morally & physically & she is afraid, that the Cabinet do not see sufficiently the great danger, of letting Egypt slip from under our control. Lord Beaconsfield would have foreseen this at once, & acted with great energy. Sir Henry Ponsonby must know well, that the Queen *cannot* communicate frequently & openly with Mr. Gladstone, as he does not possess her confidence ; & *that* was *one* of the reasons, why she so strongly objected to taking him as her Prime Minister, as she felt & feels how false & painful her position is with regard to him. The Queen trusts from what Lord Spencer writes to her, that Mr. Gladstone & the Cabinet will be firm about the Prevention of Crime Bill, as he seems very strong upon it himself & that the Government let themselves be guided by Lord Spencer.

From *The Queen* (on the subject of Lord Derby's Inclusion in the Liberal Government)

Windsor, Dec. 15, 1882

Would Sir Henry tell Mr. Gladstone *how* unpleasant it is for her to have Ld Derby as a Minister for she utterly despises him ; he has no feeling for the honour of England & the language in the French press & the alarm felt in Germany (she had a letter from her daughter hoping it was not true) show what a *very bad effect* his name will have on the Gov^t. All will believe that a " cotton-spinning ", " peace-at-all-prices " policy is now to be favoured ! Tell this *all* to Mr. Gladstone. It is too bad of Lord Granville *not* to give her a hint of this before it was too late. He has not once (since he came into office) been of the slightest help to her at all & it is a *gr^t shame*.

Mr. Gladstone will have to resist Ld Derby's foreign views at any time. But in the Colonies he may also do gr^t harm — by letting everything go. . . .

From *The Queen*

Windsor, Dec. 16, 1882

The Queen was *gr^tly shocked* when Mr. Gladstone proposed Mr. Chamberlain in these uncomfortable words " Sir C. Dilke says *his friend* Mr. Chamberlain is quite ready to exchange with him " ! The Queen gr^tly objected & was told Mr. Chamberlain had never said anything like [it to] Sir C. Dilke. But she maintained her objections & she said that there might be other arrange^ts. The Queen is determined *not* to have a man like Mr. Chamberlain to hold such a personal app^t & Mr. Gladstone sh^d be told the Queen will NOT have him. If Sir C. Dilke & Mr. Chamberlain are such " friends " their power for mischief may be *very great*.

Ld Granville's silence in all this shocks the Queen gr^tly. Ld Hartington is the most straight forward & reliable & far less radical.

To *Edward Hamilton* (Gladstone's Private Secretary)

Windsor Castle, December 16, 1882

From your criticism I think you do not at all understand her feelings about Lord Derby. What she said could not have reflected in any way on Mr. Gladstone.

She disliked Lord Derby under the late Government but respecting his traditionary connection with the Tories she did her best to be friendly with him.

He threw her over at a critical moment. You will object that it was not " her " but " her Government ". But She looks upon it that England was on the eve of disastrous consequences, and that his action nearly ruined the country — and that what ruins the country is a crime against her and not against her Government.

That acts of this sort are above party consideration and that now he comes to her as one not who feels with her for the honor of the country as she believed he formerly did — but as one who is ready to sacrifice it at any moment.

Taking this from her point of view you will admit these are very different circumstances. She feels this more strongly than the Republican pill as you call the Member for Chelsea,[1] as she believes to some extent in his determination and energy on behalf of the country. And in his case it was a personal attack upon her. This she is willing to pass by if some expression of regret for it is made. And I imagine this will be made.

From *The Queen*

Balmoral Castle, Sep. 16. 1883

The Queen is a good deal surprised & she must say annoyed at Mr. Gladstone's " Progress ". He " was not to cross the border " and yet he has been landing & receiving Addresses from many places in Scotland & now is off to Norway.

The Queen thinks it *most unusual* & not she thinks respectful towards herself that the Prime Minister should go to a foreign country without mentioning it to the Sovereign. And she thinks considering the extraordinary & tactless publicity given to every single movement & trifling act of his, his presence in Norway when affairs are very critical seems indiscreet & ill-judged.

Sir H. Ponsonby is in such frequent correspondence with Mr. Gladstone's Private Secretaries that she wishes him to tell them what she feels (& she does so very strongly) on this subject. Why does Mr. Gladstone not try to stop this sort of Court Circular which the Queen believes never appeared for *any* other Prime Minister & which is not approved of by many.

From *The Queen*

Windsor Castle, [?] 1885

Sir Henry sh[d] tell Mr. Goschen that she hopes he & those he hopes to act with will be *truly patriotic* & will not be in a hurry to try & turn out this Government which is doing its best in a most difficult position. Her hope is that if they are obliged to give up it will be for a Coalition Gov[t]. She prays the country may be spared from Mr. Gladstone who has done the country almost impossible harm deluding himself with the belief of the reverse. He can convince himself black is white & wrong is right which makes him so dangerous.

In addition to the letter which Sir Henry Ponsonby wrote on December 19, 1885, the Queen herself wrote to Mr. Goschen on December 20,[2] and repeated the last sentence, which Ponsonby probably omitted.

---

[1] Sir Charles Dilke.
[2] *Letters of Queen Victoria*, Second Series, vol. iii, p. 713.

From *The Queen*

Aix-les-Bains, Ap. 15, 1885

With respect to Mr. Gladstone the Queen does feel she is always kept in the dark.

In Ld Melbourne's time she knew *everything* that *passed* in the Cabinet & the different views that were entertained by the different Ministers & there was no concealment. Sir R. Peel who was completely *master* of his Cabinet (& the Prime Minister *ought* to be) was, after the 1st strangeness for her [who] hardly knew him, also very open. Ld Russell less communicative but still far more so than Mr. Gladstone & Lord Palmerston too. They mentioned the names of the Ministers & their views. Ld Palmerston again kept his Cabinet in g^t order. Ld Derby was also entirely master of his Cabinet. Ld Aberdeen most confidential & open & kind — Ld Beaconsfield was like Ld Melbourne. He told the Queen everything (he often did not *see* her for months) & said : " I wish you to know everything so that you may be able to judge." Mr. Gladstone never once has told her the different views of his colleagues. She is kept completely in the dark — & when they have quarrelled over it & decided amongst themselves he comes & tries to *force* this on her.

The Queen feels gr^{tly} aggrieved at the utter ignorance in which she is kept. It is very wrong & Mr. Gladstone cannot expect the Queen to have any confidence in a Minister who never tells her the different views of the different people in the Cabinet. He speaks of the result, of " one or two members ", etc., & she stands alone & unsupported & unable to know what goes on ! The Queen has never been treated so badly by any Ministers or Minister in this respect as the *present*. Sir Henry cannot wonder if the Queen w^d not be sorry if Mr. Gladstone retired. She is sure Ld Hartington w^d not do this. . . .

The prolonged negotiations over the Franchise Bill are referred to elsewhere. In June 1885 the Government were defeated on the Budget, and resigned. Lord Salisbury was at first unwilling to take office without certain assurances from the Liberals. On June 11 Ponsonby received a letter from General Sir Alexander Gordon, M.P. :

It may be useful for you, and perhaps also for the Queen, to know that *before the Whitsuntide recess* I knew that the Cabinet, or at any rate some members of the Cabinet, were arranging that the Government should be defeated on some minor point, so as to give them an opportunity for resigning and thus to escape out of their responsibilities.

My information came from so confidential a quarter, that I am unable to make it public, but the mere fact of my having been told it, together with what has now taken place, seems to show that there was good foundation for what I heard.

Had the Government made known their intention to take the division as a vital one, as they ought to have done, I should have voted for them in order to defeat such a dirty trick.

During the next few days Ponsonby had to be very active. In a letter to his wife on June 23rd he wrote :

> Windsor Castle, June 23, 1885
>
> It is a comfort to have a minute or two of peace after the racket of the last 48 hours. I saw Gladstone 5 times yesterday — and Salisbury 4. Salisbury has been here and has kissed hands and is now Prime Minister. But as I am sure he had settled this yesterday morning why try and get these extra assurances from Gladstone ? He certainly made me believe he would not accept without such assurances — guarantees. He said some of his party wouldn't. So I telegraphed to the Queen I thought he would refuse. But about the same time Henry Manners his Private Secretary told Lady Bolsover who I sat next to at dinner at Strathnairn's that it was all right — and that they had accepted. H.M. is in good spirits about it all.

And the next day Edward Hamilton wrote :

> 10, Downing Street, Whitehall, 24 June, 1885
>
> . . . However Mr. Gladstone will not recede one inch. Lord Salisbury will have to content himself with the papers down to and exclusive of the Queen's last letter to him, or else Mr. Gladstone will tell the whole story.
>
> The fact is Lord Salisbury was not at all straightforward with Mr. G. on Monday. He kept on haggling about terms and trying to beat down Mr. G., while all the time he had definitely and finally determined to take office. This I know as fact.
>
> Lord Salisbury told me he wished to prove (at least I understood him so to say) that it was the Queen who had forced office upon him against his will.

This was followed up by a statement to Lord Salisbury :

Windsor Castle, June 24, 1885

Any statement made should avoid giving a mistaken impression that the Queen forced office on Lord Salisbury.

The Queen's intention was to facilitate the progress of the movement for putting an end to the Ministerial Crisis.

Towards the end of the year the Queen was beginning to be anxious about the possible return of the Liberal Government.

From *The Queen*

Balmoral, Sep. 23, '85

[End of a letter] But she is most anxious that the Liberals sh^d be *detached* from those dreadful socialists Mr. Chamberlain & others & that all should try & separate from him, or the country may be ruined. How can Mr. Gladstone at 76 with a broken voice stand again ? The Queen has thought of writing to him & Lord Hartington an appeal.

The Queen's ingrained animosity against a Liberal Government, of which more examples will be given, by no means however covering the whole ground, yet perhaps becoming wearisome to readers, would hardly be believed were the illustrations not given in her own words. Partly she hoped to convert her Private Secretary to her own political views and partly, knowing he was friendly with Liberal Ministers, she expected him to pass on some of her emphatic remarks. He was not converted, and only when specially enjoined to do so did he actually quote her more severe strictures to the people concerned.

CHAPTER X

Ireland

THE two subjects forming the headings of this chapter and the next in which Liberal Governments were concerned may be detached and considered separately. They gave rise to frequent expressions of indignation on the part of the Queen and consequently involved a great deal of correspondence.

Home Rule stands out from the early eighties to the mid-nineties as the main theme of controversy. It produced a bitterness in society unequalled by any other political clash since those days. The Queen simply regarded it as an attempt to separate Ireland from the United Kingdom leading therefore to the disruption of the realm over which she reigned. The high motive which inspired Gladstone is best explained by J. L. Hammond in his book *Gladstone and the Irish Nation* : ". . . he believed that free discussion and self government were essential to man's dignity and self-respect", and further : " With his strong sense of the value and place of self-respect in the life of a nation, Gladstone saw the whole of the Irish problem with very different eyes from his contemporaries " (among whom, we may add, must be included his own colleagues). This is exactly what Ponsonby found. In spite of his intense admiration for the character and power of this amazing statesman, unmoved by the abuse of him which so often came to his ears and uninfluenced by the Queen's sustained prejudice against the Liberal leader, yet Ponsonby himself had serious doubts about Home Rule, more especially when at various stages he discussed it with leading Ministers in the Liberal Government. Noticeably they lacked any of the enthusiasm of their leader and often they fell back on such phrases as " What else can we do ? " So the Queen in this case is hardly to be blamed. Gladstone, we may be sure, never attempted to explain to her the high ideal which drove him forward with such persistence. Nor if he had would she have understood what he meant. So it was that blind prejudice on the one side and incapacity for explanation on the other drew the two steadily and fatally apart.

The published correspondence on Home Rule is very full. The following letters do no more than supply some links which were omitted. They do not divulge at any stage features or facts which alter the general trend of the embittered dispute. But while the published letters of the Queen to her Prime Minister, although at times severe and even censorious, are on the whole written with restraint, the letters here included show that in writing to her Private Secretary any restraint was set aside in her apparent desire that he at any rate should fully understand her inmost feelings and perhaps pass on to others some intimation of the strength of her indignation. The utmost vigilance and care in personal guidance and official steering on the part of the Private Secretary was therefore essential.

Lord Carnarvon,[1] it will be remembered, believed in the possibility of a solution by the Conservatives of the Home Rule controversy. In conversation with the Queen he mentioned his scheme but before the Cabinet had pronounced any opinion on the subject. In reply to a letter from Sir Henry Ponsonby on the subject Lord Salisbury wrote :

> Foreign Office, November 29, 1885
>
> I have some difficulty in answering your letter — because the matter of it, the gravest that could possibly be discussed, has not yet been laid before the Cabinet for their decision. I did not anticipate that Lord Carnarvon would trouble the Queen with this question at this stage. I hold that the Queen should not be troubled with the divergent opinions of Ministers, until they have ascertained by discussion that they cannot agree. These opinions of Lord Carnarvon have been mentioned at the Cabinet : and they were repudiated by all the Ministers who spoke ; but no general discussion was opened ; and it was agreed to defer the matter until we should have ascertained by the Elections how far the matter was a practical one for us. I am, therefore, speaking only for myself in what follows.
>
> My opinion is that a Central Parliament for Ireland is

---

[1] Henry H. M., 4th Earl, Lord-Lieutenant of Ireland 1885–1886.

practically Home Rule : that is to say, it will involve either at once or in a very brief space so much independence as to reduce the connection between England and Ireland to a personal union expressed in Her Majesty's Sovereignty. In every other respect the two kingdoms will be independent.

In my judgment, this result would be principally hurtful in that it would expose the Loyalists — the Classes who have made themselves unpopular by backing the policy of England — to utter ruin. Their properties would practically be taken from them. Such a result seems to me scarcely consistent with the honour of an English Sovereign, or of English Statesmen.

I believe that any policy of utter surrender to Mr. Parnell, such as this would be, would be profoundly repugnant to public opinion in this country — and especially to the opinion of the Tory Party — and that it could only be carried out, *now*, at the cost of a great disruption of parties, and an entire loss of honour among public men.

Draft of letter to *Lord Salisbury*

Dec. 2, '85

The Queen thinks it only fair to Lord Carnarvon to observe that she sent Mr. Gladstone's letter to him and that his reply is in reality a criticism upon Mr. G.'s proposals.

H.M. hopes you will not remonstrate with Lord Carnarvon for writing openly to her.

From *Lord Salisbury*

Dec. 2, '85

I have said nothing to Carnarvon ; and I will not mention the matter to him. I think he was wrong : for — if it had not been for the Queen's extreme frankness with Her Ministers — in fact if I had been dealing with anyone else — I might have been put in an awkward position. Remember the history of Lord Loughborough and Catholic Emancipation.

Note by *Ponsonby*

December 4, 1885

In 1801 Mr. Pitt discussed with his colleagues the proposals for admitting Roman Catholics to office.

Lord Loughborough — Lord Chancellor — wrote to the King the objections against this measure — thus privately reversing the views of the Cabinet.

The King accepted Lord Loughborough's views and Mr. Pitt resigned.

Draft of letter to *Lord Salisbury*

Dec. 4, '85

When I recalled to the Queen's memory the circumstances of Lord Loughborough's communications with the King on Catholic Emancipation, H.M. desired me to point out that the essential difference of the two cases lay in the fact that Lord Carnarvon's views were elicited by her and that he did not attempt to advise her on the course that should be followed more than by giving his opinion when she asked for it.

We may well hope that the final Act in that transaction differs from what may result in present incident.

From *The Queen*

Osborne, Dec. 19, '85

The Queen sees with satisfaction that except from the very Radical papers, there is a universal feeling of indignation at Mr. Gladstone's extraordinary & most mischievous conduct. The Queen thinks that Mr. Goschen must *now* work strongly & earnestly to gather & unite all who wish to maintain the constitution & the Empire, so that a split between these theoretical radicals headed by a wild fanatical old man of 76 (who very likely may not see what ruin he is devising for himself & his Country) — & the moderate constitutional Liberals who the Queen w^d fain hope are patriots before they are party men, may take place when Parliament meets.

Patriotism *must now* be the *one aim* of *all* who love their country & are loyal to their Sovereign. *No* time must be *lost* in working hard for this & the Queen expects [this] of people like Mr. Goschen & she would fain hope Ld Hartington.

Letters from Osborne

January 2, 1886

As Lord Lyttelton says that the published scheme is Gladstone's there is no use doubting that any more.

He does not however put it forward and awaits to know what Lord Salisbury will propose. Rowton says he imagines Lord Salisbury will give to Ireland what he gives to England — large local Government. This will be a large measure in England. How will it work in Ireland? Under the rule of terror the County Boards will obey the Parnell orders. Lord Carnarvon thinks this would be made safer by a large Board in Dublin. Still it seems to me that this will also be under Parnell. So that this measure alone which will not satisfy the Parnellites will still lead to trouble.

Trevelyan's [1] was a good speech and H.M. liked it. I

[1] Sir George Trevelyan, Secretary for Scotland.

find she has been privately writing to Goschen and she tells me his answers are most satisfactory. But what is Goschen ? In a Cabinet under Gladstone he would no doubt have great influence. But by himself or outside he can do nothing. He wouldn't have half a dozen followers and as to his being at the head of the middle party, I don't see where that party is to come from. What Liberals could form such a party ? To which Rowton replies And what Tories would join it ? There are no half hearted Tories. This is true so I don't see how this party can be formed. The Liberals who may break away from Gladstone about Ireland will not quarrel with him on anything else.

January 3, 1886

Campbell Bannerman's suggestion that there should be a union of parties to deal with the Irish question always seemed to me to be the most practical and when I told H.M. of it she agreed. I also thought that if they could get some reasonable Parnellite in also — if such exists — it would be useful. This has occupied my thoughts and yesterday I got a letter from E. Hamilton to the same effect — pointing out that Parnell should be compelled to say what he wants. If he refused an invitation to discuss these matters in conference he would show that he was an irreconcilable. The Queen having told me she was in communication with Goschen I wanted to hint to her that he had no following and that if Salisbury goes — he must be succeeded by Gladstone. So I wrote a letter simply saying that Goschen in Gladstone's Ministry would be powerful but out of it would be powerless. And I went on to suggest whether Salisbury would meet Gladstone on the Irish question and perhaps these two would ask Parnell to join. When I came home from Church Lady Ely saw me with a message that the Queen wanted time to think over my letter and therefore hoped I did not require an immediate answer, but one thing she wished me to understand at once. There was no question of Mr. Gladstone who had resigned to the Queen the lead of his party and she would not hear of his being mentioned as forming a ministry — or as being consulted. I could only reply to the latter by observing that if the Queen would communicate with Lord Salisbury he would advise her as to which of the opposition he would meet. Of course I am sure what Lord Salisbury would say. I also mentioned that as Rowton was here he might carry any message she wished to send to Salisbury though I thought the Prime Minister would prefer hearing direct from her. The first question is the conference and I need not discuss with H.M. whether Gladstone or any one else could follow Lord Salisbury — as Prime Minister — at present. But I know this makes her angry with me. She said last time that my partiality for Gladstone made me press him on her unfairly — and so she was furious with me. I only tell her facts. However for the moment I hope she will consult Lord Salisbury as to whether he will confer with one of the opposition. Hamilton in his letter says he is uninspired and that no one knows of his letter to me. Still I suspect he is cognizant of Gladstone's feelings and that Gladstone would be ready to meet Salisbury. You will have seen the *Pall Mall Gazette* written almost with authority, at least so they say, of Gladstone. I was going to point this out to the Queen and to tell her about Hamilton's letter. But after Lady Ely's message she will think I wrote the article and will be wrath at my having letters from Gladstone's late Private Secretary.

January 3, 1886

Soon after I wrote to you this morning Rowton told me he had seen the Queen who had shown him my letter and had asked him to see Lord Salisbury as I had suggested. He is all against the proposal and came to talk it over with me and to find out what he should say. He observed that the case of '83 and the present were quite different and that even then many men condemned the principle of a secret agreement between Chiefs unknown to the followers as unconstitutional and that the whole principle of our Government was that questions should be openly discussed in Parliament.

I replied that it was precisely because Parliamentary Government would be impossible in the coming Session because of the Parnellites — that this unusual course was proposed and that it was most desirable to ascertain what Parnell wanted.

He did not see why we should want to know a Traitor's views. Parleying with Treason was like negotiating with a pickpocket. I would not allow that Parnell had as yet proved himself a traitor but assuming he was — you must either parley with him or crush him — was the Government going to do the latter? Rowton musingly thought the question difficult. Then he said I had no right to dictate that Salisbury must confer with Gladstone. I quite agreed — I had not meant to do so. But I asked Rowton as a man of sense would Salisbury confer on the subject with anyone else. Rowton thought Salisbury might fairly ask Hartington — after his letter — whether he would support him. That I said " was another question. I am talking of a conference between the two leaders which will to a certain extent bind the parties. Can Hartington answer for the Liberal party apart from Gladstone — who would follow him if he did ? "

Rowton smiled. " I suppose Goschen would — and — and — well I don't know of anyone else." He went on to say it was undesirable the Queen should take any prominent step. I quite agreed. I did not think it advisable to bring her name forward. The matter was a pure secret between us. I had told her what I thought. She might ask Salisbury. If he disapproved there was an end of it — nothing could be done without his full concurrence. Nothing more would be said — as of course I should not mention it to anyone.

Surely I urged — whether good or bad the Queen had a perfect right to consult her Prime Minister on any subject — the best way would be to talk it over with him. One of Rowton's best arguments was that the Orangemen would be frantic if they heard of Salisbury discussing with Parnell any Home Rule Scheme and that the Tories would not support him if he proposed anything of the sort. Gladstone's scheme was Home Rule. If he and Parnell agreed, what would happen ? I replied that if Lord Salisbury did not agree he would withdraw from the conference — he would be beaten in the House of Commons and no doubt joyfully resign his office to Gladstone who would have to undertake the job. I of course have not said a word to him about having heard from Hamilton as it would not be fair to Hamilton and at this moment would look as if I were pressing on Gladstone's suggestion.

My belief is that it would be by far the best mode of meeting the difficulty. But it must of course be with the consent of all concerned — so that if anyone says no — the proposal falls to the ground.

January 5, 1886

All that you tell me of your visit to Hawarden is most deeply interesting. I should have liked to have heard you discussing Ireland with Gladstone. What is most important is what you say about his having approached Salisbury through A. Balfour. This is coming to the point and proves that he considers himself the head of the Liberal party (of which I had no doubt) — and that as long as he does — no other chief is possible. A special messenger came to the Queen from Lord Salisbury late last night — and very probably this may have been the subject of the box.

The Queen talks to me upon every other possible subject except this one so I don't know if she will let me hear of

Salisbury's letter — for it will prove I was right that we must
count on Gladstone and on no one else if Salisbury goes.
Rowton asked me if — supposing Gladstone and Salisbury
came to an agreement on Ireland this would mean that
Gladstone came into office. I said certainly not — it would
mean he would support Salisbury. Then asked Rowton
does it mean that he would not attempt to turn him out on
other questions ? I could not answer this.

January 6, 1886

I saw Rowton this morning and he told me of the negotiations thro' Arthur Balfour and that Lord Salisbury had
declined because he did not see his way to their leading to
any good — because his views and Mr. Gladstone's were
hopelessly divergent and because his party would not
support him if he came to any private understanding with
Gladstone on the subject.

All this was answered on the present state of affairs.
Circumstances might arise when other counsels might
prevail. Thus ends this episode. You argue against this
system of private arrangement and I quite admit it is a bad
one and ought not to be used often. It is not however a plot
for deciding anything — but an attempt to agree or disagree
which each of those who conferred must bring to his party for
confirmation or not. Lord Salisbury as Prime Minister has
a right to speak on behalf of his party. Gladstone has not —
but he knows that the majority will support him. Parnell
if he came would have shown his hand and it would have
been for his party to decide what to do with him. I imagine
that Rowton's mission to Salisbury went further than this
and that he was directed to ascertain whether Salisbury
would feel his way with some of the other Liberal leaders
as to whether they would support him. Because he said to
me : " I find that Lord Salisbury agrees with you that it
would in the present aspect of affairs be useless to approach
Hartington or Goschen — tho' the latter has a far greater
following than you think ".

But the moderates appear to look up to Hartington as
their chief and there does not seem to be much chance of
his supporting Lord Salisbury.

January 7, 1886

The North in America was united against the South. But
we are not united against Ireland. That is why I wanted
the meeting between Salisbury and Gladstone before the
battle began as I do not believe that the two programs were
irreconcilable. It would be for them to decide whether they

would send for Parnell — I should. Cowper's [1] second letter also repeats exactly what I have said — that the extension of a large Local Government measure to Ireland will be Home Rule. He says — what I said — that it will throw great Power into Parnell's hand — but he believes in the ultimate settlement by this means.

I imagine Salisbury is going to propose Home Rule for both countries. At least he said so at Newport and I therefore think that if he and Gladstone had met they could have come to an agreement. However as Salisbury won't — it is useless to go on. Rowton hinted he might later.

From *The Queen*

Osborne, Jan. 27, 1886

The papers speak as if the Gov^t w^d resign but as Lord Salisbury never gave a hint of this to the Queen, she thinks it must be premature. To call upon Mr. Gladstone *with his radicals* to form a Gov^t the Queen will NOT do. Would it be well to telegraph to Ld Rowton to come here at once so that the Queen c^d send him back with a message to Lord Salisbury. She would like to cypher to Lord Salisbury as follows :

" Regret defeat but must ask for no precipitate action. You never prepared me for resignation on this amendment & I cannot accept it until I see a chance of a moderate & safe Government. Have telegraphed to Lord Rowton to come here at once & you could send the papers through him & he take any one from me."

From *The Queen*

Osborne, Jan. 29, 1886

Has Sir Henry had no telegram from Mr. Goschen? Her letter went at 7 — & she asked him to telegraph the hour of his arrival.

The Queen does not the least care but rather wishes it sh^d be known that she has the gr^{test} possible disinclination to take this half crazy & really in many ways ridiculous old man — for the sake of the country. In asking to consult Mr. Goschen (if the Duke of Argyll had been in England she w^d have sent for him) she only follows the precedent of '51 & '55 when she consulted Ld Lansdowne & the Duke of Wellington & followed their advice.

She will not throw herself blindfold into incompetent hands.

---

[1] Lord Cowper, Lord Lieutenant of Ireland.

Note by *Ponsonby* [1]

January 30, 1886

Lord Salisbury at Osborne resigned in the morning. The Queen sent me up at 5 to see him again. Saw Lord Salisbury who told me he had had telegram from the Queen wishing me to see Goschen so I had better do so. This was causing delay. But I had to obey. Lord Salisbury said that Gladstone had put forward no authorized plan and therefore as Queen had nothing before her to object to she must send for him. Went up to Portland Place — Goschen out. I sat with Mrs. Goschen till 12, when he came home. Agreed with me that delay was serious and attributed to Queen's absence. Advised me to see Gladstone at once. Went off to Carlton House Terrace. He was just going to bed.

I said to him that Lord Salisbury had resigned and the Queen wished to know if he could form a Government. She had doubts as he had so often expressed wish to retire. Gladstone asked if I had brought letter. I said no. He was satisfied with this verbal summons. He was grateful for consideration shown him on account of his age. Had the late Liberal Government remained in office — he would have retired. But matters had changed since then. In Lord Spencer's time Parnell would have accepted local Government. Now that policy of Lord Spencer had been discredited and Parnell wanted independent Parliament.

Situation was grave. His age might command respect and he would place his services at the Queen's disposal.

From *The Queen*

Osborne, Jan. 31, 1886

Could not Sir Henry cypher or telegraph to Mr. Gladstone that the Queen is anxious to hear something about his chances & proceedings *before tomorrow*? Also if any Household can be formed. People she is very anxious NOT to have again as *Lords* are : Ld Sudeley & Lord Wrothesley — both insufferable bores. They c^d get something else perhaps they take office when they know Mr. Gladstone's intentions. The Queen would like young Lord Camoys.

Note by *Ponsonby* (on letter from the Queen, January 28, 1886)

Osborne, Midnight

Rowton was sent for. He did not like coming and hoped it would be unnoticed. But it got into the papers. He asked

---

[1] See Sir H. Ponsonby's letter to the Queen, *Letters of Queen Victoria*, Third Series, vol. i, p. 27.

me what the Queen's views were. I said she abominated
the idea of sending for Gladstone and was angry with me for
saying that this was inevitable. He asked why not Hartington. I said Hartington himself would not like that as he
must decline to form a Government unless Gladstone had
already failed. Rowton agreed with me that Goschen
would not do. He told the Queen that he thought she must
send for Gladstone and must give him a free hand. She
thought I had said Hartington would not in any condition
join Gladstone. I explained that he would not in Irish
policy. If that were postponed I did not know what he
would do. The Queen wanted me to see him. But this was
given up. Lord Salisbury saw the Queen and resigned.
She could not accept it till she had new minister. In the
evening he sent cypher to Manners, his Private Secretary :
" Tell Goschen Queen will settle nothing till she has seen
him." I suppose to consult ?

Note by *Ponsonby* (on letter from the Queen,
February 1, 1886)

Osborne

Mr. Gladstone asked me not to send him unpleasant letters
at night as it prevented his sleeping. He was much put out
at the Queen's objection to Childers for War Office. Said
he was moderate man. Wouldn't hear of Harcourt for that
office. Queen wouldn't hear of Childers. I showed him in.

From *Edward Hamilton*

2 Feb. 1886

I do not like the outlook ; and greatly wish Mr. G. were out
of it altogether. I have not been able to keep my fingers out of
the political pie altogether ; and so have been giving him a
helping hand on the sly in starting ; but must now stand aside.

Mr. G. with whom I had a long conversation last night
seemed none the worse for his long journey. He was on the
whole pleased with his visit. The removal of the great
difficulty about Lord G. has been an incalculable relief to
Mr. G. I am afraid there will be plenty of other personal
difficulties. Chamberlain is certainly an infernal fellow to
deal with. I do not believe that there is anything lasting in
the Govt ; though what the alternative to it is I cannot see.

After the formation of the Government, Ponsonby wrote in a
letter to Horace Seymour, Private Secretary at Downing Street :

I can't conceive why Mr. Gladstone at his age tackled a
question which is too big a one for a statesman of 20. — I

hinted this to him delicately and he said it was exactly because he was an old man that he felt he could deal with the subject. Everyone was violent about it. But everyone would pay respect to age and to him.

Windsor Castle, March 8, 1886

I told the Queen last night that the feeling against the House of Lords was increasing and that some Reform must take place if the Institution was to remain.

She asked who wanted to touch it. I said Lord Elgin's brother — " Every one knows he is a radical " — Lord W. Compton — " He is the same " — Lord Wolmer — " Really ! I wonder what Lord Salisbury says " — Albert Grey — " Albert Grey ! Impossible " —

Today I talked to Lord Spencer at the Council. What makes me uncomfortable is that he does not seem keen. In all great reforms the leaders are always keen. Say those who want to abolish the H. of Lords such as Chamberlain and Dilke. They speak of the Reform as a great gain — an improvement. But those who talk of Home Rule talk more in the " What else can you do ? " tone.

Osborne, April 11, 1886

H.M. pines for news but of course things must go steadily. She says everyone is against the Bill. Well — no — though as yet very few except Irish have spoken for it.

I said " Irish representatives ". She jumped down my throat. " They are not Irish representatives. They don't represent the Irish people and Mr. Gladstone knows it for Mary [1] told him so." We must wait and see how the country takes it all. I want to hear the democracy speak. Lord Cowper is all very well — but we want to see what the working man thinks.

Osborne, April 18, 1886

I thought Spencer when he was here for the Council in much higher spirits about the Bill than he had been and bitter against Hartington for agitating against the Government. But his language was not that of affection for or confidence in the Irish Parliament. It was all " They'll find themselves much mistaken if they intend to do that ", " We can easily stop them doing so and so ". But he repeated that all depends on how they — the Irish — take it and he believes they like the scheme and will make it work harmoniously. I cannot help thinking he is over sanguine.

In the mean while the Queen who seems convinced —

---

[1] Lady Ponsonby.

more convinced than I am — that the Bill will not pass the second reading discusses naturally with much anxiety what is to happen if this Government is turned out and Whigs and Tories refuse to coalesce to form a Government. All I can say is that it is too early to talk of such matters yet — parties are dissolving and we don't know what course matters may take — and it is possible the present Government may mould the scheme into a more acceptable form.

The second reading of the Home Rule Bill was moved in the House of Commons on May 10. In the division on June 8 the Government was defeated by 343 votes against 313.

To *Edward Hamilton* (in reply to a long letter reviewing the situation)

St. James's Palace, May 26, 1886

I am much obliged to you for your letter which I had studied just before I had a disquisition with H.M. on the subject. She is dead against Home Rule as calamitous for Ireland, hazardous for England and tending towards separation but she says she is convinced Mr. Gladstone undertook the work from the highest motives and with the perfect belief he would settle the question and if he is right and she is wrong so much the better. She thinks that one of the misfortunes was — that you were not his private secretary when he undertook this work and that your more distant advice was therefore not so well listened to. I used some of your arguments to her but they had not much effect. Lord Spencer's advocacy for instance. What he said to her last year is still ringing in her ears — and now all his devils are angels — how can she be sure that in a month or two all his angels may not be devils again.

If it is such a good measure why are all the Government to drop it for a time ?

No one seems to like the measure. No one speaks of it with the enthusiasm which is excited by great reforms. Everyone is apologetic for it and intelligent people as the Attorney General [1] boasts are opposed to it including the Scotch nation and only excluding the present cabinet.

Notes from *The Queen*

Balmoral Castle, June 2, 1886

The news given by Sir Henry Ponsonby on Monday & Tuesday was very *welcome* & fortunately arrived before his very unsatisfactory acc[t] in his letter was rec[d].

[1] Sir Henry James.

It would be bad in every way if Mr. Gladstone withdrew the Bill. His baits for votes have done him harm & confirmed the opposition against him. Sir Henry sh^d tell him that after the defeat the Queen w^d expect Mr. Gladstone to send a Minister down if he is unequal to come himself, to report on what he intends to do. If he proposes Dissolution it must be immediate.

Balmoral, June 5, 1886

In case of the rejection of the 2nd Reading the Queen w^d wish to say that she does *not* wish the Minister to be sent to be either Ld Kimberley, Sir Wm Harcourt or Mr. Morley. The Chancellor or Ld Rosebery w^d be best or Mr. C. Bannerman.

June 9, 1886

. . . She is greatly relieved at the large majority against the Bill.

From *The Queen*

Balmoral, June 25, 1886

The Queen sends Sir Henry Ponsonby a strange letter from Mr. Gladstone whom she is very glad *not* to see as she *must* have expressed her g^t dissatisfaction at the way he *stumps* the country using violent language of abuse of his friends for their honourable & patriotic conduct. What a strong letter Mr. Bright has written !

The Queen also sends Mr. Gladstone's answer to her letter w^h Major Edwards sent him & the article in yesterday's *Scotsman* (which she has marked) which has had one of the same kind every day. She heard from private & very reliable sources from Edinburgh & Glasgow — that Mr. Gladstone's receptions were organized that no one one knows were at his meetings & that the mobs were of the lowest description — It is grievous to see a man of his age behave as he does & lower himself to an ordinary demagogue which is what the late Sir C. Trevelyan called him in speaking of him to the Duke of Argyll. If he could only be stopped !

This was conveyed to Mr. Gladstone in what is described as " a gracious and frank letter from Balmoral " (Morley's *Life*, vol. iii, p. 344).

From *The Queen* (on newspaper report of Mr. Gladstone's speeches and messages at the Elections)

Windsor, July 6, 1886

This is so monstrous & wicked that the Queen wishes Sir Henry to try & see some one who can speak the truth to Mr.

Gladstone. He is trying to revolutionize the country & to
ruin his own reputation. He has done incalculable mischief
in (. . .) & Mr. Goschen's defeat is very serious. Still the
Unionists are double the number of Gladstonians & have
had an addition of 5 more clear gains today.

Sir C. Dilke's defeat is a subject of gr^t rejoicing.

From *The Queen*

Windsor Castle, July 17, 1886

Has Sir Henry read this *new* Letter of Mr. Gladstone's ?

It is really too disgraceful & so untrue ! The article in
The Times is one of the strongest the Queen must think ever
written against a Prime Minister & quite true. This is very
painful for the *Sovereign* to have a Minister who can be spoken
of in the leading papers in this way.

Osborne, July 31, 1886

There can be no doubt that a conversation with Gladstone
is interesting and I am sorry mine was cut short yesterday.
He asked me to walk with him down to his boat but just as
we started the Queen sent for me. I therefore ordered his
carriage to take him and walked to meet it, only a few
minutes. He began at once : " Now about Ireland — I
cannot for the life of me see that any other plan generally
speaking is practicable besides that which we put forward."
I observed, " and which was rejected because it gave Ireland
an existence separate from England." " Good heavens no
— in what way ? " I replied, " It gave Ireland a Parliament—— " He interrupted, " A Statutory Parliament for
the management of her own affairs." I said " But co-equal
so far, with the Parliament of Westminster." He interjected,
" Not co-equal. The power of all the Governments possible
could not create a co-equal Parliament." But I remonstrated,
" You destroyed the Imperial Parliament — the Governing
body of the United 3 Kingdoms." " No, no, no, a hundred
times no. The Imperial Parliament remained in complete
enjoyment of all its powers. (Footman : ' Carriage is ready.')
Yes — yes, I tell you of all its imperial power." " Minus," I
shrieked, " of the independent Irish Government." " It
wasn't to be independent in that sense. (Footman : ' Time
you should be starting.' ' Yes, Yes.') No, I say if there had
been a repeal of the Union, a restoration of Grattan's Parliament (pushed in to the carriage by the footman) that might
have been an independent Parliament — but what we
demand is a Statutory body for the management of Irish
affairs alone which we have failed to manage from West-

minster and this is what ——" Most of this was spoken to me out of the carriage window near the box of the policeman who stood in awe, and the speech was cut short by the carriage driving off. Most unfortunate : I think I was getting the best of it. I rushed to the Queen who told me of her interview with him which as they avoided the Irish question was most amicable.

From *The Queen* (Sir Henry asks leave to go to London)

Windsor, Feb. 22, '87

Certainly & try & see your *friend* Sir Wᵐ Harcourt who does nothing but make himself disagreeable. But foreign politics are really too dangerous to be trifled with.

In 1892 the question of Home Rule came to the front again on the eve of Mr. Gladstone's return to office when he became Prime Minister for the fourth time at the age of eighty-two. The Bill was introduced in the House of Commons, passed its Second Reading by a majority of 43 and on Third Reading was carried by a majority of 34. When it reached the House of Lords it was rejected by a majority of no less than 368 (41 for, 419 against). Mr. Gladstone favoured an immediate dissolution but his colleagues disagreed. Some agitation consequently arose against the House of Lords.

From *The Queen*

Oct. 8, 1891

The Queen deeply deplores Mr. Smith's [1] loss which is a very serious one, but he cᵈ never have continued to lead the House of Commons, that was certain ; but no one expected that we shᵈ lose him all together & his advice now wᵈ have been invaluable even if he cᵈ not hold active office.

He was so good, so honest, so amiable & of such a modest & unselfish character that every one respected him. He died from devotion to his work.

What a startling event is Mr. Parnell's death ! But what a contrast ! *He* was a really bad & worthless man who had to answer for many lives lost in Ireland.

There is a note of a dinner party on June 3, 1888, at which Home Rule was discussed :

Dined with Rosebery. The Prince of Wales, Prince G. of Mecklenburg, Lord Spencer, Fife, Randolph Churchill,

---

[1] W. H. Smith, 1st Lord of the Treasury and Leader of the House of Commons. His widow was raised to the peerage as Viscountess Hambleden.

John Morley, F. Knollys, Mr. Spring-Rice, C. Sykes, Sir Charles Russell and Lord W. Beresford. Sir C. Russell [1] spoke strongly about Home Rule, like a lawyer, and said that Parnell and Dillon were Tories at heart and that if they had Home Rule the representation would be changed and improved. He objected to a superior West[r] Parliament because all bills would then be liable to be thrown out by the H. of Lords, but if bills came in the usual way they could only be rejected by the Govt. which represented the H. of Commons. Same view was uttered by J. Morley who objected to the central Parl[t], but Spencer and Rosebery were rather in favour of it and said the liberal party insisted on it and therefore it must be. Morley admitted this but feared the Irish members w[d], if any of their measures were rejected, come over and turn out the English Government on some side issue. Sir C. Russell thought that Lord Spencer w[d] be the head of the liberal party when Gladstone retired. . . . Lord William Beresford, fresh from India, told me that Lord Dufferin was the pleasantest Viceroy he had ever served under, that D[r] T. was the damnedest snob in India and that the Duke of Connaught was a really very good officer. Mr. Spring-Rice [2] fresh from Washington said Mr. Chamberlain devoted himself to the ladies when out there on his Fishery Commission, first a Miss Grant and then Miss Endicott daughter of the Secretary of War, one of the oldest New England families. He believed they were engaged. But as Chamberlain, tho' personally popular, was condemned by the Irish for his political views, the announcement of his marriage might influence the Presidential election by turning the Irish vote against the government !

At the beginning of 1892 the Queen again became apprehensive at the prospect of the return of a Liberal government.

From *The Queen*

Balmoral, May 20, 1892

The Queen is sorry to say that the Dissolution is to take place at the end of next month for the reasons given by Lord Salisbury in this letter. . . .

The Queen is therefore more than ever anxious that *some* of her views sh[d] be known to those who may attempt to form a Gov[t] so that there is no mistake on those subjects. First of all however she must say how dreadfully disappointed

---

[1] Attorney General in 1886, subsequently (1894) Lord Russell of Killowen, Lord Chief Justice.

[2] Later Sir Cecil Spring-Rice, appointed in 1912 Ambassador at Washington.

& shocked she is at Ld Rosebery's speech which is radical to a degree to be almost communistic. Hitherto he always said he had nothing whatever to do with Home Rule & only with F. affairs & now he is as violent as anyone. Poor Lady Rosebery is not there to keep him back. Sir Henry must try & get at him through someone so that he may know how grieved the Queen is at what he has said . . . after the Gov^t defeat the Queen meant to send for him 1st but after this violent attack on Lord Salisbury, this attempt to stir up Ireland, it will be *impossible*. And the G.O.M. at 82 is a *very alarming lookout*. The points she mentioned to Sir Henry already are the C. in Chief must not & cannot be thought of & *Egypt* cannot be evacuated. Then that she positively refuses to take either Sir C. Dilke or that equally horrid Mr. Labouchere. To them however she must add Ld Ripon *not to have anything to do with India*. . . . She hopes they will not change Ld Lansdowne tho' he may refuse to serve under a Home Rule Gov^t but he ought to be asked to remain. Ld Carrington whom the Queen has heard mentioned w^d be totally out of the question since his speech.

If as they seem to be doing, Home Rule is — contrary to all expectations to be brought to the front — the Opposition are at once doing what they can to bring about a Civil war & to commence with divisions & difficulties in their own ranks. In short the Queen does not see how they can form. Anyhow the Queen foresees a g^t deal of trouble. But her views sh^d be known. She thinks sometimes it will come to Sir Wm Harcourt being sent for ! ! ! But he w^d command neither respect nor confidence.

From *The Queen*

Balmoral, June 1, 1892

The Queen has rec^d Sir Henry Ponsonby's answer [1] to her letter which she considers unsatisfactory. She said positively to Sir Henry that it be known that *she* would *never* allow such horrid men to enter the Gov^t as Sir C. Dilke & Mr. Labouchere — not that the *position* of the one was not yet known & the other w^d refuse ! — That is not the right way of putting it. But the Queen & many *still hope* the Queen *& the Country* may not be exposed to such a misfortune as to be in the hands of *such* dangerous & reckless people as Mr. Gladstone & his crew.

Better say nothing more if Sir Henry does not speak more positively. But it might appear as though the Queen

---

[1] Printed in *Letters of Queen Victoria*, Third Series, vol. ii, p. 121.

anticipated a change which she really begins to hope may not be the case.

From The Queen

Balmoral, June 4, 1892

. . . Should the time unfortunately arise for such a contingency [change of Government] Sir Henry will have to act on what he knows to be the Queen's views & she *will* be firm in her conditions.

Independent of the real misfortune for the country & Europe, the idea of a deluded excited man of 82 trying to govern England & her vast Empire with the miserable democrats under him is quite ludicrous. It is like a bad joke !

From The Queen

Windsor, July 13, 1892

The Queen, as Sir Henry will easily believe, is much distressed at the prospect of all the trouble & g^t anxiety for the *safety* of the *country* & Empire w^h these most unfortunate Elections have brought ab^t. . . . *Till* yesterday all pointed to a small majority but this has changed. Mr. Gladstone's majority being reduced by 4000 is very cheering.

Tho' she supposes she will have that dangerous old fanatic thrust down her throat — she thinks she w^d like to see Ld Rosebery 1st when the time comes, as she must have security for F. A. & she thinks Sir H. who knows all these people well c^d in an indirect manner let him & others know that the Queen will *resist any* attempt to change the foreign policy, any attempts to abandon our obligations towards Egypt & any truckling to France or Russia or giving in to any attempt of these 2 Powers to frighten or bully us. . . .

. . . The Queen mentions the necessity for *some* understanding *beforehand*, as before Sir R. Peel came in, in 41 — some time before Mr. Anson communicated with Sir R. Peel & Baron Stockmar did — & also Genl Grey in 1868 (the Queen thinks it was) with Mr. Gladstone. . . .

The Queen writes again in the same strain (Osborne, July 23, 1892) saying the Government are " greedy place seekers who are republicans at heart ". She adds :

In former times when there were changes of Gov^t, tho' often painful to part with those she liked & esteemed, it was to have to do with gentlemen like Ld Russell, Ld Palmerston, Sir R. Peel, Ld Aberdeen, Ld Grey, etc. But now it is with utter disgust that the Queen thinks of it. To *support* them is impossible for her. Her hand is forced.

She ends by saying she " is glad that Mr. Gladstone is determined about his Home Rule as this is sure to bring him into
great difficulties ".

From *The Queen*

Osborne, July 26, 1892

The Queen c^d not *personally* communicate with L^d
Rosebery but indirectly something might be done through
the P. of Wales. He *must* be Foreign Minister.

The Queen cannot make up her mind to send at once
for that dreadful old man (not because she has any personal
dislike to him) as she utterly loathes his very dangerous
politics, the language he has held, the way in which he has
used every artifice to get in & whom she can neither respect
or trust.

In '80 she sent for Ld Hartington & Ld Granville. Why
not send for Ld Rosebery or some other person ? She will
resist taking him to the *last*. In 1846 after Ld Melbourne
had been ill, the Queen wrote to him saying she w^d have
asked him to form a Gov^t but that she did not on acc^t of his
health. She might write to Mr. Gladstone leaving the option
of his not accepting on acc^t of the gr^t fatigue of the position
at his age. He might decline.

One must not be *quite* sure either of the present Gov^t
being beaten or at least in *what way* & how Mr. G.'s " united
majority " will behave.

In a further letter of the same nature in the following month
she refers to a letter from Mr. Gladstone which " ought to be
kept in a glass case ".

From *The Queen*

Osborne, Aug. 10, 1892

. . . Sir Henry will if necessary & if an opportunity offers
say the Queen will *insist* on Ld Rosebery as M. for F. A. also
on Mr. Campbell Bannerman for the War Office & L^d
Kimberley for India which he understands.

Sir Henry may say that Ld Rosebery is necessary to quiet
the alarm of the F. Powers who are beginning to intrigue
right & left ag^st us & Sir Henry may foreshadow that Mr.
G. will find the Queen very determined & firm on *all* that
concerns the *honour, dignity & safety* of the *Vast Empire* confided
to her care & w^h she wishes to hand down unimpaired to her
children & their children's children.

From *The Queen*

Osborne, Aug. 10, 1892

The Queen forgot in her letter to say that the Peerage (an Earldom) might be mentioned as a means of enabling him [Mr. Gladstone] to go on w^h he cannot if he remains in the H. of C. as Prime Minister & Leader.

Later in the year, on November 20, Ponsonby in a letter to his wife gives an account of the Queen's correspondence with Gladstone :

Windsor Castle, November 20, 1892

. . . I think I told you that H.M. wanted to have the last word with Gladstone after his memo. I wrote it, on the lines she gave me. I should have preferred silence. But however she wrote what I suggested but seasoned with plenty of mustard and pepper. He answered at once in three sheets — an excellent answer, much more clear than any I have seen. She said that he told her the class she usually saw were very imperfectly acquainted with the views of H.M. Government on Ireland. She replied that this was true and further she could not find any class or person in Great Britain who could say what was meant by Home Rule. And to threaten the House of Peers with some dreadful punishment if they did not agree to what he himself said they did not understand was absurd. He replied that no measure has ever been proposed which has been more completely explained than Home Rule. Broadly speaking it is explained in the bill of 1886 which " has not been altered or modified ". But an addition has been made in the retention of the Irish representation in Westminster (not modified !). The Queen quoted his first letter that " Home Rule was a conservative measure and did not infringe the Act of Union " and says that is all she knows from him about it — and she doesn't understand it. He replies that it is conservative in the sense of restoring peace and making people contented and that as the Imperial Parliament is not destroyed the Act of Union is not infringed. He said in his Memo that the Unionists would not believe the Irish representatives and would not trust them with the same liberties as the British. The Queen observed that the Unionists did believe the Irish Representatives who declared they wanted Separation and it was Mr. Gladstone who disbelieved them — and that as to some liberties she asked how did this come out in the Evicted Tenants Commission where the conduct of the Commission was not what Englishmen call fair play. He replied that the Irish have never spoken of Separation since 1886 — and about Judge Matthew he will ask Mr. Morley. The concluding paragraph of his letter made me laugh : " Mr. Gladstone cannot conclude without thanking Your Majesty for the frankness of Your Majesty's letter, which is the greatest kindness of Your Majesty's exposition ". . . .

From *Lord Houghton* [1] (Lord-Lieutenant of Ireland)

The Castle, Dublin, Feb. 9, '93

The first Levée and Drawing Room of the Dublin season were held on Tuesday and yesterday : the Queen may, I think, wish to hear some account of the two ceremonies.

The Levée was largely attended, nearly 700 people being present. Most of these were official or military, but I am glad to say that a fair proportion of Dublin people were there, many of them Unionists in politics.

All Her Majesty's judges who were in Ireland attended, except the Lord Chief Justice, Sir Peter O'Brien, who not only absented himself, but, as I am told on good authority, did his best to induce others to stay away. This appears to me to show such marked disrespect towards the office of Viceroy, and to be conduct so improper in one holding his high position, that I am compelled formally to bring it to H.M.'s notice.

The most notable feature, of course, was the prearranged absence of the landed class — with very few exceptions. I confess I do not understand the position taken up by these gentlemen, some of whom have told me in private that they would like to come, and think they ought to come, but that they are afraid of their followers.

Consequently, with perhaps less excuse, they follow the bad example set by the Nationalist party, many of whom, but for the same poor reason, would certainly pay their respects to H.M.'s representative.

Of course I make no complaint of any unwillingness to accept invitations to my parties — even the State entertainments. Those who do not wish to accept the hospitality of a political opponent must use their own discretion. Such a sentiment is happily almost outside one's English experience, but it clearly is one which people are entitled to hold. I can only say that I do not hold it myself and that I should be very glad, myself, to see them.

But these ladies and gentlemen could quite well have attended the Levée and Drawing Room and stayed away from the Dinners and Balls, if their principles impelled them to do so.

[1] Afterwards Marquess of Crewe.

I understand that those of them who are in the habit of going to London now say that it is sufficient to attend a Levée or Drawing Room there. But this is surely not the case. The ceremonies are held in Ireland for Irish people, who are expected to attend them. And attendance in London does not affect the obligation.

In fact, if these gentlemen's argument is sound its converse must be sound as well ; and one must assume that they attended Lord Londonderry's and Lord Zetland's Levées not out of respect of H.M., as would be supposed, but as an act of attention to a political ally.

What I have stated as to the Levée and the absence of the landowners applies also generally to the attendance at the Drawing Room yesterday. About 580 people attended, as against about 680 at Lord Z.'s first Drawing Room last year.

In reference to what I ventured to call the mistaken attitude of these gentlemen, I am specially anxious to assure H.M. that personally I have done my best to keep the Viceroyalty clear from party politics. For instance, though I was in London at the opening of Parliament, I did not attend the H. of L., not wishing to take any part in the opening debate, though direct attacks were made upon acts of administration for which I share the responsibility.

To *Lord Houghton*

Osborne, February 13, 1893

I gave your letter to the Queen and have only just got it back with rather a mixed expression of opinion on your observations. I think Her Majesty entirely agrees with you in thinking it uncivil that the Irish Gentry should abstain from going to your Court when you are officially representing the Queen, but then she added you were a Member of her Government and consequently a political representative, and attendance at your levées used to be considered in Ireland as a mark of support to the measures of the Government.

It certainly was a very strong measure for the Chief Justice to absent himself and I should have thought that even among political partisans this would scarcely have been approved. Still you appear to have had a large assemblage.

. . . Of course it is nothing new that the opponents of the Lord Lieutenant's policy will not go to his Court — though I think they are wrong. I believe Lord Normanby's levée was the smallest ever seen. But that is ancient history and the new era which is to open tonight will amend all this — ?

To *Lord Houghton*

Balmoral, September 2, 1893

I gave your letter to the Queen.

I do not reveal the names of my correspondents among the Gladstonian peers but all — that is not many — express delight at being saved from speaking on Home Rule and do not show any enthusiasm at the prospect of voting.

The Commoners are more cautious but by no means enthusiastic. I am anxious to find a hearty Home Ruler but, except Mr. Gladstone, he is not easy to find.

However these are things one must not write to a Lord Lieutenant but you are now on leave.

From *The Queen*

Windsor, March 12, 1894

The Queen is very much displeased with Ld Rosebery's allusion to the House of L^ds in his speech this morn^g which was not in " the Program ". She hopes Sir Henry will tell him so & Sir Wm Harcourt's speech is very republican. The Sovereign is nowhere and must be abolished *next*. But they *cannot* abolish the House of L^ds *one* of the 3 components of the Constitution so much wanted.

The only good thing in Ld R.'s speech is the omission of all allusion to the Scotch Church. The Queen ans^d the letter she rec^d from Ld Rosebery this m^g in answer to the Note she wrote him last night of w^h she encloses a very rough copy.

It is degrading to be the so called Sovereign when such desperate Radicals are in Power. Lord Clarendon used to say the Liberals' creed is Party 1st then the country & the Sovereign & so it is always she grieves to say.

On March 3, 1894, Mr. Gladstone had retired and Lord Rosebery succeeded him as Prime Minister. It may be noted that the Queen personally made her peace with Ireland by her visit to Dublin in 1900, the last year of her reign, when she received a gratifying and enthusiastic reception. Her Private Secretary was not there to hear her impressions. Although six years his senior his aged royal mistress outlived him by five years.

CHAPTER XI

Egypt

To the military measures which were adopted in Egypt in the early eighties the Queen paid very close attention, the failures as well as successes. Her letters show her indignation at the indecision of the Government and at not being fully informed.

As a preliminary there is a letter from Evelyn Baring which shows by its date that he was, at the time he wrote it, British Commissioner of the Egyptian Public Debt Office. His conspicuous talents in the duties he had to discharge in this capacity led to his appointment in 1883 as Agent and Consul-General after an interval in India :

Cairo, Dec. 29, 1879

You may like to know how things are getting on here.

There is a decided change for the better and I am more sanguine of being able to put matters straight than I was when I left England. The new Khedive is a very decided improvement on his father. He is perhaps not quite so *sharp*, but infinitely more honest and he has plenty of common-sense. I see a great deal of him and like him very much. He has chosen the best Ministry the country can produce and I really think that both the Khedive and the Ministers understand the fact — so fatally unappreciated at Constantinople — that they must set their house in order for that in the long run their existence depends on their good behaviour.

In point of fact the Turk with an Arab element in him is a much easier creature to deal with than the Turk pure and simple. With the former it is perhaps possible to do something. The latter is to my mind a Humpty-Dumpty, so utterly degenerate that no Asia Minor Conventions or anything else will ever put him on to the wall again.

The French are working very cordially with us and I see no present reason why the Government policy should not turn out successful here. They sadly want a success somewhere.

A brief preliminary epitome of events in the period covered

by the letters may be given as a framework into which they can be fitted.

Egypt was under the suzerainty of the Sultan and controlled by an agreement between Britain and France. In 1882 a revolt broke out under Arabi, the leader of the Egyptian nationalists whose cry was " Egypt for the Egyptians ". Britain took action alone. Alexandria was bombarded and Arabi driven from the coast. Sir Garnet Wolseley was sent out and Arabi was defeated at Tel-el-Kebir. A peerage was conferred on Wolseley and Sir Evelyn Wood was appointed Sirdar (Commander-in-Chief) of the Egyptian Army. In 1883 Evelyn Baring became Agent and Consul-General. In the following year the Mahdi, a fanatical " prophet ", gained power and instigated an insurrection in the Soudan, leading his Arab followers against the Egyptian garrisons. There were deliberations as to the best method of relieving the garrisons and it was decided, not without some hesitation, that General Gordon should be appointed by the Khedive as Governor-General of the Soudan. He took up his residence in Khartoum. In 1885 the situation was more serious and Wolseley was sent out again to Egypt. After vacillations in policy and delays in action a force was sent to the south to relieve Gordon and the garrison in Khartoum. The relief came too late. Khartoum fell and Gordon was killed. There was great indignation in public opinion and in Parliament at home and the Queen expressed herself forcibly. The question of the continuance of the campaign in the Soudan against Osman Digna, the Mahdi's chief lieutenant, became a matter of dispute. The final decision was to evacuate the Soudan. Not till 1898 was the destruction of Mahdism accomplished after the victory at Omdurman.

In guiding the Queen Ponsonby found himself confused by different and contradictory reports as well as by rumours of jealousy among the commanding officers. At first the Queen was not inclined to be favourable to Sir Garnet Wolseley, but later her attitude towards him completely changed. Ponsonby, after hearing many reports of the General and having had an opportunity of meeting him, wrote the following impression of Wolseley in one of his daily letters :

He does not inspire any love among those who serve under him though I think they have confidence in him and I

believe his staff like him. He knows a good man and selects
him and throws over all other considerations therefore his
staff are excellent soldiers. He has a talent for organization
and energy to carry it through. He thoroughly believes in
himself and this makes others believe in him and above all
he is a lucky General. Of course this last qualification is
fanciful but it is a useful fancy and has always backed him —
though his enemies use it against him as much as his friends.
He is hard and very likely unfeeling but this is useful if unpleasant in a general and he has a power of writing capital
letters which please the receivers.

To *General Sir Garnet Wolseley*

Osborne, August 25, 1882
Although the Queen had heard the good news of your
restoration to health, by telegraph, she was also glad to
receive the assurance of it in your letter which I gave her
yesterday. You will have got my telegram asking you to
write and telegraph direct to her as the Queen likes letters
from you straight without any intervention.

We are surprised and delighted at the perfect success
of your plans which have been accomplished with so little
loss — but I can understand your desire not to allow the
least check to occur which would encourage the rebel
Egyptians. Your utilization of the correspondents was a
bold stroke which created some misgivings in the press and
an inclination to abuse you — but nothing is so successful as
success and the ill-humour vanished when you appeared
suddenly at Ismailia instead of Aboukir as they had announced.

I need scarcely say that the Queen is very much pleased
with the progress of the Campaign and with the vigorous
manner in which you acted at once, the moment you arrived
in Egypt.

A very short letter occasionally written to the Queen will
please her quite as much as a long one for which you will
never find time.

From *General Sir Garnet Wolseley*

Cairo, 27th September, 1882
Many thanks for your kind note of congratulation which
reached me this morning.

I have heard from home that I am wanted there to resume
my duties so I expect to reach England about the end of
next month to reoccupy my chair at the Horse Guards. I

prefer a saddle, even in the desert, to the best of chairs in peace : but peace has its triumphs, and I think this war has shown that the much run down British Soldier is as good now as he has ever been at any period of our history. I never doubted it, and I hope that those who insisted upon believing in his deterioration will now be silenced. No men could behave better than the men are now doing. As the Judge Advocate said to me yesterday, their conduct is so good, that he has nothing to do. Facts speak for themselves.

To *The Queen*

Balmoral, September 8, 1882

General Sir Henry Ponsonby humbly begs leave to enclose Lord Dufferin's 393 (which evidently is the same as that referred to by Mr. Gladstone) but he does not quite see how it answers Your Majesty's enquiry as to whether the Government will still trust the Sultan and accept his troops.

Lord Dufferin [1] distinctly advises the acceptance of the Convention and the troops. The Khedive protests against the Troops. Does Your Majesty's Government intend to accept Lord Dufferin's advice and throw over the Khedive or support the Khedive ?

This he thinks is the question Your Majesty wishes to have decided.

Note by *The Queen* on above

Yes. Put it *plainly — strongly & ask* for an *answer*. The Queen is half distracted ab^t it & this trifling with her question won't do. Put it very strongly.

The Queen's emphasis and reiteration in this note would seem to be an instance of her suspicion that her Private Secretary was apt to water her strong wine. It is true that he was sometimes anxious that the violence of her expressions should not be mistaken for an exhibition of mere petulance on her part. But when she was on strong ground, he always gave her full support.

From *Sir Evelyn Baring*

Cairo, Jan 14, 1884

Many thanks for your letter of the 5th. I hope you will take an opportunity of expressing to H.M. my most respectful and grateful thanks for helping me in the way of getting quick answers — not that I really have much to complain of — for no one could be more kind and considerate than

---

[1] Ambassador to Turkey then resident in Cairo.

Lord Granville, and, moreover, I know that my questions have occasionally been very disagreeable — but it is of no use shirking the facts because they are unpleasant, and of course the more rapidly I get answers the better I am pleased.

I have not written to you much as I scarcely have a moment's leisure and, moreover, Evelyn Wood keeps H.M. informed. He is a very good authority, and I congratulate myself on his being here. He has all the qualities necessary for a delicate position — especially he keeps a cool head, which is a great point.

I got over my ministerial crisis better than I expected. I thought at one time that a combination was going to be formed to prevent any Ministry taking office, with the view of putting us in a difficulty. But I let it be known that I was quite prepared for any emergency, and this produced the desired effect. In case of necessity I had quite made up my mind to go down to Chérif's office and provisionally to take in hand the direction of affairs myself, but fortunately no such necessity arose.

In some respects I am sorry to get rid of Chérif,[1] as I like him. He is honest and a gentleman. I annoyed the society of Cairo by giving a great dinner in his honor immediately after he resigned. The common practice in the East is to worship the rising rather than the setting sun.

Nubar is much more clever, and on that account a more satisfactory man of business to deal with. He is just now in a state of great nervous excitement, and I am not sure whether he will have the moral courage to withstand the inevitable unpopularity which will attend many of his measures.

Having now decided what to do, the next thing is to do it. The withdrawal from Khartoum &c. is an exceedingly difficult operation. If we bring away the soldiers, civilians, women and children, without a disaster, we may think ourselves lucky. We must do our best.

The financial difficulties will ultimately be very great indeed, — but they must be faced. An undue optimism — which has generally prevailed ever since I have been concerned in Egyptian affairs (now some 7 years) — is to be deprecated.

As to whether the present arrangements will last, I cannot say — I should myself have been inclined to have had some Englishmen in the Ministry, as I doubt if the policy of dummy Ministers advised by Englishmen can stand the

[1] Prime Minister.

strain now being put on it. But there were, no doubt, many objections to the adoption of this course. Anyhow I will do my best to work the coach on the present basis. . . .

The next letter from the Sirdar of the Egyptian Army, although long must be given practically in full because it contains an admirably comprehensive survey of the situation in Egypt at that moment. Moreover it shows how Ponsonby was able to get important information from the man on the spot failing full reports from Ministers at home.

From *General Sir Evelyn Wood*

Ministère de la Guerre, Le Caire

February 1st, 1884

I can well understand all the perplexities of the Gordon appointment having felt them myself, but for two and a half months about I have been trying to persuade Sir Evelyn Baring to press his appointment. Nevertheless I feel all the difficulties which may arise, and Baring shakes his fist at me whenever my favourite runs off the rails. This he does often. The Pachas all hate Gordon — 1stly because he killed or degraded they say all the principal Chiefs in the Sudan — it is right to add they were also the principal slave owners — and dealers — 2ndly because he steadily declined to cover the merciless exactions of Egyptian officials, and continually snubbed the Cairo Government. To take one instance — they wished to employ in the Sudan a man whom Gordon disliked. Three times this man was appointed and sent to Khartoum. Three times did Gordon decline to receive him, and send him back.

Baring's doubt of Gordon Pacha's appointment comes from the impossibility of inducing him to carry out any policy of which he does not approve. This arises from a very noble frame of mind, but it is obviously a drawback. Less so in this instance for Gordon virtually drafted his own instructions.

When I start by saying I regard Gordon as the grandest character in 1884, you will not I hope misunderstand my stating I think his heart is better than his head. Either because he takes his inspirations from the Bible, and applies them literally to daily life ; or because there is some want of fixity of purpose in his mind ; he is occasionally ludicrously inconsistent. For example — on Thursday, i.e. yesterday week, he showed me in the steam launch between Port Said and Ismailia a powerfully written memorandum against the idea of telling Zebehr Pacha to go back to the Sudan — he advocated his detention in Cyprus. He enforced his written arguments with vigour. Imagine my astonishment when in Council on Friday he expressed a wish that Zebehr might accompany him to the Sudan. Gordon has many black friends here, and I received a message from the black man whom Gordon most trusts begging me to use my influence to keep Zebehr here, as his return to the Sudan would make Gordon's death a certainty, probably by poison. Again Gordon as you say, distrusts the Khedive — and says he is a wretched creature. Yet Gordon was vexed with me for stating he should nominate the man to be restored to Darfour out of the many ex-Sultans in stock at Cairo. Gordon exclaimed — " Why ! you deprive the Khedive of his prerogatives." I observed the Khedive probably neither knew nor cared anything about them. This is accurate. He chose a boy of 18 — with 42 wives and a confirmed taste for gin ! Now we are assured there is an equally legitimate candidate 30 years of age — and a man with less female encumbrance, and more abilities. Gordon moreover has telegraphed his companion, the youthful monarch having taken to drinking, Baring should not listen to anything he says.

Still with all these drawbacks Gordon stands out in my mind as the Bayard of the 19th Century, and I rejoice in his being *en route* for Khartoum.

I will now talk a little about Sir Evelyn Baring with whom I have been intimately associated for three months. He is I think one of the biggest men now serving the Queen's Government — clever — patient and determined — *il ira loin* as our French friends say. I see some of the papers write he should have kept the Sudan withdrawal policy a secret — ! It would be as reasonable to blame a man for not concealing a diamond or gold field discovery. Each Pacha tells his wife or wives all that goes on in Council, so far as I can judge. To my direct knowledge Ministers and H.H. the Khedive talk most freely with newspaper correspondents. The Chérif Ministry resigned on the Sudan abandonment question, and Nubar came into office pledged to carry out the withdrawal. How all this was to be concealed, it would puzzle any one to say.

It may be imputed to Baring, that had he forced on a Ministerial crisis early in December, he would have given the Sudan garrisons a better chance of escape. This is so — but then on the other hand the English Government has hitherto tried hard to fulfil its avowed policy of letting the Egyptians govern themselves, and 'tis only now that the Queen's Government has begun to comprehend the utter

incapacity of the Pachas. So long as it was possible to keep
Chérif in office, it seems to me that to carry out the former
policy Baring was right to avoid a rupture — Chérif is very
indolent — easy going — not wanting in ability, and very
honest. He carries more weight than a dozen Nubars,
because the latter is *novus homo* and a Christian. Lord
Dufferin made much of Chérif and as long as he was here,
Chérif was sufficiently pliable for the English purpose.
When Lord Dufferin left Chérif came daily more under the
influence of Tigrane Pacha, Nubar's nephew, and like his
uncle a Christian. Tigrane was born in Armenia? — educated in Paris — cannot write, or even speak but a few words
of Arabic — is about 35 years of age — clever — industrious
and ambitious : in his position of Under Secretary for
Foreign Affairs he acquired really a knowledge of all the
Minister's work. With this knowledge, came Power — and
although possibly Tigrane never formulated his ideas, yet
he pictured to himself I believe, a time when he would be
Prime Minister, and persuaded himself that the English
should devote men and money to reconquering the Sudan
for Egypt. Tigrane encouraged Chérif in resisting Sir E.
Baring. He was I believe the author of the silly threat of
giving up the Red Sea littoral, believing it would bring Lord
Granville down at once.

Tigrane was greatly astonished at the result. Sir Evelyn
Baring has discussed with General Stevenson and me every
possible scheme for sending armed assistance to the Sudan
to aid the retreating garrisons.

. . . The numbers under English officers available were
about 2000 Infantry, and 300 Cavalry. All the non-
commissioned officers and soldiers have been enlisted since
February 1883.

The English officers are very eager to take their Egyptian
soldiers into action, but when I put this question — " Are
you confident of ensuring the success bearing in mind we
do not object to any risk of your lives, but we must not risk
a disaster ? " they all including their brigadier, answered
" No — we are not confident, and however anxious we are
to have a fight, we should like to have a backing of English
soldiers at hand." I do not however feel any doubts as to
the soldiers' loyalty to their English officers. They will I
think remain true as long as the Khedive is true to us. The
Egyptian officer-ed brigade is not worth its cost ; but then
on the other hand it offers the only road to promotion for
Egyptians, and they may resent our breaking it up.

The fears of a popular rising are in my opinion unfounded.
Nearly all rebellions or even disturbances in Egypt originate

from the ruling class. Just now we English are the men in possession.

I have written at length because I think you may like to hear what I think. I cannot affirm I am accurate but I try to be.

The decision to appoint Gordon to go to the Soudan in 1884 to relieve the Egyptian garrison was received in some quarters with considerable doubt, as this letter shows. But the Queen approved when she received the following telegram from Lord Granville of which this is the rough draft :

Baring having now expressed wish to have Chinese G.[ordon] [1] I have assumed Y.M. will approve his proceeding to Egypt. He starts tonight accompanied by Col. Stuart (? Herbert S.) with instructions to report on general military situation in the Soudan or measures for the security of Egypt^n Garrisons and European populations at Khartoum ; on best mode of evacuating interior and of securing safe and good administration of sea coast by Egypt^n Govt. also as to steps to counteract slave trade. He is to be under Baring's instructions and to perform such other duties as may be entrusted to him by Egypt^n Govt : thro' Baring. He will place himself in communication with Baring who will probably meet him at Ismailia and concert with him whether he should proceed to Suakin or go on himself or despatch Stuart to Khartoum up Nile.

Note by *The Queen* on above

Osborne

This is good news — but I only hope it is not *too late* ! The news Reuter sends is very bad.

Please cypher to Lord Granville Much relieved to hear Chinese Gordon is going to Egypt. May it not be too late ! Trust he will be put in communication with Sir E. Wood who commands the Egyptian Army.

The failure to relieve Khartoum and the death of Gordon very naturally produced a public outburst of indignation. The Queen was so much overcome that she sent a telegram *en clair* to Gladstone which he regarded as a public censure on his Government. Ponsonby drafted a letter to Edward Hamilton explaining the Queen's feelings. He submitted it to her and further strengthened it on receiving her note on his draft. His letter is printed in the *Letters of Queen Victoria*. But we can

[1] Nickname given to Gordon because of his services in China (1860–1865).

give here the Queen's original note. Her reference to " Mary P." arose from the fact that Lady Ponsonby shared to the full the Queen's exasperation.

The first announcement of the disaster reached Lady Ponsonby in a dramatic way. She was sitting after breakfast with her two daughters in the drawing-room of Osborne Cottage which adjoined the royal grounds of Osborne House. Voices in the hall made it clear that someone had arrived at this unusual hour. The door opened and in came the Queen unattended and unannounced. Standing and without any preliminaries she simply said : " Khartoum has fallen. Gordon is dead."

In one of the few letters of Mary Ponsonby's which remain the following sentence occurs on the Egyptian campaign : " We lose splendid men and brilliant officers, and we come away without having saved one garrison or effected one single purpose unless the slaughtering of some thousands of Arabs for no reason whatever can be called an object worthy of all this demonstration. It is enough to make the very stones cry out."

Sir Henry's apparent failure to be " half indignant enough ", as the Queen puts it in the following letter, is only one more instance of his feeling of the need of restraint when there was ample excuse for anger and his realization that the result of so serious a catastrophe must fall heavily on Gladstone and his Government. If the Queen's violence of expression were encouraged, this was undoubtedly a case in which it would lead to Ministerial resignations.

To *The Queen*

Osborne, February 7, 1885

As Mr. Gladstone was rather excited about the telegram — which he called a censure on the Government, may Sir Henry Ponsonby send the enclosed to Mr. Hamilton ?

The Queen's Note

Quite right but you might add that the Queen's feelings are so strong for the honour of her Gr^t Empire that she with difficulty abstained f^r saying *much better* [these two words are difficult to read. Ponsonby in his letter interpreted them as " much more strongly " [1]].

---

[1] *Letters of Queen Victoria*, Second Series, vol. iii, p. 603.

The humiliation of this *defeat* NO one feels more keenly than she does but *dear Mr. Gladstone's* feelings are *much more thought* of than the Queen's suffering ! This is too bad, w^d be glad if it *was* known.

Mr. Gladstone has no chivalry, no sense of the *real* honour and dignity of his country. Mary P. w^d quite agree with the Queen. Sir Henry is not half indignant enough. She cannot excuse her anger.

This was followed by a full letter on the same day :

Osborne, Feb. 7, 1885

The Queen did not misunderstand Sir Henry ab^t Mr. Gladstone & she is glad he told him what passed but she *meant* that Mr. G. should remember what SHE suffers when the British name is humiliated as in the present instance — & he can go away & resign but she MUST REMAIN & she has suffered so cruelly from humiliation & annoyance from the present Gov^t *since* the unlucky day when Mr. Gladstone came in — that she was boiling over with the indignation & horror which *everyone* in this country felt & feels ! Mr. G. *never* minds loss of life etc. & wraps himself up in his own *incomprehensible delusions & illusions* refusing to read what is in every paper & everyone's mouth.

She makes no secret of what she thinks & w^d repeat it to Mr. Gladstone. How c^d she be silent when the news came & how c^d she NOT say what she did ? She named *no one.* Sir Henry stated the exact fact to Mr. Hamilton. Is it possible that Mr. Gladstone's *adulators & worshippers* (who do him much harm) *ignore* the universal feeling ? Some of the newspapers even fear Ld Wolseley may not be aware of the real feeling & that he may still be influenced by Cabinet views. She *thinks* not.

In the Queen's heart (& in that of many others she knows) she holds *Mr. Gladstone responsible* by imprudence, neglect, violent language for the lives of many 1000^ds tho' unwittingly. The Queen w^d not object to making him a peer but she will not give him the Garter, not from personal but from public motives as she honestly thinks he has *done such incalculable harm* to the country. Look at our relations abroad ! No one trusts or relies on us & from '74 to '80 especially the last 3 or 4 years of that time England stood very high.

It is a terrible grief to her. The Queen blames Lord Granville very much for he is as many people truly say " quite past " — weak & indolent & not able to work hard. Sir Henry must speak very seriously to Ld Hartington

as to eventualities but without making him *think* that he *is
certain* to be Mr. Gladstone's successor. We cannot tell
what may happen.

From March onward changes in Government policy ending
in the decision to abandon the Soudan were the chief subject of
correspondence. In April the Queen was at Aix-les-Bains
and Ponsonby with her. Undisturbed and with more time on
her hands she was able to nurse her grievances.

To *Sir William Harcourt*

Windsor Castle, March 15, 1885
The Queen has been much distressed to observe that the
Cabinet show signs of not fully supporting Baring and
Wolseley — both men selected by them — in the very
difficult positions they occupy in Egypt.

The Queen refers especially to the question of the appointment of Wolseley as Governor General and of his proclamation and as she fears you belong to that section of the Cabinet
which objects to entertain these requests of Lord Wolseley
Her Majesty commands me to ask whether you do not
think that the refusal to listen to our agents places them in a
most serious position and that it will lead to the ruin of all
that is requisite for the honour and safety of this country.

From *Sir Evelyn Baring*

Cairo, March 21, 1885
I gave the Queen's letter to the Khedive. He was much
pleased. It is very good of the Queen to support me. H.M.
has always been most kind and gracious to me in all my
difficulties, which are considerable. The great thing is to
get Ministers to decide *quick* on the points which arise. The
scene is constantly shifting, and unless an opportunity is
used when it turns up, the moment passes by, and the lost
time cannot be regained.

The financial settlement is not a good one, but we must
make the best of it. . . . The best thing now — as regards
the Soudan — is to come to terms with the Turk if possible.
It is too late for anything else.

Graham should not have been sent to command at
Suakin. He is a fine fellow but no general. Someone else
should be appointed in his place.

I have written officially — but will you also tender
privately my humble thanks to H.M. for conferring the C.B.
on me. I value it because it comes from the Queen and I

hope I may regard it as a proof that H.M. thinks I have done my best in a very difficult position.

From *The Queen*

Aix-les-Bains, April

The Queen is quite furious at the way in w^h the Gov^t continue to insist on a change of Policy against Ld Wolseley's advice & her *positive* opinion. Pray repeat I ought to have been told that the Gov^t meant to reverse their policy & that Ld Wolseley was to be consulted. I am much displeased at this being done during my absence having been assured on leaving that there was to be no change. What is the reason ? I agree with Ld Wolseley as to the political effect. *No change or withdrawal must take place* immediately. On this I INSIST. The effect w^d be serious. There may be no war with Russia & then we shall have brought our troops away for nothing. The Queen feels quite upset. The Gov^t will not learn by experience — are quite incurable . . . & changeableness is (. . .) the poor country its name & honour . . . [scribbled in pencil almost illegible].

From *The Queen*

Aix-les-Bains, April

The Queen cannot express her indignation at Mr. Gladstone's behaviour. No Minister has ever yet set her positive orders at such utter defiance. How she prays he may give up — for he is insufferable arguing & never *listening* to anything said against his *own wise notions. It is unbearable.*

From *The Queen*

Aix-les-Bains, Ap. 16, 1885

The Queen thinks she ought to write to Mr. Gladstone tomorrow & to remark on the want of attention paid to her opinion & views — which are solely actuated by the desire to save the Gov^t from committing further blunders & to remind them of the following points on which she insists.

1. That we ought to inquire if some means c^d not be found to get hold by money of the other Tribes of Osman Digna.

2. That there sh^d be *no hurried retreat* & *no reversal of policy* as *announced* which would make us look ridiculous. That any change sh^d be first *upon* the *heat.*

3. That we must protect the friendlies & altogether *not do* what the Queen pointed out viz : scuttle out after killing some 1000^{ds}.

Lastly to remember how my warning of him which was *disregarded* had *come true* & that if we retreat in indecent haste our conduct of last year w^d show most lamentable & grievous weakness & want of all principle & purpose to the world.

The Queen would like to write something like this by tomorrow's messenger. Sir Henry sh^d write much more strongly to Ld Hartington ab^t his (. . .) of purpose & perhaps confidentially to Mr. Hamilton ab^t Mr. Gladstone's want of openness of communication to leave the Queen entirely in the dark.

The worry ab^t this affair of the Soudan has quite upset the Queen & she is not very well today. She had been feeling much less nervous but this behaviour of her Gov^t & the mistrust she has of their conduct & concealment has brought back her nervous existing feeling of exhaustion which she suffered so much from latterly.

Sir Henry might answer Ld Wolseley : We'll await letters : Have not cyphers : Am apprehensive of intentions.

The Queen's letter to Mr. Gladstone is printed on p. 638 of *Letters of Queen Victoria*, Second Series, vol. iii. It is strong but Sir Henry's hand can be traced in softening the above draft.

From *The Queen*

Darmstadt, Ap. 23, 1885

The Queen cannot understand how Mr. Gladstone can allude to Geo. III excepting with a view to make her appear as blinded as her grandfather was about America w^h would be most irrelevant as well as unjust.

The Duke of Argyll spoke as he ought to do & it is shameful of Mr. Gladstone never once to have noticed even her anxiety about " the poor friendlies " & the Gov^t of the Soudan but he cares not how many lives are sacrificed or how civilization is advanced provided his Franchise & (. . .) Bill pass.

She will not trouble herself to keep him straight but Sir Henry must look up the allusion to Geo. III & should remind him that he has never answered the Queen about the Tribes & the Gov^t of the Soudan.

Note of *Mr. Gladstone*'s Reply [1]

With regard to Y.M.'s gracious declaration as to the absence of reserve in these difficult and trying communications Mr. G. is sensible of the great advantage derivable from Y.M.'s unfailing frankness . . . he is confident that the basis of

[1] See Morley's *Life of Gladstone*, vol. iii, pp. 180-181.

action has not been the mere change in public view (which however is in some cases imperative as it was with Geo. III).

From *The Queen*

Windsor, May 2, '85

. . . She thought Sir Henry ought to see what L⁴ Wolseley writes. Clearly much discussion has been concealed from the Queen. The present people behave shamefully to her & if Sir Henry sees any of them tonight he sh⁴ tell them *how* they *estrange* numbers from *her* who wishes to help them to do what is good for the country.

In the summer Ponsonby had an opportunity of a talk with Wolseley.

Osborne, July 15, 1885

Wolseley has just arrived here. I said : " Do you think you could have saved Khartoum ? " He looked round and said : " May I speak confidentially ? " I said : " Yes." He replied : " I haven't a doubt we could have done it. Wilson was useless as a military commander and lost his head. He lost nearly three days. If he had gone on at once a rapid move would have encouraged our friends and Gordon would have been saved."

Osborne, July 17, 1885

The Queen told me that Wolseley was low when he talked to her, his expedition was a failure. He had gone to rescue Gordon and his garrison and had not done it. Checked by the Government at home, delayed by Ministers and badly served at the critical moment by a good man but inefficient soldier, he missed his object by 48 hours. When he spoke of Gordon his voice broke — He told me he liked Hartington who backed him up, but some evil genius at home always neutralized what Hartington promised should be done.

This correspondence may be concluded by a letter written seven years later :

From *Lord Cromer*

Cairo, June 28th, 1892

I have only been waiting for the official announcement of my peerage to beg you to submit to the Queen my respectful and very sincere thanks for the great honor which Her Majesty has been pleased to confer on me. I cannot express how gratified I feel that Her Majesty should consider any services I may have rendered here as worthy of such a reward.

May I add that I can never cease to remember with the utmost gratitude the personal support I received from Her Majesty in the dark Gladstonian days when pretty well every one's hand was against me, and when the position here was, in truth, one of extreme difficulty. Her Majesty has, I dare say, forgotten a few words of kindly encouragement sent to me a few years ago when things looked very black. But I can assure you that at the time they were like Manna in the Egyptian Wilderness.

This is the first letter I sign with my new name — curiously enough on the anniversary of my marriage.

Very sincerely yours,

CROMER

Note by *The Queen* on back of above

The Queen will be glad to support him again in *fresh* dark Gladstonian days.

CHAPTER XII

Relations with Ministers

WHEN he had settled down in his office, Ponsonby found that the visits of Ministers, particularly at Balmoral where they stayed for some days, constituted the most interesting part of his work. He could learn from some of them more of the political situation than could always be gathered from their audiences with the Queen. He was thus able to study their personalities and this came in useful in all future dealings with them.

In 1870 a Liberal Government was in office. The first Minister who came to Balmoral was Lord Halifax. As Sir Charles Wood (raised to the peerage in 1866) he had held high offices including those of Chancellor of the Exchequer, First Lord of the Admiralty and Secretary of State for India. In this year he was Lord Privy Seal. He had married a daughter of Charles, Earl Grey, and was therefore Mary Ponsonby's uncle. He is generally referred to in the correspondence as " Uncle Hal ". The Queen had great confidence in him although in the correspondence she charged him with un-patriotic behaviour in 1879. Ponsonby was on intimate terms with him. He found him "impatient, lively and active and was at all times ready for an expedition. He trotted up on a pony to the top of Lochnagar in 2½ hours, which rather disgusted those who were accustomed to make a great ex-pedition of it." At this time he was seventy-one. But ten years later Ponsonby refers to him at a dinner given by his daughter Mrs. Meynell Ingram as " Uncle Hal, the boy of the party ".

Extracts from two letters of Lord Halifax's may be quoted, one on the Franco-Prussian War, the other on the Bradlaugh case :

Oct. 1st, 1870

. . . I am alarmed at the prospects of Europe and indeed of Prussia herself if she takes Paris. There will be little better than anarchy in France. With whom is Prussia to treat? I cannot think Bismarck can seriously think of conquering France with the Emperor. From whom is he to get the pecuniary indemnity? How in short is Prussia to get anything but the actual possession of what she chooses to hold : and to do which she must maintain at great cost a large Army? It seems to be essential for Prussia, in order that she may realise what she wants to gain from the war — that there must be a Government in name with whom she can treat, who can undertake to pay the indemnity she wants, and who can bind France to keep the terms which are agreed upon. Bismarck is urged on no doubt by German feeling, but he may easily push his success too far for his own purposes.

It would be advantageous even for Germany, according to my view of matters, that they should have a little check and find out that the price they pay for success and glory may be serious to them in the end.

May 26, 1880

. . . I agree with you that this Bradlaugh matter is most disagreeable, and it is most unfortunate for everybody that it has been made almost a party matter.

I seldom have known the House of Commons deal with a matter of this semi-judicial kind, in which they did not get themselves into a great difficulty — and they have contrived to do so on the present occasion. Mr. Staveley Hill, a conservative barrister who was on the committee, told the Attorney General on the preceding evening that in his opinion Bradlaugh was entitled to *affirm*, but the next day in the committee voted against his being allowed to do so, with his party.

And in the debate most of the Opposition have declaimed against Bradlaugh as an atheist and a republican, instead of speaking to the question of whether he could be allowed to take the oath. Beresford Hope put the objection to it on the real ground, in which for myself I quite concur. The only chance however of coming to a decision with any appearance of fairness is what Gladstone proposed and what is now agreed to, a committee with an amended form of reference.

In such cases the proper course would have been that the leaders on the two sides should have agreed on the best course in order to extricate the House of Commons from a difficult situation, and that there should have been no pretence for alleging party views on either side. Whatever Bradlaugh's character may be, the legal and constitutional rights of a man chosen by any constituency must not be set aside.

J. G. Goschen (1st Lord of the Admiralty) the youngest member of the Cabinet came to Balmoral next.   Ponsonby describes him as

> very cheerful and pleasant, desperately shortsighted, a very ugly walker but walked any distance. He was far more open in talking of political matters than any of the others and though extremely Liberal was bold in his views and considered the functions of Government were to govern and not to follow the varying opinions of the House of Commons especially such an uncertain House as the present.
>   The Queen wished to endeavour to stay the horrors of war and sketched her idea of a telegram to the King of Prussia.   Goschen altered it a little and sent it to Lord Granville and begged Odo Russell [at the Foreign Office] to translate it and said he could keep it till a convenient moment arose.   But the Queen preferred her own German and begged it should be sent as soon as possible.   It was to the effect that the King would offer terms that the French could accept.   He replied he must secure the peace of his own country but that compatibly with that he would offer the best terms he could as he wished earnestly for peace.

On the subject of the above-mentioned telegram and the reply sent, Goschen wrote in a letter to Ponsonby :

> As regards the publication of the telegraphic messages between the Queen and the King of Prussia, I am inclined to think it would be of some use.   Firstly it would disprove, if disproval were needed, the foolish suggestion that the Queen favours the Germans from dynastic ties.   Secondly, it would prove the Queen's warm interest in current affairs. Thirdly, I think that the telegram is in itself creditable to her, that it is friendly and complimentary to the Germans and yet in the interest of the French.   On the other side, would not the telegram imply the consent of the Government to its despatch ?   I am doubtful as to Lord Granville's opinion.   Of course the Queen would not think of publishing the telegrams without the cordial assent of Lord Granville. Again what would the Prussian King say ?   I think the answer is " intended for publication ".   Bismarck is plainly impressed on that last article " protection of Germany against attacks from France which no generosity will prevent ".   There is a certain snub in that answer which shows

the spirit in which Germans receive our suggestion. If I had to act on my own responsibility, I should recommend the publication of the telegrams on the whole, if I knew the King of Prussia did not object, but I feel a delicacy in giving my opinion without knowing Lord Granville's.

In September 1876 Goschen was staying at Braemar and although he was then in opposition the Queen asked him to dinner at Balmoral.

> Goschen dined here last night. He had a very long conversation with the Queen after dinner. Before dinner he seemed inclined to talk of Gladstone's speech, in fact he rather thought she had invited him for that purpose. But I cautioned him against plunging uninvited into that topic, for she is very tetchy on what she considers an attack on the Government.

The Queen continued to have a high opinion of Goschen's abilities and he certainly was successful in the way he approached her. The full correspondence, most of which is published, shows her confidence in him at the time of the secession of the Liberal Unionists. She overestimated however his power to form an independent party. Writing at the Queen's direction Ponsonby says in a letter on December 9, 1885, to Goschen that " the Queen is convinced that if all who have true patriotic feelings will free themselves of the trammels of party and faction a strong and honest Government could be formed which would be heartily supported by the Country ".

After a visit from Lord Hatherley, the Lord Chancellor who seemed " more devoted or rather acquainted with his own law business than with Cabinet matters ", W. E. Forster (Vice-President of the Council) came to Balmoral. Of him Ponsonby writes :

> Rough, uncouth but agreeable and pleasant and I should imagine the cleverest of all. At first a little distrustful of us, whom he generally termed " you swells ", but gradually more communicative. He generally avoided much discussion on radicalism and used to say his friends the radicals would condemn him for having turned courtier. But he was always firm in his opinions and though anxious beyond measure to do the Queen's bidding and to please her, always let her know his opinion.

R

The Queen took to him which showed that polished manners were not a necessary passport to her favours. Forster gained confidence. In a letter of October 20, 1870, Ponsonby writes more of Forster :

> His thirst for knowledge on royal and aristocratic affairs is great. She can turn him round her finger — up to a certain degree. But Forster has ideas. I am in a horrid fright that he intends to speak out his mind before he goes. He said to me about some question she was aspere about, not getting an answer from London : " Here is a splendid peg. Couldn't I hang on it an argument against her absenting herself from London at such an important moment ? " I gave a sickly smile and said " No." He put his tongue out about a foot and a half, jammed his foot into the grate and said : " Well, I think it's an opportunity." But wisely he did not take it.

Cardwell (Secretary of State for War), whose Army reforms Ponsonby later did so much to support, never gained favour with the Queen. In his sketch of him Ponsonby writes :

> Cardwell in general society sat far back in his chair, gazed at the ceiling and told long anecdotes with the tone of a dissenting preacher. But talk to him individually and he seized on the subject and discussed it, always pausing before answering. He talked to me pretty freely on military matters, lamenting the want he had of military assistance in the House. He is far too much afraid of the House of Commons. He does not seem to consider that the functions of a Minister are to lead. He dreads proposing anything the House will reject and in talking over desirable reforms he said it would be of no use thinking of such, the House would not have them.

There is an undated draft referring to this period of a letter from Ponsonby to the Queen which shows yet again his support of measures which he was convinced were beneficial in the face of the Queen's strong opposition :

> As Your Majesty so graciously condescended to speak on some Military questions yesterday to General Ponsonby he most humbly asks permission to submit his opinions on the subject for what they are worth. . . .
> General Ponsonby is convinced that Mr. Cardwell's earnest desire is to raise the efficiency of Your Majesty's Army to the highest possible pitch and to increase the power

of Your Majesty over the Army to the fullest extent. He holds that Your Majesty is the sole and entire Head of the Army and that he is Your Majesty's responsible adviser for all things military.

The recent reforms introduced by him, many of which were rendered absolutely necessary by the improvement in other Armies, have secured the pre-eminence of the British Army small as it is — in every matter which it is possible to judge of in time of peace — except perhaps the Control system which is not by any means perfected.

The powers of the Commander-in-Chief have been enormously increased and his responsibilities proportionately enlarged so that it becomes absolutely necessary that the harmony between the Horse Guards and the War Office — which improves daily — should be complete.

All Mr. Cardwell's schemes may not at once be crowned with success, but the abolition of purchase will soon produce its beneficial effects and be one of the grandest military reforms which will adorn Your Majesty's reign.

General Ponsonby fully believes that Mr. Cardwell is one of Your Majesty's most loyal and honest advisers and deserves your Majesty's most complete confidence and while he will gladly listen to the suggestions that Your Majesty should at any time direct should be made to him, he will not by any false step imperil the safety of Your Majesty's kingdom.

In a subsequent Liberal Government H. Childers at the War Office was just as unsuccessful in his approach to the Queen. Ponsonby says : " Childers certainly contrives to rub up the Queen unnecessarily. He had an opportunity of talking over matters with her at Windsor but said nothing." Immediately afterwards however he sent down the names for two very important appointments, one of which the Queen disapproved.

We now come to Ponsonby's dealings with and opinion of the two great political leaders. No novelist or dramatist could have invented two characters for rivalry who were so diametrically opposite in disposition, genius, method, tradition, accomplishments and even appearance as these two Prime Ministers. Nor indeed has political history previously or subsequently described two so strongly contrasted champions confronting one another in the parliamentary arena who could rouse their two camps of followers to such a frenzy of animosity against one another. Enough has been said of the Queen's attitude towards them. But her intermediary's judgment of them is not without interest. Admittedly his own political opinions gave him a bias towards one rather than the other which may appear in his critical notes on them personally. But his scrupulous fairness in delivering messages to them and from them, and the very favourable estimate both of them formed of the Queen's Private Secretary, show that his passing opinions of their personalities were private and only conveyed in confidence to his wife.

The difficulty with Disraeli lay in his method already described of corresponding with the Queen direct. While Ponsonby did not resent this, in fact on occasions welcomed it, he found it hampering in his work when the complete sequence of communications with the Prime Minister was so often broken and he was left in the dark. He also found at once that any word of criticism to the Queen of the Tory Prime Minister was out of the question. Some of the comments in his letters from Balmoral may be quoted.

October, 1873

Disraeli writes with his tongue in his cheek. He is most clever. But he seems to me always to speak in a burlesque. All the time I saw him about the crisis I could scarcely help smiling. In fact I think him cleverer than Gladstone with his terrible earnestness. But how anyone can put faith in Dizzy is what I don't understand.

October, 1874

What I saw of him [Disraeli] here made me think him clever and bright in sparkling repartee but indolent and worn out. He did not seem ever to take up any question or to discuss any problem. But he shot little arrows into the general discourse pungent and lively and then sat perfectly silent as if it were too much trouble to talk.

I so fully believe that Disraeli really has an admiration for splendour, for Duchesses with ropes of pearls, for richness and gorgeousness, mixed I also think with a cynical sneer and a burlesque thought about them. When he formed the Government he spoke in the highest delight of the great names he had selected for the household offices and the minor offices — " sons of great Dukes ". His speech here on the Palatial Grandeur, the Royal Physician who attended on him, the Royal footmen who answered his beck and nod, the rich plate, etc. — all was worked up half really, half comically into an expression of admiration for Royalty and the Queen. Yet there might also have been a sarcasm under it all.

October, 1874

Bids [Sir Thomas Biddulph] thinks that Dizzy is a perfect slave to the Queen and that she is always at him about something that we know nothing of. If so I pity him as he will have work enough of another nature soon for Cabinet meets next month to discuss parliamentary business.

The private correspondence between the Queen and Beaconsfield was by no means a question of fancy on Ponsonby's part. This is shown by the Queen's letter to Beaconsfield after his defeat in 1880 when she asks him not to use the formal third person " when we correspond — which I hope we shall on many a *private* subject and without anyone being astonished or offended, and even more without anyone knowing about it ".[1]

In April 1875, writing from Osborne of the Queen's increasing devotion to Disraeli, Ponsonby adds :

He has got the length of her foot exactly and knows how to be sympathetic. You and I know that his sympathy is expressed with his tongue in his cheek. But are not her woes told in the same manner ?

Later, in May of the same year :

No, I don't think in reply to your very flattering remarks on my political aptitude that Dizzy tries to get me out of the way that he may have his own. For it seems to me that he communicates nothing except boundless professions of love and loyalty and if called on to write more says he is ill. He is said to be ill now, at any rate, whatever is the cause, the ignorance I am in of the communications between the Queen and Government which may be important, but which I suspect are nil, makes it impossible for me to watch the progress of events and to call for more information if required.

The letters from Disraeli to Ponsonby are nearly all formal and official. But on September 10, 1877, he relaxed into a more personal note :

I have recovered youth by doing exactly what my medical friends have, for years, warned me not to follow : drinking very good wine.

How delightful in these days of irreligion to owe your recovery to a divinity !

<hr/>

[1] *Life of Benjamin Disraeli*, Buckle, vol. vi, p. 527.

Ponsonby sent this up to the Queen, who wrote on it :
" The Queen quite agrees. Ld Beaconsfield's letter is most
amusing."

On the occasion of one of Lord Beaconsfield's visits to the
Queen in 1878, on a Sunday morning coming back from
Whippingham Church, near Osborne, Henry Ponsonby
walked with the Prime Minister while his three sons followed
at some distance behind. Disraeli was dressed in a dark-blue
frock-coat with a top-hat partly covering his curls. He wore
rings *over* his white gloves. He turned round and waited till
the boys came up and then addressed them : " Which of you
boys can tell me what is the capital of Cyprus ? " There was a
silence. The youngest felt he was not called upon to reply
but his elders were equally ignorant, so the walk was resumed.

In a letter from Windsor dated July 16, 1878, Ponsonby
gives an account of Beaconsfield's return from the Congress
of Berlin :

> I went on to Downing Street where I settled myself with
> the Queen's letter and the Queen's bouquet. There were
> a good many people in the Street chiefly M.P.s of all sorts.
> I did not know many. However I talked to Cust [1] — Cust
> always amuses me. I said it was a glorious day for him —
> and he replied " Your saying so is the only thing that makes
> me doubt it. They say he is to have an equestrian statue
> opposite George IV." None of the Tories were exultant.
> The most rejoicing came from a lady I didn't know who
> said very loudly that she heartily welcomed him — " the
> only mistake he had made was giving anything back to
> Turkey at all — however they have gone bag and baggage
> out of Bulgaria ". There was I believe a considerable
> crowd in Whitehall — he drove up in an open carriage with
> Lady Abergavenny, Lady Northcote and Lord Salisbury.
> Lord Beaconsfield wore a long white coat. As he entered I
> gave him the letter and bouquet, shouting " From the
> Queen " — as there was so much cheering. He looked
> tired — thanked me and went in. I shook hands with Lord
> Salisbury — who was laughing as if he thought it all a good
> joke. Lord Beaconsfield came out to a window and spoke
> to the people. Then sent for me while he wrote a few lines
> to the Queen. He said " Well, we have done it. — And I
> trust it will be approved — the work, the trouble, the deep
> great anxiety, the incessant interviews knocked me up at

[1] Henry F. C. Cust, M.P. for Grantham, *b.* 1819.

last — but Kidd set me up and here I am tired and done but I must say gratified with my reception at Dover and here." He gave me the letter.

After the attempted assassination of the Czar by a bomb towards the end of 1879, the Prime Minister wrote to the Private Secretary in some concern for the Queen's safety :

From Lord Beaconsfield

Hughenden Manor, Dec. 5, 1879

This Russian catastrophe makes me nervous.

Although I really believe there never was a time when there was less disaffection with the institutions of the Country, and that the Queen especially, and the Royal Family in general, are popular and beloved, still human nature is essentially mimetic, and often commits crime, not so much from absolute and organic wickedness, as from vanity and a diseased self-consciousness.

I hope, therefore, indeed I feel sure, that you are taking all due precautions about the movements of our Sovereign Lady, whether in walks or rides, and that you have adequate experts hovering over the towers and terraces of Windsor.

During his administration from 1874 to 1880, and more especially in 1873 before he took office, Disraeli's intercourse with Ponsonby was frequent and full and he remarked to a political friend : " I believe that General Ponsonby used to be a Whig, but, whatever his politics may once have been, I can only say that I could not wish my case better stated to the Queen than the Private Secretary does it. Perhaps I am a gainer by his Whiggishness as it makes him more scrupulously on his guard to be always absolutely fair and lucid." [1]

So through all the moments of political strain which the Queen's interventions did little to relax, there was never a breeze between the Conservative Prime Minister and the Queen's Private Secretary.

Of all the tributes which Ponsonby may have received none can surpass in sincerity and cordiality the note Lord Beaconsfield wrote him when he was appointed in 1878 to the office of Keeper of the Privy Purse in addition to that of Private Secretary :

---

[1] Quoted in Buckle's *Life of Benjamin Disraeli*, vol. v, p. 210, which also gives Ponsonby's memorandum in full.

Hughenden Manor, Oct. 9, 1878

MY DEAR GENERAL,

I learn from the Queen, with entire satisfaction, the important changes Her Majesty has been pleased to make in Her Majesty's Household, in consequence of the lamented death of Sir Thos. Biddulph.

You are in your right place.

I shall have the pleasure of carrying on affairs not only with a man of business, but with a man of the world : but, what is of still more importance, with one whom I personally regard, and in whose honor, and kind feeling, devotion to our Sovereign, and abilities for his high and delicate office, I place, and have reason to place, unbounded confidence.

With my kind remembrances to Mrs. Ponsonby,

Yours sincerely,

BEACONSFIELD

Sir Henry Ponsonby's letter to Beaconsfield on his retirement from the office of Prime Minister in 1880 confirms in its expressions of gratitude the friendly relations which had existed between them,[1] and in the letter of April 20, 1880, announcing that he was submitting Ponsonby's name in his honours list for a Privy Councillorship Beaconsfield himself wrote : " We have passed five years in the conduct of great affairs without a cloud between us ".

The last time Ponsonby saw Beaconsfield was at a dinner party of which he kept a note :

In the evening Mary and I dined with Sir William and Lady Harcourt and Lewis Harcourt in Grafton Street — Lord and Lady Granville, Lord Beaconsfield, Lord and Lady Lytton, the Duke of Sutherland, Sir Henry James, Hartington and Lady Dorothy Neville. . . .

Lord Beaconsfield looked rather worn but was in good spirits and made himself very agreeable to Mary at dinner. Afterwards he went away early — that was the last time I ever saw him. At dinner Hartington chaffed Lady Dorothy — who was well able to sustain and reply. We talked on riches and Lord Granville asked Lord Beaconsfield who he thought the richest man. Lord Beaconsfield said the man who had most ready money. Lytton added — " in his pocket. If you have a hundred pounds in your pocket you are much richer than with a thousand in Consols." Someone observed that money was more respected than rank in

[1] Buckle's *Life of Benjamin Disraeli*, vol. v, p. 474.

England now.   Lord Beaconsfield said :   " Perhaps — by
radicals but they have a deep respect for a title too " — looking at Hartington the Liberal leader who has both.

On the death of Lord Beaconsfield expressions of the Queen's
sorrow have appeared in the published volumes.   The letter she
wrote to Sir Henry Ponsonby was rather more political in tone
and seems to suggest between the lines that the high value of
the deceased statesman was insufficiently appreciated by her
Private Secretary :

Osborne, Ap. 22, 1881

. . . She is terribly distressed at the loss of her most devoted
& invaluable friend who on all & every occasion supported
& helped her.   She could turn to him for wise & dispassionate
counsel.   Where is she to find that now & where will the
honour & dignity of her g^t Empire ever find such a *Champion* ?

The Queen feels quite bowed down with this misfortune.
Till Thursday we were full of hope.   He died the very day
of the year he reached office !

Her grief & anxiety at the unfortunate elections while she
was at Baden were it w^d seem a foreshadowing & a presenti-
ment of this dire event.

Poor Lord Rowton is quite broken hearted.   Such unselfish devotion & affection on the one side & such love &
confidence on the other are rare & beautiful to see.

With Gladstone Ponsonby's relations were more intimate
than with any other Minister.   They were both great walkers
and their walks often provided an opportunity for conversations on public affairs, and the Liberal Prime Minister could
express without restraint his feelings on the ups and downs of
political life.

Before he was Private Secretary, Ponsonby as Equerry-in-
Waiting was sent down in June 1869 to meet Gladstone at
Cowes and escort him to Osborne.   This was the first conversa-
tion he had with him and he records it in a note :

He had evidently been lately accustomed to popular
receptions for he looked round to see if there was anyone to
bow to and nervously touched his hat to the few people on
the pier for Cowes is not a demonstrative place.   He was
agreeable as we walked up and, talking on the Election trials,
said Disraeli ought to have all the credit of that measure
(Reform Bill of '66) for he passed it against strong opposition

on both parts of the House.   He is very fond of talking on
Church matters specially about the Bishops. . . . I should
think he was a strongly religious man ; though a little shy
or nervous in manner there is a great power in his discourse
and I should *think* his conviction for the time would carry
him through everything.

We talked of the resemblance I have frequently heard
made and which I saw between the character of the Prince
Consort and William III.   He entirely disagreed.   William,
though a great statesman and able warrior winning campaigns although losing battles, was hard, cold and cruel.
The Prince whose only resemblance was his shyness was
warm and kind.   The Prince could never have effected the
revolution : he had not the indomitable will of William nor
could he ever have perpetrated the Glencoe massacre.
Macaulay's apology was unworthy of Macaulay.   I said they
were both unpopular with the English.   But Gladstone
denied that the Prince was.   He was unpopular with smart
society but the people liked him.

In September 1871 Gladstone was in attendance at Balmoral
as Minister.   The Queen had not quite recovered from her
illness so he was told not to speak to her of anything that might
excite her.   He saw very little of her.   But at Household meals
he was very talkative and always talked across at Ponsonby
" as if I were the Chairman ".   During a walk he had with
him in the rain,

> he never ceased talking but kept the conversation in his own
> hands, never suffering me to turn it to the subject I wanted.
> He conversed much upon the state of affairs.   He did not
> think the Queen's absolute retirement a serious matter but
> was concerned about the stories of the Prince of Wales
> gambling at Baden about which there had been newspaper
> comments.

In Ponsonby's letters in August 1873 after several walks with
Gladstone at Balmoral it is curious to find references to Gladstone's desire to leave political life at that time :

> He said he thought he would never return to Balmoral.
> He would be glad to retire from public life and should an
> opportunity offer would do so.   To attempt to govern with
> a party who pretended to support him and in reality thwarted
> him was simply impossible. . . . I sometimes think him
> rather mad — earnestly mad and taking up a view with an
> intensity which scarcely allows him to suppose there can be

any truth on the other side. But looking back on his visit here although he was physically well and although he was in good spirits, he was not the same man that he was two years ago. He seldom or never spoke of the political future. He was looking back not forward. There was no keenness about future measures and he made little or no stand against anything the Queen insisted on. He gave way. There was a sort of want of interest in the political future which was not like his old self. As to expeditions and amusements he was very ready for them. . . . I am very sorry he has gone as he was most pleasant and agreeable and talked to me very openly on most matters.

When Lord Granville succeeded him at Balmoral he wrote in a letter to Gladstone : " The Queen told me last night she had never known you so remarkably agreeable ".[1] Rather later Ponsonby describes a conversation in which Gladstone expressed views which surprised him :

He praised George III for having opposed Catholic Emancipation, because this was the popular feeling and what is more still is the popular feeling. Fortunately the measure was passed before the Commons was reformed. A House like the present which represents the feelings of the people would never pass it. " But," I said, " that sounds as if the Reform Bills have done more harm than good." So they have undoubtedly as far as the composition. Statesmen on the old lines are becoming impossible. We have scarcely any rising young men in the House now.

Towards the end of 1874 after the ecclesiastical discussions on the Scotch Patronage Bill to which Gladstone objected, and after his retirement from the leadership of the Liberal Parliamentary Party, the Queen wrote to her Private Secretary her earliest letters of general criticism of him, to the first of which Ponsonby ventured to reply.

From *The Queen*

Balmoral, Nov. 18, 1874

These are very curious ! But pray write to Ld Derby to say that Pr^ce Bismarck's opinion of the C. P^ce is wrong & *unjust*. The C. P^ce *hates* intrigue & is very straightforward & honest & kindhearted but rather weak & to a certain extent obstinate not *conceited* but absurdly proud, as all his family are, thinking *no* family *higher* or g^ter than the Hohenzollerns.

Not proud to those below him that is to the people, but proud & overbearing to other *Princes*.

Bismarck's conduct to the Emp^r is perfectly disgraceful. He wishes to make the Emp^r feel that he is the Master.

Mr. Gladstone's sending his Pamphlet [1] is significant. She (. . .) thinks Sir A. Paget gives it its right name. She must say to G^l Ponsonby, tho' he may hardly like to believe it, that *she* has felt that Mr. Gladstone w^d have liked to *govern* HER as Bismarck governs the Emperor. Of course not to the same extent or in the *same* manner ; but she always felt in his manner an overbearing obstinacy & imperiousness (without being actually wanting in respect as to form) w^h she never experienced from *anyone* else & w^h she found most disagreeable. It is the same thing w^h made him so unpopular to his followers & often even to his colleagues.

Draft of *Ponsonby*'s Reply

Balmoral, November 18, 1874

General Ponsonby presents his humble duty and will write as Your Majesty desires.

Are Prince Bismarck's accounts of his conduct to the Emperor accurate ? May he not pretend to have greater influence than he possesses and does he not as in the Military question throw the blame on the Emperor for measures he himself approves of ?

The great difference between him and Mr. Gladstone is that the latter is honest and true. When once convinced of an idea he runs at it with such desperate energy scarcely listening to any remonstrance. It may have been this eagerness which displeased Your Majesty as General Ponsonby feels sure that he is so loyal and devoted that he would never have presumed on Your Majesty's favour.

His pamphlet has exposed him to several attacks from both extremes — whether it was well timed may be a matter of doubt but it is his character to dash headlong down a line which he is convinced is right without fully weighing the immediate consequences.

From *The Queen*

Balmoral, Nov. 19, 1874

The Queen must just say a word with respect to Mr. Gladstone. He certainly means to be honest & the Queen has always said so, but he is not considered so by many people for his sudden changes & want of, as Lord Halifax said,

[1] *The Vatican Decrees in their bearing on Civil Allegiance : a Political Expostulation.*

adherence to a respect for the real " Landmarks of the constitution ". This is what makes him so unreliable & appears so insincere & certainly the Queen thinks Ld Palmerston was *not* wrong when he said to the Queen " he is a very dangerous man ". No one can be sure for a moment what he may *persuade himself* to think right, & hence the impossibility to place confidence in him. His conduct *now* is beyond measure strange & as he holds these ritualistic & sacerdotal views no one can treat [with] him on that subject. He was loyal & meant to be so, but he was often very harsh & as the Queen said yesterday very dictatorial & wished the Queen to do what *he* liked & w^d listen to *no* reasoning or argument.

Bismarck is a bad man & the Queen also thinks that he boasts of what is not true.

Writing from Osborne on January 23, 1875, to Gladstone, Ponsonby makes a reference to his retirement from leadership :

I cannot say I was surprised at your late resolve, but I was startled when I read the correspondence.

Although it is natural that a leader who has led his not too submissive followers to victory, and secured peace and prosperity for his country, should withdraw from that post when they are in their peaceful encampments, it is also natural that the soldiers now recognizing his value more than ever should lament the loss of such a general and regard their future with apprehension.

There is a rough draft of a letter on the subject of the power of the Monarchy which comes into this period :

To *Mr. Gladstone*

Windsor Castle, July 13, 1875

I have to thank you very much for sending me a copy of your article on the Prince Consort. I had read it when it came out in the *Contemporary* with great interest. I was much struck with the paragraph in which you briefly touch on the altered character of the Regal office and describe this as the substitute of influence for power. Yet, I imagine the power still remains, though unused.

I have heard that the Prince often struggled to enlarge her power while equally jealous of his demands. I can understand his feelings for in my small way I feel it my duty to point out everything that tends to weaken the Royal power and possibly I may sometimes urge Her Majesty to do more than she does with a view of maintaining her position. But I am appalled at the tremendous results whenever she does move. A wish complied with seems to (. . .) the law. Take for instance her eagerness that some public denunciation of Railway carelessness should be published. It certainly was her persistence that induced Fortescue to write his circular ; and then the country was full of it for days afterwards, Parliament founded debates on it, now a Royal Commission is sitting on the matter and possibly legislation may follow — and yet the Queen's name never appeared at all.

In some ways the dormant power is so great that it might almost be dreaded if we had a bad and clever King and a weak Minister. This is most unlikely but I only allude to it to support my argument that the latent power exists and though it is dormant indeed is the force which gives to the royal influence the strength it possesses.[1]

In spite of the Queen's fears of Gladstone's "revolutionary" policies, a letter from Edward Hamilton shows how punctilious he was with regard to the correct observance of the proper practice where the Queen personally was concerned. Hamilton wrote (December 7, 1880) of the exact procedure in eliciting the Queen's wishes with regard to her presence in opening Parliament, adding, " He is the most extraordinary Conservative ' stickler ' for forms and ceremonies ; and unless I can give him ' chapter and verse ' he won't be happy ". Ponsonby replied :

Mr. Gladstone is quite right — I meant that the Prime Minister had done so in the course of conversation. But I asked Her Majesty. She told me that no one put the question. She herself announced her intention or not as she pleased. One or two had asked her. But she preferred that the initiative should come spontaneously from her. She said she certainly would not be able to open Parliament on the 6th of January.

When the Liberals were again in office, the Queen took exception to speeches by Chamberlain and Bright :

Mr. Chamberlain & Mr. Bright sh^d both be told that they cannot *speak in public* as irresponsible people. It will become very serious.

[1] See p. 95.

From *Mr. Gladstone*

Dec. 22, 1880

The Queen is anxious that I should speak to Bright and Chamberlain about passages in their speeches.

The enormous gravity of the questions raised in Ireland with regard to repression, and especially to land, makes me unwilling, unless under necessity, to enter upon secondary issues, which, in smoother times, it would be easy enough to deal with.

I am not however fully aware what are the passages or sentiments in the speeches delivered at Birmingham, which H.M. has particularly in her mind. You may have heard the Queen refer to them : and I should be much obliged if you could give me any light.

The Queen has named to me words about the House of Lords used by Mr. Bright : I imagine those commented upon by Lord Carnarvon. It is certainly not the business of a Minister to raise or suggest questions respecting the root of a body which, while unhappily opposed to every Liberal Administration (except Lord Aberdeen's, under which it showed great wisdom) yet is undoubtedly a co-ordinate historic portion of her Legislature. On the other hand Mr. Bright is to some extent an exceptional man without official traditions : and there is no *suite* or latent purpose in these occasional utterances.

There is a rough memorandum giving the substance of Ponsonby's reply :

The Queen objected to Mr. Bright's reference to the House of Lords and thought that he and Mr. Chamberlain did not sufficiently condemn the outrages in Ireland. Her chief objection was to the tone of both the speeches made on the eve of an important Cabinet Council. But I certainly think with you that it might scarcely be desirable to repeat these remarks to these two Ministers.

In the same month in the course of a letter on official matters Gladstone explains the pressure of the work which was falling on him :

It is very good of you to miss me at Windsor. But the actual object of time presses me hard. On *no* day, I may say, do I get more open air than the minimum necessary for health — and every day is a continuing recurrence of effort and arrears. It was not the fear of two more journeys, three days after getting here, but my knowledge that I should have much difficulty in getting through my necessary work while staying here, and that the bulk of two days expended in going and returning would make it hopeless. Eight hundred folio pages of print at this moment stare me in the face, with which I ought to have made progress, but which are not yet begun. I hope then that my humble petition through Sydney [1] could not seem to show an insensibility to the honour done me by H.M.

In March 1881 Ponsonby went to see the Prime Minister in order to arrange an appointment for him to come and see the Queen. After a discussion on the Wolseley Peerage question, he records in his letter Gladstone's subsequent remarks :

He went on to say " My day is drawing to a close and when a man gets worn out he gets gloomy. Formerly I saw no reason why Monarchy should not go on here for hundreds of years, but I confess that the way Monarchy has been brought to the front by the late government in political and foreign affairs has shaken my confidence and I dread any shock that may weaken the power of the crown with the rising mass of politicians. Some of those you live with probably accuse me of being a radical. I am not. But, I believe that I have the confidence far more than I deserve of those that are extreme radicals but who as long as I am here pay me that respect of following me in most of what I do even though they do not think I am advanced enough. But when I am gone younger men who take my place will either be far more advanced than I ever have been, or will be forced on by the extreme liberalism of the masses. I dread this, and I dread appearing in antagonism to the Crown, which I am not, for this would encourage both now and hereafter those who are dangerous to the Monarchy." He was rather agitated and spoke in a mournful way, then he stopped and said the cabinet was going to meet on the Irish Land Bill at once, so I left him.

Later in the year some malicious gossip, repeated to Gladstone, stated that " the Queen hated him ". When she heard of this she was much annoyed and declared she had never said anything of the kind. Ponsonby adds in his letter : " But everyone tells me that he is sore at his treatment by H.M. No wonder he gets angry if these things are said to him."

[1] The Lord Steward.

In July of the next year, 1882, Ponsonby's report from Balmoral was good :

Gladstone was in very high spirits last night. He seemed stronger and fresher than ever ; and although he talked of " the time must come " when he could no longer bear the fatigue, he didn't look like it now.

There are three letters of Ponsonby's in 1884 worth quoting. They have a certain amount of atmosphere as a setting. The first from Osborne is dated February 2 :

Gladstone has been here in a most suave mood. He said something to me about this Parliament being dissolved in the summer of '85 " when my business will cease ". I said " Why ? " He got very excited — " No, no, impossible, I could not go on through a General Election — impossible, I have retired once. I fully made up my mind ten years ago to give up public life and for two or three years you will scarcely see my name mentioned. I seldom even spoke. But the Turkish cruelties were too much for me — they dragged me out of my privacy and forced me into the front rank again. I regretted it but I couldn't help it — I could not keep silent and I did not — "

He talked at dinner on many agreeable subjects with the Queen — she and he alone remembering some of the persons named and I sometimes having a faint glimmer of the man. The Queen said Lord Westmorland was the last man who wore a pigtail. I said no, my grandfather was — but cut it off on the passing of the Reform Bill. Gladstone said he couldn't have been the last then for Lord Westmorland wore it up to the Queen's reign. H.M. said so too. However he was the last Cabinet Minister.

The next is from Claremont where the Queen used to stay from time to time in earlier years :

Much to the disappointment of Warren, the rector of Esher, Dean Davidson was sent for to perform the service — in the house. In the long room where the sacred picture by Doré of the disciples saved in the storm stands side by side with the portrait of a P.B.[1] The house is really very pretty and poor Leopold had taste or employed those who had in the things he bought. But it cannot be thoroughly lived in by the Duchess [of Albany] with her present means. The Queen reads carefully the Ministerial speeches and immediately writes to Gladstone if she observes the least threat

[1] Professional Beauty.

against the House of Lords as he promised her that no threats should be used. Gladstone replies that he has not time nor eyesight to read all the speeches and Hamilton complains to me that if these criticisms go on there must be an Assistant Prime Minister to do nothing but read and expostulate with wild members of the Government. Gladstone says that he does not want to touch the House of Lords. All he asks is that they should use their power with moderation.

This third is from Balmoral and shows completely friendly relations. In fact after it Ponsonby in a letter to Horace Seymour, one of the Private Secretaries at Downing Street, writes, " H.M. gets on so well with him, it is a pity these meetings are so few " :

> Mrs. and Miss Gladstone came here to luncheon and saw the Queen, after which she saw Gladstone for some time and we took him out for a drive. He talked the whole time. We went to the Linn of Muick which was beautiful and as we all stood at the foot of the fall he called me up to him and pointed to the foaming rushing cataract and then to the rock dividing it from a little spout of water that trickled down also and said " There, the first is our agitation — the other is the Tory agitation. I could not have found a better simile."
>
> When we got home in the evening we found there was to be a ladies' dinner. I was rather surprised — but one never knows the Queen's ways. But by the time we had got to fish at our dinner they came to tell me there had been a mistake and that Mr. Gladstone and I were to dine with the Queen. He laughed very much at having to eat two dinners, and as of course we couldn't begin at once again with soup he got the start in conversation — and kept it up the whole of dinner, the Crown Princess and Queen backing him up well. I thought him most agreeable. The Queen blew us all up afterwards for not reminding her she had left him out.

In his letter from Windsor on June 24, 1885, Ponsonby writes : " Gladstone was full of praise of me today and shook my hand most warmly at parting, saying God bless you — it rather brought a lump to my throat ".

Dated the very next day there is a brief note or memorandum written in an unusual form which seems to show Gladstone restraining his exasperation at the misrepresentations by his opponents of his speeches :

10, Downing Street, Whitehall

Mr. Gladstone to Sir H. Ponsonby.

25 June, 1885, 9.30 A.M.

I understand the Queen to be disposed to express her belief that my words are used with sincerity & loyalty and may reasonably be so accepted and to this I can offer no objection : but the incessant attempts from the other side to extend them obliges me once more to say that I can in no way be a party to any construction or interpretation placed upon them.

After the fall of Lord Salisbury's Government, which only lasted from June 1885 to February 1886, correspondence and meetings again continued showing that the aged statesman who twenty years before used to speak of retiring from public life was full of drive and vigour :

Note of Dinner with Mr. James Knowles (Editor of the *Nineteenth Century*) on April 1, 1886

Mr. Gladstone, the Duke of St. Albans, Mons. Waddington, Mr. Phelps (American Minister), Mr. Holman Hunt[1] and Hamilton Aïdé dined with Knowles. Mr. Gladstone full of Eton and of stories of flogging which was very common in his day. A whisper went round as to whether he had ever been flogged and they poked me up to ask him, which I did. " Yes, indeed, once and only once — for good nature in not reminding Keate[2] as I ought to have done that there were three friends of mine awaiting punishment — " Knowles said no one had ever written more than one book. We disputed this as also his saying to Hunt — and no one ever painted more than one picture. Knowles said G. Eliot's *Middlemarch* would live long beyond any other — including Scott — he did not care for Scott — Mr. Gladstone upheld Scott — and *Middlemarch* too. But the two foreign Ministers said that in France and America *Middlemarch* was scarcely known while every one read Scott.

I told Mr. Gladstone he was asked to dine at Windsor. He said he could not possibly come. He could do nothing till the 8th (his speech). His work was enormous and he had to do in the midst of the Session in four or five weeks what ought to occupy four or five months out of the Session.

[1] The Pre-Raphaelite painter.
[2] John Keate, Headmaster of Eton 1809–1834.

Note of Dinner with Gladstone, June 2, 1886

M. E. P.,[1] Betty[2] and I dined with the Gladstones. Although
in the midst of his Irish Bill he was in high spirits and told
me he wanted to make me acquainted with the redoubtable
Canon McColl (H.M. had refused to promote him because
of his High Churchism). Mr. Hutton of the *Spectator*, Mr.
Illingworth M.P., Mr. and Mrs. Stephen Gladstone, Lord
Acton and Lord and Lady Rosebery were there. Hutton
did not show any shyness in attacking Gladstone on the
Irish Bill as he disagreed with him and they got to Bright's
letter. Rosebery said he went in a cab with Bright who left
him to pay the cabman — but the man refused as he had had
the honour of driving Bright. Someone hinted that he must
have been an Irishman to have allowed his feelings to overcome his pocket and Illingworth observed the Irish were not
grateful to Bright but were most grateful to Gladstone — to
which Mr. Gladstone assented. Rosebery at once objected
and said " I agree with you in most things, Mr. Gladstone,
but not on that for I think the Irish have been most ungrateful. You have passed more Bills for their benefit than any
other Minister and they have opposed you on every occasion
— and even now may probably do so again." Illingworth
denied it and told some story of Healy having expressed
himself as if Gladstone was a divinity — which shut up the
conversation and two loud raps at the door took us to the
Ladies. It was Betty who had rapped by Mrs. Gladstone's
leave to remind us it was time to go to the Queen's Ball.
. . . The Queen's Ball was a bright and pretty one. I had
some talk with Hartington there who in certain conditions
would be prepared to answer the Queen's call if Gladstone
resigns.

At the end of July Gladstone went to Osborne and they
had some talk, as shown by Ponsonby's letter of August 1, 1886 :

When I went in to Gladstone's room on Friday to fetch
him for the Queen I found him absorbed in *Kidnapped*,
R. L. S. I asked him : " Do you find time to read much ? "
He said, " Why, what else could I do coming down here ?
I have no time to pick up novels but when I hear of a good
one I read it." He told me he was going to reduce his correspondence. When in office he and his private secretaries
wrote about twenty-five thousand letters a year.
I hear the Tories are terribly afraid of his agitations. He
is keen to be at something and I think will attack at once.

---

[1] His wife.   [2] His eldest daughter, later Mrs. Montgomery.

The Queen wrote to appeal to his patriotism not to prevent any measure being carried for the benefit of Ireland. She ended by writing that he should not encourage the Irish to expect they would ever get Home Rule as that was impossible. I asked her to change this as I am not sure how far she could ask any one in opposition to do this and of course he would answer it was not impossible but on the contrary very probable. We altered it at last into a hope that he would say nothing that could be construed as an encouragement to those who openly defy the law. This I think she might fairly say though it would have been more prudent to have said nothing.

James Knowles gave another dinner which is referred to in a letter of February 28, 1890 :

> Knowles gave a very good dinner to what he called an Octave, that is to eight besides himself : Gladstone, Randolph Churchill, Ferdinand Rothschild, Philip Currie, Sir James Paget, Sir T. Lubbock, Mr. G. Ryder and me. I sat next Gladstone who was in full talk though he and Randolph were I think a little afraid of each other. Much discourse on books, on which he has just written an article in the *Nineteenth* — and how many books would make a good library. It was generally agreed about twenty thousand of which Rothschild immediately made a note. Also we discussed *Origin of Species* and Wallace on Darwin of which of course I knew nothing and I think Gladstone less but R. Churchill and Lubbock (very quietly) held forth on it — and to the origin of all things, on which Knowles remarked that Tennyson said to him : " The vast majority of Englishmen picture to themselves God as an illimitable clergyman with a long beard." Gladstone said " That is the best argument in favor of the Established Church which I have ever heard."

A sentence in a letter from the Queen (October 8, 1891) shows that her animosity against Gladstone was still very pronounced. She writes :

> What a monstrous speech w^h Mr. Gladstone made ! Such wicked & mischievous proposals ! But he surely has gone too far & will shock all more moderate men. He states such falsehoods.

In 1892 Gladstone formed his Government. Ponsonby in a note wrote about his visit to Carlton Gardens on August 13.

After discussing the Queen's absolute refusal to have Labouchere in the new Government, he goes on :

> I then gave him the Queen's letter calling him to form a Government. He replied that there were points he wished me to explain. That Home Rule was a very Conservative measure as it would bring peace and contentment to Ireland — probably make the Irish Tories and at any rate make them loyal instead of being always opposed to every English Government. That at one time he thought the Tories would bring in Home Rule but instead of that, urged by the perverse conduct of the Liberal-Unionists, they took up Coercion and then he (Mr. Gladstone) opposed them fiercely and had now carried the day and he would make a strong and united Kingdom. But the defection of the Liberal Unionists had also another evil effect. By weakening the leading Liberal party who were therefore now compelled to take on extreme men the forces of Socialism and Democracy had attained such force that they must be recognized. All this for the Queen. He then wrote his reply to H.M. I settled with West [1] his journey for Monday and asked about Rosebery. Mr. Gladstone feared that he would refuse. He had told Rosebery of the wish of the Queen that he should take the Foreign Office, but Rosebery said his nerves were unstrung. He never slept now and that work was impossible. There was no political difference between them.

There is a letter from Gladstone in which he writes of the Poet-Laureateship just vacant on the death of Tennyson, 1892 :

> I have taken much pains about the Laureateship without arriving at any conclusion. A book has been lent me by Mr. Walker Hamilton which throws much light on the history of the office. So far as I have yet got, it tends towards the conclusion that when an illustrious holder could not be or had not been found, the holder, and the office through the holder, is apt to become an object of sarcasm and ridicule. So I imagine it may at all events stand over for a while to avoid the chance of a false step, and in considering the matter I shall be anxious to learn the exact state of the Queen's thoughts and wishes.
>
> The question has brought to my acquaintance a junior poet named William Watson who is certainly of very distinguished ability. In the *Illustrated News* of some days back

---

[1] Sir Algernon West, Private Secretary to the Prime Minister.

there was published a monody of his on Tennyson, by far, very far the best thing I have seen on the occasion.

Although undated the following letter comes in about this time :

From *Miss Maud Stanley* [1]

No doubt you know what Gladstone feels about you but when he was with us two days ago, he was so enthusiastic in your praise that I hope you will not think me impertinent in repeating it to you. He said he had the very highest opinion of you, of your tact and your powers, that he could not say how fond he was of you, that he loved you, and much more. He seemed so genuine in his admiration. . . .

The last dinner referred to in a brief note was on November 18, 1893 :

Dined with Mr. Gladstone. Mrs. Gladstone the only woman, Lord Elgin, Judge Wright, Acton, Mr. Milner, Burne-Jones and Edward Clinton. Mr. Gladstone in high spirits and talked all the time, chiefly on Montaigne. He declared we had no complete book on Montaigne in Windsor Library. I find he was right. From that he went off on fat people, saying that fatness was going off. You never saw a fat man now. In the House of Commons he did not know a single fat man and looking round the table observed " Curious, I have not a single member of the House of Commons here — and no fat man either." After dinner he took me off on business, that is on the appointment of Herkless [2] to St. Andrews and on the Duke of Coburg's financial affairs. And on both was most pleasant and amenable.

This summary of Ponsonby's relations with Gladstone can be fittingly concluded by Gladstone's last letter to him (which has appeared before in print) :

March 5, 1894, 10, Downing Street.

MY DEAR SIR H. PONSONBY,

The first entrance of a man to Windsor Castle in a very responsible character is a great event in his life : and his last departure from it is not less moving.

But in and during the process, which led up to this termination on Saturday, my action has been in the strictest

[1] Daughter of Lord Stanley of Alderley.

[2] The Rev. T. Herkless, D.D., afterward Regius Professor of Ecclesiastical History at St. Andrews University.

sense sole, and it had required me in circumstances partly known, to harden my heart into a flint.

However it is not even now so hard but that I can feel what you have most kindly written. Nor do I fail to observe with pleasure that you do not specify absolutely in the singular. If there were feelings that made the occasion sad, such feelings do not die with the occasion.

But this letter must not be wholly one of egotism.

I have known and have liked, and have admired, all the men who have served the Queen in your delicate and responsible office : and have liked most, probably because I knew him most, the last of them, that most true hearted man, General Grey.

But forgive me for saying you are " to the manner born " and such a combination of tact and temper with Loyalty, intelligence and truth, I cannot expect to see again. Pray remember these are words which can only pass from an old man to one much younger, though trained in a long experience.

Believe me always
and most sincerely yours,
W. E. GLADSTONE

The fitful and incomplete correspondence and casual notes show that while high politics brought the two men in contact with one another, their official acquaintance ripened into warm personal friendship. There are indications (no doubt more if we had fuller acquaintance of their walks) that Gladstone was not invariably oppressively serious. Had he been it is doubtful if Ponsonby would have enjoyed his intercourse as much as he did. The picture of their relations would have received many finishing touches had space allowed for the inclusion of the very full correspondence of Ponsonby with his opposite number, Gladstone's Private Secretary, Edward Hamilton. His wise, friendly and illuminating letters often disclosed facts, circumstances, relationships and trends of opinion with which it was important the Queen's Private Secretary should be fully acquainted.

John Bright came to Balmoral in 1873. This was not his first visit to Court. In spite of his advanced speeches, the Queen had a soft corner for him because he had stood up for her publicly against attacks and criticism in the earlier days of her retirement. He was devoted to fishing and said he was sick

of politics as it took him from that sport. " Indeed," he added,
" I should like to live in a country where there was no Government." He entered into the Balmoral life, seemed quite at
home and played billiards with Prince Leopold. In the course
of conversation he told Ponsonby of his admiration for William
Morris as a poet. He was a strong advocate of Disestablishment so that the clergy might be free and not forced into a
groove and made narrow. He expressed himself strongly
against Papal tyranny — " an old man who knew nothing
of what was going on, advised by a dozen old men equally
ignorant, pulled the strings and excited trouble in every
State ".

When Bright died in 1889, General Lynedoch Gardner was
sent to his funeral as the Queen's personal representative.

With Hartington Ponsonby does not seem to have had
much intercourse on his visits. There is a reference to his visit
to Balmoral in one of the letters in the early years :

> Hartington has talent and tact but terrible idleness. If
> he has work to do, no one does it better but he takes things
> very easy indeed. . . . He talked a great deal at dinner.
> Perhaps too much. Whereon he was rather set down as a
> bore. He don't quite know where and when to stop.

There is a brief but rather curious note from Hartington
to Ponsonby, dated December 5, 1884, written from Devonshire House on his return from being Minister in attendance.
It asks for something he left behind in his bedroom to be sent
to him — not his sponge or toothbrush as one might expect
— but a loaded revolver " which I usually carry about with
me in London ". (It was at the time of the Fenian outrages.) [1]

There are many letters from Granville about official
matters. He was on terms of too great intimacy with the
Ponsonbys for any description or character sketch of him to
appear in Henry Ponsonby's letters to his wife. The Queen
felt he was a friend but expected too much of him and was
therefore disappointed in him. Although foreign policy was

---

[1] The present Duke of Devonshire writes that the revolvers were a constant
source of worry. " He was always losing them and buying new ones, and there
were certainly no less than twenty of them knocking about Devonshire House
when he died."

certainly not the strong point of the Liberal Governments, the Queen seemed to think that Granville should convey her reprimands to his colleagues and divulge to her differences of opinion in the Cabinet. Granville's policy of paying as little attention as possible to what she said was not successful. When he went off fishing at Balmoral so as to be out of the way, the Queen made comments on his fishing too often.

The packet of the papers dealing with Sir Charles Dilke's republican speeches in 1871 and the Queen's desire that he should make a public recantation of them in 1882–1883 before joining the Government is a bulky one. It consists of letters from Gladstone, many from his private secretary Horace Seymour, and Ponsonby's attempts between the Queen and the Prime Minister to prevent the matter getting out of all proportion. The Queen's attitude was not unreasonable. As she herself put it in a note to Ponsonby : " The Queen does not blame people for *having* republican levelling views, *if that* is their *conviction*, but she does for taking office *under a Crown* ". The matter was finally adjusted by a passage inserted by Dilke in a public speech which was accepted as a recantation. As Ponsonby had no personal correspondence or dealings with Dilke, he makes no estimate of his abilities or character. But as the Queen wanted a far stronger protest to be made against his Newcastle speech in 1871 favouring a republican form of government, Ponsonby sought the advice of other Ministers as to whether Gladstone should be approached by the Queen to do this. The following reply was received :

From *W. E. Forster*

I think the impression produced by Dilke's speech is on the whole not discouraging. Many who might have been supposed to have some agreement with him appear to me shocked when brought face to face with such opinions, and still more are disgusted by his vulgarity and bad taste.

His letter to the *Daily Telegraph* the day before yesterday seems to show that he himself feels he has made a false step. Still it is a bad sign that such a speech *can* be spoken by an M.P. of apparent respectability.

With regard to the second point on which the Queen graciously asks my opinion, I confess I doubt whether it *would* be advisable for Mr. Gladstone as Premier to seek an opportunity to give the speech the importance of a *second* notice.

Upon this point, however, he must be a far better judge than I can be, and I feel sure he would be very glad to receive from Her Majesty any expression of her views or feelings, especially as I can not doubt he must be anxiously considering the possibility of having to deal in Parliament with this reckless talk which it is not safe to treat only with contempt.

Lord Halifax wrote in the same sense, advising that a public condemnation of the speech by the Prime Minister would only have the effect of drawing more attention to it and it was therefore better to leave it alone. The speech in question was warmly supported by Joseph Chamberlain.[1]

There is an early reference to Joseph Chamberlain in a letter of Ponsonby's to his mother Lady Emily in 1874 (November 6) :

To *Lady Emily Ponsonby*

November 6, 1874

We were all watching how Mr. Chamberlain the ultra radical Mayor of Birmingham would receive the Prince of Wales. It seems to have been most successful and the speeches made by the Mayor were far better than any I have read on so trite a subject as Royalty. He welcomed them with dignity and independence. The Duke of Richmond was much struck with it.

We then jump to November 27, 1883, when Chamberlain's speech at the National Liberal Association produced great indignation on the part of the Queen. She wrote to Sir Henry enclosing a full press report :

From *The Queen*

November 1883

This is incredible. It is not one *particular* word or two — it is the general tone — the democratic views held by Mr. Chamberlain of which everyone is full, that requires checking. . . . She has written strongly to Lord Granville [2] to call on Mr. Gladstone to point out again to Mr. Chamberlain the impropriety of his conduct as a Cabinet Minister holding such language.

---

[1] *Short Life of Sir C. Dilke*, Gertrude Tuckwell.
See *Letters of Queen Victoria*, Second Series, vol. iii, p. 458.

An interchange of letters between Horace Seymour and Henry Ponsonby may be inserted here.

In one of his letters to Horace Seymour in this year Ponsonby says : " We don't like Joe's speeches here," and in another : " In controversies respecting Chamberlain we must remember he is on the right side of fifty. Most of the Cabinet on the wrong side."

From *Horace Seymour*

10, Downing Street, Whitehall
9 Dec. 1883

Do you know to which particular passages in Joe's speeches H.M. particularly objected ? I don't suppose there is anything to be objected to in his preference for manhood suffrage, or electoral districts. It is a matter of opinion, and there is nothing unconstitutional in the desire for these blessings. Considering that it is impossible almost to carry such a matter as the extension of the household franchise in Counties, no one need alarm themselves much about manhood suffrage, if they object to it.

Personally I think he is defeating his own objects in going in advance of what is immediately practicable, but I suppose H.M. will hardly weep if the enthusiastic Joe succeeds in breaking up the Liberal party ?

It is possible, however, that H.M. has not read the speeches, but only goes by what she is told by friends on the other side, who see High Treason in the Prime Minister's shirt collars. If rumour is true I fear there are many of these. I have a holy horror of backstairs influence — but perhaps it doesn't exist — rumour is a great liar : at least, so we find him here.

To *Horace Seymour*

Windsor Castle, December 10, 1883

You ask me what part of Chamberlain's speech " we " did not like.

Did you ever hear of Lady Tatton telling her coachman to look at a horse she wanted to buy — and he advised her not to buy it. She said "Why? What part of him is bad?" The coachman replied " Why, My Lady, I don't like 'is 'ocks nor 'is ass nor anything that is 'is."

A note on a dinner party about a year later reports some of Chamberlain's conversation :

Monday, November 3, 1884

Dined with J. Knowles, the editor of the *Nineteenth Century*. Waddington the French Ambassador, Chamberlain, Herschel the Solicitor General, Sir H. Holland,[1] F. Harrison the positivist, Dean of Westminster, Dalhousie and Major Collins.

Of course the early topic was the House of Lords. Chamberlain said he must confess he hoped they would not give way as in that case the Institution would certainly be abolished as he wished, but he admitted there would be a row about it and he felt convinced that if the Peers did give way the agitation would cease at once. Waddington strongly advised us to keep our House of Peers. No doubt it had plenty of faults and the anomalies were great but neither the faults nor the anomalies were half so great as in any other assembly. We certainly had the best form of an Upper Chamber and had better keep it. Harrison did not agree : he would be ready to abolish it but he wouldn't mind abolishing the House of Commons at the same time. Sir H. Holland strongly defended the House of Lords. Chamberlain talked of the war in Egypt as sad — but he said we must win and indeed could easily do so if we sent enough troops and spent enough money, but the war in South Africa was a war against the people and he did not see how we could come out well from that. He was more afraid of the financial state of affairs in Egypt than anything else.

Knowles was a very good host putting in a crucial point if ever the conversation flagged. He was originally an architect and was rather proud of his early calling. Chamberlain told me that he saw every one laugh at him for being a screw maker which he now was but he did not understand why they did not chaff him about being a cobbler, for that was his original occupation — at least the firm he originally was engaged with was one for making boots. Chamberlain spoke out his views in a very convincing manner. Thus he said he could not support the Anti-Vaccination Movement. Still it did appear hard to send a man to prison because he would not — as he believed — inflict what might be a deadly injury on his child for no advantage to anyone. " Yes," I said, " the advantage was to stamp out smallpox." " Exactly so," replied Chamberlain. " You say that vaccination preserves you from the smallpox — therefore be vaccinated and you will be safe from the non-vaccinated child who may itself die — but cannot hurt vaccinated people — "

Other speeches of Chamberlain's came in for strictures by

[1] M.P., later Viscount Knutsford.

the Queen. But a good illustration that it was political views and not personality which influenced the Queen in her relations with Ministers is shown by the fact that later, when Chamberlain broke with Gladstone, he came into high favour with the Queen, in spite of having been at one time Gladstone's " evil genius."

Ponsonby appreciated Chamberlain's abilities. After a speech in January 1885 he writes in one of his letters : " I don't think people can find fault with what Chamberlain said. Of course he is very advanced in his views on taxes, land, etc. All his arguments however are fair and one had to collect one's thoughts to see why one disagrees with him."

Sir William Harcourt was unfortunate in seldom pleasing the Queen. " He argues as with a man ", writes Ponsonby. " On Hares and Rabbits Bill he sends defence of it and three sheets of letter paper. The Queen wouldn't read it, said he was tedious. With her you must be short." On another Bill he sent a still longer memorandum which was never read. He was also very touchy and resented criticism.

In a letter to Ponsonby dated June 18, 1882, he writes :

> I have been working like a galley slave in the face of incredible difficulties to get the Prevention of Crimes Bill through the House of Commons. The progress I have been able to make and the success I have had in resisting all material alterations in the Bill have received the acknowledgments of all parties, the Tories as much — perhaps still more than the Liberals. And yet I get letter after letter from Balmoral as if I was an incompetent sluggard. This spurring of a willing horse who is already worked to death is a very disheartening sort of treatment and makes public service a very thankless task.

Ponsonby calmed him down in his reply, assuring him the letters he gets " are intended to support you ". Next year he resented the " wigging " he says he has been sent for having taken too many police precautions on some official occasion. He defends himself by saying :

> If anything had occurred I should have been justly censured for want of care. . . . It is foolish to expect any gratitude for all the trouble one takes for other people, for one is not likely to get it. But it is a little embarrassing to be

constantly worried, first of all to do a great deal that is unnecessary and then to be blamed for doing what is prudent. . . . I must endure the reproach of having protected the Queen too much, but I shall not face the blame of having protected her too little.

Writing after a Council at Osborne in 1881 Harcourt says with a refreshing absence of any disparaging remarks, which were not uncommon with other Ministers :

> I had a very pleasant time at Osborne. I am not one of those who think it fine to vote the thing a bore. On the contrary I find your society a good deal more agreeable than that of the Lobby and the Home Office and find a Council jaunt a very pleasant holiday.

In August 1881 Harcourt objected to the Queen asking why a man called Redmond was pardoned. He had killed his wife but not on purpose and was sentenced to be hanged — commuted to penal servitude for life. Harcourt said he must resign if the Queen objected to commutation. This was Ponsonby's reply :

To *Sir William Harcourt*

Osborne, August 18, 1881

I agree with you so far as that I think it would be better not to touch upon these questions at all — but I also think that as H.M. has to sign her approval to the remissions she has a right to enquire into the reasons. Not with a view of rejecting your advice, but of making her opinions known to you and receiving from you some further explanations, for as you truly say she has not the smallest knowledge of the facts of the case.

In the present instance a man who has killed his wife is pardoned because he did not mean to go so far. Without insisting on this man being hung the Queen may surely ask for your observations.

Ponsonby approached Ministers by letter, visited them or asked them to call on him. But on occasions he buttonholed them at parties. After dining with Mr. and Mrs. Cyril Flower [1] in July 1890, he writes in a note :

> Harcourt came out on the Balcony and I said " As I have met you I must deliver a message to you which I would

---

[1] Afterwards Lord and Lady Battersea.

not otherwise have done. The Queen said ' Do you remember the last time you were at Windsor how you impressed
upon her the necessity of withstanding the clamour of the
Irish agitators and the necessity of subduing their criminal
acts, and yet now you are supporting them.' " He was
rather taken aback and said " I also warned her that if she
allowed the Tories to have their fling they would drive
Ireland into semi-rebellion. Look what a state of things at
present — " I observed " I don't think that is quite an
answer to me and if I repeat your words H.M. will no doubt
say that Ireland is quieter and more contented now except
among the agitators than it was when you were in office."
He answered that a quiet surface did not prove the absence
of a volcano underneath, but added " It is not for me to
bandy words with my Sovereign so please say that I am
much gratified that she should have retained any remem-
brance of me at all."

In 1891 Harcourt had a bitter audience with the Queen.
Ponsonby was away working elsewhere. Arthur Bigge reported
to him and told him how Harcourt remarked afterwards to
him : " My connection with politics may not last much longer,
but believe me a Court more Tory than Tory with a country
becoming daily more democratic is a serious outlook." Bigge
declined to admit his definition of the Court.

Lord Salisbury was bored at Balmoral and was seldom very
communicative. There are a couple of references to him in
the daily letters during his visit in 1875.

Lord Salisbury admired Gladstone in some points but one
thing that surprised him was that Gladstone ever heard a
sermon without " rising to reply " :

Macgregor preached yesterday. He is very energetic
in the pulpit. His sermon was not bad but nothing remarkable in it. In the evening Lady Errol said to me " How
beautiful his prayer was for the Prince of Wales." " Well,"
I said, " I don't know that it was a bad one, but I didn't
understand what he meant ' Oh bless abundantly the objects
of his mission '." She replied, " Oh, all the good he may
do." I said, " The object of his mission is amusement."
" Yes," said Salisbury, " and to kill Tigers, perhaps he
meant to bless the Tigers."

Salisbury declined the Kirk yesterday saying he had a
very bad cold. I suppose he really had a cold as he declined
coming out in the afternoon. We all dined with the Queen.

I am sorry Salisbury has gone though I did not see much of him. He refused to walk out and did not conceal his entire abhorrence of the place and the life here. He positively refused to admire the prospect or the deer which Lady Ely pointed out to him, and though he lived with us he did not like us — or rather I should say our ways. But when I did talk to him he had no hesitation in expressing his opinions. They were positive and decided. . . . He looks as if he could break forth indignantly when opposed but bottles up his opinion on party politics.

Among the few of Salisbury's letters which are purely official there is one in March 1889 in which he writes : " The Germans are seriously anxious to be on good terms. The difficulty now is the hateful Herbert." (Count Herbert Bismarck, who was coming over.)

In December 1886 there is a note of Lord Randolph Churchill dining with the Queen at Windsor two days before his resignation of the office of Chancellor of the Exchequer. The Queen read of the resignation in *The Times* before Lord Salisbury had a chance of letting her know. This led to much correspondence in which the Prince of Wales, who had received a letter of explanation from Lord Randolph, was involved.

In a letter to Ponsonby at this period Sir Francis Knollys wrote : " The fact is Randolph is no more a conservative at heart than Mr. Chamberlain. All his instincts and feelings are liberal, *very* liberal, and I say this from having known him intimately in former days, and from having been again brought into contact with him latterly."

Arthur Balfour, who was Chief Secretary for Ireland, visited Balmoral in 1890. With his conspicuous social gifts he was a great success :

Balmoral, September 1, 1890

Arthur Balfour has gone. He did very well here. He has an opinion on various questions and gives it — but not roughly or over-decidedly as if every one else must be wrong but himself. Still his opinion is good and he sticks to it. And he enters into the Queen's arguments and discusses matters with her showing that he does not agree which makes her think over it — and not opposing her slap which never fails to make her more strong in her own views.

T

September 3, 1890

I was pleased to find that Balfour quite agreed with me on poetry and far preferred Dryden and Pope to Browning. I confided to him that except some ballad here or there I couldn't read Browning and he replied with a similar confidence to me. I asked him who he would make Laureate if he were Prime Minister. He said that W. Morris and Swinburne were obviously impossible and that he therefore would name Lord Lytton. I don't know enough of his poetry.

He came again in August, 1891 :

August 30, 1891

Balfour is able to talk on any subject and does not repel any interpellation because it is not in his department. He discusses anatomy with Reid — Ireland with me — and is now engaged on a controversy with Bigge on the abolition of the two troops of Horse Artillery — and he is excellent on foreign affairs as he is not hampered with the minutiae but takes the broad comprehensive view of our policy and has an excellent opinion of the value of our different Ambassadors. I think the Queen likes him but is a little afraid of him.

In the Rosebery packet one would expect to find examples of his wit and charm. But these were no doubt reserved for conversations. The letters are mostly on official matters. The downs and disappointments and the ups and successes are fully dealt with in Lord Crewe's *Life of Rosebery*. It will be seen that occasionally he unburdened himself to Ponsonby whom he knew intimately and to whom he wrote on the celebration of his silver wedding : " I have come to the conclusion that so indefatigable a writer as yourself cannot have too many inkstands. So pray accept this and use it sometimes."

With a view to explaining Rosebery's resignation from the office of Under-Secretary at the Home Office in 1883, and as an instance of the useful and valuable information Edward Hamilton was able to give, a letter of his may be quoted which although wrong in one conclusion throws considerable light on the somewhat difficult disposition of the capriciously brilliant statesman :

From *Edward Hamilton*

1883

I am sorry to say that Rosebery has been in a discontented frame of mind for a long time. He has had no difference of opinion whatever with the Government ; and the Government have in deference to his wishes promised to bring in a Bill to improve the arrangements for the conduct of Scotch business. But he has long been bored by the routine of his office and disappointed at not getting promotion and downcast at his political prospects. He has also been far from well, worried and sleepless. In fact his personal position has been on his brain. The difficulty he has been met with all along, since last Christmas when he first gave expression to his feelings, has been to find a plausible excuse for resigning. After trying several expedients he has resorted to the somewhat flimsy excuse of a discussion which took place last Thursday night in the House of Commons, taking exception to his holding the Under-Secretaryship. It is no doubt true that it is desirable as a rule, and it has generally been the custom, that the Home Secretary should have a Commoner as his Under-Secretary. But there was no necessity for making a change in deference to the Parliamentary criticisms. At the same time, viewing the subject all round — Rosebery's mood, state of mind, etc. — Mr. Gladstone after consulting with Lord Granville and Lord Hartington thought he was perhaps not justified in declining any longer to accept the resignation ; and perhaps this excuse (viz. the Parliamentary view of his office) was as good an one as any to give out to the world.

I am extremely sorry about this business. On whatever ground it may be put, Rosebery's resignation will be a distinct loss to the Government. It is no small grief to Mr. Gladstone. The hope is that he may be induced to rejoin the Government in some more congenial office before long, when an opportunity occurs, either as President of the new Scotch Board contemplated in the Bill about to be introduced or in some other capacity.

I have known him intimately for twenty-three years — we were next each other at Eton for about five years and a half and afterwards at Christ Church together — and yet I have never really understood him. He is an extraordinary mixture. He has brilliant abilities and in many ways special aptitude for political life ; but I fear his over-sensitive, thin-skinned nature will sadly stand in the way of a really successful political future.

Please make as *little* use of this letter as you possibly can. All that we can say to the outside world is that he has offered himself up for the good of the Government and for the sake of improved administrative arrangements.

I thought you ought to know exactly the position of affairs, which Mr. Gladstone himself could not have explained to Her Majesty. . . .

A considerable amount of correspondence passed between Ponsonby, Edward Hamilton and Sir Francis Knollys in 1892 before the general election in August, when there was a certain prospect of the return of a Liberal Government. The Queen thought this calamity might be mitigated if she could depend on Lord Rosebery accepting the post of Foreign Secretary. It was considered however inadvisable, if not unconstitutional, that the Queen should communicate with a prominent member of the Opposition before the election. Ponsonby took this view. Similarly the intervention of the Prince of Wales was turned down. But eventually the matter was settled. Rosebery accepted the appointment, it having been realized that " his game was to be made much of " and indeed there was nobody so well qualified for the position.

There is nothing of note in Rosebery's private communications with Ponsonby till August 21, 1892, when he had just assumed the office of Foreign Secretary :

From *Lord Rosebery*

Many thanks for your kind wishes and words. I was, I confess, vexed at Lord Salisbury's not receiving me. For seven years I have worked hard to make the foreign policy of this country continuous, whether I was in or out of office, and the task is sufficiently difficult even under the ordinary conditions and courtesies of political life. Moreover the state of Europe is delicate, critical and complicated.

However he has condescended to write a letter to Philip Currie [1] to be communicated to me. But I cannot say that he has acquired good manners with the Windsor uniform ! which I thought never clothed any but chivalrous bosoms.

I attended a meeting of the Cabinet on Friday. I thought I was at a public meeting, and nearly moved Mr. Gladstone into the Chair.

There is a word of caution in 1893 about the Queen's messages to the Cabinet :

From *Lord Rosebery*

Foreign Office, January 24, 1893

I entirely shared the Queen's views in this business, but I have great doubts of the wisdom of her sending rescripts to be read at the Cabinet. Such is the jealous temper of

---

[1] Permanent Under-Secretary. Afterwards Lord Currie.

Britons that these utterances are more likely to produce reaction than compliance ! Cromer's telegrams have caused me a peck of troubles. They may have been admirable expressions of agony but they were hardly calculated to mollify or persuade the Cabinet !

On Gladstone's resignation the Queen in the published correspondence [1] was in communication with Lord Rowton and speaks of " consulting Lord Salisbury ", an idea however which she fortunately abandoned. Judging by the following letter Rosebery must have heard of this :

From Lord Rosebery

Foreign Office, St. David's Day, 1894

I am not quite sure from your letter if I *did* make myself quite clear. I suppose, constitutionally speaking, that the Queen has a right, when the Prime Minister has resigned and the Cabinet therefore is technically at an end, to consult whom she pleases. But though all things are lawful, all things are not expedient. Should she summon *to an audience* a member of the Opposition, it would give rise, I conceive, to the belief that she was making an attempt to get rid of the party in power, and this would cause an injurious impression. On the other hand, it is easy to consult without audiences, and that I presume would be unobjectionable.

Remember, I am not giving, and did not yesterday give, advice as a minister or a politician, but entirely from the Queen's own point of view.

The Queen viewed the prospects of Church Disestablishment with dismay, as is clearly shown in the published letters. Rosebery's reply to her pressure that the measures should be dropped when he became Prime Minister is also printed. But in this letter to Ponsonby he puts it more strongly, in fact to the point of resignation :

From Lord Rosebery

Foreign Office, March 9, 1894

I am afraid this is a fatal announcement, for it is impossible that I can face Parliament without the announcement of these two measures. The Welsh party would simply vote the Government out on the address, and the Scots would follow suit.

---

[1] *Queen Victoria's Letters*, Third Series, vol. ii, p. 368.

The Disestablishment of the Welsh Church is the first article in the programme (I say Welsh Church for brevity). These measures were practically announced last session and we cannot withdraw them.

If the Queen insists on her view I have I am sorry to say no resource but to give up the Government.

I cannot tell you how disheartened I am, for you know how willingly I would do everything possible to meet the Queen's wishes. But this is impossible, and there is unfortunately no time for discussion.

Note by *Ponsonby*

Mentmore, September 12, 1887

Came here with M. E. P. Rustem Pacha in the train and E. Hamilton. The others who were here on and off were Sir James Lacaita, Mr. and Mrs. Phipps, H. Calcraft, H. Primrose, M. and Mme. de Falbe, Lady Gerard and Mr. Henry James. Rosebery most agreeable and amusing. I attacked him on his Secretary of Scotland Scheme and said the present Government were enlarging the powers of the office and would give the Secretary for Scotland the power of pardon in capital offences. " I mean," I explained, " that it will be for Lothian to advise the Queen as to the prerogative of mercy in the case of a Mac Lipsky." Rosebery solemnly observed, " You have wounded me in my two tenderest points — as a Scotchman and as a Jew." The Turkish Ambassador was low — " So would you be if you had just received a despatch saying your Government intended to cease paying you your salary." We made various suggestions as to who would be Prince of Bulgaria when Ferdinand goes. One advised Teck — another Lorne — " No," I replied, " the Prince must be rich." " Then," said Rosebery, " put Vanderbilt on the throne of Bulgaria —" on which Rustem sharply said, " There is no throne of Bulgaria — it is a dependency of Turkey." Rosebery told me he did not see how Hartington could rejoin the Liberal Party. He was sorry for it. The Unionists had modified the extremists and their loss would throw the Liberals into the power of the Radicals instead of preserving a proper balance. He thought that Hartington and others could have modified the Home Rule Bill at the Round Table Conference if they had chosen but now the severance was complete. The Unionists must either join the Tories or disappear from Public Life. He afterwards modified these words as regards Hartington. He could never join while Gladstone led — but if Gladstone disappeared the Liberal Party would probably dissolve and reform in a new manner. Hartington could become Prime Minister of a Tory Unionist party now. Harcourt would be the leader of the Liberals after Gladstone. But with the power of Gladstone's name gone it was possible that some Liberals might prefer Hartington. But by that time Hartington would probably be in the House of Lords and that would make his leadership more difficult.

There is a brief reference to Hicks Beach [1] in the seventies. " Beach is not a communicative man or a talker on general subjects. When he discusses business he does it briefly and to the point, but otherwise does not talk much."

In November 1889 Ritchie [2] came to Balmoral. He was the President of the Local Government Board. Ponsonby writes of him :

> Ritchie is really made *du bois dont on fait les Radicaux* and starts large views very well. He talked to me for a long time as to whether the Queen would throw open Buckingham Palace Gardens, when she is not there, to the public. I told him he might as well ask her to dance a fandango. He expatiated on the popularity it would give her and how hard it was on the people being kept out of a beautiful garden which was used by no one. I asked what he thought the Prince of Wales or A. V. [Albert Victor] would say as they would probably live there more than H.M. He looked with a curious smile and said, " *When* they come to the throne — ah ! they will have to take care of themselves pretty sharply then. I am only talking of a popular Queen."

It is rather surprising to find a man of the calibre of James Bryce favoured by the Queen. He was certainly learned and suspiciously clever. But he had knowledge of the world. His visit to Balmoral occurred in November 1892. There are two references to him in Ponsonby's letters :

November 6

Bryce is a success. He makes himself very agreeable and talks to H.M. on literary matters which highly pleases her. I don't discuss Home Rule with him, but his Home Rule allusions are of the mildest sort and his allusions to Irish members do not show much admiration of them.

---

[1] Afterwards Lord St. Aldwyn.
[2] Had carried Bill creating County Councils. Home Secretary 1900, Peer 1905.

November 7

Bryce is not only theoretically fond of "access to mountains" but practically so — and went off at an early hour this morning to ascend Lochnagar. They will have a fine view for it is a beautiful clear day. He is very pleasant. I had two long walks with him yesterday but protested against his going up all the mountains he saw and limited myself to Craig Gowan and Carrop.

He talks openly on all political questions and does not mind my saying "I can't see why you are a Home Ruler." Evidently his wish is to get rid of the Irish out of our Parliament so as to enable us to go on with British legislation. The Queen likes him — but is rather afraid of his "Access to Mountains Bill" which she says will ruin the deer-stalking in Scotland. He says it won't if properly managed but then he is not an admirer of modern deer-stalking of animals who are enclosed in a wire fence, and all mountains forbidden to anyone but the proprietor.

In March 1893 the Queen even suggested that Bryce might be invited to come out to Florence while she was there (he was Chancellor of the Duchy of Lancaster) :

The Queen thinks Mr. Bryce might do to come to Florence. He has travelled much and knows so much and so many languages that he might be agreeable and useful there — besides having been Under-Secretary for Foreign Affairs.

Early in 1894 there is an exchange of letters between Asquith who was Home Secretary and Ponsonby on the subject of the explosion attributed to Anarchists. On the strength of an instruction from the Queen who wrote that she " trusts that firmness & energy will be shown to check the Anarchists after the dreadful events in France " :

From *Mr. Asquith*

Home Office, 19 February, 1894

Thank you for your letter. I will keep you fully informed about the explosion and the Anarchists. The newspapers are full of sensational rubbish. We are having the whole thing most carefully investigated and the results are not yet complete. But so far we see no reason to suspect anything in the nature of a serious conspiracy. Every hole I think has been stopped. Her Majesty need be under no apprehensions for her own safety, so far as foresight and care can secure it.

P.S.   You will see an announcement affecting me in tomorrow's *Times*.   Have I to ask the Queen's consent !

The P.S. refers to his engagement to Miss Margot Tennant. On the back of this letter the Queen wrote :

How curious that *he* sh^d abuse the papers so much & *that he* sh^d ask if my consent is required to his marriage.   If this *was* required the Queen w^d not give it as she thinks she is most unfit for a C. Minister's wife.   V.R.I.

Mrs. Asquith was of course treated with every courtesy at Court when her husband was in office.

Other Ministers with whom Ponsonby associated and whom he consulted came to Windsor and Osborne when he was living with his family and therefore there were no daily letters to his wife in which he could relate what he thought of them.   But in October 1892 Campbell Bannerman came to Balmoral. Ponsonby wrote :   " He is rather a new man to me as I only knew him officially before ".   The Secretary of State for War, as he then was, had several talks with the Queen who as usual was alarmed at prospects with a Liberal Government in power. She had a good opinion of his judgment and appreciated the help he eventually gave by his tactful handling of the delicate matter of the Duke of Cambridge's retirement from the post of Commander-in-Chief.   Campbell Bannerman was Minister in Attendance at Osborne in 1893 and was present sitting next to the Queen at the amateur performance of *She Stoops to Conquer* in the Council Room.   The part of Tony Lumpkin was played by Sir Henry Ponsonby's third son, who twelve years later was appointed Principal Private Secretary to Campbell Bannerman when he became Prime Minister.

The extracts in this chapter from the papers and correspondence give some idea of the use Ponsonby made of the easy intercourse he gained with leading politicians which brought him into close personal relations with several of them.   It often helped him to smooth by a word of caution or encouragement awkward situations which might arise in their audiences with the Queen.   But more especially it was useful in enabling him to mitigate any sudden animosities to which Her Majesty might give utterance by suggestions of a more reasonable interpretation of the character and intentions of those who at the moment were not in favour. All of them found the Private Secretary an accessible intermediary and a wise guide. But it could not always have been easy for him to assume at once a completely sympathetic attitude towards the new Ministers on a change of government although it was absolutely necessary ; the more so as the Queen, in the case of the advent of a Liberal Government, hardly made any attempt to do anything of the kind.

SIR HENRY PONSONBY AND HIS SON ARTHUR IN PAGE'S UNIFORM

CHAPTER XIII

Journeys Abroad

THE Queen greatly enjoyed her periodic journeys abroad. She liked most of the places she went to and treated her visits as a real holiday. Princess Beatrice accompanied her, there was a Lady-in-Waiting in attendance and some of her other children occasionally came and stayed with her. She could not be bothered by Ministers, or if, as happened very rarely, one came out she hardly saw him. This did not prevent her from sending fairly tart letters on political affairs from wherever she might be. Needless to say, to the inconvenience at times caused by her absence so far away she paid not the smallest attention.

Ponsonby was in attendance on these visits fourteen times : Lucerne 1868, Baden and Coburg 1876, Baveno 1879, Darmstadt and Coburg 1880, Mentone 1882, Darmstadt 1884, Aix-les-Bains and Darmstadt 1885, Aix-les-Bains 1887, Florence and Charlottenburg 1888, Biarritz 1889, Aix-les-Bains and Darmstadt 1890, Grasse 1891, Hyères (called by the servants Highers) and Darmstadt 1892, and Florence and Coburg 1894.

During the holiday in Switzerland at Lucerne the party had frequent expeditions up the mountains and behaved very much like ordinary tourists. On one occasion they went up to a monastery at Engelberg. Colonel Ponsonby accompanied the Queen into the large church. She had never seen a Roman Catholic service before. " I am not quite sure whether it is not high treason to advise the Queen to enter a Roman Catholic Church." She was deeply interested, but on the whole she was not favourably impressed and " there is no danger of her forsaking the Protestant faith especially while there is a bitter Protestant like me at hand ". On relating her impression she was understood to say to Canon Duckworth, who was one of the party, that the chanting was very fine,

" Like the chanting of the Georges ". Duckworth, puzzled, asked What was the chanting of the Georgian era ? or did George IV chant and had she heard him ? But Prince Leopold explained that she had referred to St. George's (at Windsor).

All the later visits were more formal and for Ponsonby were very far from holidays. In addition to his ordinary political work which was sent out to him, he had to watch the royal courier in making the travelling arrangements, and hours of his time were occupied in the careful observance of the necessary punctilio usual in foreign places such as leaving cards, arranging introductions, writing letters of thanks to all officials, guarding the Queen from undesirable visitors and coping with British and foreign pressmen. Only towards the end did he have with him a congenial colleague such as Bigge, Edwards or Reid with whom he could escape for a few hours' relaxation. Yet in the daily letters to his wife which give a full account of these visits only occasionally is there any reference to boredom or weariness, although there is mention of only an hour in the morning when he is undisturbed and of how his writing-table is covered with letters.

The Queen's " Highlander " attracted attention in villages and towns. But John Brown was insufferably bored and made himself intensely disagreeable. He generally managed to prevent the Queen going out till after four o'clock as was her custom at home. At Baveno in 1879 Ponsonby writes of a drive to a lovely place. But the Queen did not get out of the carriage. " We believe it was because Brown would not allow her to get out. He is surly beyond measure and today we could see him all the way — a beautiful drive — with his eyes fixed on the horses' tails refusing to look up." At Mentone (1882) Lady Churchill, who was the Lady-in-Waiting, defied Brown and took the Queen for a little expedition which gave her great pleasure.

It was during this visit to Mentone that there were alarms about Fenians. Three Irishmen were supposed to be coming to Mentone from Paris. The local police were making the most of it and Brown, detesting the place, told the Queen. The British police who accompanied the Queen thought it was a hoax. Nevertheless special precautions were taken. The Queen herself was not nervous but she was sorry for Brown's anxiety.

From *The Queen*

Mentone, March 20, 1882

The Queen thanks Sir Henry Ponsonby for his kind letter which has much reassured her tho' she cannot say *she* felt so much alarmed but it gave her a great shock as she was forgetting the 2nd of March [1] & she trusts Sir Henry will also reassure Brown who was in such a state heightened by his increasing *hatred* of being " abroad " which blinds his admiration of the country even. The Queen thinks that one principal cause of all this (wh was *not* the case in Switzerland) is that he can communicate with *no* one when out, nor keep anyone off the carriage nor the coachman either. At Lucerne we always had Hoffmann & *now* when Greenham [2] is not with us we take him walking we have *no one* and that is what puts Brown so out and makes him so anxious.

How long would it take to drive to Ventimiglia & to Bordighera & to Monaco ? Perhaps Sir Henry will make inquiries about a china manufactory near here & a Monastery.

In short find out about any excursions within reach.

At Hyères (1892) the Queen had her Indian servants with her. The flies were very troublesome. " At dinner she has one of her Indians with a gold whisk of cowstail which he sweeps about over her head. It has quite an oriental look. But the flies come to us instead."

Sometimes Ponsonby and others were lodged in a separate building but generally they were in the same villa. At Aix-les-Bains (1887) he writes :

She [the Queen] told me that on the previous night about 12 o'clock she had heard noises below her room and, not being sure whether it was the regular rumblings of an earthquake or what, she sent for Hyam the Footman in waiting who had the audacity to say " I think it must be Sir Henry." It is true I do live just under the Queen and it is true I went to bed early, but I don't believe it was my snoring. However the anecdote has caused great hilarity in our circles, in which I do not join.

Two letters from Baveno in 1879 give a full account of the days' doings :

Villa Clara, Baveno, April 16, 1879

Our expedition to Milan was a failure. The Queen was annoyed two days ago because Paget [3] wanted to telegraph

---

[1] When she was shot at near Windsor station.
[2] The English detective.   [3] British Ambassador in Italy.

about it. Her idea was that she could go quite incog.
(arriving by Special and driving about with a Highlander
on the box) and it was only on my pressing it that she allowed
him to notify her coming at all. Then it poured. I hinted
at a postponement but she said no she would go. So we went.
There was a crowd at the station but the people were kept
back. At the Cenacola not many and a dozen police, but
even here H.M. thought they were too close to the carriage.

We saw the pictures in peace but in haste. At the
Cathedral there was a crowd on the steps which increased
inside and we had to walk round her. At the tomb of
S. Carlo we kept them out — but in the Cathedral itself they
thronged round. Not a very great many but still a crowd
and this perturbed her and she complained to me that there
were not more police. If she had gone as Queen we might
have had fifty police there, but she had repeated over and
over again that she would go quite privately — so there were
only a few police — enough to keep them back — but not
to prevent them crowding round. I believe they tumbled
Jenner down the steps which has made him wrath with the
boys of Milan — but he enjoyed the sights very much. As
it rained the Queen drove in a shut carriage. She wouldn't
go to the Brera — so we drove for an hour. And she wouldn't
have Paget in her carriage — and didn't ask Lady Paget to
come. So with Brown on the box who never raised his head
to look at anything — she saw nothing. We men opened
our carriage as it ceased raining and saw a great deal. I
stopped the carriage once and ran back to tell her these were
San Lorenzo's columns. But this stopping of the carriage
was coldly received and a crowd began to assemble to see
the Highlander, so we went on — and I didn't trouble them
again. In the evening the Queen began to reflect she had
seen very little. True. But whose fault? She said she never
expected the mob at Milan to crowd as much as they did,
seeing how civil the Baveno people are. But Milan is a great
city. I admit the people were rather rude and pushing —
but unless regular precautions are taken this can't be helped.
And Baveno is a little village with very few people in it.

Villa Clara, Baveno, April 17, 1879

Yesterday was occupied by the Duchess of Genoa —
mother to the Queen of Italy — who announced her intention
of calling here from her villa at Stresa where she arrived two
days ago. Due at 1 — so the Queen came in drenched at
¼ to 1 — with her two ladies and gave orders she was to have
ample notice of the Duchess' coming. I was giving the

orders when the Duchess appeared on the Hill. Carriage
and four preceded by an outrider something like ours but
wearing a sword. The postillions in blue velvet very well
got up on 4 splendid black horses — the footmen in long
scarlet cloaks walking by the side of the carriage. This I
think was not state. But our hill is stiff and the footmen
heavy. Of course no one was ready. Edwards and I fortunately had our frock coats on and ran out. I took the
Duchess to the Drawing Room and talked to her, apologizing,
till the Queen came in 5 minutes and Edwards took the others
to the Billiard Room. Our ladies came down as fast as they
could. The visit lasted half an hour. All well and good.
Lady Paget who was to have presented the Duchess did not
arrive till 10 minutes later. It poured all the time. After
luncheon as the Queen sent to say she did not want the
Gentlemen we started — at 3.30 — and took Miss Cadogan
with us — as we said she must come to write her name down
at Stresa — and leave cards. Of course we were all in walking clothes — but drove, and I had on my white ulster.
Rather a crowd at Stresa but we drove up in our shay. Our
horror was great to see the Duchess of Genoa on the top step
— her household around her — and obvious preparations for
receiving the Queen. Jenner said " Dear me." I jumped
out — ran up the steps in my ulster and accosted the swells
in hats and white kid gloves and most smartly dressed. I
encountered a short — fat — most cross looking man and
said I hoped they were not expecting the Queen and explained we had come to write our names down. The
Duchess of Genoa a few yards off glaring at me through her
binocles.

The fat cross man sent for the book. Said : Oh no we are
not expecting the Queen. The Duchess is merely taking a
promenade in the garden. Then he couldn't help saying
plainly — " *Est-ce-que la Reine vient ?* " To which I replied
" *Je n'en sais rien.*" On which he disappeared looking more
cross than ever.

There were 8 servants in scarlet drawn up in line. Two
valets de la maison in purple tights — obviously full dress —
and a venerable *chef de la maison* old and bewildered. He
was evidently an old family servant given the best place to
see the Queen — and he didn't make out whether I was the
Queen or not.

However the book was brought. I called Miss Cadogan
and Edwards to come to me — Edwards also in a lively
ulster. Jenner remained unmoved in the carriage. So all
eyes were turned on him — while we inscribed our names.
The lady and gentleman then came to us, overwhelmed us

with civilities so as to cover any awkwardnesses, and we departed. Obviously they had expected the Queen — so we reported on our return home, where we hurried back in thunder, lightning and hail.

There is an account of a luncheon in Florence at which the presence of insufficient Kings to pair off with the Queens caused complications :

> The Emperor of Brazil and his wife came up to see the Queen — looks very old — and has been very ill — but still works from 8 A.M. to 8 P.M. incessantly at everything. She is very groggy on her feet. Then at 2 we went to luncheon at the Pitti.
> The complications of not having Kings enough caused the King to adopt " *Una Costuma tedesca il sandwich* " which was that as in Germany — he and the Emperor each took in two ladies. I couldn't help laughing to see the King of Italy with our Queen on one arm and the Empress of Brazil on the other walk slowly in to luncheon — while the Emperor took the Queen of Italy and the Queen of Servia. I took in Princess Strongoli — a woman with spectacles — really agreeable and we talked during the whole of luncheon — on my other side the Servian lady who, as she only spoke German, I did not get on much with. There was a long talk after with some thirty or forty people. I aired my Italian everywhere and swaggered about having been presented in my youth to Carlo Alberto which only one other man there had been. I was introduced to Crispi. He talked away without saying anything — that I expected as I did not expect him to develop his program to me — but Savile says that is what he does to everyone so that no one really knows his political intentions which he adopts according to the sentiments of the moment. He is clever and to a certain extent popular as he is quick in seizing popular ideas but he has no fixed policy.

Ponsonby received a letter from a newspaper correspondent in Florence giving further details of occurrences on this occasion of which the following is an extract :

> There was one incident in to-day's proceedings which may perhaps be not known to you. The King and Queen of Italy on leaving the Palazzo Pitti this morning to visit the Emperor and Empress of Brazil were surrounded outside the Palazzo by an enormous crowd, which was kept back by the Gendarmerie. The King stopped his carriage, summoned the officer commanding the Gendarmerie to his side, and ordered him to remove his men. The crowd im-

mediately cheered him loudly. At the same time he held out his hat, and received in it numerous letters and documents from the surrounding people. Other letters were also thrown into his carriage, which proceeded only at a walking pace for some distance, while this continued.

The only contretemps I have heard of during Her Majesty's stay has been the prominent position given to the servants at the Bigallo when H.M. viewed the *Scoppio del Carro*.[1] By the Italians, it was considered a great slight on the Queen of Servia, that the Queen's servants should have been allowed to occupy the adjoining loggia to the Queen of Servia, as was the case. It so happened that both the Queen of Servia and the Dukes of Edinburgh and Leuchtenberg had been seen in the identical loggia only five minutes before Her Majesty's dressers and Indian Servants took up their places there. I have stated to everyone who has talked to me on the subject that it was an entire mistake that they were where they were.

However, the day-to-day doings with their humours and worries which are recorded in almost diary form cannot, in consideration of the space they would occupy, be related in full. A few of the major episodes must be selected.

When she visited Germany the Queen was brought into close contact with the unfortunate circumstances which politically as well as domestically darkened for many years the life of her daughter the Crown Princess, afterwards Empress Frederick. We catch a glimpse of her in 1876. The Queen had come over from Baden to Coburg and the Crown Princess visited her, bringing her son Prince William, the future Emperor, then about sixteen years old. He looked pale : "The Princess is said to work him too hard". The old Emperor William also came over. He was seventy-nine and still very active.

The next mention of the Crown Princess is in 1885. The occasion was a visit from Sir Robert Morier who having served in several German Courts had a close knowledge of German affairs. At this time he was British Ambassador at St. Petersburg. The question under discussion was Count Seckendorff's influence over the Crown Princess. Ponsonby writes :

[1] The ceremony of conveying the holy fire by means of a mechanical dove on a wire from the altar of the Duomo to a cart in the Square drawn by white oxen.

Morier explained that Bismarck only employed Secken-dorff to restrain the Crown Princess and that he would not support Seckendorff.   He — S. — decides what friends she shall see and what not and controls her completely.   I suspect much of this comes from young Stockmar — an oldish man now — and he sees very little of the Crown Princess.   If Seckendorff has this complete control how is it he does not prevent her Anglomania from continually oppressing the Germans ?   Morier says — and others say too — that her constant praise of England is the cause of the Court irritation against us.   Prince William her son sees this — he opposes his mother on all these points and is furious about Seckendorff.   His tutor Hinzpeter — whom I met years ago at Baden — taught him to be " thorough " in everything he undertook and this is now his character. He enters most deeply and heartily into Military and Civil matters — is beloved in the Army, is very popular elsewhere — dislikes the English, is energetic, clever and ambitious and it would not take much to induce a rising on his behalf against his father if the father in any of his visionary schemes came to grief with Bismarck.   Bismarck likes Prince William and does not care for the Crown Prince.

I have given you a benefit of these German stories.   I was interested in all Morier told me.   I believe he has told H.M. all this.

It will be remembered that the old Emperor William died on March 9, 1888, and the Emperor Frederick reigned little more than three months.   The Military Attaché in Berlin wrote the following letter before these events happened :

From *Colonel Swaine*

Berlin, Dec. 9, 1887

The other day I dined with Prince William and shot with him yesterday and on both occasions he expressed his deep regret that he and his English Relations did not appear to agree and that rumours were circulated in England by his relations which were neither just nor true.   He said that considering that they never took an opportunity of corre-sponding with him, or when in England to try to know some-thing more of him, it was impossible for them except from hear-say, to know what his feelings, opinions and aspirations were.

For instance, he said, that when he suddenly went to San Remo he received a request from the Queen to give Her Majesty an account of how he found his father.   He wrote

Her Majesty a long letter on the subject but neither received a letter in turn, nor any acknowledgment of it in any shape. He feels bitterly that such action leaves him out in the cold and will never tend to bring him nearer to his English Relations.

Rumours have also gone abroad that he is very anti-English and most warlike. He has again begged me to use all my endeavours to dispel such statements. " It would be monstrous if I in my position were to run my country into a war. I fully endorse the policy that the Chancellor is carrying out and we mean to do absolutely nothing to provoke or irritate either Russia or France. As to my being anti-English it is an unkind mis-statement of facts. It must be remembered that above all and in first line I am a German Prince. I am personally attached to the Czar, because he has always treated me most kindly, and when I am with him he makes me feel as if I were talking with a Prince of my own nationality. But for all that I am no more Russian than I am anti-English. As regards my English feelings I long to think that the two countries should go hand in hand in all political questions and that we two being strong and powerful should uphold the Peace of Europe. You with a good fleet and we with our great Army can do this and if my English Relatives will only give me the opportunity I would tell them this myself. But if they don't write to me and don't speak to me when the opportunity presents itself how can they ever know what my feelings really are."

I send you these lines to show you what Prince William really feels. You know how anxious I have always been to bring about a better understanding in the Royal Family and enable the English Branch of it to value Prince William's merits. A better understanding amongst the Relations will tend also to produce a better impression in both Countries and looking into the Future both near and far I uphold that it is our duty to try and bring this about. So little is really necessary to accomplish this, and I should be so glad to hear from you that you see your way to giving the necessary aid by throwing in a little word here and there and smoothing over all difficulties and misunderstandings.

The Queen's comment on this letter was written from Windsor on December 13, 1887, to Sir Henry Ponsonby :

You might say 1st that there was no intentional illwill or coldness between Pce William and his English relations but that they had been shocked & pained at his behaviour towards his Parents for some time past — passing them over

& settling things behind their backs with the Emperor, which is so contrary to what the Queen has ever been accustomed & her children and g^dchildren dreamt of doing that it is impossible for them to be as cordial towards him as they w^d wish to be. That at San Remo specially he had shown so little feeling & respect towards his mother before strangers unknown who were much shocked at it at a moment of intense distress & anxiety that the Queen was greatly pained to say the least.

As regards his Anti-English feeling this comes to the Queen's ears from many quarters.

Let him be a dutiful & affect^{te} son trying to help & support his Mother in her terrible anxiety instead of opposing & annoying her & his Father who sh^d in no way be annoyed or irritated & she sh^d be most happy to be on friendly & affect^{te} terms as when he was a child. The Queen has today written to thank William. She had purposely delayed doing so — but now that the news are so much better she has written.

This is merely the substance of what Sir Henry might write. Col. Swaine flatters W^m far too much. He sh^d speak to him openly & strongly.

Sir Henry accordingly wrote on the same day :

To *Colonel Swaine*

Windsor Castle, December 13th, 1887

I lost no time in making the Queen aware of the substance of your letter.

I am afraid there must have been some little misunderstanding as Her Majesty was undoubtedly hurt at what she had been told of Prince William's relations with his parents for she said that if the Prince would support and be kind to his mother in her time of trouble and affliction, the Queen would gladly welcome him as an affectionate grandson. The Queen was glad to hear from you that the Prince was not anti-English, but she said this had been repeated to her from so many quarters that it was difficult not to suppose there was some truth in these allegations.

Her Majesty had already written to Prince William who will have received her letter before you get this.

The full account of the Empress Frederick's distressing years of suffering caused by her husband's illness and death and the conduct of her son to her is contained in *The Letters of the Empress Frederick*, edited by Sir Frederick Ponsonby, Sir

Henry's second son, who was the Empress's godson and to whose care the letters were entrusted. The volume also includes letters from Colonel Swaine and from Lady Ponsonby.

But the Empress had another cause of trouble in the case of her eldest daughter Princess Victoria. This came to a head during the Queen's visit to Florence in 1888. What at first seemed only an ordinary royal betrothal of Prince Alexander of Bulgaria to Princess Victoria of Prussia developed into an acute controversy in international politics. Ponsonby appears to have avoided referring the matter home and was content to keep in communication with Sir Edward Malet, British Ambassador in Berlin. The trouble was largely confined to royal personages.

Prince Alexander (generally referred to as " Sandro ") was brother of Prince Henry of Battenberg. This brought in Princess Beatrice as an interested party. Prince Alexander was a nephew of the Tsar Alexander II and on Russia's proposal was chosen as first sovereign Prince of Bulgaria in 1879. He was closely under Russian influence. In 1881 the Tsar died and Russian influence waned. After troubles, which need not be entered into here, he abdicated in September 1886. To give the full story it will suffice to quote a letter from Ponsonby to his wife and the draft of one he wrote to Sir Edward Malet :

Florence, April 10, 1888

So many conversations go on about this marriage affair that one gets bothered. The Queen really would like the marriage but only on condition that Crown Prince William welcomed him as brother-in-law — which he won't. The Empress wrote yesterday to the Queen that on the 6th, the day on which the articles about it appeared in *The Times* and *Cologne Gazette*, she had had a long and very satisfactory interview with Bismarck and that the Queen was not to believe the stories which would be published in the papers. What can this mean ? The story which I gather from letters and conversations seems to be this :

Some five years ago or more the then Crown Princess pushed on the then Sandro of Bulgaria who pledged his troth to Princess Victoria. The then Emperor, Crown Prince and everyone at Berlin was against it for political reasons. The Bulgarian reason has disappeared (though the Russians fear the marriage would revive it) and the present Empress, feeling that her tenure of power may be short, wants the marriage to take place now — at least we suppose so. The Queen wrote to her three weeks ago not to press it on if William was against it. Sandro was invited to Berlin on the 5th April. He is not particularly keen on the marriage — his love having somewhat cooled and the prospect of a poor marriage and general dislike shown to it making him still more opposed to it. But he feels himself bound to it. So packed up his things. Suddenly he got a telegram " Don't come " so he did not. Two days later he received a letter from Crown Prince William. " If you marry my sister I shall consider you the enemy of my family and my country."

In the meanwhile rumour at Berlin said that old Bismarck had for some time been bored with the love story till he discovered that Herbert [his son] was in love with Princess Victoria. He was rather pleased with the idea. Herbert tells everyone he intends to marry Victoria and the Empress having heard this is determined to get the marriage with Sandro completed. Herbert therefore stirred up Crown Prince William, has managed to drag in the Russian Scare, and has met the Empress' move by telling the newspapers that his father will resign if the marriage takes place. This is the story as conjectured.

If it had been a mere love story I think it might have been left to the principals concerned. But as it affects the Queen — and her immediate movements — the quarrel becomes very interesting here. What I wonder is — Is the story about Herbert true ? Is it not put forward to aggravate us here ? If so it has succeeded — for whereas we were cool on the question a week ago — the idea of Herbert Bismarck cutting out Sandro — and of Malet telegraphing that the excitement against the Queen as roused by the Chancellor is so great that she had better not come — has roused H.M.'s indignation and she is now determined to go. Sandro's love had certainly cooled. But he won't stand being insulted by William or cut out by Bismarck, so he is now full of fire again.

Princess Beatrice made me help her to write a letter to Sandro yesterday — which she really made very good. She has advised him to answer William that he cannot discuss his marriage with a brother, while the whole question is in the hands of William's father and mother. And has also advised him that he, Sandro, cannot give up Princess Victoria himself but if (as she, Princess Beatrice, hopes) he does do so to avoid unhappiness to both — the breaking off should be done by his father, old Prince Alexander of Hesse. Prince Henry comes back on Friday from Malta and I hope will quiet the excitement here. Reid tells me that M. Mackenzie says the Emperor's general health is beginning to suffer and that he is going back.

To Sir Edward Malet

Florence, April 13, 1888

I am commanded by the Queen to thank you for your letter of the 7th instant which Her Majesty received last night by messenger, in which you communicate to her an account of Prince Bismarck's reasons for intending to resign which you consider were of such a private nature that you could not give them in an official despatch but which were communicated to the newspapers immediately after or possibly before His Serene Highness had spoken to you.

The Queen is quite unable to understand how the visit of a private individual, such as Prince Alexander of Battenberg is now, could have aroused distrust in Russia to such an extent as to have made such an event a cause of danger to the peace between the two countries, and she must confess that she is surprised that Germany should be dictated to by the Czar who has, you say, a craze against Prince Alexander which as far as the Queen can learn is not shared by the Russian nation.

Nor is it easy to see how the marriage of Prince Alexander and Princess Victoria could in any way cement the Union of Russia and France against Germany or cause estrangement between England and Germany. Surely the prognostications of such great European changes arising out of a marriage of this sort are absurd. Prince Bismarck appeals to the Queen who he supposes favors the marriage. He is as much mistaken in this supposition as he is in his other conclusions, if he imagines that the Queen has urged this marriage. No doubt she would be glad if the Prince and Princess wished to marry and if the Imperial family of Germany welcomed such a proposal, that it should take place, but all the details could have been easily and privately discussed without making a state affair out of a family matter.

As far as the Queen can learn the Chancellor allowed his intended resignation to be announced to the world before consulting the Empress upon this question and it would appear that after he had seen Her Imperial Majesty matters were arranged.

This storm might therefore have been avoided if Prince Bismarck had only taken the trouble to inform himself more fully of the facts of the case.

The Queen went to Charlottenburg straight into the hornets' nest. On April 25, 1888, Ponsonby wrote home from there :

The Empress was very nice in talking to me of you both in the afternoon and in the evening but at the last time when I spoke of the Emperor as being better she said " No, he is not really better " — and then I saw her eyes fill with tears and she was silent — " but it has done him a temporary good to see Mama." So it is quite clear she knows his condition. Many people here say she does not. Radolin is the most hopeful — or rather he says the doctors agree that it may go on for months, though it may end at any moment. He and Seckendorff speak now though I don't think much.

In the meantime the state of tension between the Empress and Prince William [then Crown Prince] seems to be increasing. H.M. is troubled and wants to re-establish harmony. But all depends on the reason of disagreement. Swaine is strong on the honesty and excellence of Prince William but says he is no doubt narrow and aggravated by his mother's English praises. There are faults on both sides. How are these to be got rid of? The Empress declares she has no friends, all her family are against her and all her surroundings.

M. Mackenzie tells the Queen that the Empress is betrayed and has no one to consult. She does not care for Malet and there is no other person who can advise her. (Why not Seckendorff?) However Sir M. Mackenzie has alarmed the Queen and I am to see him. Reid cautions me at the bottom of all Mackenzie's arguments there is — self. Besides which why should the Empress alone be right and all the rest here wrong? Bismarck is coming to see H.M. this morning. But Bismarck is said to be against the Empress, otherwise I should have said consult the big man. What I have advised H.M. is to speak to Prince William himself and to hear what he says and also to Prince Henry [of Prussia]. Every one says that Prince William is not a bad fellow — but will not be commanded or ordered about by his mother or any one else. Then when the Queen knows Prince William's views and feelings she could speak to the Empress.

I sat between Bruhl and Countess Eulenburg at dinner. A reception in the evening. About fifteen Royalties dined alone together. Radolin said to me " They all insist on coming and they all hate each other." This family dinner takes place once a week. Countess Perponcher is in very good force and all are most civil to us.

I have had a long talk with Seckendorff. He is a

Mackenzie-ite — but laments the manner in which this doctorial controversy has become international. I declared that many English were against Mackenzie. He said that may be so but the conviction in Berlin is that he represents England and that the Empress for this reason backs him up. Seckendorff is doubtful about any rejunction [?] of the Empress and Prince William but hopes the Queen will try.

On the same day in a hastily scribbled note he writes : "Just seen Bismarck, only just a conversation with him. Most civil and almost nervous at seeing the Queen. I took him through the rooms and he only talked about them and I handed him over to the Empress to take in."

They left for England the next day. So this is one of the instances in which the correspondence breaks off suddenly as Ponsonby and his wife were shortly to meet. That Bismarck was nervous is well known. That the Queen was not in the least nervous may be taken for granted. But it would have been interesting to have the Queen's impressions of the interview, which no doubt she confided to her Private Secretary.

In her journal [1] the Queen wrote a fairly full account of the subjects discussed at this interview. But curiously enough there is a certain formality in her diary-writing, as if she were conscious that the pages would one day be given publicity. It appears also that the blue pencil or even the scissors have been unwarrantably used for the excision of her natural and characteristic indiscretions. To her Private Secretary she would give, no doubt, some personal impressions and touches which would illuminate and enhance any description of Prince Bismarck's audience with her.

Four years later in a letter from Hyères (April 17, 1892) Ponsonby writes :

> The Emperor is certainly a most excitable man and proposes all sorts of wild schemes for England. . . . Lord Salisbury observes, if he is in this excitable mood he may be dangerous and that a few hours' conversation with the Queen can appease him. So he hopes H.M. will see him at Darmstadt, which she does not at all want to do. She said to me " No, no, I really cannot go about keeping everybody in order."

In contrast to the rather serious and distressing events

[1] *Letters of Queen Victoria*, Third Series, vol. i, p. 404.

which came to the front during the Queen's visit to Florence and Charlottenburg in 1888 there was some comic relief connected with her visit to Biarritz in the following year. The Count de La Rochefoucauld had lent the Queen his house, the Pavillon. The Countess was an English lady divorced from a previous husband and Ponsonby had heard from the Foreign Office that " the details of her divorce were more than ordinarily unfit for publication ". There could be no question of the Queen receiving her. But the whole visit was punctuated by her attempts to reach the Queen. It began at once :

> March 7, 1889
>
> I jumped into a *calèche* on arriving and rushed to get to the Pavillon before the Queen, to present Comte de La Rochefoucauld who was going to give her a gold key. I had written twice to Madame la Comtesse to tell her not to appear, so I was flabbergasted to find the whole family on the steps. She rushed and shook me by both hands. . . . I thought How on earth can I get rid of her ? When she enquired how should the Queen be received, I said by the Count alone. She said, " May I stand behind the door ? " I didn't like to say no. So I said " If he alone receives the Queen and you stand in the recess that will do." But not at all, she rushed forward and gave the Queen a bouquet. . . . She plunged at Lady Churchill and embraced her. . . . H.M. sent for me afterward and was very indignant. But what could be done ? Nothing.
>
> March 8, 1889
>
> Our trouble is the Comtesse de La Rochefoucauld. From what we hear, she apparently thinks that her disgrace only lasted while G. C. [her former husband] was alive. But that as he has died of drink a month ago, she is now restored to virtue.

There were reports in the local paper that the Countess had intended to leave Biarritz but the Queen begged her to stay. Ponsonby refused to contradict them. The Count then took up the cudgels for his wife and begged through Prince Henry of Battenberg that the Queen should receive her. He also had " a terrible interview " with Ponsonby, when he implored, wept and threatened. His claim was that his wife was a foreigner and so should be received. Ten days later :

> For one hour before breakfast La Rochefoucauld poured forth his griefs and his arguments to me. Some were curious

in that he, one of the La Rochefoucaulds, a family that had
not its equal in Europe, was not to be treated like the rest
of the world. I thought the story " *Le bon Dieu pensera deux
fois avant de condamner un La Rochefoucauld* " was a fiction but
it was true yesterday with him.

He went on to relate how her former husband had beaten and
robbed her. He had protected her and finding her defenceless
had married her. Subsequently he sent Ponsonby " an immense packet of letters to read ". At last the Queen on March
30, 1889, wrote very clearly on her black-edged and ciphered
notepaper :

> The La Rochefoucaulds are quite intolerable. The
> Queen will *not* see her on any acc^t & if she forces herself
> forward the Queen will not look at her.

In the midst of these invasions from the Count and fear
on the part of the household of meeting either the Count or
Countess in the street, all the arrangements for a meeting on
the frontier between the Queen and the Queen of Spain,
by no means a simple matter, had to be attended to. This
event passed off successfully.

An episode which amounted to a sort of farcical melo-
drama, if irreverently such an expression may be used of the
doings of royalty, took place at Darmstadt in 1884 when a
large assembly of royal personages were invited there for the
marriage of Princess Victoria of Hesse and Prince Louis of
Battenberg.

Princess Alice died in 1878 and the Grand Duke of Hesse,
Prince Louis, had been a widower for six years and was a
great favourite with Queen Victoria. Ponsonby had of course
come across him before. He wrote to his wife an amusing
letter about an expedition with Prince Louis from Osborne as
far back as 1875 :

Osborne, April 21, 1875

Yesterday Byng [1] and I rode with Louis of Hesse to Park-
hurst and saw the barracks there. Louis understands all
the machinery of soldiers very well and delighted the officers
and men by trying their arms, pulling at their belts, examining their buttons and hooks and putting his nose into their
cartouche cases and pouches. It happened also that I was
very knowing on the subject of the new equipment, having

---

[1] Colonel Byng, Equerry, afterwards Earl of Strafford.

been on the Committee, so that I explained and discussed learnedly on the valise and mode of putting it on. Byng meanwhile had fallen a victim to what he called the melancholy Major who talked to him of nothing but sickness and death. I then got into very eager discourse with the Officer Commanding the 49th, having told him I was once in that corps, which excited him greatly and he asked me if I knew Stiggins and Wiggins and Biggins, etc., which of course I didn't. I suppose our converse grew warm for Louis of Hesse enquired what it was about and I mentioned my services with the 49th which produced a series of " *Ach so* — how shall I say — *Ach so* " for some time and was duly reported to the Queen so as to form a topic at the dinner last night.

On the occasion at Darmstadt in 1884 the Grand Duke was the hero, the villain or the clown, whichever role seems to suit him best. The Queen had come for the marriage ceremony. The Crown Princess arrived for it but she was more preoccupied by her daughter Victoria's possible marriage with Alexander of Battenberg. Prince Henry, the third Battenberg brother, was present with his mother Princess Battenberg (of Russian origin). The Prince of Wales came for the ceremony. So the uniformed chorus of royal personages with their suites was tremendous and the Hessians were very proud at being able to attract such an assembly at Darmstadt. The popular Grand Duke was jovial and radiant at the station receiving them all. The festivities and functions were elaborate and heavy. On one day there was a royal confirmation in the morning to be attended in full uniform, a banquet which lasted two hours, the christening of a royal baby in the afternoon, again in full uniform, later a " Punch " and a heavy dinner in the evening, after which a Russian Colonel " played beautifully on the pianoforte ". Henry Ponsonby was then asked to play (never having done so in his life) so " I said I had left my music behind ". At a subsequent banquet Princess Victoria remarked in the course of conversation to Ponsonby (exactly what her mother Princess Alice had said to Lady Ponsonby many years before) : " I dare say Royalty is nonsense and it may be better if it is swept away. But as long as it exists, we must have certain rules to guide us." The scene was set, the palaces resplendent, the treasures on view and the streets crowded with gorgeous uniforms and state carriages.

Now some months before there had been gossip about a pretty lady called Alexandra Kalomine, a Russian. She had recently divorced her husband Kalomine, a Russian diplomat, and had been " taken up " by the Grand Duke. Princess Victoria had often accompanied them in their walks together. No one at first paid much attention to the gossip and Princess Victoria declared " Dear Papa will never marry again ". But gradually the rumour spread, although only by whispers, that he would marry Kalomine. Ponsonby found himself drawn into all the functions connected with the great marriage celebrations, discussing with the Crown Princess her Victoria's marriage with Alexander of Bulgaria and hearing in every corner more gossip about Kalomine. He writes : " So you see we are in the midst of love matters ". The Queen was hearing details from Hessian Court ladies. The Prince of Wales was angry that the Queen had been kept in the dark. The Crown Princess said if the Grand Duke were engaged to Kalomine the marriage must be broken off. The Princesses' governess declared the Tsar should order the lady back to Russia and Ponsonby wrote :

> The Grand Duke has behaved very badly in not telling the Queen before she came to Darmstadt because it places her in a most awkward position. If she goes away it will create a scandal, if she remains it will look as if she approved the marriage.

Gladstone wrote to Ponsonby :

> It must cause continual and painful embarrassment to the Queen, and I am wholly at a loss to conceive how the conduct of the Grand Duke in not giving her notice before her journey, can be justified.

But at Darmstadt everyone went about pretending they knew nothing about it. The great marriage ceremony of Prince Louis and Princess Victoria was duly performed and then came the thunderclap. The Grand Duke married Alexandra Kalomine *the same evening* !

Ponsonby sums up the situation :

> Darmstadt, May 3, 1884
>
> Like a novel, our romance comes to its definite conclusion. Whether alarmed by the family conclave or whether in

accordance with his settled arrangement which certainly we were warned of — the Grand Duke married Alexandra Kalomine on the evening of the great marriage here. At least that is what is believed by us English and Prussians, and this — which oozed out — though we are still keeping it dark here, yesterday morning was telegraphed to Berlin by the Crown Princess.

I was inspecting the treasures of the Schloss Staat Library with Lady Churchill and the fair Kohausen at 4 — and we separated with tender vows of meeting again for victuals and renewing our literary researches today — but at 5 a thundering answer came from the Empress ordering the immediate return of the whole party from this contaminated court — and after a hurried dinner they all rushed off in the evening. Tyrwhitt-Wilson, the Prince of Wales' Equerry, told me that H.R.H. had only heard it from the Crown Princess at 5 — and that he apparently approved of this moral decision. We don't hurry. But we go as settled on Monday. And we trust nothing will become public till we are well away. I am really sorry for these Hessians. Westerweller is miserable. He apparently is not aware that the marriage has taken place. Werner has taken to his bed — and von Herf prefers to continue in a state of ignorance. The glory of the Hessian Court is its alliance with other great ones — Baden, Würtemberg, Bavaria, etc. may swagger — but a family event in the Hessian family brings to Darmstadt Royal England and Imperial Germany and all this to be lost for the sake of a frail woman. I asked Westerweller what the feeling of the Hessians would be. He shook his head. " They won't like it at first — but you know human nature — they will accept it — and nothing more will be said. To us the real friends of the Grand Duke it is destruction — for we love him and are sure he cannot really be happy. But for the rest — she will simply be his morganatic wife — or we shall descend to the condition of Meiningen." (The Duke of Meiningen married an actress — so no one goes there except to see the opera and theatre as he now devotes himself to that.)

These Hessians have been so kind and civil to us that I am really sorry for them. Fraulein Kohausen (Prussian) kept on asking me last night before she started whether I was sure the Prince of Bulgaria was still here — whether I had seen him — whether he was going, etc. — so I apprehend that that little affair is also coming to a point.

The Queen was said to be in the tantrums yesterday on all this — but she was certainly not when I saw her though we never allude to the painful subject. She has not

mentioned it to Lady Churchill or any of us except Lady
Ely. . . .

Since I began this letter I find that it was not the Crown
Princess who telegraphed the news of the marriage to the
Empress but it was Stumm who sent the news to his Government — with the consequence of recalling the Prussians to
Berlin. Stumm has gone off on a special mission to Carlsruhe
today to be out of the way. Starck the Prime Minister who
married them is very ill — no one can see him. Jocelyn
[the Consul] however saw him driving unbeknown. There
were two witnesses to the marriage as required by law —
Prince Sternberg, who with his wife has cooked up the
affair from the beginning — and M. Chapska who is Madame
Kalomine's brother.

Ponsonby returned home from Darmstadt to Windsor. At
Norman Tower he was in time for breakfast. His wife and
daughters who had read of the Darmstadt romance in the
English newspapers immediately bombarded him with questions. With imperturbable calm he gave them the diplomatic
courtier's lie : " It isn't true, he hasn't married again." But
there is no record of his conversation when he was alone with
his wife or of her laughter penetrating through the door.

The morganatic love affair however did not last, as
Ponsonby was informed by Hermann Sahl, formerly German
Secretary to the Queen, who now lived in Darmstadt. In
a letter after the marriage ceremony of Princess Ella, another
Hessian Princess, to the Grand Duke Serge in June of the same
year he wrote :

Thanks for your note. Our dull little place is now
without its sovereign ruler, since the Grand Duke and all
his family (including the two Battenbergs) left here for St.
Petersburg — on Thursday evening, quarter before seven.
Poor Princess Ella had a very quiet and unofficial departure
— although she had been the decided pet of the public of
Darmstadt. *How differently* would the sympathies of our
people have made themselves felt — but for this most unfortunate and most stupid " Columbine " business. You
will be glad to hear that *substantially* the untieing of the
morganatic knot is now accomplished, and by degrees the
formal severance will be pronounced by a Court of Law con-
vened for this purpose. Diplomatists and Lawyers are never
embarrassed about finding a suitable *form* — as soon as they
have secured a convergence of views and aims in *substance*.

During the visit to Aix in 1890, the question arose of a meeting between the Queen and Carnot, the President of the French Republic. That it was not a simple one is shown by the following letter to Ponsonby :

From *Lord Lytton* (British Ambassador in Paris)

Paris, 10 March, 1890

I returned to Paris last Wednesday, and saw Spuller the same afternoon. I told him that if, in the course of next month the President (who, I had heard, was intending to visit the South of France about that time) should happen to be at, or near Aix, I believed the Queen would be very pleased to have that opportunity of seeing him. Spuller at once replied that it would be impossible for the President to go to Aix. The object of his journey South was to visit Toulon and there inspect the fleet and Arsenal. On account of the *Conseils Généraux* which meet on the 14th of April, and the Municipal Elections, which take place at the end of the month or the 1st of May, the President (he said) would probably not be absent from Paris longer than a week ; and his tour would be confined to Toulon, Marseilles and Montpelier, with perhaps a flying visit to Nice. Aix would be quite out of his route.

Last Saturday there was an official ball at the Ministry of Marine ; and, meeting there General Bergère the President's Aide de Camp, I repeated to him what I had said to Spuller. He gave me exactly the same reply, adding that he would communicate what I had said to the President, who would he felt sure be glad of an opportunity to see the Queen on her way through Paris. I said at once that Her Majesty would, I believed, be only passing through Paris late at night, that she was always obliged to minimise the fatigue of her journeys, and I felt sure that it would be quite impossible for her to break her journey here.

Yesterday, Sunday, the Carnots asked us to their box at the Conservatoire Concert ; where I had some talk with the President himself. But in consequence of what General Bergère had said to me the previous night, I purposely refrained from saying anything to him about the Queen's movements. My reason was that, if I had done so, I should probably have elicited from him some expression of a wish to see Her Majesty on her way through Paris — I knew that any such proposal would be unacceptable ; and coming directly from the President himself — perhaps in the form of a definite proposal, it might be embarrassing.

XIII*Journeys Abroad*   305

My impression is that, in the present state of French political parties the President (a timid man) would fear the comments he might provoke from the Radical and the Pro-Russian Press here, if he went ostentatiously far out of his way to wait upon the Queen at Aix. On the other hand, if Her Majesty were to break her journey in order to see the President at Paris, that event would certainly be advertised from the Elysée as a signal tribute to the increased international confidence acquired by the French Republic under the Carnot Presidency.

If the Queen particularly cared to see the President I think it could be arranged for him to meet Her Majesty at Cherbourg. But of course the meeting would also be regarded as a political event. And therefore, unless I hear from you to the contrary, I propose to let the matter rest where it is, and say nothing further about the Queen's movements, till the time comes to ask for the usual facilities. . . .

We are again in a Ministerial Crisis here, and the inability of the Republic to produce a stable Government seems to be inveterate. The Chamber had no wish to turn out the present Government — was indeed rather anxious to keep it in. But it is breaking up from internal dissensions, and Ranalle's budget will probably give it the *coup de grâce*.

After the visit to Hyères and Darmstadt in 1892, the last visit on which Sir Henry Ponsonby accompanied the Queen was to Florence and subsequently to Coburg in March 1894. He describes his room in the Villa Fabricotti. " I live in a drawing room made up as a bedroom. I am told Pauline Borghese died here and there is a picture of her without too much clothes on the ceiling. But though a gorgeous room, it is not comfortable."

Although Colonel Arthur Bigge was with him he was beginning to find the work heavy and there is a notable change in his usually bold and clear handwriting. He was hard at it most of the day " engaged in receiving Questors, Ambassadors, correspondents, Prefects, Syndics, Architects, etc., until I am tired of them, the last Prince Meiningen has just gone ". But needless to say he never missed his daily letter to his wife.

The King and Queen of Italy came to pay a visit to Queen Victoria which made Ponsonby quote Pope :

" Ye Kings and Queens your distance keep
In peace let one poor poet sleep.

For the moment I am inclined to agree. They spoilt all yesterday and they are spoiling all today." Not only was he tired but bored to a degree he had not shown in other visits. " Sono grumpeggio, which means I am old and crusty without any reason."

At Coburg, whither they went in April, the change of climate revived him. The chief function here was the marriage of the young reigning Duke of Hesse to Princess Victoria Melita, daughter of the Duke of Edinburgh. There was an immense assembly of Royalties: "I never saw so many". They included the German Emperor William II, the Empress Frederick, the Cesarevitch (afterwards the Tsar Nicholas II), the Duke of Edinburgh (now Duke of Coburg) and the Prince of Wales who both wore the uniform of German Generals. So what with " uniform and not uniform one is all day dressing or bothering ". No occupation that can be imagined could Ponsonby have detested more. After the main function he writes :

> The Cesarevitch would not take Alice's " No." But persisted and the Emperor William backed him up. So she consented and he, the Emperor, rushed into the Queen's room with the good news. Of course we drank healths and *Hochs*.

As usual getting home and seeing his wife again was what he looked forward to most.

In the last five years of her reign the Queen visited Cimiez three times. But this was after Henry Ponsonby's day had passed.

CHAPTER XIV

Letters Received

APART from family letters and the almost complete series of Ponsonby's daily letters to his wife there are over forty boxes of letters from an extraordinary variety of correspondents. This itself is only the selection of letters considered worth keeping. Some of them have already been quoted. Those given in the following pages are no more than samples covering a wide range of different subjects. Some are answers to letters from him, others written on the initiative of the writer, but in either case his own letters have seldom been procurable. Statesmen, governors, ecclesiastics, diplomats, sailors and soldiers, most of them knowing Ponsonby personally and hoping that through him the Queen might be reached almost direct, took advantage of this to write reports, requests or grievances to him far more frankly and informally than they would have to their official chiefs. Civil servants were anxious to give full information to one whose position gave him special influence which it was important should rest on being closely in touch with the trend of events.

There are many letters on Army reform, in which he was specially interested, constant reports from Dublin, while the Irish Question was prominent in the political field, and of course controversy over the series of wars gave an opportunity to administrators and military commanders to express their views more or less confidentially. Interspersed with these there was the usual flood of letters, only a few of which remain, on subjects such as requests for the loan of pictures, the submission of presentation books, subscriptions for philanthropic objects, letters about honours (not infrequently eloquent claims by the writer for himself) and correspondence about lies in the press which he often thought inadvisable even to refute. Letters from celebrities are not included just to bring in a well-known name but only if the subject matter is of interest. On the other hand good letters from people whose identity it has been impossible to trace have had to be omitted and those in which the subject of the letter is insufficiently complete to be intelligible.

Eminent men do not always write good letters. Many of their long reports on subjects of importance at the time have had to be excluded. Obscure people sometimes write good letters on subjects of little importance.

Home politics and foreign affairs are the chief subjects discussed. With regard to the latter there are examinations of events and discussions on policy, notably from Germany and Spain, which have a familiar ring judging by the course of events in later years and to which the tag " history repeats itself " might be applied. Curiously enough, however, there is one country frequently referred to on all sides disparagingly and the future doom of which is repeatedly prophesied — namely Turkey, on which the chorus of detractors has been proved to be in error.

There is a large number of the letters exchanged between Henry Ponsonby and his brother Arthur. They corresponded regularly before 1868 and at great length. But their letters record little else than their movements and occupations and discussions on military matters, with some references to public affairs. Henry did not develop his effective and racy epistolary style till after he married, and curiously enough his brother Arthur, a very amusing, original and unconventional man, was quite colourless in his letters, although he touched on questions of interest.

Colonel Arthur Ponsonby was quartered at Corfu in 1858 when Gladstone arrived on a special mission. The future Prime Minister had been chosen by Sir Lytton Bulwer, the Colonial Secretary in Lord Derby's Government, to investigate the unsatisfactory state of the Ionian Islands which were still under British control and were in many parts restive and anxious to be returned to Greece. Gladstone as a Homeric authority was considered to be an appropriate person to undertake this duty.[1]

---

[1] See Morley's *Gladstone*, vol. i, chap. x.

From *Colonel Arthur Ponsonby*

Corfu, November 28, 1858

Mr. Gladstone arrived last Wednesday. A Neapolitan Secretary, Gordon and Mr. Glyn, brother-in-law and Chaplain. Guns were fired and there were Guards of Honour; with the latter Mr. G., like all civilians, was highly pleased but did not know what to do. So whilst they presented arms Mr. G. remained with his hand on his heart and the General walked on thinking he was by his side. However we got him up to the Palace and handed him over to the Civil Power. The Greeks with their usual cunning thronged the way, taking their hats off and showing great respect, this is not their custom with the Lord High Commissioner. Mr. G. has come out with the idea that these Ionians are the finest race on earth. He flatters himself that they bought up and read his Homeric Studies. Why, they have not even read Homer. There is positively not a copy (except one or two in the College) in the Island.

29th — These rascally Greeks now say that we (England) are afraid of them. They do not see that it is a most tremendous compliment paid to them sending Gladstone out. . . . They have drawn up a petition to Sir Lytton Bulwer (but have not sent it through Mr. G.) to ask the Government to give these islands over to Greece. The feeling between the English here and the Greeks is getting worse and worse. They however know that our Four Biggest Guns are pointed straight at the town, to say nothing of smaller ones. The lower orders (peasantry) are a quiet, certainly idle but contented people and like the English. It is the Signori Landlords or rather Squireens, who do all the mischief. They all live in the town and gamble day and night, are all in debt, talk nothing but politics and are intensely ignorant. The Press is the vilest in the world. All this is, there is no doubt, brought on by giving them a Constitution and a free Press. The Signori in order to meet expenses grind their servants down and tell them they are forced to in order to meet the taxes laid on by the English. . . .

The islands were handed over to Greece in 1863 by Lord Palmerston. So the " rascally Greeks " had their way.

A letter from his younger brother the Rev. Frederick Ponsonby may be inserted here. Although undated it must have been written soon after his acceptance in 1877 of the living of St. Mary Magdalen's, Munster Square, and not long after the passing of the Public Worship Bill by Parliament.

This Bill, which was by way of being an attempt to curb ritualistic practices in Church of England services, was found in practice rather to encourage than restrict them. Constant litigation kept the controversy between the Evangelicals and the Tractarians or Ritualists continually to the front. Frederick in his church indulged in highly ritualistic practices. His brother was distressed, not because of the vestments, the incense, the candles and the confessional, but because he knew Fred's admirable work in his poor parish and extreme popularity among working people fitted him for a high position in the Church, while the practices in his services would be an insurmountable barrier to any promotion. Frederick, who had no personal ambitions, was not going to trim his sails to please the high authorities. He was not going to abandon his firm belief in beautifying his services. He had found his parishioners by their crowded attendance at his church approved.

From The Rev. F. Ponsonby

" Sufficient unto the day is the evil thereof " so I don't quite see why I need alter things here, until I am attacked for the use of them. Unless there is to be a distressingly rigid enforcement of rubrics there must be a certain amount of tolerated lawlessness. My predecessor spent between £20 and £30,000 of his own fortune on the Church Schools, etc., and he introduced " these unlawful things " as they are called, and the congregation now wish them to be continued, as I know from a large memorial to that effect, signed to the Patron. So my reasoning is this — The Law (we won't argue the question of right, it has got might which is sufficient for present purposes) has decided (after what seem contradictory decisions in previous cases) and decided as it declares finally, that the only garment lawful for the Minister to wear at Holy Communion is the " Surplice " and in Cathedrals " the Cope ". Now I use another vestment, the Dean of Windsor uses another vestment, the Archbishop uses another vestment, etc., at this Service than that declared by law to be alone legal.

H.M. would be bothered beyond measure at seeing the black gown abolished, if not the Archbishop, (*peut-être un Gallio*) many a good low church Bishop would be exceedingly distressed at having to wear a cope and my congregation (some of whom have consciences and all of whom are not fools) would be equally distressed if the surplice were introduced during the whole of the service to the exclusion of the vestments. If there is to be rigid uniformity, it must be enforced equally all round and not onesidedly against the High Church or Ritualists or whatever they may be called.

I grant that Custom gives some sanction to the Black gown and militates against the introduction of disused vestments, but I suspect the period in Church History when that custom arose for even Shelley (atheist as I suppose he was) could say that this Religion was " Christless, Godless ". Of course if three aggrieved Parishioners (creations of the precious Public Worship Bill) who have felt no grief for ten years, suddenly have their righteous souls vexed at my proceedings and complain to the Bishop, I for one shall not be inclined to defy his authority but as I began — Sufficient unto the day, etc.

Don't think, that in writing this, I am blind to all the thoughtful kindness and real wish for my success which is the motive of your letter : I do see it and thank you more than I can say for it.

The following letter rather baldly recounts an adventure in the streets of Dublin which had been greatly exaggerated by rumour and gossip :

From *Lord Arthur Wellesley* (afterwards 4th Duke of Wellington)

Jan. 4th, 1870

Colonel de Horsey tells me you wish me to send you an account of my accident. It is this : I left Barracks walking in the afternoon of Monday, Dec. 27th. A party of six or seven men followed up Northumberland Road towards Mount Street. They did not throw any snowballs. One of the party tried to trip me up. I hit him with my umbrella. The remainder then set on me, except one man of the party who tried to keep them off. One threw a stone which cut my left eyelid. The others used their fists, which did not hurt much as they were all rather drunk. A policeman came up and they all ran off. He did not catch any of them. They seemed to be nothing but ordinary roughs. The men are constantly being attacked in the same way. They never attack two men or the N.C.O.s who carry side arms, only one man by himself. I think that is all I have to report.

The frequency of railway accidents much disturbed the Queen, who was instrumental in securing an official enquiry. One of them is here graphically described :

From *Lord Colville of Culross* (formerly an Equerry to the Queen)

23 January, 1870

I sent you a reply to the Queen's most gracious message last night — and, as I thought that some details of the " accident " of Friday last might be acceptable, I added, that " I would write — "

It was a frightful catastrophe, and the horrors of the scene were much enhanced by the state of the weather. In that part of the country it had been snowing all day — it was snowing when I went down to Yorkshire early that morning — and where the collision took place, in a deep cutting, the snow lay deep — it was still falling in heavy showers and a strong wind was blowing.

Although the first collision, between the Scotch Express and the coal-train, was a frightful one, I do not think that any great loss of life or damage had taken place. But, when the engine of the " down-train " dashed in, sweeping before it the débris of the first accident, that was the climax of horrors and a sight that I never shall forget.

, I had *two* miraculous escapes. I was in the third carriage from the front. The compartment was full. I was in the far seat with my back to the engine. Opposite to me was an Officer of Artillery, who I subsequently saw, a good deal shaken.

The centre seats were occupied by two very nice looking lads, apparently travelling together, and in the remaining seats, by the door, were two gentlemen.

There was no warning — but, in a moment, there was an awful shock, and utter darkness. The end of my carriage seemed to sink down on the rails. I doubled myself up — and put my arms over my head to protect my surviving eye. The cushion from the opposite seat fell on my head, and, I believe, protected me much. When, at last, we stopped — I was still in my seat, but I *stepped off my cushion into the snow* — NOT THROUGH THE DOOR, *the whole side of the compartment was gone* —

A few minutes after this, being uninjured and in full possession of my senses — I, with another gentleman, assisted a Scotchwoman and " her lassie " as she called her — out of a portion of a shattered carriage laying across the down line — we had JUST got them into an uninjured carriage in the Scotch Express, when the engine of the down-train, having leaped over the tender of the Scotch Express engine which was laying across the down-line, dashed past us, and turned over on the top of the very carriage from which, *two minutes* before, we had rescued the Scotchwoman and her " lassie " ! !

I remained at the scene for upward of four hours after the catastrophe — and as I never saw either of the lads who were in the carriage with me, I felt certain that something had happened to them. I mentioned this to Mr. Cockshott, a Great Northern official who had arrived on the spot, and I described their dress, etc., etc. He told me yesterday that their bodies had been found — *the lowest down of eight*, under the wrecked carriage the engine had fallen upon — so disfigured he could only recognise them by my description of their dress. How *they* got there, and *I* did not, God only can tell, *I* shall never know. I had my feet on the same footwarmer with one of them when the collision took place !

Count Schouvaloff was in one of the last carriages which was uninjured — but his servant, poor fellow, had his leg frightfully fractured. His master took him to the hospital at Huntingdon.

Letter on Henry Ponsonby's retirement from the command of the 1st Battalion of the Grenadier Guards :

From *Colonel de Horsey*

Chelsea Barracks, July 4th, 1870

In the name of the officers of the 1st Batt^n Gren^r Guards I beg to thank you for the very beautiful piece of plate you have given us. The design, taste and execution are quite perfection. But we shall value it for your sake and therefore value it very much. Let me take this opportunity of again expressing in my name and that of the officers of your old Batt^n how much we regret your having left us, and how heartily we join in assuring you of our united sentiments of respect and affection. If we did well at the Inspection today we owe it to you — you made us, we think, the best Battalion in the service, and it shall be our endeavour to keep up to your standard.

Although he never succeeded in being elected to Parliament the writer of the following letter was well known in his youth as a radical politician and figures as the hero in George Meredith's *Beauchamp's Career*. His profession was the Navy, from which he retired in 1867, eventually reaching the rank of Rear-Admiral. Subsequently he was an opponent of Home Rule and in the eighties became a follower of Mr. Joseph Chamberlain. The year date of the letter is missing but the reference to Beales gives a clue. Edmond Beales, a lawyer, was President of the Reform League. He was organizer of the Hyde Park meeting in 1866 when the rowdier section of the crowd broke down the railings and swarmed into the Park. In 1871 mention was made in a vote of censure on the Liberal Government of the appointment of Beales to a judgeship of a County Court. It seems probable that the " remonstrance " refers to this and the mention of the Franco-Prussian War seems to confirm this date :

From *Admiral Maxse*

October 16th

I was very much gratified to receive your letter. The tolerant spirit in which you discuss my views makes me desirous to recognize whatever errors they may contain : my most anxious wish is that they should fall or stand by their real merit. There is a great deal in what you say : nevertheless I believe the remonstrance I have just published to be sorely needed. Of Beales's capacity I say nothing — but I hold that his political and private character is as un-impeachable as any of H.M. Ministers. What I regret is that it appears to be sufficient for a man to have the confid-ence of the Working Classes to ensure him the abuse of the Upper and Commercial Classes. They are treated intoler-antly, ridiculed, and jeered at. I maintain that they are valuable agents and should receive the same honourable treatment (when of weight with their class as are the men I name in my manifesto) as other politicians who profess to represent a different order of opinion. A republican party is forming itself slowly in England now, simply because the Upper and Middle classes refuse to recognize that the work-ing classes have great grievances : I know a number of honest, conscientious and able men (of unblemished private characters) who simply *despair* of obtaining redress for the evils from which their class suffer, through the present parliamentary machine and corrupt electoral system. I differ from some of them in their views, and because they have confidence in me and know I believe in human pro-gress — they receive any criticism I offer with the utmost desire to render it justice. They are only rendered intolerant by intolerance. Of course the working classes have differ-ences of opinion and different leaders ; this is no reason why they should not be listened to. No great task is de-manded in this as they have but few prominent leaders. I have taken four typical men in my remonstrance — Beales,

Odger, Applegarth and Bradlaugh. I especially name the
latter as he is the particular mark for religious and political
persecution : — and by far the most powerful man of the
four. He is not to be listened to because he is an avowed
atheist — but examined, this atheism simply means that
upon the great question of the Unknown he differs in opinion
from other people : he is in conflict with what he earnestly
believes to be *human* error and the cause of much misery
— his opponents declare that in combating them he combats
God, theologians have always done this and in doing this
manage to affix an unpopular stigma upon their adversary.
Bradlaugh's atheism consists in denying the revelation of an
external Providence or supernatural Being. It is a religion
with him to do so : of course a difference of opinion is to
some people an " insult " — as Protestantism is to Roman
Catholicism so is Free Thought to Protestantism — this however is because we are as yet incapable of religious tolera-
tion. However whatever Bradlaugh's views are he is a *power*
in the country, though his speeches are not reported in *The
Times* or *Daily News* : he has a large gathering at his taber-
nacle and an organ the *National Reformer* (this week's number
of which I forward by post) and possesses considerable
talent as well as courage. His political opinions and position
are I maintain entitled to respect : his religious opinions no
one need put himself in the way of hearing.

One final remark on this subject. You say Beales (a
pious man by the way, horrified at Bradlaugh's opinions,
but respecting him personally) should have tried the Hyde
Park Paling case or rather " right of entrance " case, by law :
he proposed to do so, but the Government refused to give
him any facility in the way of expense and neither he nor
his friends could muster £500 to purchase justice with.

The Continental struggle is indeed ghastly. I hold
Bismarck's attitude to be simply *criminal* : he has the effron-
tery to demand as terms of *peace*, terms of *war* (avowedly, for
he says he does not believe in peace) — that is he offers an
armistice during which he is to hold certain strategical
advantages (at the expense of the 1½ million Frenchmen
held captive in annexed provinces) in anticipation of renewal
of conflict ! And England does not even offer an opinion —
but declares that the only remedy is for the combatants to
murder themselves out ! !

There are several letters from the biographer of the Prince
Consort, often rather long-winded and didactic. This one gives
a view of the Franco-Prussian War which was held by many
people at the time :

From *Theodore Martin*

26 December, 1870

Thanks for your letter just received. I quite agree with you, that, as matters now stand, there is nothing for it but to let the French and Germans fight out their quarrel. Whether this has always been so may be open to question. My own conviction is, that in our present utterly helpless condition, in so far as the power to take the field, or present even a menacing front is concerned, we could not have intervened with any effect. But to what a pass are we come, that we are made every day to feel that France is fighting *our* battle, and that our chance of making head against the two most formidable military despotisms the world has ever known is dependant on whether France shall be able to hold out for the next six months against the long trained skill and deeply studied organization of the Germans. What I as an Englishman complain of is, that our statesmen did not look one inch before their noses, when this war broke out, and were not even startled by the revelations of what Germany had been about in the way of preparation for an attack on France into taking *instant* measures for strengthening our armaments both by land and sea. " United Germany " in a certain sense was all very well, but it surely required no great knowledge of Prussian hereditary policy or of human nature to know, what was likely to ensue from such immense military preponderance and such unprecedented success. I believe Englishmen are now fully alive to the sense of danger to our prestige and our commerce ; and it will not at all surprise me to see the present Ministry go to the ground, with a fall as ignominious as its rise was great, solely because people have begun to feel that they have not shown due foresight in the measures necessary to make this country respected in the altered position of the European States. I have within the last months had many opportunities of observing in which way the current of opinion is setting in the great manufacturing and commercial cities, and this is the conclusion I have come to. When some of the more important facts as to our want of preparation come to be known, as they will be before long, I expect a storm of indignation against the Ministry, which they will find it very hard to face. Just take this one item of powder. I have reason to know, that the Government have lately given orders for powder, on which we shall have to pay about £600,000 over the market price, or the price for which they could have themselves manufactured it ! ! Then I believe we have not at this moment one single torpedo in store !

And this when the Germans are proclaiming on all hands the intention to attack us the moment they have settled accounts with the French. It is the misfortune of the English Court, that it does not hear what is to be heard on all sides in the best informed quarters of English Society as to these matters. But I assure you, the state of feeling that now exists both as respects alarm and distrust of what is being done by the government is very serious. Add to this, there is great depression in trade and a great deal of unemployed labour, to increase the complications.

Forgive this long letter. The subject haunts me night and day, and it is little consolation to me to see that people are *now* alive to the perils of England's position. Still that is better than the delusive complacency in which we were wrapped, while we ought to have been straining every nerve to make ourselves secure against insult or aggression. We may yet do so ; but we want time, and men to lead us, who think of something more than party-success. The French will, I trust, give us the first. It will be the nation's fault, if it does not find out the latter.

When the Grand Duke Wladimir, son of the Tsar Alexander II of Russia, visited England in 1871, one of the Queen's Equerries was attached to him. In an entertaining series of letters, most of which have already been published, a full account of the visit is given. This one of the series has not previously appeared :

From *Colonel the Hon. Arthur Hardinge* (afterwards General, K.C.B., and Commander-in-Chief at Bombay)

Thursday. [1871]

It is the pace that kills — and as the Grand Duke has rather challenged our endurance — we have cut out the work without mercy — and I think this afternoon galloped H.I.H. to a standstill. After attending the Levée yesterday the Grand Duke paid formal visit to the Duchess of Cambridge and the Grand Duchess of Mecklenburg, then to Hurlingham from Marlborough House. Dined at Lord Granville's, where the Russians were given precedence over the English peerage, then to a drum at Mrs. Gladstone's. This morning we started at 10.30 from Claridge's, went all over the Bank of England, saw a bank note for a million, 25 million in bullion — glittering in a cellar — and 300 millions of bad paper in the form of old notes. Then to the Post Office, threading the narrow streets to the telegraph offices, where

400 damsels, with prodigious Chignons, but with small hands, were manipulating the electric wires. Onwards still to the Mint — to see gold, silver and copper receive alike the impress of Majesty. The marvels of coining culminating in a piece of legerdemain worthy of Mr. Freemantle, as ex-Secretary of the Ingenious Benjamin. A medal was struck instantaneously, as commemoration of the Grand Duke's visit to The Mint. The process was so miraculous that I need hardly confess, to a person of your worldly experience, that I suspect it was prepared beforehand — *n'en parlons jamais !*

I forgot to include in our programme an inspection of Printing House Square, where copies of *The Times* danced like Marionettes through every form of production, with the neatly folded editions that consuming 125 miles of paper will tomorrow confirm our proceedings upon the Breakfast table of Balmoral.

We had luncheon with the 1st Battalion of Coldstream Guards in the Tower. Lord de Ros did the Honours of the antiquities and a steam-launch brought us just now to Westminster Stairs.

Tonight we dine at the Russian Embassy — Ball to follow. The Grand Duke receives the guests so the Royal carriages are ordered for a punctual eight.

I have prepared the Grand Duke for the Honour of being received by H.M. before the Breakfast at Buckingham Palace on the 23rd. He seems confounded by the idea of presenting himself to the Queen in plain clothes.

I am writing against time, so you will I am sure make the best of my slips and slops.

The subject of the following letter seems of remote interest, but the letter is a good one :

From *T. Villiers Lister* (Assistant Under-Secretary for Foreign Affairs)

Foreign Office, Aug. 25, 1874

I opened your letter to Tenterden about the Bishop of Central Africa and enclose a Memorandum which will I hope answer most of your questions.

Central Africa being neither under the Home, nor, as yet, under the Colonial Office, is considered to belong to the Foreign Office. Why a Bishop should be wanted there I cannot say ; there are, it is to be presumed, no Christians except the Protestant Dissenters converted by Livingstone of whose numbers we have no trustworthy statistics, but we may hope that a Right Reverend Father with the Thirty-

Nine Articles in one hand and the Public Worship Bill in the other will compete successfully with the native creeds and human sacrifices, and that by the exercise of great tact and judgment he may acquire as great and as beneficial an influence as if he had been appointed to a Diocese in England.

If you are really anxious about Central Africa, I think you might comfort yourself with the consideration that the Bishop will probably return to this country in a few months.

The same writer in October 1876 gives some useful definitions. He writes :

I really could not venture to explain to a General the difference between a suspension of arms and an armistice. It seems however that the former is easy to break and the latter difficult to make.

The difference between a note and a protocol is much of the same kind. But a protocol is a legal international document, and it is felt to be more humiliating for a foreign government to sign a protocol engaging to make internal reforms, and thereby acknowledging a right of interference in such matters on the part of other countries, than to write a note promising to do the same things.

The *Mistletoe* accident [1] no doubt made the naval officers of the Royal Yachts very cautious. The following is from the captain of the *Victoria and Albert* :

From *Captain Prince Leiningen, R.N.* (cousin of the Queen)

6th April, 1876

Biddulph has just spoken to me about the yacht going into " Calais " or " Boulogne ". The former place simply is an impossibility and the second is not safe on account of size and length of ship and the strong tides which run across the entrance of harbour. Neither is Dover or Folkestone fit for the yacht to go alongside of on this side of water. If any more questions are asked please let it be understood that I *most positively decline* and *refuse* to take the *Victoria and Albert* either into Calais or Boulogne, in fact into *any* harbours on that coast except Cherbourg or Antwerp.

What I predicted has happened : the Admiralty have published the most unjust and undeserved reprimand which they thought fit to send Welch and myself in December last. Just watch the row there now will be ! !

Please let me know when convenient on what day and

[1] See p. 42.

where H.M. will re-embark, as I have to inform the Admiralty officially.

During the Russo-Turkish War the Comptroller of the Household of the Duke of Edinburgh wrote giving the Russian view :

From *Colonel Sir W. J. Colville*

Peterhoff, 2nd August, 1876

. . . The difficulty of arriving at the truth as to the results of the fighting which has taken place has been great indeed — Of one thing however there can be no doubt, that is, the intense satisfaction felt here at the receipt of any news of a favourable nature as far as the Servian cause is concerned.

The feeling in its favour is very strong indeed and takes its outward expression in the form of collections of money for Sick and Wounded. The Empress herself shows great interest on the subject and the ladies of the Court, old and young, go to St. Petersburg and make *quêtes* from house to house. I met one of the latter the other day on board a steamboat with her little brass box into which her fellow passengers dropped their contributions. . . . I daresay that large sums will be eventually collected and no doubt they will be required.

And with this strong sympathy for the Servians there exists an intense hatred of the Turks and, I regret to say, a very sore feeling against England, who alone, they declare, supports and encourages the latter and has thus made herself responsible for the horrors which have taken place.

It is difficult to answer these attacks with arguments in favour of the balance of power. One is told, over and over again, that Russia has not the smallest desire to possess Constantinople and that the only feeling on the subject is one of sympathy for co-religionists and an earnest desire to drive from Europe a race which is incapable of civilization and progress and which has ground down and oppressed the Christian population of these regions far too long already.

The statement that our Government has sent £40,000 to pay the Turkish troops is implicitly believed by many, and I have more than once vainly tried to point out the impossibility of such a thing.

A friend of mine, who is certainly very well informed, tells me that although the feeling for the Servians is deep and widely spread there never was the smallest chance of its forcing the Government to take up arms for them. . . .

Without exception all sensible people to whom I have spoken appear to think that a great blunder was made when the Berlin Memorandum was so suddenly decided upon without consultation with us. The discomfiture of the Russian policy has no doubt caused a very painful feeling throughout the country. I was told the other day that, were it not for the great confidence felt in the Emperor and Prince Gortschakoff the cry would have been " *Nous sommes vendus aux Anglais* ". The hard things that have been said in the papers have of course caused much annoyance. A man of very high position expressed to me the other day his sincere regret that — now that our policy has been successful — a few words of a friendly and conciliatory nature should not have fallen from some member of the Government in Parliament. He was convinced that they would have had a most salutary effect.

Information from Berlin came chiefly from the Military Attachés and was very full.

From *Major-General Beauchamp Walker* (Military Attaché in Berlin)

Berlin, 15th January, 1877

The Hermit of Varzin [Bismarck] is to me an undefinable quantity, as the mathematicians say, and him I never pretend to fathom. Further than this his stomach is very much out of order which is, in my opinion, quite sufficient to account for any vagaries, political or personal. He is a huge feeder and takes no exercise, lives in an atmosphere like that of a forcing house, and smokes powerful tobacco. One's only wonder is that he does not blow up altogether, instead of only blowing up his subordinates. To me he is as inscrutable as the other Sphinx, and I look upon him with much the same awe and wonderment, not a little thankful that no roll of the ball can ever bring me into the position of being required to read this human riddle.

He has just reaped the crop of one of his sowings, and I am puzzled to say whether he is disappointed or pleased with the result of his husbandry. Universal suffrage has sent something like twenty Social Democrats to the German Diet. Whether *he* inflicted Germany with universal suffrage out of a great and enthusiastic philanthropy, or whether he gave it with a cynical wish that it might become apparent how delusive and worthless an institution it is, is not for me to say. Far less am I able to judge his conduct during the present crisis. I learn that Lord Odo Russell thinks that he has been sincerely desirous of acting with England, and, as I have no other means of judging at present than what I hear from

Y

Lord Odo, I do not like to form any opinion at variance with that which I derive from him. I have not seen Bismarck to speak to for more than a year. The one opinion however which I hold in regard to his general line of action whenever Russia is concerned is this — the only point on which he dare not openly differ from the Emperor is Russia. Need I say more. As regards the man generally I always recur to my first conversation with Mr. O. R. when he arrived at Versailles and asked me to describe the man with whom he had to deal. My answer was : " The greatest and most unscrupulous liar who ever cumbered the earth, most dangerous when he is most frank, but — the greatest statesman of the day." I subsequently added, " He is the only man in Germany who knows what he wants and *will* have it." I do not think that everybody will agree with me in this estimate of Bismarck's character, but I myself see no reason to alter my dicta.

I hope most sincerely that no war will grow out of the present complications, still less a war between England and Russia. I hate war, like most old soldiers ; I hate it for its own sake, I hate it for its brutality, I hate it for its consequences, for the sufferings which it inflicts, for the disturbance to progressive civilization, for the deplorable traces which it leaves behind it and for the consequences which ensue. But at present I also think that a war with Russia would be singularly inopportune, and trust that the Emperor Alexander may close his reign without its being darkened by a war between Russia and England, much as it would be to my own interest that this war should come before the judgment of " too old " is pronounced on me.

Russia will have to fight someone and that someone is either England or Germany. Now Germany will put off the fight with all the means available because — war with Russia means an attempt on the part of France to recover the lost provinces. And this I think is the clue to Bismarck's policy throughout. He always sees France before his eyes, and would be glad to see Russia weaken herself in a contest with some power other than Germany. As regards the allusion made in your letter he totally and absolutely denies that anything of the kind has taken place. . . .

To those among my friends who give me the name of Turkophile or Russophobist according to the present childish fashion I answer plainly that I neither love the Turk nor fear the Russian, and that if they want to know what I am they may spell the word Anglophile.

. . . The Germans are very fit, always fit, but the Germans have as much idea of going to war on the Eastern question as they have of meddling with the moon. They have quite enough to occupy them at home, and have no intention of giving France the hoped-for chance at present. . . .

From *A. P. Stanley* (Dean of Westminster)

Feb. 24, 1877

I forwarded your inquiry at once to the Archbishop of Canterbury, but have had no answer. Possibly he may have replied direct to the Queen or to yourself. At any rate I wish you to know that the delay is not any neglect of mine.

I sincerely hope that there will be a Burial Bill, and that, if there is, it may not be the miserable subterfuge of closing the existing churchyards (Imagine the closing of the "Country Churchyard" at Stoke Poges !) and establishing cemeteries with two rival Chapels up and down the villages in Every English County.

Unfortunately we have not Ponsonby's reply to the following interesting controversial letter. But the second letter shows that he answered promptly and fully.

From *Colonel William de Horsey*

January 8, 1877

Many thanks for your letter. We all look through spectacles more or less coloured. War is a dreadful thing. So are executions and all severe punishments for offences against the law. But it would be disastrous to nations and to individuals if they were to shrink from carrying out existing laws. The treaty of Paris of '56, with its amendment in '71, is at present an international law. Russia broke this law openly in Servia. This, I believe, is not contested by any one conversant with the said treaties. Why " the miserable Turk " ? He is brave, temperate and enduring. Up to the present time all our great statesmen have held the protection of the Ottoman Empire to be a condition of our Indian Empire. The Queen is Empress of 40 millions of Mussulmans and one of our greatest boasts is that all her subjects, whether Christians, Jews, Mussulmans or of any other creed, are all equal before the law. This is also the case in Turkey. There Christians have but one disqualification — that they may not carry arms. We have found it at times necessary to disqualify the Irish in like manner. But now consider the intolerance of other countries — Russian and Servian intolerance to Jews, Spanish to Protestants. You may think that I am looking through very coloured spectacles when I attribute a great part of the Bulgarian atrocities to Russian intrigue — that Russian " *agents provocateurs* " prepared the Servian rebellion, and that Ignatieff recommended the Sultan to use, not regular as he had intended, but irregular troops to put down the insurrection in Bulgaria. It was necessary to put it down with a strong arm and this cannot be done without many lamentable excesses. See what we were obliged to do in India. Think what a handful of English may be obliged to do again should Shere Ali and Scindiah, shocked at our abandoning the treaties we have made, in behalf of Turkey, attempt to regain their independence.

Think of centuries of Russian atrocities in every country she has subjugated and these Bulgarian atrocities, however much to be deprecated, will appear to you as insufficient in justifying England to alter a policy which has been looked at through the spectacles of many great statesmen, at many times, for many years, which spectacles, although varying in shade, have ever shown the same distinctive colouring, and, I believe, not without sufficient reason. Canning's policy, and Navarino, is the lamentable exception. It is presumption on my part to write all this to you whom I recognise to have information and ability very superior to mine. But you, perhaps, not without your knowing it, labour under one disqualification from which I am exempt — Government by party, without doubt full of advantages in questions of domestic policy, has disadvantages where foreign policy is concerned. Few statesmen are exempt from the feeling " If I were in office I could do so much good ".

With this idea, I fear that, if they do not encourage, at any rate they do not manfully put down, any popular cry, got up by those politicians who are more liberal, or illiberal, than their leaders, " *plus royaliste que le Roi* ", their motive being the good of the country they ignore the harm they may bring about.

Well, you, being a distinguished member of a distinguished Whig family, how can your spectacles not be tinged by the very natural strong feelings of admiration for the many great men past away and the few present ones, of the Whig party ? Is it not natural that you should wish to see those, whom you consider the best men, in office again ? My spectacles may be coloured by ignorance, a fatal colour, but never having been mixed up in political life I praise either party, or blame them, according to my relative ignorance without bias — I blame Lord Salisbury for bullying the Turk — a fatal error — for he is not a creature to be bullied, although he may be led easily enough — I blame Lord Derby, who, to my mind, has neither courage nor principle. I blame them for fearing that, which you refer to, *not war, but an unpopular war.* If they think the country will not support their policy why have they not the courage to resign? Disraeli has had fearful difficulties to combat. Himself, in domestic matters, a thorough going Liberal, he has had to educate his party and has succeeded — for the domestic policy of the present Government appears to me to differ in no way from that of the last. He has now had to educate his Cabinet, who as a rule are very ignorant of any other country but England. What chance has Lord Salisbury, who cannot understand a German, or indeed any foreign newspaper, to understand other countries? He sees through very imperfect spectacles. What a child he is in the hands of Ignatieff.

If you have not thrown this long scribble into the fire long before this you will have treated me with very great consideration.

From *Colonel William de Horsey*

Jan. 10th, 1877

One line to thank you for your admirable letter. It is very good of you, with so much important correspondence on your hands, to take the trouble to write to me as you have done. I consider it a very great compliment.

Your arguments are those of a statesman and are doubly valuable from the information, from all sources, which must reach you. One real good will come from this protracted Eastern question, namely that many important subjects will, where great authorities differ, through discussion, become better understood than they have been hitherto. Such as how far the Muslims of India are interested in their co-religionists in Turkey. Also Russia has shown her cards and all nations will see that it is the interest of none that she should acquire great territory.

The next letter has a singularly prophetic last paragraph.

From *Mr. Edwards Pierrepont* (United States Minister)

17, Cavendish Square, January 30, 1877

I am obliged by your letter in which you express much gratification that my countrymen manifest so much admiration of your Queen. I sometimes think that it would save me a world of annoyance were it less, though I cannot say that I would diminish it if I could, and Mrs. Pierrepont would increase it fourfold. When the Prince of Wales visited America sixteen years ago, the Mayor of New York selected the heads of twenty families to meet the Prince at breakfast. Mrs. Pierrepont and I were of that number : the reception of the Prince was truly enthusiastic and genuine, not on his own account, in the least, — he was but a boy, and had as yet done nothing — but on account of the Queen, his mother, he was hailed with honest greeting. My countrymen and *countrywomen* then believed that the Queen was in every relation of life a *true and most exemplary woman* ; that she gave an elevated moral and religious tone to the nation, and time has confirmed them in that belief, and if the Queen, on her way to Canada, should pass through the United States the demonstration would be UNPARALLELED.

There is a universal belief that the Queen, in our late Civil War, was on the side of freedom, and opposed to slavery ; and that she prevented a recognition of the rebel states, and thus prevented a prolongation of the strife, and thereby saved the lives of many thousands of our countrymen. Hence the affection towards her is very deep and would amaze her were there a chance for expression.

There is not a bit of love for kingly government in the United States, but a deep hatred of it — and yet towards your Queen there is a deep honest and sincere admiration, and should any misfortune befall her it would awaken universal sympathy and condolence.

In the fullness of time a great war will surely arise and a combination be made to humiliate England and despoil her of her vast riches and power ; meanwhile if her statesmen have any forecast and address they will so conduct affairs that the inheritors of her blood, her laws, her religion and her liberties will be her powerful allies and her natural friends.

There are several letters from Lord Lytton during the time he was Viceroy in India (1876–1880). This one is supplementary to a full account of the Delhi Durbar, which was addressed direct to the Queen. It describes a significant new departure in the usual ceremonial :

From *Lord Lytton* (Viceroy of India)

Benares, 12 January, 1877

. . . There is only one detail of any importance which I omitted to mention to Her Majesty in my account of the proceedings at Delhi. Will you kindly allow me to repair the omission now ?

It has hitherto been uncustomary for any female members of the Viceroy's family to appear in any public ceremony to which natives of rank are admitted ; the notion being that the strict seclusion, not to say suppression of the female sex is so prevalent throughout the East, that the appearance in public of any Englishwoman of the least rank or position, would shock native prejudices, and lower her in the eyes of the natives. I was however persuaded from my previous personal intercourse with the better class of natives in India, that this was merely one of those anachronistic official traditions of our own which have lasted so long because no one has taken the trouble to question the sense of them, and that the danger apprehended by all my official advisers as likely to arise from the abrogation of it, was a purely imaginary one. Nobody admits more readily than I do the duty and propriety of forbearance and conciliation towards native sentiments, and even towards native prejudice, in all matters that concern exclusively the domestic or religious life of the natives *themselves* ; but I cannot admit that we are bound to conform *our own* social life and custom to the low standard of those whose masters we are by reason of our superior social enlightenment.

In any case, the particular prejudice which this un-English custom was intended to satisfy, appears to me to be one which it is not only beneath our dignity and self respect to adopt and incorporate into our own manners and customs, but also contrary to the acknowledged principles of our policy and the best interests of our Government, to encourage and perpetuate on the part of the natives themselves. We have put down *suttee* with the strong hand, and have done much to improve the position of Hindoo widows, and Mahomedan wives. We are establishing Zenana schools throughout India, and exhorting the better class of natives to educate their women, and humanize female life in their homes. Is it consistent with such a policy to stultify our precepts by our practice, or to select for conforming our own conduct to a prejudice we deprecate and deplore, those occasions, of all others, when our power is most conspicuously displayed, and our wisdom most publicly proclaimed ? To me the adoption of such a course seemed singularly inappropriate to the solemn proclamation of the title of a female sovereign to the Empire of all India. We had already decided on a great innovation in another direction by taking occasion of the Imperial Assemblage for doing away with the worn out and inconvenient system of exchanging presents ; and it appeared to me that the occasion was a singularly fit and favourable one for introducing a more rational procedure in this direction also. I therefore decided that Lady Lytton should accompany me in my State Entry into Delhi, and also have a place on the Dais behind the Viceregal Throne at the Assemblage. I trust that Her Majesty will not disapprove of this arrangement. I can truly say that the effect of it has been most satisfactory. So far from shocking the Native Princes, it has, to all appearances, greatly flattered and pleased them. Each of those who were present at the Viceroy's subsequent receptions spontaneously asked to be presented to Lady Lytton, and all of them shewed her the most deferential and courteous attention. When she afterwards appeared at the Races, they rose, greeted and conversed with her as respectfully and cordially as the most polished English gentlemen could have done. Such conduct on their part was an entire novelty, surprising to many and gratifying to all who witnessed it : and I fully believe that the course adopted in the ceremonials at Delhi, if judiciously followed up, will help to bridge over, at least some portion of the inconvenient and deplorable gulf which unavoidably exists between English and Native Society. . . .

After arduous service in India, Sir Bartle Frere was appointed High Commissioner of South Africa in March 1877. His ideal was the confederation of all the states and colonies. But he was frustrated by wars and rebellions and became the target of parliamentary criticism and censure. He wrote a number of letters to Ponsonby, as also subsequently did his daughter, Mary Frere. The following letter was written a year after his appointment as High Commissioner :

From *Sir Bartle Frere*

King William's Town, March 6th, 1878

I have received your kind note telling me that the Queen had been graciously pleased to order a copy of the third volume of the Prince's Memoirs to be sent to me. I intended to have written by this mail to express my grateful sense of Her Majesty's goodness to me, but I have delayed in hopes of being able to say that this sad war was ended. I have been so often disappointed, by some fresh outbreak of rebellion, that I am afraid to be too confident — but I am sanguine that in a few days I may be able to follow up the withdrawal of Martial Law, which was notified last week, by an amnesty to all but ringleaders in rebellion.

But I fear there is trouble in store for us in other quarters.

There is much unconnected evidence to show that this war
on our frontier was only a premature outbreak of a hostile
combination intended to embrace the whole Kaffir race ;
and that Kreli, and his follower and ally Saudilli, precipitated
an outbreak which was intended to be simultaneous up to
the Portuguese Frontier and beyond it.

Sir H. Bulwer in Natal, and Sir Theophilus Shepstone
in the Transvaal are both evidently more alarmed by the
attitude of the Zulus than they were some weeks ago, and
have asked me to enquire into reported importations of
Cannon into Zululand expected through the Portuguese
port of Delagoa Bay ; and Shepstone tells me he apprehends
trouble from the Boers in the interior of the country about
Pretoria. Taking advantage of Shepstone's absence Mr.
Paul Kruger has departed from the terms of his understanding with Lord Carnarvon ; he has contrived a sort of
Plebiscite, on a Memorial to the Queen, and proposes, if
the votes are adverse to Annexation, to summon the Volks-
raad, and appear as their Vice President. These Boers may
not be so difficult to manage as the Zulus, but they will
require very careful handling.

Altogether General Thesiger [afterwards Lord Chelms-
ford] has not come too soon, and I hope that if the war here
is really ended, we may be able to strengthen both the Zulu
border, and the interior of the Transvaal. Fortunately I
find the new Colonial Ministry working much better than
the old one. I did not tell you of the attempt of two of the
Ministers, Messrs. Molteno and Merriman, to usurp something more than the Queen's prerogative, to remove Sir
Arthur Cunynghame and the Queen's troops, and to establish
a sort of military Dictatorship of their own. They declined
to resign, when I told them they had forfeited my confidence, and I fully expected they would have resisted
dismissal. Fortunately their conduct was so bad that I
hope, when Parliament meets, the new Ministry will have
a majority, and that I shall be supported in what was, in
a country under responsible Government, a very extreme
measure.

Hitherto the new Ministry has worked much better than
I expected, and the Press with a few exceptions has come
round to them in a very satisfactory fashion — but they
will have enormous difficulties to contend with — the war
and its consequences — besides an empty exchequer —
bad seasons and consequent diminished trade. They are
pledged to Confederation, and some form of union of these
Colonies is likely to be materially advanced by their coming
into office.

In the following letter one of Lord Beaconsfield's private secretaries throws a somewhat lurid light on the question of the conferring of honours :

From *Mr. Algernon Turnor*

10, Downing Street, Whitehall
13 May, 1878

Lord Beaconsfield desires me to tell you that on the day on which Sir Bartle Frere, in a public despatch, sent to H.M. Government " some very enthusiastic praises of Sir Arthur Cunynghame ", he wrote a private letter to the Secretary of State informing him that Sir Arthur was utterly incompetent, and that if he were not removed Sir Bartle could not answer for the consequences.

This ingenious dealing on the part of Sir Bartle has involved the Ministry in some disagreeable circumstances into which, Lord Beaconsfield says, he cannot now enter. Suffice it to say that H.M. Government directed a trusty person to investigate the matter, and he reported, as the result of his enquiry, that he could not make up his mind which was the most incompetent person : General Cunynghame or Sir Bartle Frere.

Lord Beaconsfield is extremely dissatisfied with all that has taken, or is taking, place at the Cape. The troubles commenced by Lord Carnarvon, who, he says, lived mainly in a coterie of Editors of Liberal papers who praised him and drank his claret, sending Mr. Froude, a desultory and theoretical littérateur, to reform the Cape, which ended naturally in a Kaffir War.

Lord Beaconsfield cannot recommend the Queen to confer a Baronetcy on Sir Arthur Cunynghame.

If the Secretary of State for War thinks the General has been rather scurvily treated by the Government, it is open to him to recommend the Queen to confer on him the G.C.B., and Lord Beaconsfield will not object to such a step under all the circumstances.

A Liberal government came into office in April 1880. In October the Queen, alarmed at Liberal foreign policy, sent for the Secretary of State for Foreign Affairs to visit Balmoral. Ponsonby was away and received the following note on the visit, which is another illustration of the Queen's dislike of verbal arguments and preference for written communications :

From *Lord Granville*

18, Carlton House Terrace, S.W.
Oct. 1, 1880

Your letter of the 22nd was most acceptable and useful. I found things much as you described. Edwards, who was most goodnatured to me, saw me on my arrival and hinted that the Queen was much perturbed. I gave him some explanations, which he thought I had better state myself to the Queen.

Then arrived Prince Leopold, " *abondant dans mon sens* ", suggesting the arguments which would have most effect, boasting of his endeavours to smooth matters. I was not sent for as I was told to expect, but dined. H.M. very civil, and very general in her remarks upon Foreign Policy. The next day, I was sent for. H.M. attacked some of my colleagues, for whom I hope I was able to say what was iudicious, but she shunned argument. I then overate myself greatly, was confined to bed all Monday — a very critical day, disagreeable cyphered messages coming in at every moment. Leopold sent to know what was to be done — all the time the trivial messages of a sanitary kind.

I then asked leave to go up for the Cabinet — answer that the Queen had hoped I should stay some time, but that she would allow me to go, but as she had so much to say to me, it could not be till Saturday or Monday. Fresh explanations that the Cabinet could not be postponed. Leave refused for the next day on grounds of health, and of necessity for much talk. (Compromise for Thursday.)

On Wednesday afternoon I was sent for. Never had a pleasanter hour and a half — of which scarcely five minutes were on Foreign Affairs and Gladstone's Russian proclivities — which I absolutely denied.

I was told that I might be wanted again. But instead of that, I received a present of prints and an invite to dinner.

But as soon as all chance of conversation and argument was over I received a very strong note on Turkey, Afghanistan, and Ireland, which have been followed up by some telegrams.

Harty Tarty [Lord Hartington] is to appear there on Monday, and will I presume inspire still more dislike to controversial argument.

The controversy over the retirement from Kandahar is dealt with by the Private Secretary to the Secretary of State for India in 1880 :

From *The Hon. Reginald Brett* (afterwards Viscount Esher)

India Office, 8 November, 1880

. . . With regard to the Kandahar Despatch the difficulty is this, that the longer a public announcement of the intended retirement is delayed, the greater the risk of disturbances in Southern Afghanistan, and the greater therefore the danger to the fabric which has been raised with so much difficulty at Kabul.

One of the good effects of retirement will be sacrificed unless the intention of the Queen to withdraw her troops is publicly stated some time before the withdrawal actually takes place.

Lepel Griffin — who has just returned from Kabul — told me on Saturday that the effect of the English having kept their word — which was given to the effect that they would not annex Afghanistan — has created a great impression both in that country, and upon the Native Princes in India, with whom he has since come in contact. He has had a great experience — for without him the Abdur Rahman negotiations would very likely not have succeeded — and while he is in favour of postponing the retirement from Kandahar for a few months, he is strongly in favour of announcing the intention to do so now.

That is exactly the position of affairs. I believe your description of the official state of the case to be quite correct. The decision has been arrived at and communicated to the Viceroy, but it has not been made public, and that is now what is required.

The Prince of Wales travelled to Russia for the funeral of the Tsar Alexander II who was assassinated in 1881. The following is from the British Ambassador at St. Petersburg :

From *Lord Dufferin*

1st April, 1881

I am happy to say that the Prince started all right yesterday. I am glad to find that you did not disapprove of his coming. I confess I was all in favour of it. Considering that almost all the other representatives of the Crowned heads of Europe were present, it would have been very much remarked if so near a Royal relative had stayed away, and especially if his absence were to be attributed to fear. Now the Prince has shown in the face of all Europe his readiness to stand by his Brother-in-law, in spite of any personal risk to himself. Not that I really thought the risk appreciable, though where such unreasonable madmen are concerned one can never be quite sure of anything.

The Garter Ceremony went off admirably. The Prince did it so well, and made a nice graceful little speech. It was quite a pleasure to see these poor people have something else given them to think of than assassination and funeral celebrations.

The Private Secretary at the Colonial Office kept Ponsonby well informed on some of the critical colonial affairs. This letter throws light on the defeat at Majuba in the Boer War :

From *Mr. Robert Bickersteth*

Colonial Office, 18th May, 1881

. . . We have had another visitor, Colonel Stewart, who was taken prisoner after Majuba, and who has a great deal that is interesting and curious to tell.

He says that — contrary to what we have hitherto heard — Colley *did* receive an immediate answer to his last letter to the Boers. The answer was that Kruger (to whom the letter was addressed) was at Heidelberg, and that they should therefore require six days instead of forty-eight hours before giving their definite reply : — the forty-eight hours for consideration, with four days for the post to Heidelberg and back.

Meanwhile no forward movement was to be made on either side, but the Boers evidently considered that this agreement left them at liberty to strengthen and extend their entrenchments, and Colley accordingly determined to extend and strengthen his by occupying the " undefended " position of Majuba Hill. It is difficult to follow the process of reasoning by which poor Colley convinced himself that this would not be a " forward movement " or likely to pre-cipitate a conflict before the Boers' answer came back, but this was so clearly his view (according to Col. Stewart) that he abstained from covering his movement by shelling the front of the Boers' position for the very reason that by so doing he considered he would be violating his understand-ing with the Boers. He looked upon Majuba as an " un-defended " position because the Boers had made no entrench-ments there, though they occupied it every day and only withdrew their men at night.

As to the disastrous morning itself, Stewart generally corroborates what we know. If only Colley had entrenched himself at once as he intended to do when he began his march it is Stewart's opinion that no number of Boers could have turned us out : but when our men arrived at the top of the hill, Colley thought the position was naturally so strong that he could take his own time for constructing the three earthworks, the position of which he had already decided upon.

The day was lost by the extended outer line being broken, and running in upon the supports just as they were in the act of moving out in response to the appeal for reinforcements, and so not in a formation steady or solid enough to check the panic with which they too were immediately infected.

Stewart was close to Colley who was as cool as on parade, doing his best to rally the men : but he must (Stewart thinks) have seen that everything was lost just before he was shot himself.

Col. Stewart's story of his own adventures afterwards is interesting enough, and his account of the hospitality of the Boers after he fell into their hands very curious : but you will begin to think my letter is never coming to an end.

There are two further letters from Mr. Bickersteth with regard to the reception of the Zulu Cetewayo in England :

> Colonial Office, 13th July, 1882
>
> There is no escaping Cetewayo now ! The Mayor of Plymouth has been here, eager to know if he may attend in scarlet robes and chain of office to receive Cetewayo on his landing, and offer him a Royal reception and a Royal luncheon. We replied " Certainly not ", but it looks as though Cetewayo's custodians would have enough to do to prevent their charge being lionized !

On the back of this letter the Queen asks " why, when the C. Office said Sir H. Bulwer was to give his advice did they so immediately go agst it ? Why will this Gov^t listen to no local advice when it does not suit them ? "

> Colonial Office, 19th August, 1882
>
> I send you a loyal address surmounted by a representation of something between a " burning bush " and a Christmas tree.
>
> I have written to Mr. Shepstone about M. Sohn, but they (the Zulus and company) are all at Windsor to-day, so I have had no answer yet.
>
> Did you hear that in the middle of his luncheon at Osborne Cetewayo exclaimed " The Queen's champagne is

much better than the champagne they give me at Melbury
Road ", a remark which gave proof of rapid progress in the
ways of civilization and which also necessitated a change of
brand for the household in Melbury Road !

Cetewayo told me that to complete his happiness he wanted
some *dogs*, especially big dogs, to take back to Zululand.
Somebody has already promised him three.

When Cetewayo went to see the Queen at Osborne he stopped
for a moment at Osborne Cottage. Some of the Ponsonby
family watched him from the top of the stairs and observed
bedded in the hair of the frock-coated figure the iron ring of
the Zulu chief.

Controversies at the War Office form the theme of a large
number of letters. When a Liberal Government was in office
or where the Duke of Cambridge was concerned they may be
said to have raged. This is one of them with ramifications
on which it is unnecessary to enlarge :

From *Mr. Hugh Childers* (Secretary of State for War)

5th Nov., 1881

. . . About Wolseley and Roberts I hardly know what to
say. From my point of view the *first* mistake was made by
the Duke in not speaking to me about the approaching
vacancy in July or August, and in fact in only writing when
Ellice pointed out to him the extreme inconvenience his
reticence was causing. The *second* was the Duke assigning
untenable objections to Wolseley, which I was absolutely
forced to combat, and the *third* was his shewing to the Queen
my letter, only intended as (and marked) " Private ", and
written for his eye alone. I should not have written to the
Queen myself, certainly not at that stage, had she not
written to me about my correspondence with the Duke. I
had then no choice but to tell her the whole story, and to
give my reason for recommending the joint appointment of
Wolseley and Roberts. To this letter I received no answer
for three weeks : but I then, after a long interview with the
Duke, at which I fully discussed the question in all its bearings,
wrote to her again. I understand that the Duke then complained that under the Order in Council, the submission of
the names to the Queen should have been by him, not me.
I told him distinctly that my two letters were not the formal
submission, which would be made by him on the usual
printed form ; but that my writing to the Queen was the
direct result of his shewing her my private letter, and of her

letter to me. Today in conversation he admitted frankly that this was the case, and that he withdrew any suggestion of my having acted irregularly.

As to the point in discussion itself, I can say nothing until I have seen Mr. Gladstone on Tuesday. My inclination always is for harmony and conciliation, but the extravagant pretensions in certain newspapers, such as the *Morning Post, Army & Navy Gazette,* etc., as to the government of the Army, compel me to be very cautious.

It is greatly to be regretted that " irresponsible chatter " at Service Clubs should give the public an inkling of these differences.

In Ireland the Land League had been suppressed by proclamation a few months before the Lord-Lieutenant wrote the following letter :

From *Lord Cowper* (Lord-Lieutenant of Ireland)

Vice Regal Lodge, Dublin
Dec. 3, 1881

I wrote to the Queen on Thursday evening — and I hope my letter will give Her Majesty the information she requires.

I fear the list of outrages is very little exaggerated and there is no doubt that the state of the Country is as bad as possible. The break up of the Land League was necessary as a first step towards bringing about a better state of things — but the immediate result has been, as was predicted, an increase of crime.

We had intended to visit different parts of the Country this winter but, now that we have done Belfast, there is no other place to which we could go with the smallest prospect of being well received — and to go anywhere with the result of being hissed and insulted would only do harm. We shall therefore remain quietly here for the present.

The signing of the marriage contract of the Duke of Albany is described by the Permanent Under-Secretary for Foreign Affairs :

From *Sir Thomas Sanderson* (afterwards Lord Sanderson)

Foreign Office, April 27, 1882

The exchange of the ratifications of the Marriage Treaty was a fitting climax to the previous proceedings. Baron Stockhausen confided his Ratification (such as it was) to his servant — and when he got to the Foreign Office forgot to ask him for it. The servant wandered away with it in his pocket and knowing no language but his native German was at once lost in the mazes of the Metropolis.

Baron Stockhausen, on discovering his omission, wished to run after his servant, and they would both have utterly disappeared but Bergne [1] held him back by the coat tails and brought him to Lord Granville's where he went through the process of exchange with a " bogus " document — I believe an unsigned copy of the Treaty.

Everything is to be set right afterwards. I sincerely trust that the Baron has got nothing to do at the ceremony. If he has he will certainly do it wrong. . . .

One of several letters on the campaign in Egypt may be quoted from a writer who was on the spot :

From *Admiral Lord Charles Beresford, M.P.*

Oct. 4th, 1882

I am delighted that my letter interested you. The Queen asked me to dinner two nights ago and H.M. took much interest in many anecdotes I had to tell. H.M. may be really pleased with the duties performed by the Duke of Connaught, he has been really good about his men and their comforts. I wrote a quantity of notes on various matters connected with the future government of Egypt, while I was in Egypt. Lord Granville asked me for them, and has sent them to Mr. Gladstone who I hear is much interested and wishes to see me. I sincerely hope to be the smallest use to the poor Egyptians who, although totally wrong, and misguided by Arabi, etc., have many fair and square grievances which could easily be put right for them. The " Heavies " did really well at Kassasin, and indeed saved the campaign as if they had not charged when they did, and as they did, Graham's brigade would have been annihilated, and the other brigades rolled up like a ball, particularly as the Guards were *en route*.

And an extract from a letter from the same writer at a later date when he was one of the Lords Commissioners of the Admiralty on the subject of Lord Randolph Churchill's resignation from the Chancellorship of the Exchequer :

Jan. 10, 1887

Randolph's jib is a terrible blow to us, but I believe he will run straight with the party, although the party underrate

[1] Head of the Treaty Department, afterwards Sir John Bergne, K.C.M.G.

Z

his power and influence. I am a people's man like Randolph and I know he can upset us tomorrow if he gets wicked. If he does Gladstone will sail in on the troubled waters, and after that we better wish for the judgement, as this country would go to pieces and never be right in our day, or perhaps any day.

Randolph will get immense sympathy in and out of the house if he takes the line of having retired on the Mal-Administration of the finances in the great Spending Departments, in years gone by, and up to the latest date. He retired too quickly and in a huff. A torpid liver, and an energetic disposition are dangerous when combined. But I can see he has the elements of a grand defence. I am amazed at the want of organisation I found here, and should have resigned and published my reasons in every paper in England if my suggestions had not been attended to. But we are doing our best. Randolph's resignation will help. He is sure to come to the top again before the session is over. If our party do not irritate him he will work with us. If they do he may upset us, and then, Gladstone! How dreadful a thought!

The attitude of Italy after the bombardment of Alexandria in 1882 is described in an extract from a letter:

From *Sir Augustus Paget* (British Ambassador in Rome)

Rome, July 15, 1882

. . . I hope those who patronize Arabi, amongst whom are the Italians, are now satisfied with the exploits of their hero. The Italians may perhaps have been behaving decently officially — but God knows what they have been about otherwise. The Italian Press is *too too* disgusting. They accuse us of firing on the town and of having caused the conflagration and consequent ruin and devastation. I have just relieved my mind on the subject in a dirge to the F.O., which I venture to recommend to your perusal. I hope no one will ever talk to me again of the friendship and sympathy of Italy for England. If we had always been their worst enemy instead of best friend they could not vilify us in a more outrageous manner.

Vivid and entertaining letters were received by Ponsonby from Lord Henry Lennox (M.P. for Chichester and a junior Lord of the Treasury) during debates in 1882 from the House of Commons, which he describes as " this very turbulent and not over respectable assembly ". On July 3, after the debate on O'Donnell's suspension he writes that there were "cheers, groans intermingled with catcalls" and adds : "One thing is clear, we have wasted another night in bickering, ballyragging and blundering". But however well described, old parliamentary debates are seldom entertaining reading.

Between the years 1875 and 1892 by far the most voluminous correspondent Ponsonby had from abroad was Sir Robert Morier. He had entered the diplomatic service in 1853. After serving in small German posts he was appointed Minister at Lisbon, subsequently Ambassador in Spain, and ended his career as Ambassador at St. Petersburg for nine years. Over twenty-five of his letters are contained in the correspondence. Morier was a man of considerable ability. His reputation was due more to his knowledge than his judgment. But he rendered conspicuous service when he was in Russia. He had too the fault not uncommon with diplomatists in the days before the amalgamation with the Foreign Office (which now allows a diplomatist a term at home), namely to overestimate the importance of the post he was in. He was a scholar and a good linguist, and his letters were often highly entertaining and were useful in exposing trends of policy and international intrigues. He had many critics and even enemies. He was not accommodating in his manners. Ponsonby was a friend to whom he could write privately and unofficially. One of his letters is marked "Diabolically Confidential". In 1872 Ponsonby refers to him in describing in a note a house party at Strawberry Hill :

> Morier grows larger and heavier and more philosophic every time I meet him. I believe he is one of the deepest enquirers in the diplomatic service, but he plunges too deeply into causes and effects in general conversation. Odo Russell told me last January that Morier was a clever man but used very big words. He always puzzled Enfield [1] when he began upon "Units".

Some extracts may be given from a few of his letters showing his lighter as well as his more serious vein. The long disquisitions on the trend of policy in the various capitals are now too much out of date to be subjects of interest suitable for quotation.

---

[1] Parliamentary Under-Secretary for Foreign Affairs, afterwards Lord Strafford.

From *Sir Robert Morier*

Munich, 18 May, 1875

. . . In the mean time Princess Alexandra died and was buried (in part at least — the heart having been sent to Alt Ötting) and . . . had to remain for the funeral. But the King [of Bavaria] left Munich the day before which has caused great scandal. But much more scandal still was caused by H.M. taking advantage of the theatre being closed for the two days immediately following the Princess's death, to have his favourite Louis XIV plays acted all for himself. Of course the " personnel " who were done out of their holiday were furious and spread it all over the town (though under strict orders to keep it a secret) and the public which was done out of its operas on the plea of mourning for the King's Aunt were furious that H.M. should be the only one who profited by the death of his Aunt to amuse himself. . . .

Munich, 30 May, 1875

. . . As regards Prince Otto [heir to his brother King Louis II] I am not likely to hear anything more about his proposed journey [to England]. There can be no doubt that the reason I have not heard is that his state has very much worsened during the last month and the whole town is talking of an *esclandre* which happened on the occasion of the Corpus Christi festival three days ago. The King who is cross with the Church would not attend the procession or allow the princes to take part in it. This seems to have worked on Prince Otto's mind (whose hallucinations have of late taken a religious turn) and just as the procession was entering the Cathedral he burst through the cordon of soldiers lining the streets, rushed in (dressed in a shooting jacket and wide-awake) and threw himself on the steps of the Altar immediately behind the officiating Archbishop and began in a loud voice a general confession of his sins. It was with the greatest difficulty that he was conveyed to the vestry and got into a quieter state of mind. But from all I hear there is now no doubt that he will have to be treated as seriously out of his mind. On the whole it is certainly as well that this scene did not occur in St. George's Chapel [Windsor].

(Prince Otto went out of his mind and the King also was declared insane.)

Munich, 13 April, 1876

. . . I cannot bring myself to believe that there can be a serious intention on the part of the Great Chancellor [Bismarck] to break the peace but he certainly does not allow his poor Germans to *sleep* on their laurels and these perpetual alarums do not tend to increase the general sense of European security. When a nation of nearly 40 millions of inhabitants, all the males of which are trained to arms, have the good or bad fortune to be ruled absolutely by an almighty master it is a very decided disadvantage that such a master should be afflicted with " nerves ". . . .

King Luiz of Portugal visited Madrid in 1883. Morier had known him intimately in Lisbon. In his letter he describes a scene with the King after a state luncheon :

Madrid, 16 July, 1883

. . . You must know that I was the unfortunate cause of his taking to translate Shakespeare and to spend large sums in putting Shakespeare on the Portuguese stage ; whenever we meet therefore I have to look for a Shakespearean sitting.

Well, at a great breakfast party, given in his honor and where the Spanish society were to be presented to him and the Queen, he espied me and though (knowing that all eyes were upon us) I tried to dodge out of the way he pinned me and, full of lunch and Shakespeare, plunged in wild excitement into *Otello* and began the narration of its successful representation at the Royal Theatre at Lisbon. The preliminaries went smoothly enough — but when, having explained for about twenty minutes the *mise en scène*, the designs for the armour, the dresses copied from pictures at Venice (we two alone on a lawn, surrounded at a respectful distance by a circle of bearded and inquisitive Senors and lovely Senoras, the observed of all observers), he began to give me his interpretation of Otello's character and thence to show how he had taught the actor to carry out this interpretation, which consisted in a gradual crescendo from the perfectly civilized *Grand Seigneur* General to the final catastrophe where the wild beast appears in all his glory, the true martyrdom began — for he acted each scene, repeating all the passages in Portuguese (not a word of which I understood) first *sotto voce* in my ear (being still conscious of the presence of an admiring crowd who listened but could not hear), then louder losing himself entirely in the inspiration of the moment — all the while gesticulating appropriately and clearly seeing in me only the Cassio or whoever else was on the stage. Three times came Chamberlains to inform him that the Royal tea table was laid and the rest of the Royalties waiting. He neither saw nor heard them. I saw the terrible moment approaching when I should be called to be the passive Desdemona to the "wild beast in all his majesty" and sure enough there we were in the fifth act — always describing the great actor, whom he had himself created, he said : Here the wild beast came out — and (His Majesty crouching down as if to spring at my throat) he jumps twenty feet across the lawn — at this moment at the very nick of time the Queen (who I suspect had had a hint) came and separated us *et la session fut levée.* His Majesty was in the profusest perspiration — I in a cold sweat !

In 1885 Morier was in his second year as Ambassador at St. Petersburg. He was being sharply criticized, more especially by the Queen, as being too pro-Russian and not giving sufficient support to Prince Alexander in Bulgaria. Ponsonby was instructed to write to him which he did very fully. Morier's reply covers twelve quarto pages. He begins :

St. Petersburg, 15 December, 1885
Had I not chanced to catch sight of your signature on first opening your letter, I should have fancied I had received one of Pio Nono's encyclicals,

and ends :

I cannot hide from you that I feel vexed at this having got me such a headwashing as that contained in your letter.

He defends himself on all counts and would appear to be on strong ground when he gives definition of the duties of an Ambassador :

I can only say that your ideas and mine about the duties of an Ambassador differ. I have to guide myself by the Queen's instructions which tell me I am to do all I can to foster good relations with the country to which I am accredited. Now the very first condition of good relations is to prevent *malentendus* and misconceptions on either side, and consequently the very first duty of an Ambassador is to endeavour to place before his Government as fairly as possible the version of their conduct which the Government to which he is accredited desire to be so placed. The next is by every means in his power to test the truth and correctness of this version. I have endeavoured to do both. I may not have been successful. I can only say I have done my best. If I have failed so much the worse for me.

He also wrote formally to the Queen in a letter which she condemned as " humbuggy ". But this breeze did not prevent the correspondence from continuing. One more extract may be given from a letter dated St. Petersburg, August 1, 1886 :

> . . . I have I regret to say no spare moments for studying Russian. The game of mutual buzznagging which the two Governments seem to find so entertaining leaves me no time for more profitable employment.
>
> Pray note the term *buzznagging* — a beautiful American addition to the dictionary — from *buzz*, the irritating sound made by a mosquito when preparing to attack you — and *nag*, an occupation indulged in mainly by vicious females — to *buzznag* — to say and do irritating things, for the pleasure of irritating.

Ponsonby wrote to his first cousin asking : " Why there are more rowdies in Ireland than elsewhere ? "

From *Lord Bessborough* (6th Earl)

> Bessborough, January 30, 1882
>
> . . . Because there are more unemployed and therefore discontented. This has always been the case as long as I can remember, but it is more felt now, owing to the improved Education, manner of living and knowledge of the world than formerly. I do not mean the unemployed Labourers and their families only but I consider the most dangerous class of people in Ireland are the members of Farmers' families (male and female) who are not to succeed to the farm. They are too well educated — the men especially — to sit quietly at home or work for their fathers — they think themselves fit and *are fit* for something above a Common Labourer's position and after failing (as the large majority must) in getting situations by Competitive Examination or by interest somewhere, they become discontented and see nothing but emigration before them. This they consider a hardship and will enter into any row or conspiracy before they go. They tyrannize over their parents and force them into becoming bad tenants — they make them pay them for all work they do. . . .
>
> That is the state of those classes and with the ruffians of secret societies to entrap them into outrages and the teachings of returned Irish Americans they become ready for any row and in some cases for crime and outrage. Now these very young men, if got hold of and given employment, would turn out well. I have had lots of Boys at Coolattin and here

out with me shooting and beating, and all my English
friends have said " What nice boys." I always answered
" Yes — and in two years (when they are eighteen or
nineteen) they will be gloomy, discontented men, unless I
can find something for them to do." I sent a great many
over as Clerks, Porters, etc., to the Great Western, and they
almost always turned out first rate men, rising rapidly in
the service, and as one of the Superintendents told me,
" often making very eligible marriages ". There is in my
opinion the difficulty of Ireland, and I believe if ruffianism
of secret societies and rowdyism of unemployed could be
got rid of there would be very little trouble in the country.
What can be done is a more difficult question to answer, as
it would not be consistent with English ideas of Government
to take steps which might in a great measure meet the
difficulty.

Lord Odo Russell (created Lord Ampthill in 1880) was
Ambassador in Berlin from 1871 till 1884. There are several
letters from him. But before quoting extracts from them an
account of a conversation with him may be given from a letter
Ponsonby wrote to his wife from Osborne on August 11, 1876 :

Certainly Odo Russell is a most agreeable man. He and
Lady Emily arrived yesterday afternoon and I took a walk
with him. He was full of his interview with the Emperor.
He never expected to see Bismarck and only hinted he was
at Kissingen. Bismarck at once insisted on his coming with
him to Würzburg — as he was going to resign if the Emperor
persisted in sending a note of remonstrance to England.
Bismarck talked the whole way — six hours. The enthusiasm
for him everywhere was remarkable. Odo went to see the
sights of Würzburg but was pursued by a Royal messenger
and brought to the Emperor's hotel.

Pückler said the Emperor would see him and at that
moment Bismarck came out from the Emperor's room.
The day was hot and Odo's forehead was marked with
black from his hat. " You can't go in like that," said
Bismarck. " Give me a room to clean myself," said Odo.
" Impossible," said Pückler, " the Emperor is waiting and
you must go in." It is on occasions of difficulty that Bismarck's true greatness appears. He pulled out his enormous
pocket handkerchief — all truly great men have enormous
pocket handkerchiefs — wetted it with his mouth, rubbed
Odo's forehead clean and handed him in to the Emperor.
He said the Emperor was furious with England. He was
ready to throw over Bismarck and go any lengths against

her. But Odo appeased him and Bismarck thanked him afterwards.

I said the Czar stirred him up against us — why do so ? Odo replied : " The Czar has no cause to like us. We have thwarted him on every occasion. When he proposed the Softening of War conference, we spoilt it by refusing to join. It was ridiculous of course — but we might have humoured him. It could never come to anything. When he proposes things about Turkey — we refuse to join. Of course the Berlin note was impracticable. But if we had joined we might have converted it into something. By holding aloof we broke up the common understanding and appeared in the character of supporters of the Turk — not intentionally. But such we were supposed to be. The Czar wished for peace — but this split made it impossible for him to restrain the Servians — and thus came the war. If we had adopted a dull steady policy working with the rest — there would have been no outbreak. But our Government preferred the brilliant stroke of genius which has undoubtedly been heartily supported by the English nation — and it may turn out to be the right one. But you see it is natural that the Czar should feel hurt at his schemes for peace being upset and himself and his Ministers distrusted."

From *Lord Odo Russell* (later Lord Ampthill)

British Embassy, Berlin
27 Dec., 1880

My wife desires me to beg of you to have the kindness to send the enclosed letter to the Queen, thanking Her Majesty for the high honour of a Peerage so graciously conferred upon us, — and which gratifies me more deeply than words can ever express.

Things are going on much as usual here, and the event of the winter will be Prince William's wedding, to which, it is ardently hoped, *all* our Princes will come.

Prince Bismarck, who likes the institution of the " European Concert ", is seeking to establish his personal influence absolutely over its proceedings, and he has already secured the obedient co-operation of Austria and France, who live in dread of the formidable forces at his command.

His object appears to be the maintenance of peace and the postponement of the Collapse of Turkey, which he imagines Mr. Gladstone's policy is calculated to hasten on more rapidly than he likes. He is in favour of letting Turkey vegetate unmolested, and believes that the Reforms we press upon the Porte are merely nails in her Coffin, which it would be more prudent not to drive in with too much force if we wish Turkey to live and last a few years longer.

Extract from letter from *Lord Ampthill*, August 1882 :

You ask what Bismarck wants ? He wanted, as you may remember, that Austria should hold Bosnia, France take Tunis and England occupy Egypt, and with his usual good luck he is gradually getting what he wants. He settled the Austrian occupation of Bosnia, through the Emperors at Reichstädt, the French invasion of Tunis with Waddington at the Berlin Congress, and now that the State of Egypt imperatively calls for a policy of action he whispers to the Powers in concert consulted : " Be thankful for England will settle Egypt for us, better than we can singly or in concert ". What he will want in the future will be the prolongation of our occupation of Egypt during his lifetime.

Lord Beaconsfield said to me in reply to a private message from Prince Bismarck about Egypt : " Tell Bismarck from me not to trouble himself about Egypt — *I* will take care of Egypt ! " And now that England is taking care of Egypt the policy of H.M. Government is immensely popular at home and abroad.

Extract from letter from *Lord Ampthill*, October 6, 1882 :

Bismarck is favourable to us, and as I told you before, must wish from his personal point of view for a prolonged occupation of Egypt by England.

While he wishes for the maritime supremacy of England in the Mediterranean, he would not like England and France to quarrel, because he holds to the Anglo-French Alliance as an element of peace and order in Europe, since it excludes the possibility of a French-Russian alliance, which would be a permanent threat to Germany in his opinion. His influence on France will be favourable to a continuance of those friendly relations which Lord Granville knows so well how to maintain between England and France — and France at the present moment cares more for the regular payment of the " Coupon " than for Glory !

Austria and probably Italy will also be guided by Bismarck's attitude.

Russia I fear may give trouble and seek advantages elsewhere, but on the whole I do not anticipate any difficulties which H.M. Government cannot overcome with time and patience — and the longer the time we take, and the more we try the patience of the Powers, the better for us and for Egypt.

From *Lord Wolseley*

Paris, 21st December, 1882

. . . I am here until the end of the year, trying to have a few days' rest of which I stand in need ; no one I think except those who have experienced it themselves can tell how great is the strain upon a commander's brain during such a high pressure campaign as that we have had in Egypt. If I could have a month of perfect rest in some country part of England where no one could get at me, it would be worth many boxes of Parr's pills, even assuming they possess the charm which their inventor claimed for them. But it would seem as if I never should have any rest and the consequence will be that I shall be worn out before my time. . . .

At a later date in 1887 (month omitted) there is a letter on uniforms, a favourite subject in royal circles :

From *Lord Wolseley*

War Office, Saturday

I entirely agree with all you tell me the Queen thinks about the incongruity of dressing men of the same Regiment differently merely for economical reasons. It is the same wherever any expensive headdress or taildress is worn by the Line Battalions of the Regiment. The answer given to our remonstrances is " Given fourteen millions to be spent on the Army, have you no other more pressing want than feather bonnets and bearskin hats for your Militia Staff ? "
What can one say to such a question ? Why, upon the supply of some of our wants depend the safety of the Kingdom. We are this year more than ever cheeseparing all round and yet we have to wipe out items asked for upon which we know the health, comfort and well being of Her Majesty's soldiers depend. Under these circumstances, there is no likelihood of our getting the ornamental things we ask for. No one can regret it more than I do. I am heartily sick of the whole thing and if I could afford a little place in the country I should like to retire and give the struggle up to younger men.

On questions which concern pictures, copies of pictures or reproductions, the President of the Royal Academy is from time to time brought into the correspondence. The note attached to the following letter explains it :

Note by *H. P.*

March 23, 1883

Sir F. Leighton asked me to " submit " Machette's etching of Mason's Harvest Moon to the Queen. I asked what "submit" meant, as Dunthorne the publisher was fond of advertising these for his own benefit. Leighton said merely " submit ". I submitted. The Queen said it was good. I told Leighton the Queen liked it. After a time he asked might Dunthorne advertise what the Queen had said. I replied " Certainly not." The Queen's words could not be used as an advertisement.

From *Sir Frederick Leighton*

I was an idiot even to doubt that it could be otherwise — but to be an idiot in the service of others is the least disgraceful form of imbecility. Thanks for your letter.

One of the many letters from Gladstone's Private Secretary :

From *Edward Hamilton*

10, Downing Street, Whitehall
24 Sept., 1883

You may perhaps as well know (if you have not heard direct) that on Saturday Mr. Gladstone received the somewhat blowing-up letter which you anticipated would come, questioning the wisdom of a Prime Minister hobnobbing with Crowned Heads without the Foreign Secretary at his elbow and without instructions from his Sovereign, etc., etc. Mr. Gladstone did not like the tone of it ; but, in his reply which was apologetic and becoming alike a gentleman and a statesman, carefully concealed his displeasure, though he did not lose the opportunity of hinting that the only two Organs of the Press in this country which had taken exception to his Danish visit never could see anything but guilt and folly in every action of his.

He was delighted with your visit on Friday ; but I will spare your right ear from a very severe fit of tingling and not attempt to reproduce his warm and appreciative expressions. You will let me know if you hear anything further of the Balmoral mood ; and also anything of the proposal to add to the Poet Laureate's crown of laurels one of gold ?

Although the year date of the following letter is missing, it would seem to belong to the early eighties. The writer was Equerry to the Duke of Edinburgh and was entrusted with the duty of escorting the Duchess, her children and suite to

Coburg. Although it does not touch on any serious international matters the letter is too amusing to omit. The scandals of the court of Coburg led to prolonged differences between the reigning Duke and the Duke of Edinburgh who succeeded him in 1893. There are in the letter several more pages which concern them :

From Lt.-Colonel Arthur Haig

Coburg, 28th May

. . . The journey terminated successfully on Saturday evening about six o'clock. We took no courier, and as no one else has had the grace to thank me for the arduous duties, which in that character I performed, I must take this opportunity of expressing to Haig our extreme gratitude for the untiring energy and unparalleled skill with which he conducted Her Royal and Imperial Highness to her journey's end. It is true that there was a slight mishap at Brussels. We got there at six in the morning. I put the Duchess and Miss Corry into one carriage and the children into another. Then I ran back to the platform, where I was instantly transfixed with horror. Hutchins, our page, was seated on a silver night-stool, the *only* article of all our luggage that he had succeeded in securing. The rest of the luggage, the nurses and nursery-maids, the dressers, footmen and valets were scattered to the four winds. Some of the luggage was at the Gare du Nord, some at the Gare du Midi, some had gone on to Cologne, the rest in a fit of disgust had gone back to London. And *all* our money in my despatch box amounting to nearly £3000 had gone off in an excursion train towards Antwerp. It was a general débâcle. The menservants were stupefied and the women " stood crying and wringing their hands ".

My first idea was to send in my resignation on the spot — and to return by the next train to Scotland, but I overcame that temptation, and by dint of superhuman efforts I actually succeeded in rallying our beaten forces and in recovering all our lost luggage at Cologne in the evening.

The next time I travel on the Continent in charge of

A Royal and Imperial Highness,
3 Royal and Imperial Children,
A Lady-in-Waiting,
An Equerry,
4 Nurses,
4 Ladies' Maids,
A Page,
and 4 Footmen,

without a courier — may I be — never mind. I will *not* do
it again. And am I not to be rewarded for all this ? What !
No decoration ? Oh try and procure me the Cross of
Ernest The Second-rate.

But no matter ! I have much to tell you. Coburg is
in a state of intense fermentation. It is moved, I may say,
to the very dregs. On the 1st June will take place, with great
pomp, the celebration of the 50th Anniversary of the Foundation of the Ducal-Saxe-Coburg-Gotha Opera ! There will
be a performance of unequalled brilliance in the Great
Theatre ! where also the most distinguished artistes of the
Thuringian theatre will be crowned with laurels. Ernest —
the Great, the Good, the Chaste, the Second, the Father,
nay the grandfather now of many of his subjects, will appear
in state. His Consort and all his other Consorts will be there
— all, those that have been — that are — and that are going
to be — all. Imagine ! — but I have not paper enough to
imagine it upon. Send out a Hogarth quick to paint the
picture " *La Famille Ducale et demi-Ducale* ".

After the theatre there is to be a grand ball in the Giant's
Hall of the Great Palace. There all are invited, the First,
the Second, the Third Societies and the Great Actors and
Actresses. How fortunate a man I am, to be sure ! I am
wild with excitement, and I would not have missed this
sight for anything.

Ah ! but there is something much more important than
this to tell you. Hush ! " *She* " is no longer here. She has
gone. Those little dinners " *à trois* " are a thing of the past.
A Burgher of Leipsic has made her an honest woman and
taken her to his own home. It seems that after the last
visit the Duke of Edinburgh paid to Coburg she saw that
he had an invincible dislike to her — so she went to the other
Duke one morning and said " May it please Your Highness !
You are growing old, and you will probably die soon. Your
successor hates me and will certainly drive me penniless
away. Therefore, my August Master, you must purchase
a house and a husband elsewhere for me and I will go — "
She is coming to the ball though, so I may see her once
again. . . .

The Colonial Secretary writes on the expedition under
Sir Charles Warren which was sent out to South Africa in 1884
to check the efforts of the Boers at territorial expansion. The
territories in question were occupied without a shot being
fired. The expedition cost a million and a half.

From *Lord Derby* (15th Earl, Secretary of State for the
Colonies)

Colonial Office, Nov. 20, 1884
Antrobus has shown me your very pertinent query. I hope,
and expect, that there will be no fighting. But everybody
insisted on an expedition. You ask why?

(1) The opposition, in order to spend money, and spoil
our next budget.

(2) The military party, because to them the sending out
of expeditions, anywhere and for any purpose, is the chief
object of human existence. Besides, they have not forgiven
Majuba Hill, and hope to pick a quarrel with the Trans-
vaalers.

(3) The philanthropists, headed by Forster, who want
South Africa to remain a negro state, and see with extreme
jealousy the inroads of white civilisation.

(4) The colonists, to whom a war, or preparation for
one, means fat contracts and double value for their produce.

(5) The Radicals, chiefly to show that they are not
peace-at-any-price men.

I believe M. and the other chief would have sold their
lands for a tenth of what this business will cost. But that
would have suited nobody. The trade road question will
be settled amicably between the Cape and the Transvaal.
The majority of the white colonists are of the same race as
the Boers, and love them much better than they do us.

There are three letters describing incidents in the Egyptian
campaign in 1885 when a force was sent forward from Suakin
against Osman Digna. The first two are from the commander
of the 2nd Infantry Brigade (one of the Queen's Equerries) :

From *Major-General Sir John Carstairs McNeill*

Camp, Suakin, 5 April, 1885
Only a line to tell you what you might know already, that
for the last fortnight I have had a hard time of it. I was
retired [?] from the Service yesterday after a fortnight,
without a chance of changing or washing, the only Regiment with me all through was the Berkshire. I objected but
could not refuse to do what Graham wished. I said that I
had a great many too many camels to look after as a fighting
force and *I* knew we should have to fight. I was told to go
eight miles but finding the huge convoy all adrift I only went
six and made the best arrangements I could for protection

while cutting bushes for the fence. The attack came with a vengeance and all would have gone well had not the 17 N.I. bolted. As it was we halted them in twenty minutes and killed 1500. Their force was 5000 at least, all desperate men, who had cut their hair and put on Mahdi uniform. I wrote a very short report and did not mention anything about difficulties, and I shall say nothing on the subject.

It is a rotten business and a rotten country. Wolseley's force never will go up the Nile again and I do not think the Rail will ever go beyond Handoub. If active operations cease I should like to leave, I believe myself that I have had the fight of the season. Climate lovely at present, hot in the day of course.

Suakin, 8 April, 1885

Many thanks for your letter. We also received all the papers and the abuse, for which I care nothing. I am only thankful that things went as well as they did. Had I gone to the point I was ordered to or had I not taken the precautions I did we should have had a very great disaster. Of course one cannot calculate on a Regiment bolting. I was sent two days ago to clear out that post with four Regiments and over 3000 animals : had we been attacked exactly the same thing would have taken place. You can not control 3000 frightened camels with drivers mad with terror. We are obliged to march in Square, for if a dozen of these mad Arabs got inside stabbing camels and men our people would fire on each other. They come on to the bush in groups of five and six as fast as horses and quite straight. A man will stand ten yards from a square and let fire go on till he is killed. If you try to give them water when wounded they will kill you. You will see my report. It is a plain story. The Queen sent me a most kind letter. The sooner we are out of this the better — no good can come of it. I write in the usual dust storm with flies and stench.

The third is from a young subaltern in the Guards, who was a cousin of Ponsonby's :

From *W. F. B. Tighe*

Suakin, April 7th, 1885

Thanks very much for your letter. We returned from Tamai on Saturday, having been marching in the sun and sleeping on the ground without a wash for more than a week. We relieved the Coldstream and Scots at the Zareba and stopped there five days. The dead camels, etc. are still lying round, only a few buried. They came up from Suakin on Wednesday, arriving at 7 A.M., and we all went on to Tamai, thinking that at last we should have a go at Osman Digna, as the Mounted Infantry had reported him to be strongly posted. We marched as usual in square. I suppose it is necessary, but it is the most difficult formation. The camels and mules lag behind, and break through the rear face of the square, and the heat and dust are awful. We had a balloon out that day but the man in it wanted to get out after he had been in an hour, and it went up too fast and was torn nearly in half. We arrived at O. Digna's position at about four. It was very strong among rocks, but he cleared out of it before we came. We formed our usual zareba at the weak places and stopped for the night. The enemy came and fired at us most of the night as they usually do, but very few men were hit, and we started for Tamai at seven next morning. We advanced in an enormous square which was rather broken over the rocky ground, but they wouldn't attack us, so all we could do was to burn the place and come away. They fired at us a good deal. Mildmay had a spent bullet hit his buckle. We arrived at McNeill's Zareba that evening, slept outside on the ground and off again to Suakin next morning, where we arrived at about three, with dirt on us in flakes. Some of us went and had a bath on the Hospital Ship. Just as we arrived our dragoman came running out to us with soda water and oranges ; I think we were never more glad to see anybody.

Our men behave wonderfully well. The most trying time was when we were retiring from Hasheem, in square ; we were the rear face, *i.e.* leading. The enemy were firing into the square from all round, and we had to go very slow to let the camels and ambulance keep up, and couldn't see anything to fire at, but the men marched perfectly steady.

The outpost duty was very hard at first. The camp was pitched with as large a front as possible, apparently. We were in a long line right out into the desert, and had to defend each side of it, often having *five* companies out to guard *three* and if anybody had fired, they would probably have shot into some other regiment. It is a little better now.

One of the officers rather amused us when we were at Tamai. We were on about two pints of water, and he came to the water guard saying he must have ten watercarts for his men. The fight at the Zareba was a very near thing, but was not entirely McNeill's fault. They sent him with an enormous convoy and a very small force, and if he had gone on as far as he was ordered would have fared worse.

Please give my love to the family.

2 A

A note from Charles Gore (Commissioner of Woods and Forests), formerly Private Secretary to Lord John Russell, records that his son Charles, then thirty-two years old (eventually Bishop of Oxford), had been through the ordeal of preaching before the Prime Minister at Hawarden :

January 13, 1885

Son Charles has been on a visit to the G.O.M. and had to preach before him on Sunday. He seems to have had a deal of talk and walk with him and was astounded at his powers and kindness.

The Viceroy of India discusses policy with regard to Burmah :

From *Lord Dufferin*

Camp, Bhurtpore, Nov. 22, 1885

. . . I am thinking of going to Burmah myself in order to determine what is to be done with the country. A " buffer " should be elastic and possess some power of resistance. These qualities may be said to be possessed in an imperfect degree by Afghanistan, but there is as little elasticity in Burmah as in a pat of butter. On the other hand, the Chinese show an inclination to raise difficulties, and it would be very unwise to come to loggerheads with them on the subject if we can possibly avoid it. Our Empire is certainly large enough, and nothing would have induced me to have extended our territories if it could have been avoided, but unless we had acted promptly a very difficult situation would have been created in the Valley of the Irawaddy hereafter, as Theebaw was determined to get the French in, and was becoming more and more hostile in his attitude towards us. I am in hopes that we have sent a sufficient force to reduce the chances of opposition to a minimum, and that there will not be much loss of life on either side. The Burmese are a nice people, easily managed, and I cannot bear the thought of making war upon them. I have enjoined our Commander to do everything he can to get the better of them by strategy rather than by direct conflict. It will be by no means a paying affair from a purely financial point of view, as was the annexation of Lower Burmah. For some years we shall certainly be out of pocket by a few lacs if we annex, but annexation is still an open question, and we have not yet sufficient information really to form a sound and conclusive opinion. Whatever information I submit will certainly not be the product of any Jingo impulse. . . .

And two years later on Russian intrigues in India :

Calcutta, 15th Feb., 1887

I sent off by last mail a letter to Her Majesty contradicting in the fullest manner the rumours she had heard about Russian intrigues and native disaffection in certain towns in India. It is impossible to conceive anything more unfounded than the whole story, and the tremendous " tamasha " which is about to be held from one end of India to the other will be a sufficient reply to these foolish fabrications. In the history of the world there will never have been such a spontaneous and unanimous exhibition of affection by a people towards their Sovereign.

Will you inform Her Majesty that all the ladies of Calcutta are ordering jubilee bustles.

The next letter from one of the Prince of Wales' Household, although of no consequence illustrates the sort of language Ponsonby was sometimes obliged to listen to :

From *Sir Dighton Probyn*

Marlborough House, Pall Mall, S.W.
Feb. 4, 1886

. . . Don't talk to me about Gladstone. I pray to God that he may be shut up as a Lunatic at once, and thus save the Empire from the Destruction which he is leading her to. If he is not mad, he is a *Traitor*.

I am worried over Lord Spencer. I have always looked upon him as being an honest Englishman, and a Gentleman — one who put party *far far* behind Country. But he has fallen into that Traitor's clutches, and is lending a direct helping hand to a fearful Civil War — God help him, and put him straight before it is quite too late. He had a " hang-dog " expression last night. I never saw a man look so altered. Everybody must have remarked it. A man of that sort advocating Communism shakes my belief in anything mortal.

The above letter was a deliberate personal attack on Ponsonby's political views. But just to show how he never allowed himself to take offence or shut off correspondence with writers of such letters with whom he was obliged to be in communication, a letter of amusing chaff to Probyn a few years later may be inserted (Probyn when on active service in the army had been awarded the Victoria Cross) :

Osborne, December 29, 1890

MY DEAR PROBYN,

In urging the claims of Mr. Mackay for a Chaplaincy to the Queen, and to preach before her, you base your argument on the services he rendered during the mutiny and you say " surely his services in the field deserve this recognition ". Well — I did not know that gallantry in action should be rewarded by Chaplaincies. If so you ought to have some very high ecclesiastical appointment and I fully recognize your claims. Please arrange so that you may preach here on Sunday next. I will ensure your having a good congregation.

Happy New Year to you.

From *Sir Lyon Playfair* (distinguished scientist, afterwards Lord Playfair)

25 June, 1887

On coming back from the Abbey last Monday impressed deeply with the ceremony, I tried to form an index of the progress of Civilisation during the Queen's reign. The result may interest you. The price of rags as indicating the demand for paper has always appeared to me the best index of progress and the following facts are striking :

In 1837 each head of the population consumed $1\frac{1}{4}$lb. of paper : in 1887 no less than 12 lbs. Measured by this index England is now at the head of all nations in 1887.

England	12 lbs. of paper per head		
United States	10 ,,	,,	,,
Germany	9 ,,	,,	,,
France	8 ,,	,,	,,
Italy	4 ,,	,,	,,

In 1837 each person of the population spent 1/11 on books and newspapers annually : in 1887 this had increased to 9/-.

In 1837 each person sent 9 letters through the post : in 1887 this had increased to 38. An index of this kind is encouraging.

Another index of well doing is the consumption of soap, because " Cleanliness is next to Godliness ". This however has not increased so much as I could have wished :

1837 — $7\frac{3}{4}$ lbs. per head of soap
1887 — 10 lbs. ,, ,,

Still a child born today has three years more of life than if born in 1837.

From *Mrs. Gladstone*

May 21st

Of course my husband would wish Her Majesty joy of *the* birthday. Please tell me (he is a little inclined I think to write to *you* a letter you could shew) — don't you think a letter straight to H.M. would be best. Please be quite honest.

I never can make him think he is a great man ! which every one else should think, or ought to think ! Please, one line directed to ME TONIGHT, to 21 Carlton House Terrace where we sleep.

I wish you were all coming here to our afternoon, if it is but fine.

The costume of some of the Queen's visitors had to be carefully attended to, as is shown by this letter :

From *Sir Philip Cunliffe Owen*

7 July, 1886

I enclose a memo from the Executive Commissioners for British Guiana respecting the curious natives arriving this day. They are like Red Indians and may be considered as such.

The total absence of clothing of both sexes was to be compromised by bathing drawers. But I have stipulated for some drapery besides their usual garments of feathers, crowns and necklaces.

I have also arranged that the Executive Commissioners should be allowed to appear in Morning Dress.

The Memorandum I have had drawn up will I am sure interest Her Majesty.

There is a note by Ponsonby on a letter from Hallam Tennyson dated February 15, 1888 :

Prince and Princess Henry of Battenberg, Miss Cochrane and I drove to Farringford — Lord and Lady Tennyson and Mr. and Mrs. Hallam Tennyson. He though seventy-eight looking fresh. He said to me " I hear you are a Home Ruler." I said no — quite the contrary, though an admirer of Gladstone. He replied " So am I socially but his politics are atrocious." He then told several Irish stories not to the credit of Irish peaceableness. We clambered up to his study, rather cold, and there he read — Ode on the Duke of Wellington's Funeral and The Spinster — I don't very much care for his reading.

The letter from the Hon. Hallam Tennyson merely says :

It was a great pleasure to welcome you here yesterday.
. . . You hoped that my father did not feel the visit too
much for him, so let me tell you now that he thoroughly
enjoyed it.

The writer of the next letter served from 1852 onwards
in several diplomatic posts in Germany and elsewhere. He
was now at Dresden. He was by no means of the official type
but wrote with unguarded frankness as his letter shows :

From *Mr. George Strachey* (Chargé d'Affaires at Dresden and
subsequently Minister)

British Legation, Dresden
April 25, 1888

I was very sorry that the Queen passed through Leipzig in
the night.

That town, which is hyper-Bismarckian (specifically
National-Liberal), and Dresden, which is ultra-Conservative,
have shewn a maximum of hatred of the Empress and the
Queen. The Leipzig National Liberal " *Grenzboten* " (an
equivalent (in a weak fashion) of our *Fortnightly*), which has
been often utilized by Bismarck, published the other day a
long tirade against the two royal ladies, in which the insol-
ence and venom of the Prussian " reptiles " were almost
surpassed. The folly and vulgarity of the similar lucubrations
here pass belief. The " *Freisinnig* " party in Saxony is weak,
so that their voice cries in the desert ; but they have defended
the Emperor, the Empress, and the Queen, with great
courage and pertinacity, and their Dresden organ exhausts
the superlatives of eulogy every day in praise of all three. As
in Berlin, the radicals (who, after all, are only on the political
level of our Tories) are admirably loyal, while the Bismarck-
ites are behaving like Anarchists.

For the moment, it would seem as if the " reptile " press
had received a hint to prepare for a change of front. One
of the Berlin gang has the audacity to dilate on " the *Reich-
kanzler's* touching, devoted love for his all-highest master ",
which may indicate that Bismarck thinks that the Emperor's
recovery is possible.

At the great official dinner on the King's birthday, I
found that all the political *summits* agreed that Bismarck was
the moral, perhaps the material, author of the whole " *Hetze* ",
and, although the majority present were " grave-diggers ",

no one much dissented from the very undiplomatic language in which I relieved my feelings at his expense.

One of the Prince of Wales' Equerries wrote from time to time letters some of which were on serious subjects, such as the one already quoted. Others were in an entertaining and humorous vein, full of indiscretions and occasionally illustrated with excellent drawings. Describing a banquet at Marlborough House which was " very bad — everything that should be cold was hot and vice versa ", and which was concluded with speeches, he adds : " In fact there was the usual amount of forced conviviality and suppressed gloom which characterise these banquets ". He writes later, in January 1892, when the Queen put Windsor Castle at the disposal of the Prince of Wales and his Household, on the occasion of the funeral of Prince Albert Victor, Duke of Clarence :

From *Major-General Sir Arthur Ellis*

Windsor Castle, 22.1.92

. . . In every — even the saddest occurrences of life there arises a comic side — a gleam of absurdity — which helps one to bear the gloom. . . .

The Prince of Wales desires me to say that — the harem of Princesses was *not* locked into the further Zenana pew closet but the door got jambed, and adds that they were none of them wanted at all. No ladies were to attend, and the Princess of Wales especially requested privacy — and to avoid meeting her Osborne relations. So they all came.

If Princess Beatrice was annoyed it cannot be helped and she must get over it — as she likes.

We are fairly comfortable in this most conveniently built house — and most of our time is spent in a sort of game of " post " or hide-and-seek, looking for and searching for each other — and being hunted by servants who get lost.

We all admire various little economical thrifty dodges here. In the W.C.s — NEWSPAPER squares — there was one idea of sending them to Cowell [Master of the Household] in an unpaid envelope. . . . And with a cup of tea — three lumps of loose sugar on the tray ! ! It is admirable — and we now see why you are so rich.

The avalanche of telegrams and resolutions still pour in. One day over 1700 telegrams ! ! ! Average for five days

1000 per diem. We write till we feel scribblers' palsy coming
on — and it seems to have no effect on the letters. I have
appraised the Sandringham telegram bill at £2000. All
the small places in New Zealand, Australia and India sending messages, all to be replied to, at so very much per word,
is ghastly waste.

Strange for us to be installed here and writing to you
away on this side of the grave.

We all clear out tomorrow — Hallelujah ! These mem-
morial services in " Wolsey " [Chapel] are most harrowing
and upsetting. The choir boys sing like angels, but it is *too*
sad — and I cannot listen to it. It is turning the knife in
one's wound.

MacNeill is excellent, useful, cheerful and most attentive
and full of resource — and we believe if *he* cooked the dinner
also, it would even be better and warmer perhaps. . . .

P.S. We have great larks with the press, to whom I had to
say we are *unable* to tell them ahead the sex of Prince George's
future eldest child ! ! They want " early copy ".

The Military Attaché in Berlin from 1882 to 1889, and
again from 1891 to 1896, was a very punctual correspondent
who had close knowledge of all that was going on. There is a
large packet of his letters, from which a few extracts may be
given :

From *Major-General Leopold V. Swaine*

Berlin, May 16, 1885

Prince William, like most of his countrymen, is narrow
minded. His " *Hofmarschall* " and the first " *Hofdame* " of
his suite have done everything in their power to kill his
leaning towards England. English nurses have been discarded for his children and nothing but " German ", or
what is Teutonic pure and simple, is allowed for a German
Prince. Added to this his early marriage and his Grandfather's great age have stood in the way of his being allowed
to travel. His military surroundings flatter him, and the
life he leads between Potsdam and Berlin, and Berlin and
Potsdam, is not calculated to increase his knowledge of the
world or to induce him to understand either his own nation,
or that some good may be got out of seeing other countries
and other peoples otherwise than out of books. But for all
that I say he is a chip of the old block. He is a right good
young fellow, and he is the making of everything deserving
the great future he has before him. He works hard, he
reads everything that he thinks will instruct him, he is self-

willed, but has great determination. *He requires very careful leading.*

Feb. 28, 1889

. . . From the long conversations I had before leaving Berlin both with the Emperor and with Count Bismarck, it is quite clear to me that both are most anxious that the visit should be a success and that the Queen should be as glad to receive the Emperor as, I know also, the Emperor is looking forward to see Her Majesty. Nothing could exceed the attachment with which the Emperor spoke of the Queen and of the pleasure he was looking forward to at the meeting.

Count Bismarck also felt that it was a visit which not only was gratifying to the Emperor, but which it was his duty to pay.

Count Bismarck is rough in manner but he is not as heartless as he is frequently painted and there is no one in Germany who is so strongly imbued with the wish that a strong and warm friendship should exist between the two countries.

Nov. 9, 1892

Your question : how are the Germans going to pay for their new Army? is a difficult one to answer. Some say that Beer and Tobacco are to be taxed. This will make even a bigger hubbub than the Army Bill does itself. Speaking personally I think it will be to the advantage if Beer were taxed, and taxed heavily for I am satisfied that a great deal too much Beer is drunk here. Every grand looking house in every street is a " *Bier Lokal* ". It is undermining the clear heads of the population. North Germans always talk of " *die schwerfälligen Bayern* " and attribute this condition in Bavaria to the amount of beer drunk there. The Prussians are now falling into the same condition. Beer is very fattening and heavy bodies entail heavy and lethargic minds. If you go into society here, you have no sooner done dinner than beer is handed round and the fair ladies are as fond consumers of this poison as their male relatives.

I have just come from a shooting expedition in Silesia and I find there that although the people fully see the necessity of an increase in the Army, they are afraid that it can only pass with the assistance of the " *Centrum* " in the Reichstag, *i.e.* the Catholic Party, and that the Government will have to make concessions to these to gain their votes. This will not be popular.

On the other hand the Government has a strong card to play, namely the continued advance of Russian forces towards the frontier. In the last month the largest dislocation of troops in Russia has taken place since I have been in

Berlin — since 1883 — and in comparing notes this morning with an official in the General Staff Office, he replied : *" Russland steht vollkommen schlagfertig da."*

Germany is terribly handicapped by her two allies and unless our fleet extricates the Italians a war between the Triple Alliance on one side and Russia and France on the other will in my belief end in victory to the latter — and then God help the rest of Europe.

Nov. 3, 1894

The papers will have shown you that Caprivi [the Chancellor who succeeded Bismarck] got his walking ticket ten days ago. His meeting with the Emperor yesterday week was of a distinctly stormy nature. You will recollect that in the beginning of that week the Emperor received an Agrarian Deputation introduced by Count Eulenburg, Prime Minister of Prussia. Count Caprivi, annoyed at this having taken place without his knowledge and consent, tendered his resignation. The Emperor however smoothed the matter over and the resignation was withdrawn. A semi-official communiqué, considered by Count Eulenburg as inspired by Caprivi, then appeared in one of the principal papers. It dealt somewhat roughly with the latter and was intended to show that the Emperor disapproved of Count Eulenburg's action. On Friday of that week the Emperor sent for Caprivi and insisted upon his disavowing it, which Caprivi declined and intimated that he would rather retire than allow his position to be thus weakened. Upon which the Emperor said : " Very well then, you can go ; but remember that I dismiss you and that it is not your resignation which I accept." Two days afterwards the Emperor gave Caprivi the Black Eagle in brilliants ; but when he heard that Caprivi intended coming to thank him and bid him Goodbye His Majesty said : *" Das kann er sich schenken "* (he need not trouble himself to do that). Prince Hohenlohe, however, to whom this remark was made, recalled Count Caprivi's services and insisted upon the Ex-Chancellor being received. Finally Caprivi left Berlin last Wednesday night unaccompanied by a servant and without a single one of his late colleagues in the Ministry seeing him off. For his position he is a very poor man. If he has £600 a year it is quite the outside. . . .

When Bismarck was shown the door the Emperor wrote him a letter of farewell, but Caprivi received no such communication. Thus has a great man fallen ! We are all most sorry for it. He was an upright and honest man and was respected in Parliament by friend and foe.

The Emperor's behaviour is silently and confidentially but severely commented upon here. It is asked what will History report of his action, and what will the general public in other countries say in canvassing these proceedings? No sooner does he come on the throne than he parts with the Chancellor who has carried out the unification of Germany. Four years later he dismisses a second Chancellor without, as he did in Bismarck's case, consulting any of the other German Governments, and in his place he takes an old man seventy-five years old [Prince von Hohenlohe], whose age naturally limits the period of his possible usefulness. And why does he act so : in order that he may pull the strings without opposition and in order that the new man should carry out the same identical policy of the last. Is this the action of a great ruler and a sensible man?

From *Lord Hopetoun* (Governor-General of Australia) [1]

Government House, Melbourne
April 4th, 1890

. . . You ask me " Are you going to Federate? " I say " Undoubtedly — Yes ", but I do not think that it will come directly. Sir Henry Parkes says in less than two years but I think he is over sanguine. Our Prime Minister, Mr. Gillies, says it will take four or five years and I think he is probably nearer the mark. The people are keen to Federate — but Federation involves certain sacrifices such as the practical extinction of the Local Parliaments, the loss of the Border Customs, the loss of the seat of Government and the loss of the Governors from the chief Towns of each colony — all these things will make people delay before committing themselves. . . .

From *Lord Cowper* (formerly, 1880–1882, Lord-Lieutenant of Ireland)

Bordighera, March 26, 1890

I will most gladly and gratefully present Her Majesty with a copy of *The Melbourne Papers*. I say gratefully because I feel highly honoured by her being willing to receive it.

In case I may appear remiss in not having already offered it I may mention that though I approved of the papers selected and wrote the Preface I did not myself edit it. Had I done so I would have asked permission to dedicate it to Her Majesty with whom Lord Melbourne's name is so closely and so honourably connected.

[1] Marquess of Linlithgow, 1902.

The great blot upon my Preface is that I have left out all allusion to this relationship which is the brightest and most interesting incident in Lord Melbourne's career. But I felt that it would have to be done with greater skill and delicacy than I was confident of possessing if it was to be done effectively, so I hope Her Majesty will think that I was right in leaving it alone.

Report of proceedings in the House of Commons :

From *Lord Lewisham, M.P.* (Vice-Chamberlain of the Household, later succeeded as 6th Earl of Dartmouth)

April 18, 1890

. . . I am not quite sure that the slackness of Private Members is not rather a good thing for the Government, as it affords an excellent foil to the obstruction on Government nights. We had a more disgraceful exhibition on the Royal Palaces vote this year, even than usual, and the climax was reached when one Radical member proposed that Buckingham Palace should be made a place for sleeping for destitute women. However I think Mr. Labouchere even has rather overreached himself. We had a very good budget debate last night, and Mr. Goschen was in such form that in the course of a three hours' speech he actually " heard a smile " of Sir William Harcourt's. The brewers are not very much pleased with the proposals but otherwise it seems popular, especially the equipment of the volunteers and the cheaper ocean postage. A curious fact was announced by the Chancellor of the Exchequer, that £23,000 out of the £80,000 duty paid on gold and silver plate is attributable to wedding rings, whereupon Dr. Tanner wished to know if any rebate would be allowed on second marriages. To-night we are to have a debate on bimetallism. I shall not be there, but I have arranged for the usual communication, which will be very short, as the transmission of an explanation of the question, through telegraph clerks of various nationalities, will not make it any more easy of comprehension. . . .

Two opposing views on General Booth's *Darkest England* :

(1) From *W. Boyd Carpenter* (Bishop of Ripon)

Dec. 17, 1890

Thank you for your letter. I must have mistaken what was said to me ; but I certainly was under the impression that the £50 had been or was about to be given. I am obliged to you however for writing. I do not know whether to be sorry or not. As a fact, I agree entirely with you that the energy of General Booth is worthy of all praise and his scheme, notwithstanding the criticisms, seemed to me practicable. The critics found out that (1) it would not work (2) that others were successfully doing the same thing. As (2) answered (1), I felt disposed to ignore the do-nothing critic. Further, the evils, and the dangers resulting from them, are so great that it seems to be nobler to fail in trying to do something than to discredit all sympathy and earn the execrations of the sorrowful and suffering by doing nothing. The problem in some minds is beginning to assume the form of the dilemma — either a big war, or Home-Revolution.

I am one of those who believe that a little practical application of the laws of Christ might avoid either necessity. I have no sympathy with the Drum and Fife business of the Salvation Army : I have been at their meetings and they gave me a headache. But notwithstanding this General Booth preached simple self-denial and insisted on honesty and industry and love to God and love to man — and I could not find it in my heart to abuse or oppose him. No doubt there are agents of the Army who are rough, profane and empty headed and perhaps worse. But when we are face to face with a large problem, we must be glad that a large organization like the Salvation Army is being directed towards social needs, as well as suffering folk. For their religious eccentricity we are not responsible. The Church Army is a much more sober and sensible organization and has been doing good and quiet work. But there is so much to be done that there is room for all.

(2) From *General Lynedoch Gardiner*

20 November, 1890

I congratulate you upon your letter to Mr. Booth. I observed that F.M. the Heir Apparent recognized that individual as holding a military rank one grade inferior to his own and accepted the blowing of his own trumpet as loudly as his followers are wont to do in the streets as proof that he is to be trusted widely to administer funds for the accomplishment of objects which are by no means new and which hundreds beside himself (the Clergy and their visitors and numerous societies with their Almoners) have been less ostentatiously pursuing for many years past, — as I believe with far greater success — for the operation must be a slow one : (that of moral elevation). The inhabitants of Darkest England may want money — but to *give* them money is the most demoralising thing you can do — most of it will be found next day in the tills of nearest public houses : they may want better dwellings — but if these are supplied tomorrow (unless worked on Miss Octavia Hill's plan) you will find them pigsties in a few weeks' time : they may want clothes, but if you supply them you will recognize the garments a few days later at the three balls : and all this is to be cured by men and women calling themselves Captains and Colonels and Generals and parading the streets playing at soldiers and by their Commander-in-Chief writing a sensational book describing the cures he proposes and some of which are in operation but none of them new, and appealing for a million of money !

Verily, it is the age of successful humbug : sensation and advertisement seem to carry the day.

It is now asserted that Mr. Booth renders strict account of money received. He certainly did not do so for a considerable time after he assumed military rank. However he has now got forty thousand and I should like to see how he spends it before allowing his claim to more.

From *Sir Julian Pauncefote* (British Ambassador in Washington, afterwards Lord Pauncefote)

Washington, 26 June, 1891

I hope you will allow me to add my little contribution " *d'outre-mer* ", to the innumerable felicitations which have showered upon you and Lady Ponsonby from every quarter, on the occasion of the happy event in your family [marriage of their daughter Alberta], which has created so much genuine sympathy everywhere and to which the gracious act of the Queen [her presence at the wedding] has imparted quite an historical interest. There has been felt I am sure the most widespread gratification at the tribute thus paid by the Queen to your eminent services and in a manner that touches the heart more deeply than any other kind of reward.

I am still fighting the great battle of the Seals and as Blaine is hors de combat I begin to hope that truth will prevail and virtue be triumphant — but the Politicians in this country still cultivate as much as ever the arts of lying, cheating, and expectorating. M. de Bacourt who was French Minister here in 1842 wrote of them in his *Mémoires d'un Diplomate* : " *Quel drôle de monde —! ou pour mieux dire, quel monde de drôles !* "

I remember that the night I had the honor of dining with the Queen at Windsor, Her Majesty was amused at hearing that there were some towns in America where all the Municipal Offices from the Mayor downwards were filled by *women*. I enclose an extract from an American paper, giving a comical account of the female Municipality at Westward in Kansas, where man evidently does not count for much.

I hope to be able to run over next year *pour me retremper dans la civilisation*.

From *The Hon. Eric Barrington* (Private Secretary at the Foreign Office)

Aug. 3, 1891

I see that the Queen is much interested in Ja Ja, at least in his body which we hope to get Spanish leave to exhume and send to the Opobo Chiefs [Southern Nigeria]. But Her Majesty ought to know that he was a most brutal savage, capable of every kind of abomination. Little Johnston [1] who deported him when Vice Consul at Cameroons wrote a horrid book called the " *Life of an African Slave* " garnished with ghastly illustrations. One of these represented a woman tied to a tree dying of starvation. This was a wife of Ja Ja's with whom he quarrelled. He promised Johnston, who was going away for a few days that he would not kill her. When Johnston came back he found her tied to the tree, dead. He mildly rebuked Ja Ja for breaking his word. " Oh no," said Ja Ja, " I kept it. *I* did not kill her. She died." . . .

The editor of *Truth* intimated that information with regard to the discovery of documents belonging to the Queen had been communicated to *Truth*. The facts of the case, as set out in a letter from Ponsonby, were curious :

To *Mr. Henry Labouchere*

Windsor Castle, July 13, 1892

I am much obliged by your letter. The circumstances are as follow. Madame Nicole saw one of the Secretaries of the Embassy at Paris and told him that her husband, late Private Secretary to the Queen, had among the papers which he left at his recent death, three documents which apparently belonged to the Queen and which she therefore requested should be sent to Her Majesty. In recent letters to me she says she wished them sent for Her Majesty's inspection, but Mr. Lee [2] at the time reported as above. He thanked

---

[1] Later Sir Harry Johnston, Special Commissioner in Uganda.
[2] Mr. Austin Lee of the British Embassy.

her and sent the three papers to me. They were rough drafts of a letter from the Queen to the Emperor Napoleon III with pencil corrections by the Prince Consort. I am told that these letters have since been published in works referring to that time, but even if not they were of small value or importance. I asked Mr. Lee to thank Madame Nicole for having restored these documents to the Queen and to add that if he thought right to offer her 100 francs in recognition of her honorable conduct. I added to him that Nicole was never a Secretary to the Queen, and that I had not been able to discover what he was. Since then I find he was a valet to the Prince Consort but only served him for three or four months. However this of course was a matter which it was unnecessary to discuss.

I understood that when offered the money she declined to accept it — and claimed the documents back again. I explained that they were the property of the Queen and I could not get them back again. Since then (two years ago) she asks to see me to get me to give her back the letters — which I have no power to do — so I have only repeated the offer of 100 francs. There seems to have been a misunderstanding between her and Mr. Lee originally. But as the letters belong to the Queen I could not advise their being given up.

I still am ready to give the 100 francs.

This selection from over three thousand letters received, even combined with letters quoted elsewhere, is of course not comprehensive but merely illustrative. It is sufficient to show that Henry Ponsonby had sources of knowledge open to him on principles of policy, public events and personalities both at home and abroad to a greater degree than any single individual inside the public service or outside. Friends confided in him, officers trusted him, statesmen were anxious to give explanations to him, many hoped that a word in their favour might be passed on to high quarters and routine work filled the gaps. So that to the advantage of his equipment as a counsellor it may certainly be said that he was enabled fully to know " what was going on."

CHAPTER XV

Husband and Wife

MOST of the quotations in the earlier chapters are taken from Henry Ponsonby's letters to his wife. But an impression may have been given that in writing to her he confined himself to relating incidents and reflections on public affairs and to recording his estimate of royal, political and other eminent personages. While he certainly does this to a great extent, it is by no means exclusively. The beginnings of his letters generally refer to domestic home doings and his wife's activities, and there are discussions and opinions on books and subjects outside the range of his official work. There was also frequent interchange between them of published articles chiefly from the *Pall Mall Gazette*, the *Fortnightly Review* and the *Daily News*.

Country house parties and dinner parties, when husband and wife were together and therefore there was no need to write a letter, are sometimes noted on a couple of sheets of notepaper, giving the names of those present. For instance in 1872 there is a note on a visit to Strawberry Hill, then occupied by the Gladstones, where there was a large party, including among many others the Tecks, Hochschild (the Swedish Minister), Lord Strathnairn, Bernal Osborne, Arthur Kinnaird, J. Morley and William Harcourt who " was agreeable as he can be when he chooses ". Two dinner parties at Lady Stanley of Alderley's are noted : at the first they met Lyulph Stanley " who poured forth a perfect torrent of chaff the whole time". Among the guests at the second were Kinglake, Browning and the Amberleys, she announcing " à propos of nothing ' I never go to church ' ". There was a " bright little dinner and excellent too " at the Charlie Woods' (later 2nd Lord Halifax) where they met Mrs. Brand, the new Speaker's wife, and others, and Mr. George Howard (later Lord Carlisle) gave a dinner at his house in Kensington decorated by William Morris, where Mrs. Grote " was treated like an oracle ", and J. R. Green the historian, then Librarian at Lambeth, was among the guests.

In October 1867, referring to some discussion, he wrote : " You always have peculiar views on everything ". This was by no means sarcastic. As is subsequently shown, " peculiar views " were just what he liked. He was far from being the hidebound official who never mentioned anything about his work and would resent the interference of a woman on public, official or even court matters. He knew that from his wife, who was fully acquainted with his *entourage*, he could get an outside opinion which would be of value and could be stimulating in making him see what was to be said for a different or even contrary point of view. He could be certain there would be no frivolous irrelevancies and that the innate feminine instinct would here be supported by intellectual reasoning.

But the outstanding feature of the correspondence is that after they were married, from his absence for a time with his regiment in Dublin, all through his Private-Secretaryship until the end, he wrote to her every single day they were apart. From Balmoral in 1875 he writes : " Up betimes this morning to copy much and to continue my controversy with the Queen about the Indian visit. But I take part of the time in writing to you. I wish I were able to consult you more closely." Again later he confesses : " Every interest I have is an interest entirely got up by you ". The pity of it is that the other side of the correspondence is almost gone. About a score of letters from Mary Ponsonby were found and included by Magdalen Ponsonby in the book on her mother published in 1926.

She did not write so punctually every day and was sometimes reprimanded. Nevertheless his pleasure in her frequent letters can be gathered when he writes, " Your letters are so full of facts, of discussions and of arguments that I read them over and over. They form by far and away the most agreeable and delightful reading I have in the twenty-four hours." They were both argumentative and sometimes differed sharply on details. But fundamentally in spite of hot controversies they had great respect for one another's opinions and judgment. He writes chaffingly from Balmoral in the earlier years : " Yet I would rather argue with you notwithstanding your furies and your crassness, I would rather be sitting with you discussing

LADY PONSONBY
1891

the probity of Mackenzie than I would be anywhere else. To
be with you is life, happiness and joy to me. To be away is
discomfort and tediousness. The pleasantest moment is when
I am getting a letter from you or writing to you." And again :
" I pine to have a good strong wholesome argument with you ".
There is an amusing reference to one of his letters which was
put aside : " I think your putting my letter into your jewel
box unread argues a slight feeling of boration — such as I
have when I receive the fifth letter in a day from Lord Sydney
[the Lord Steward] on claret ".

In 1877 he writes :

> They say Lady Derby is a bitter Turk while Derby is
> pro-Russian ; that they have controversies possibly as fierce
> and violent as we do. But whereas ours terminate after
> you have spoken to your full without allowing me a word —
> a syllable in reply in declaring that never, no never will you
> ever say another word to me on the subject, which determina-
> tion you keep for five minutes, Lady Derby goes off to the
> Pyrenees. I am glad you don't do that.

When in 1878 Mary Ponsonby suggests going for a bracing
holiday, he replies :

> Where is bracing to be found, by the sea or on high
> ground ? That is one of your songs isn't it ? Not that I know
> your songs for you never sing to me ; though I once sang
> to you which I believe gave you a bilious attack.

This cannot have been the occasion she relates in some diary
sheets in Canada : that at a station, while passing the night
with the Hudson Bay Company's men when she was screened
off out of sight, she heard one of them say " There is a gentleman here who has a remarkably sweet-toned voice when he
speaks, I wonder if he can sing." To her astonishment she
heard " H. say ' Certainly ', and he struck up an Irish song
which was vociferously applauded ".

In 1885, referring to his depression at their constant
separation, he quotes a little poem :

> A boat at midnight sent alone
> To drift upon the moonless sea,
> A lute whose leading chord is gone,
> A wounded bird that has but one
> Imperfect wing to soar upon,
> Are like what I am without thee.

Their separation from one another, calculated by counting the letters not only in the long Balmoral periods, but occasionally from Windsor or Osborne when he was absent on business or she was away on a visit, amounted sometimes to well over four months in a year. So that he was reflecting seriously when he wrote in 1878 : " You are more use to me than a thousand secretaries. You tell me everything. You are my eyes which see the outer world and know what is going on, your advice is worth more than anyone's. . . . To be separated is the unhappiness of my life and makes me often long to give up everything."

None of the letters has the usual or any opening words. They all end " God bless you " and are written rapidly and conversationally without paragraph breaks. The transition from politics or royal functions to domestic affairs is not always easily noticeable. So that in the middle of a recital of Court events when the sentence comes " I am distressed to hear about Mrs. Ballingall ", it has required a member of the family to recollect that the lady in question was not a courtier, nor one of the Queen's visitors, nor one of the P.B.s (Professional Beauties) who are mentioned on their visits to Abergeldie. Mrs. Ballingall was the family cook.

Ponsonby related his narratives well and set out his arguments with great lucidity. But he always avoided flourishes, retained purely colloquial style and was sparing of any self-conscious philosophic reflections. He had far from a limited vocabulary and used certain favourite words, some of which were inherited. The eighteenth-century " agreeable " conveyed high praise for a person and is used constantly, and he wrote " ain't " for " is not ". He invariably described a man or woman with good manners as " civil ". " Conversable ", which is seldom used now, conveys quite well a good talker. " Tetchy " is sometimes applied to the Queen when she was out of humour. " Bosky " for drunk, occurs somewhat frequently. He was fond of " aspere " and applied it to his youngest son when he was six months old. When irritated he was apt to use the effective Turkish monosyllable " bosh ". Chaffingly he sometimes called his wife " crass " if she misunderstood his argument.

The insertion of the other side of the correspondence would of course add considerably to its interest, especially with regard to subjects where opinions differed. The few letters of Mary Ponsonby's which remain show indeed how fully she entered into the serious questions of politics and foreign affairs. Some have been printed. But, unlike her husband, she often omitted the date and even the year of her letters. To fit them in therefore would be too difficult. The extracts included in this chapter from letters written by Henry Ponsonby to his wife are no more than a very few samples, mostly of a domestic character, supplementing many already quoted. They form no sequence. His daily letters as a whole have the merit of a diary, that is to say the atmosphere, the life and the mood are exhibited by their completeness, comprising as they do the dull uneventful days or weeks as a natural setting for the more important and salient episodes. As the letters run into several thousands restricted selection is enforced.

The first two letters, written when Ponsonby was an Equerry, describe his attendance on the Sultan of Turkey, Abdul Aziz, who had come over to visit Queen Victoria and of whom for political reasons a great fuss had to be made :

Buckingham Palace, July 19th, 1867

Don't say your letters are flat for they are the real point in my day — the rushing about, the excitement and anxiety are all very well, but your letter is *the* pleasure.

To reply to your question about the Sultan, he talks no known language. He is voluble in Turkish, but almost always has a tired look — though pleased. He converses through Fuad Pasha, who is the chief Minister in Turkey, a very able man they say. Moore interprets — or the Turkish Minister, Mustapha Pasha from Paris, whom he brought over here to be useful as Musurus [1] is utterly effete — jabbers all day and does nothing. Moore says he can't talk Turkish. Certainly his English is abominable. At the Queen's dinner Fuad sat near and translated the observations.

The Sultan is very obedient to suggestion. Last night he began to shake hands with all. Moore, behind Musurus, said in Turkish " Tell him he needn't shake hands with all the people — only the Lord Mayor and Recorder." But Musurus, who is privately making friends with City people on money affairs, said in English " Ah, Mr. Moore, I don't agree with you — the Sultan should shake hands with all these gentlemen." Moore in a great rage said no one could have done such a thing but a damned Greek as Musurus is.

[1] Turkish Ambassador in London.

The City ball last night was very Civic — grand — enormously over-crowded and the authorities quite ignorant of West End ways. At the chief supper Raglan was not included — he being the Lord-in-Waiting representing the Queen with the Sultan. Raglan gave it to one of the Aldermen pretty freely afterwards. The Duke of Beaufort tried to get in. They wouldn't let him — another row. On the dais they tried to clear a place for dancing, kept everyone off they could. Duke of Beaufort saw Djemil Bey, the chief chamberlain, struggle with a policeman — he remonstrated with an Alderman who was giving the order and at last Djemil Bey was allowed in. Immediately after was Apponyi. Beaufort said " You must let him in." Alderman wouldn't, at last did sulkily and said " There, you'd better take my place and do duty here." " If I did," said the Duke, " my first duty would be to kick you out." So you see the amenities were numerous. The Sultan seemed pleased. Of course the Lord Mayor read an interminable address. The Sultan then spoke to Musurus in Turkish and Musurus read the answer in fearful English. If it had not been for the Prince of Wales the Civic authorities would have done all sorts of absurdities, but he kept them in order very well indeed.

I carried off some dozen Turks to find supper, got into one room where an Alderman said to me " Pray don't take those people to seats, we have many Earls not yet seated." I contemptuously said " Earls ! Why these are Pashas ! " I don't know what he thought a Pasha was, but he exclaimed " Oh, I beg pardon," and we went on. Of course, they weren't Pashas — they were Officiers d'Ordinaire, Beys, Effendis, etc.

The Prince of Wales went afterwards to the Agricultural Hall for the Belgian Ball. Some of our Turks went. They say it was a marvellous sight, and a mixture of vice and virtue.

Buckingham Palace, July 20, 1867

Yesterday when all the carriages were ready to take the Sultan to the Bank, etc., he sent to say he wouldn't go out. There are whispers that he was angry at being hustled at the Guildhall, and so not anxious to see the City again. Others said he wasn't well. However he wouldn't go out. Hood went to tell the Duchess of Cambridge who in her best gown with Mecklenburg and Teck awaited his visit — and was indignant. I went off to tell city authorities. I took a Pasha with me, Rassam, an admiral. At the Bank we had a bit of the luncheon intended for the Sultan, but the Directors and ladies highly disappointed. Handsome Doubrey and

Woolaston Bertie in full jaw. Then to the Tower. Told
Burgoyne. An awful row going on between Burgoyne and
Lord De Ros as to whether to wear uniform or not for private
visit. I backed up Burgoyne and said uniform. However
great disappointment about his not coming, so showed all to
Rassam. Then to Tunnel. . . . Then to Houses of Parliament, not much in common. Great crowd at the House of
Lords to hear debate about Maximilian but Lord Stratford
withdrew it. Then home. In the evening to the India Ball.
It was perfectly magnificent. I went with about two dozen
Turks an hour before the Sultan. . . . An awful thing
happened. Madame Musurus and her daughter arrived as
usual. She went to supper with Louis of Hesse, and came
out of the supper room. Dudley saw her sit on a sofa and
faint. One or two ran up and they got some people to carry
her to her carriage and send her home. But before she had
got home she was dead. I think it a most fearful thing.
Her daughter dancing quite ignorant of it. There was
everybody at the ball, Maud Stanley, Cecilie, etc., etc. Tons
of cup champagne, etc., which people helped themselves to
from a tap. The supper itself I did not see, but all was very
good. Tired, I sought a seat and someone came and sat
next to me, but didn't take notice at first, when after a bit
I found it was Julia [his sister].

In 1869, in a discussion on the functions of diplomacy and
the avoidance of wars, he writes (April 24), taking the case of
the French designs at that time on Antwerp :

You say that if France bags Antwerp, all Europe will
be against her and turn her out. True, after we have spent
no end of money and lives, and then we return to the present
position. Is it not better by personal influence to prevent
the calamity ? That is what I call personal diplomacy.
The future grand and general aspect that France if she
commits atrocities must come to grief is all very well but it
don't prevent present wars and they alone are calamities
that it is worth all our efforts to avoid.

In 1873 they have an interesting dispute about Memorials.
Mary Ponsonby favoured memorials which only rested on their
beauty as against " utilitarian memorials " such as " scholar-
ships, fellowships, parish pumps, etc." He prefers the modern
method of leaving money for specific purposes rather than
" overlords driving serfs to build cathedrals ".

There is a passage in a letter written from Osborne in 1875
in which he makes an amusing comment on his wife's habits :

One of the extraordinary points in your very extraordinary character is that when you are ill, when you are unfit to leave your room, then you are all activity here there and everywhere, settling domestic affairs, overhauling the china, correcting abuses, rushing to London, sitting on Committees, giving very strong opinions and writing to me. When you are in strong and violent health and the weather is lovely you then refuse to leave your prison corner and read *La Haute Philosophie.*

His condemnation of subscriptions for the wounded in war given under the cloak of philanthropy and neutrality is worth giving in full :

Balmoral, September 6, 1877

I said that subscribing to the Russian fund was the same as subscribing to the Turkish fund which you had just before objected to. Lewis Farley's appeal for help for the Russian wounded is full of the fiercest denunciations of the Turks and their rule. While Lord Blantyre in giving two thousand to the Turkish fund fires away ferociously at the atrocious conduct of the Russians. Consequently I maintain that both are strong partizan funds.

But you go off on the Red Cross Association subscription for supplying funds and necessaries to the sick and wounded on both sides.

The Red Cross or Crescent is a valuable association in its attempts to protect the sick and wounded in time of war. But why are neutrals to aid by subscriptions and especially us ? You say the Russians and Turks with their thoughts intent on the next action would leave their wounded to their fate. Exactly so — and that is what we are leading up to, that the principals are to fight and the neutrals to take care of the wounded, cure them and send them in again to action to fight again — and so prolong the horrors of war indefinitely. Every pound we contribute to repair the combatants enables their Government to spend another pound in war material, and to feel sure that we shall do our best to supply them with restored men as soon as possible. It makes the whole thing like a prize fight in which the backers keep restoring their men with the assistance of the spectators who here come to enjoy the fight and whose wish it is to keep up each man to the longest endurance.

It is also one of the various attempts to make war pleasant. War is most horrible and in the present one it is shown under its worst form, so why do our best to prolong it ? Besides which ones especially have a serious claim upon us ? In

India more than a million of our fellow subjects are threatened
by death. They say that every pound sent out may save one
person. We have begun by sending £50,000. Surely that
is a more legitimate way of doing charity than by sending
out doctors, surgical implements and medical comforts to
the Turks and Russians who ought to be compelled by the
united opinion of the whole world to provide for their own
sick and wounded. You compare me to the Levite for
turning away from these poor people — to our own poor
people who really have a claim on us — and who no one
else will help to relieve. But aren't you the Pharisee who
proclaims his great charities to the sensational horrors and
leaves the unobtrusive ones to take care of themselves ? I
don't believe that those who go out to assist both sides can
be purely neutral.

On coming back to work at Balmoral in 1874 he writes :

I had a message from the Queen on my arrival to hope
I had left you and the children well. She never omits these
proprieties, but I wish she would also let me be more with
you. It is such a very dull and dreary existence here that
every one gets foolish. . . .

Sometimes the discussions between husband and wife reach
rather profound depths. This is shown by a letter of Mary
Ponsonby's (not hitherto printed) towards the end of the
seventies :

Because Jenner tells you the mistake you make is to
consider life a thing in itself, instead of looking upon it as the
manner in which chemical force acts upon matter, you listen
to him. But when I had the same argument with you and
said I thought the belief in life as a *separate entity* would be
exploded in the course of time, just as the words " principle
of vitality " or " essence " (in the middle ages) were no
longer used, you treat me with scorn. Your letter is in my
box, so I don't know if I am quoting right, but I think you
said Jenner's definition was " powers of resisting decay ". I
think I like Spencer's best : " A continuous adjustment of
internal relations to external relations ". Decay is but
another form of life ; we are always dying — I mean that
every particle of us that existed ten years ago has passed
into other forms of life. Then reparation and building up
of the different parts of our organism has gone on at the
same time. But the powers of reparation get weaker and
weaker and the fire goes out from want of fuel ; but life or
chemical force does not cease, only takes another shape.

A little later he writes :

> Very glad to hear of your going about everywhere and
> to the classes in Physiology — too deep for me — as I am
> content to know that I am what I am and I have only in a
> moderate degree —
>
> > The wish to know — that endless thirst
> > Which even by quenching is awak'd
> > And which becomes or blest or curst
> > As is the fount whereat 'tis slak'd.

On religious questions there are only occasional expressions
of opinion. After her marriage Mary Ponsonby drifted away
from the very rigid high church attitude she had adopted as a
girl. Writing to his mother, Lady Emily, from Canada in
1863, Henry gives an amusing account of Mary's heterodoxy
at that moment :

> Mary is now plunged into the deepest work on the
> evidences of Christianity, and only stops to ask me where
> St. Andrew would go to church if he came to London now,
> or where St. Athanasius would have a pew. I'm sure I don't
> know, so give evasive answers on which Mary triumphantly
> calls out that the whole of my religious creed is wrong. As
> she is a Nonconformist of course we are all wrong. Just now,
> however, she is a good deal more attached to the Roman
> Catholic religion than any other because the old curé de
> Chambly brings us wild raspberries and gooseberries. And
> though attached to the Episcopal parson for whom she plays
> on the organ, she can't abide the clerk who reads the responses
> so loud. In fact, she would have broken out against him, but
> he turns out to be a Devonshire man.
>
> To-day Mary played Jerusalem the Golden at Church
> to the great delight of the men who like it very much.

There are in the correspondence occasional references
to religion sometimes arising out of ecclesiastical disputes which
were brought officially to Ponsonby's notice. He was simply
orthodox but by no means narrow. As a soldier he was inclined
to be a disciplinarian ; regarding Bishops as commanding
officers who rightly demanded obedience from their subordinates. His wife after she had taken a broader agnostic line sent
him articles by John Morley and others. He was prepared
to examine these as he did anything and everything that came
from her, in this case with tolerant disagreement. Religion

to him was a very personal and private matter differing with
each individual. It was not within the range of subjects which
could be discussed profitably with the aid of facts and definitions and it should therefore be left to unexpressed inward
reflexions. Religious observances were different, when the
outward forms seemed to be divorced from the spirit. He was
as critical as the Queen about sermons.

In 1883 Socialism was beginning to be discussed more
seriously. He writes from Balmoral (November 18, 1883) :

> Most of my studies among the recent speeches evolve the
> fact that " Socialism " is the theme most of them deal with.
> I don't exactly know what it means. It don't mean the
> Socialism of the German Revolutionists but means I suppose
> Associationalism as opposed to Individualism — at least
> that is clearly what Morris means when he says the old
> Associations of Guilds, etc., were far more artistic than now
> where every man wants to make money for himself. I
> don't agree with him that Art didn't flourish under Tyrants
> — because I think it generally did. Fawcett also talks of
> " Socialism " — and all point to advances in that direction.
> I quite agree with those who say that to oppose its advance
> is madness — but that the proper course is to adapt new
> ways to the coming ideas — but I also think that Statesmen
> can direct the current of the advancing tide and use it
> beneficially instead of allowing it to overflow and destroy
> everything. And I think our present Government are good
> for this.

There is a discussion on the extension of the franchise, Mary
having taken the line that minorities might often be right :

> Balmoral, October 14, 1884
> . . . Your most valuable letter on the situation has just
> arrived and I think your views are very good. As to personal
> abuse I scarcely think this has been confined to Chamberlain.
> Read Harcourt and Salisbury. When you go on to discuss
> the question that the majority are not always right, is not
> this an argument against extending the Franchise ? Here
> you are against both sides. At least the Tories as much as
> the Liberals declare they are heartily in favor of extending
> the franchise and Cross said the other day that any man was
> a liar who doubted him. You admit that the extension of
> the franchise has been conceded long ago — and I think
> rightly conceded. Why Culture v. Anarchy ? There are

many of the lower classes quite unfit to vote — but many of the propertied classes equally so. We want to know the real feeling of the whole people and how that feeling can be best represented. If there are large masses outside who have no means of giving their opinion won't that lead to revolution? We have had splendid statesmen and the statesmen to come if they know how to gauge and lead popular feeling will be splendid still. I don't call anything a revolution that is done within the lines of the Constitution. And if we move on steadily why should there be anarchy?

How we should reach the true feeling of the country is the problem the Ministers are solving. All agree to the extension of the franchise. But no "gerrymandering" in redistribution. Lubbock's letter on Minority representation was very good. I cannot quite go with him. The Majority must be roughly got at. The intricacies of his plan are too difficult.

A talk with the Crown Prince Frederick :

Osborne, August 4, 1884

Certainly I think the Crown Prince a grand man. He is fine to look at, pleasant to talk to and while proud of being a soldier does not push it forward. He talked to me about Egypt and said we must take real command there or else give it up to some one who would. He didn't believe the present Khedive was strong enough in any way. The late Khedive was. He saw a good deal of him when he was there. Sharp, clever and fearless and unscrupulous. Though grand in his way he had none of the instincts of Royalty but was a haggling merchant turning his dominions to his own profit without caring for the welfare of those he governed except as regarded how they would benefit him. He had great ideas of the progress of Egypt if a strong nation ruled it. He went on to tell me of Spain and his visit there. I did not know he had gone about the country so much. He had seen all the towns. He liked the King. No doubt he had his faults — but his faults were Spanish. He was a regular Spaniard. The Crown Prince expatiated on the splendors of the palace — galleries full of Murillo and Velasquez and other Spanish painters and of all sorts of things. In the revolutions these were always taken care of. The Army is miserable and how can it be otherwise when the only chance of promotion is a revolution? When there is a revolution all the officers and N.C.O.s who join the side which wins get promoted — and of course the steady going real professional men have no chance.

Press gossip was often fantastic. But Ponsonby usually let it pass without any notice. This instance amused him :

> Balmoral, November 9, 1887
>
> One of the Society papers — the low ones — gives a sketch of Prince Henry's [of Battenberg] life here and says he tries to get through the day by playing billiards with Sir Henry Ponsonby, " no mean wielder of the cue — but an astute courtier who never permits himself to beat his Princely opponent ". I never saw Prince Henry playing billiards at all.

He did not like longwinded descriptions of scenery. Nevertheless he often puts a note in his letters expressing his own admiration of it as he does in this letter :

> Balmoral, October 31st, 1883
>
> As I resume my researches among the Scotch poets, I am convinced I have no power of appreciating scenery. None of their descriptions of country stir me, while descriptions of men and women and events and passions do. In fact a wordy picture of braes, and roads, and heather is dull. Jane Ogilvie writes " Dear Scotland's heather covered hills, while gazing on you never tire mine eyes ". I don't agree and a feeling of bore comes over me. There is very little in Scott of this sort and he comes to the action of men and women ; too much dull palaver does not do. " *Allongez les Ballets, et raccourcissez les jupes* " was I believe Scribe's advice. At any rate I am protesting against these pictures of scenery and poetry "*à cause de vous*" who always want me to admire a Linnel or a landscape and not a portrait or an incident. . . .
>
> I rode round Ballochbuie with Bigge and never saw it look more lovely in the evening sun and clear sky and the place full of deer and roe. It certainly is most beautiful weather and I hope you have got it as well.

Mary Ponsonby used to relate how in 1855 before her marriage, when she was in attendance on the Queen in Paris as Maid of Honour, the royal party went to the Opera. The Empress looked very beautiful but was hesitant, gauche in her manner, and ignorant of what to do when they reached the door of the royal box. The Queen on the contrary without any hesitation stepped forward, walked right to the front of the box and received the tumultuous applause of the crowded Opera House, completely outshining her companion whose looks and dress were matchless.

The Empress Eugénie, although throughout her exile on very friendly terms with the Queen, was nevertheless nervous with her as is shown in the following letter :

Balmoral, October 28, 1889

Although pouring, Edwards and I trudged off to Abergeldie to write our names on the Empress Eugénie and were invited in. She was in full talk and said she was nervous as the Queen was coming to tea with her at half past five and she wanted to know if the room was cool enough, etc. She said that she enjoyed a visit from the Queen but that she sometimes terrified her, and told me that at dinner at Balmoral a week ago H.M. said towards the end of dinner that Lord Torrington was dead. The Empress innocently asked who will be the new Lord Torrington. The Queen thought she enquired about the new Lord in Waiting and replied " I cannot tell you " so asperely that the Empress supposed there was a doubt about the successor to the title or that he was illegitimate and she babbled out some excuse for asking. The Queen then saw her mistake and tried to explain and then got up and went to the drawing room. The Empress was so shaken by this interlude that her brain became confused and she went up to Byng who she knows very well and taking him for Sir J. McNeill asked him if Miss McNeill at the other end of the room was his sister. He replied rather severely " No." " Oh," she asked, " your cousin ? " On which the aggravated Bingo exclaimed " No, no, no relation at all," and looked so angry that the Empress went off to a photograph book and would speak of nothing but the weather for the rest of the evening for fear of making another *bévue*.

Henry Ponsonby's interest in exposing bogus stories, frauds, myths and unauthenticated legends already referred to was evidently known to the Queen from the earliest times. On his first visit abroad with her in 1868 he writes from Lucerne :

We went up to the other end of the Lake and visited Tell's Chapel and then back only just in time for dinner. . . . Discourse at dinner about William Tell. " I'm sure," says the Queen, " if there is any doubt about his existence, Colonel Ponsonby don't believe in him." " Well, ma'am, it is curious there is a similar story of one Toko of Denmark." Whereupon Bids [Sir Thomas Biddulph] split into violent clatters of laughter. I got this from *Myths of the Middle Ages*. Toko was three hundred years before Tell. Jenner horrified.

" But you don't believe in Toko ? " Of course, I hadn't
expressed much opinion, but being pressed, I denied all
belief in Tell and Toko and said the story was a very old
Indian one. Jenner indignant. Murray [? the guide book]
says — " Tell's Chapel was built by 114 people who personally knew Tell ". Louise [Princess] says that Froude says
these 114 people are myths as much as Tell.[1]

Writing from Osborne (July 22, 1889) he gives a good
instance of " second sight " :

> . . . Last night at dinner Lady Erroll said that McNeill
> had second sight and the Queen said she had heard he saw
> the *Eurydice* go down, on which Lady Erroll told the story as
> related to her by Lord Elphinstone that McNeill in Connell's
> room, Windsor Castle, cried out " Good heavens, she is
> capsizing " — at the very moment, etc. H.M. said " Most
> extraordinary," so I and the rest in chorus " Most extra-
> ordinary " except Edwards who said that he had always
> heard from Lord Elphinstone that McNeill had cried out
> " Shorten sail " when walking in the Strand at the very
> hour, etc. Miss Adeane said " No, it was in Bond Street
> that he cried out ' Close your ports ' at the very hour, etc."
> Grand chorus " Most extraordinary " and every one knew
> that McNeill had second sight. This morning we asked
> Connell. He said that McNeill was in his room at Windsor
> (so couldn't have been in the Strand or Bond Street) and
> said " That's a sharp squall " and Connell answered " Yes,
> very sudden." Next day McNeill said " Did you note the
> time of that squall ? I shouldn't wonder if it were the squall
> that struck the *Eurydice*." So ends this ghost story.

Henry Ponsonby belonged to the small minority of people
who listen. They often have to suffer. He writes, November
24, 1892 :

> To-day I have passed in talking or rather listening to a
> number of people who want to explain to me matters which
> I already know all about. It becomes wearisome. But one
> must listen.[2]

An abrupt break in this prolonged and daily correspondence is sometimes tantalizing. There are instances when an

---

[1] See *Encyclopædia Britannica*: " The popular belief in the Tell legend is still
strong, despite its utter demolition at the hands of a succession of scientific Swiss
historians during the 19th century ".

[2] Cf. Voltaire : " Si l'on veut plaire dans le monde il faut se laisser apprendre
bien de choses qu'on connoit déja par des personnes qui les ignorent ".

intriguing episode fully described in several letters does not reach
its culmination because husband and wife meet.   There is no
means of knowing what happened.   It is like witnessing the
first two acts of a play, with an uncertain inkling of the *dénoue-
ment*, and then the curtain suddenly falls and the third and
fourth acts are never seen.   Mary Ponsonby of course heard it
all when they met, perhaps more fully than she would have by
letter.

His distress at their partings and their separations, his enjoyment of her letters, his pleasure at writing to her, his desire for
her opinion and his appreciation of the way she dealt with
family and domestic affairs, constantly recurring throughout
the correspondence, show a reader their close relations to one
another more clearly than could have been the case had they,
like most couples, generally been living together.

He seemed fully to appreciate the difficulties which must
confront a young wife separated for so many months in the
year from her husband.   Moreover as years passed the separation became confirmed and, if anything, extended rather than
mitigated, because the Queen's reliance on him and need for
him increased.   It was not exactly that the Queen was markedly
inconsiderate, but she was thoughtless of all other considerations
where her own comfort and convenience were concerned.   His
anxiety to serve the Queen punctually led him into a, perhaps,
too easy acquiescence and eventually wore him down too soon.

A wife with the growing responsibilities of a mother, with
a social position which brought her in contact with prominent
people and naturally involved society entertainments, visits
and other distractions, and with notably attractive gifts and
talents, could not be expected to have a continuously smooth
course to steer.   Wise restraints and thoughtful decisions were
constantly needed ; and by her long-practised self-discipline
any slip from want of vigilance was successfully avoided throughout.   Her intellectual resources were a great help, but undoubtedly the daily letters with constant expressions of deep
affection were her support and comfort.   She carefully kept
them all.

It is perhaps permissible to quote one more letter of this
correspondence because of the way his irrepressible jesting
turns abruptly into a passionate expression of his love and
devotion :

Osborne, April 24, 1878

Curiously enough I was also having a discussion on our marriage with a person of the name of H. P. and as it is a matter which always greatly occupies our attention any reference to it is always acceptable. The question is, was it my luck — my good fortune — my moral character — my superior intelligence — my leg or my whisker which secured for me the priceless treasure ?

Am I joking ? No, I am not, for you are a priceless treasure and those words very feebly represent what I think of you. I never can be sufficiently thankful for your having been given to me, for what you have done for me and for what you are to me. Everything, every moment I am with you is a joy and a pleasure, every moment I am away from you is a lapse in my life. My own Dearest Darling Wife.

God Bless you.

H. P.

This was written a few days before the seventeenth anniversary of their wedding. So it was till the end.

CHAPTER XVI

Home and End

AFTER his marriage Henry Ponsonby as Equerry to the Prince Consort settled down with his wife in No. 6 of the Inner Cloisters, adjoining St. George's Chapel in the precincts of Windsor Castle. Four of his children were born there. When in 1870 he succeeded General Grey as Private Secretary, he came into the occupation of the Norman Tower, where his fifth child was born. This house came to be regarded by the family as their much-loved home for the remaining twenty-five years of his life.

The outstanding feature of Windsor, for which it would be difficult to find a parallel elsewhere, was the variety of distinctive elements which were incorporated within its boundaries and neighbourhood. The ancient castle with its towers and battlements on its high eminence not only dominated the valley of the Thames for miles round, but as the historic residence of sovereigns for centuries past was an emblem, as perhaps no other royal residence in the world, of the continuity and stability of a monarchical system. The frequent presence of the Queen and her Court and the visits of foreign royalties or of Ministers made the humblest residents feel they were in close touch with the centre of all authority. The Dean and Chapter of St. George's supplied an ecclesiastical atmosphere resembling that of a cathedral town. A battalion of the Guards always stationed in the barracks daily relieved guard on the Castle with their band, and a regiment of Life Guards in another barrack was ready for state occasions. So the military element was prominent. Scholastic opportunities were afforded by the close proximity of Eton, Henry VI's foundation, just across the river. Enlightened masters held classes in Windsor which young female residents in town and castle could attend. Sport, boating and racing were easily procurable.

BALMORAL CASTLE

THE NORMAN TOWER, WINDSOR CASTLE

Further there was the civic life of the Royal Borough and occasionally the excitement of a parliamentary election. Yet Windsor was not self-sufficient because London was less than an hour away by rail. It represented neither real town life nor indeed real country life. The multifarious elements were rather detached and aloof. The Ponsonby family however, as they grew up, took full advantage of the various opportunities afforded them by the different interests and there was no breach when the boys went to school, as all three went to Eton.

The Norman Tower was a curious residence, with staircases branching off in all directions, abutting on one side against the Royal Library and on the other side against the stone staircase from another entrance which led up to the Round Tower. It included the upper part of the Norman Gateway and the main wing stood in a garden in the moat at the foot of the Round Tower. The house had all been modernized and there were no features apparent of any interest, although it was composed of one of the oldest parts of the Castle. Outside and inside it was a piece with the rest of the Castle after the extensive and unfortunate restoration undertaken under George IV about 1826 by Wyatt, or Sir Jeffry Wyatville as he was called later, and subsequent rebuilding in early Victorian times.

Mrs. Ponsonby pressed at first for an entrance from the house into the Royal Library ; but this was refused. She then asked permission to remove the thick covering of plaster in two rooms which had at one time been used as prisons. Leave was given. The stone walls were bared and two windows, one with its original wooden shutter, the old hearths, a number of inscriptions on the walls and the complete upper half of the portcullis were exposed to view. In one of these rooms, made very comfortable with a log fire in winter, Mrs. Ponsonby and her husband would talk over in the morning the questions of the day when the Court was resident at Windsor. These undisturbed morning talks which were habitual at Windsor and at Osborne are referred to by Mary Ponsonby in her memorandum : [1]

> If a letter came requiring much thought and care in the
> answering H. would write a rough copy and bring it over

[1] See p. 152.

from his office, and if he had to pass its contents on with comments and advice to the Q., he would show it to me and in nine cases out of ten there was nothing to talk over. . . . Then in the tenth instance I might perhaps look doubtful and as if this or that was open to misconstruction and might not such a word be changed or cut out. He then considered it, was never annoyed, and if he agreed tore the letter up and wrote another. This was the whole extent of my influence. I never remember a single instance of disagreement or dispute on such matters. It never occurred to me to meddle or inquire about any business on which he felt obliged to be silent.

In the summer and at Christmas one of the villas outside the grounds of Osborne House was allotted to the Ponsonby family. At first Kent House, a modern gabled stone house with a pleasant garden and a mysterious wood beyond in which the children delighted ; later Osborne Cottage, which was larger and might be described as a *cottage orné*. Into these houses Mrs. Ponsonby imported a quantity of books, occupations and ornaments of her own ; and by judicious rearrangement of the furniture, improved the permanent decoration which consisted chiefly of early prints of the royal family. To Balmoral the family went once only, for reasons already explained. The children grew up to regard the Queen as a permanent institution, a sort of background to their lives. Not till they were older did they come to apprehend that they were only lodgers, that the Round Tower at Windsor did not really belong to them, and that the villas at Osborne were not theirs so that they might be with their father but the Queen's so that she might have their father close at hand. They became accustomed to the fact that their father had to be away a great deal. But they did not understand exactly what his work was. He seemed generally to be writing and the scratch of his quill pen could be heard going on and on at night as they went to bed ; and even late in the night he might sometimes be heard going to his dressing-room to put in another hour or two's work. The locked dispatch-boxes, which were put beside his plate at breakfast and sometimes at dinner, they knew were not the sort of thing all fathers had. But as he seemed only to glance at their contents after unlocking them and afterwards take them away to his office, their curiosity was never much excited. One evening in March 1881 he acted differently. The dispatch-box came in at dinner. He unlocked it, glanced at a telegram it contained, handed it to his wife and immediately left the room. She told the children that the telegram reported the assassination of the Tsar Alexander II of Russia and their father had gone over to convey the news personally to the Queen at once.

Christmas-time at Osborne was quite festive. The Queen's presents arrived punctually on Christmas Eve and were an excitement, specially so when the children were in the toy ages. Later the inkstands and blotting-books and improving volumes were less exciting. The boxes of bonbons and *Lebkuchen* from Germany — a sort of gingerbread with almonds on it — were much appreciated. The duty of having to thank the Queen with a curtsey or a bow after the snapdragon on Twelfth Night they performed very indifferently.

At Christmas-time skating at Osborne on a pond close to the old manor-house at Barton was much enjoyed by the Household, by some of the royal family and by the Ponsonby children, who joined in the hockey on the ice. Their father was often the life and soul of the game. As one of the Princesses slowly and helplessly revolved with the cork bung between her skates, he would go round her beating the ice with his stick and shouting " Don't let the Princess have it all her own way." The Queen however strongly disapproved of hockey on the ice. So when her outrider was seen coming over the hill, all sticks were quickly thrown on to the bank. The whole company turned innocently to figure skating, or some attempt at it, till the carriage which had stopped to allow the Queen to view the skating had passed on out of sight, when the game was resumed.

In appearance Henry Ponsonby was a tall distinguished-looking man with blue eyes and a slight stoop. After the period of early Victorian whiskers and the bushy Crimean beard he settled down to a small beard the exact cut of which became a matter of discussion between him and his wife. If anyone had declared that he had never looked at himself in the glass, it would not have been far from the truth. The one subject to which he could never be persuaded to turn his attention was clothes. This even included uniform and either the entire omission or wrong arrangement of his decorations.

In the mid-Victorian Court, it is true, there was nothing of " all the pleasing eloquence of dress ". The feathered hat and sweeping riding habit, the flowered and festooned crinoline and sparkling diadems of the early years of her reign had for the Queen receded into very remote history. Now in her perpetual mourning, with her black gown cut low and square at the neck and her soft and original widow's cap, she set the note and any lady who was " smart " was not regarded with much favour. The footmen, not at Balmoral but at Windsor and Osborne, brightened up things with their scarlet coats. But their stockings of white cotton instead of silk were smiled at with some contempt by the courtiers of Marlborough House. In such a setting a dandy would have been out of place. But Henry Ponsonby's not untidiness nor slovenliness but negligence was considered to go too far and became a matter of frequent comment and amusement. His frock-coat, black tie tied in a loose bow and his elastic-sided boots, which he found comfortable and easy to put on, might pass muster. But when at Balmoral he took to wearing a béret it was condemned on all sides, although he was only anticipating a fashion of much later years. Some of his sartorial failures can be recorded in his own words : one day at Balmoral in the early eighties,

> she [the Queen] sent a message about my trousers — that they are too long. Lady Ely : " No, it wasn't a message but I might tell you she had remarked they were rather long." Of course I pinned them up and of course Maids of Honour roared at our serious discussion upon the length of trousers and of course I chalked the proper length on Robertson's trousers. Whereat there was much chaff and Jane Ely said she was sorry I took it in that light as it was only a very gentle hint and not meant to offend — which it certainly did not.

But it was not only the length of his trousers. At Coburg during royal functions in 1894, the Prince of Wales began — " I sent for you. . . . Oh where did you get those trousers from ? " " Oh sir, they are winter trousers —— " " I don't care. They are the ugliest trousers I ever saw."

Representing the Queen at the funeral of the Emperor Frederick in June 1888,

> I appeared in uniform. Prince of Wales pleased but critical. Prince Albert Victor told me I had too much crape. I was covered by Gorringe and popularly supposed to be chief mourner. I sat [at the breakfast at Cologne] between the

Princess of Wales and Prince Christian. Oliver Montague, inspired no doubt, objected to my forage cap. I admit antiquated. Before we got to Hanover I removed superfluous crape and my medals blazed forth. At dinner I sat next Probyn who said " You have something wrong — I don't know what it is ; the Princess of Wales is laughing." I looked at myself and saw I had two Jubilee medals on. I removed one quickly. She at the end of the table laughed aloud and Prince Albert Victor was happier. The Prince of Wales spoke to me about it. By this time I hope I am all right.

It was the Prince of Wales he dreaded most, as uniforms and clothes were the one subject on which His Royal Highness was an expert. When the young Emperor William came to Osborne on a private visit after he had been appointed Colonel of the Royals, he expressed a wish to report himself to the senior military officer in the Household, who happened to be Sir Henry Ponsonby. Unfortunately Sir Henry had left his uniform at Windsor. The Prince of Wales went to see Sir Henry to arrange matters and having deplored the fact that there was no uniform, added, " But you can't possibly receive him in that old coat, I will go and get you a new one for the occasion." The selection of a suitable coat took longer than was expected and in the meantime the Emperor arrived in full uniform and saluted dramatically. Sir Henry shook him by the hand and welcomed him in the name of the British Army. Hardly had the Emperor retired when the Prince of Wales arrived with a parcel containing an impeccable frock-coat, only to find it was too late.[1]

There was an occasion however when Ponsonby's opinion on clothes was sought, as the following exchange of notes with Sir William Harcourt shows :

Minister in Attendance to H.M. Private Secretary

(as to whether, below the Plimsoll line, it is recommended that for the Sabbath evening the ordinary long kind with socks or the shorter kind with black silk stockings and tigsy little ribands are the more appropriate)

DEAR PONSONBY,
    Is it " knees " ?

                                 Yrs., W. V. H

[1] *The Ponsonby Family*, p. 171.

Private Secretary to Minister in Attendance

DEAR HARCOURT,

As no ladies will be present trousers will be worn.

Yrs., H. F. P.

(A good example of what in rhetoric is called aposiopesis.)

So much for outward appearance and clothes. But many men have been hampered by the tone of their voice both in oratory and in conversation. Henry Ponsonby however was gifted with what the Hudson Bay man in Canada referred to years before as " a remarkably sweet toned speaking voice ", deep but not too resonant. He also had the faculty of paying careful attention to anyone who engaged him in conversation, with complete ability to conceal irritation or boredom. This made people of all sorts very ready, too ready perhaps, to entrust him with their confidences.

But undoubtedly what helped him most in the turmoil of political controversy, in gauging the dispositions of statesmen, in the complaints of officers and administrators, in the petty quarrels of members of the royal family, in the requests of foolish correspondents and also in watching the vagaries sometimes impetuous and sometimes unaccountable of his royal mistress, was his acute sense of humour. The ready recognition of the ridiculous, even when others do not detect it, is of the greatest help in retaining a sense of proportion. With this he combined wit. The combination of the two is not very common. Many a wit is too anxious to make his joke to pay much attention to the humour of the situation. Many who have a sense of humour are content to be amused without themselves being amusing.

Ponsonby's wit did not consist in making jokes but in making without a smile or in writing some serious or even solemn remark which summed up the situation exposing its ridiculous aspect. A good instance of it he relates himself in early years while he was still an Equerry-in-Waiting. It was in 1868 when the Queen visited Lucerne. Dr. Jenner was the physician in attendance and went for an expedition one day up the Rigi with Miss Bauer, the German governess (not conspicuous for her beauty). At dinner that evening Jenner gave an account of the expedition. In his daily letter to his wife Ponsonby writes :

I do not know why my remarks are supposed always to be facetious when they are not. I simply asked what the tourists thought of their relationship. He replied " Oh, of course they thought she was Madame," which created some laughter. Then he added " The guide was very decided and made us give up the horses we rode up and come down in a chair." " What ? " I asked. " Both in one chair ? " Well, there is nothing odd in this — but everyone laughed. I turned to Mary Bids [Lady Biddulph]. She was purple. On the other side I tried to speak to Princess Louise. She was choking. I looked across to Jenner. He was convulsed. Of course this was too much. I gave way ; and we all had a *fou rire* till the tears ran down my cheeks which set off the Queen. I never saw her laugh so much. She said afterwards it was my face. At last we got a pause when Jane [Lady Churchill] to set things straight again began with " Did you find it comfortable ? " which started us off again. My laugh was at Jenner stuffing his napkin over his mouth to stop himself, at Mary Bids shaking and speechless at my side, and at Bids' solemn face.

Ponsonby had two ways of laughing : an excellent laugh aloud, quite hearty, which he called " my coachman's laugh ", completely satisfied the recorder of the joke, but was really an actor's laugh. When he was genuinely tickled, he was absolutely silent, his face grew very red and the tears streamed down his cheeks (as in the above anecdote).

Much has already been said of Henry Ponsonby's relations with his wife, the centre of his thoughts and the linch-pin of his life. Being so much away from home he could hardly feel the same absorbing interest in the shaping of the lives of the children or pleasure in their company as she, who was daily with watchful solicitude guarding, guiding and helping in each stage of their development. Nevertheless, as the letters show, he was always ready to help her in any dilemma and liked to hear all the details of their doings. There are some letters covering a time when his wife was away with her sister and he was left in charge of the five, who ranged at the time from the ages of one to ten. His reports of minor ailments, medicines, conversations and squabbles are entertaining in their conscientious exactness.

He was not in the least jealous of the children because of the attention they received from their mother. But undoubtedly they were sometimes an interruption in the longed-for and too brief intervals when at last he could be at home and see her, talk with her, consult her, confide in her and enjoy to the full her delightful company. The children were not conspicuous for their docility and most of them had inherited the argumentative powers of their parents. As they grew up they developed marked characters without any out-standing talents. Reports of the inability of the sons to pass examinations often occur in the letters. But they managed to pass the last ones and the establishment of the two eldest in the Coldstream and Grenadier Guards and the youngest in the Diplomatic Service undoubtedly gave their father pleasure. Henry Ponsonby was a very undemonstrative man. He avoided enthusiasm and not with all his children was he intimately sympathetic or companionable. When things went wrong he met the trouble not with open admoni-tions or reprimands but with morose silences. It must be remembered that he could never shake off completely the burden of his work like men who may lock the door of their office. " I am what is facetiously termed on leave and enjoying myself. But they telegraph to me every hour and I have no Assistant Secretary to unravel their conundrums ", he writes to Spencer Ponsonby-Fane. This could not fail to preoccupy his thoughts and to cloud his attention.

Nevertheless the enjoyment of domestic family life, perhaps just because it was broken and constantly interrupted, was his greatest pleasure. Not the banquet, not the Queen's dinner, not the Household dinner, not the country house dinner, but the dinner at home with just the family round the table he infinitely preferred. He was not loquacious himself but while seemingly inattentive to much of the children's talk, punctuated as it was with special words and expressions invented by his daughters, he would quietly use the very words afterwards as if they were part of the English language. He would smile at the recital of events and a story or the imitation of someone by one of them might make his face redden and the tears flow. His wife would glance at him knowing he was perfectly happy. The children much preferred having their parents present to being left to themselves. So when, as frequently happened at Windsor, sometimes at almost the last moment, the announce-ment was made " Papa and Mama are dining with the Queen," there was a chorus of protest expressed with great volubility

XVI *Home and End*

by the children and sympathetically shared by the parents. When they returned the children insisted on an account of all that happened. This was apt to go on late till their father put an end to it by saying " I think we had better go and lie down for ten minutes."

The attitude of the Ponsonby family towards the royal family appears in reminiscent retrospect to have been perfectly natural but from the circumstances of their position rather special. The children took their cue from their parents. The Queen stood apart ; seldom did they hear much criticism of her. She was kind to children but otherwise rather formidable. She bore no resemblance whatever to any other lady they knew. As they began to learn history they realized her special position and fitted her in to the sequence of monarchs, but they were never taught that awe or worship were necessary sentiments in regarding her. The rest of the royal family, some of whom were more or less intimately known, were judged by ordinary standards. More often than not the gossip and intrigues emanating from this quarter seemed rather to blight the atmosphere and obscure the radiance which might be expected to surround the crown. With ridicule and exasperation they condemned the prevalent if not universal attitude of regarding royalty down to the offshoots of the lower ranks as something sacrosanct to be venerated, flattered and pursued. The charge of having " royal-culte " was an expression of their sharpest criticism. They came to understand that their parents' method of treating Imperial Highnesses, Royal Highnesses, Serene Highnesses and even just Highnesses as ordinary human beings was calculated to draw from these exalted personages their best and most natural side.

Henry Ponsonby was not a countryman nor a sportsman, although as a young man he hunted and shot. But the routine pursuits of a country gentleman had never been open to him. All his life he lived in a more or less official atmosphere from the time of his childhood in the Governor's palace at Malta. Military life from Sandhurst when he was in his teens, up through his army promotions, service for so many years at the Viceregal Lodge in Dublin, the Crimean War, possible openings of a career as a soldier, then the Court as an Equerry and ultimately his twenty-five years as Private Secretary to the Queen, all contributed to give him as his close environment, both actual and personal, the orderly room, the barrack square, offices, castles and palaces, with fellow officers, members of the royal Household, high officials and ministers of the crown to consort with as colleagues and friends. Yet anyone less official, less aware and less inclined to make others aware of the importance of the high position he reached could not well be imagined.

He rode of course and taught his children to ride. The long walks he took away from home, not seldom alone, were not opportunities for contemplation or introspective reflection but usually with the object of climbing a mountain, seeing a house or inspecting a monument. When the children at home rather dreaded a dull constitutional, without warning he would go to the station and take tickets for some out-of-the-way place where they had fun in a " pothouse tea " with hard-boiled eggs. In his brief holiday time he liked very much going up to London on the excuse often of going to exhibitions. Indeed he loved London but he was seldom there during his Private Secretaryship except for a day or two. In a letter to Horace Seymour in 1889 he says : " Don't preach to me of London being pleasant. I know it is. It is the best place to be in from Jan. 1 to Dec. 31."

Expeditions with the family sometimes reached further afield and a log-book was kept to which everyone contributed drawings of scenery or events during the trip. A series of these little books still exists with charming sketches by Mary Ponsonby, amusing rapidly-drawn illustrations of adventures by himself and childish drawings by the children. It might be a short expedition, as when in 1881 he went off to Land's End with his eldest daughter Alberta, it might be an expedition abroad, and there is one of the whole family visiting Oxford, profusely illustrated. Following on the interest aroused by this visit the sons put their books all together at the top of the stairs at Norman Tower and instituted a lending library called the Bodeleum. Their father drew, painted and framed a portrait of " the learned Bodley ". A gallery of portraits of celebrities was arranged on the wall and a museum was attached to the institution. A quill pen broken in rage was the pen used by King John in signing Magna Charta. Queen Mary's heart was of red sealing-wax with " Calais " written on it in ink, a damp mark on a blank sheet represented the kiss Hardy gave Nelson,

1869. Mrs P. refuses to attend the established Church at Belfast

1881. Penzance. The chess players appeal to Alberta

and there were other exhibits of the same type. A decoration connected with the Bodeleum was instituted — a brass medal manufactured by their mother (with crimson ribbon) to be worn on certain occasions. However negligent Henry Ponsonby may have been about his official decorations, he never failed to wear this punctually and solemnly at dinner.

The Ponsonby talent for acting was inherited by all the children and their father would sometimes take a part in charades and plays. There were many family games, such as drawing portraits which had to be guessed, and sales where the children produced articles for sale, any defect having to be declared — " a box but the bottom is missing ", etc. If one of the Ponsonby aunts were present, she would join in with the inimitable family solemnity. Melita Ponsonby (Aunt Lily), always gorgeously arrayed in silks with an amethyst necklace, as if making a bold bid for a Rembrandt in a sale-room would call out " Fippence " (*i.e.* 5d.) for " a clock which has no works ".

One can gather in occasional references in the letters his attitude towards his children. The birth of the eldest child, christened Alberta Victoria (generally called by him Alberta although known by the rest of the family and by friends as Betty [1]), was naturally an excitement. When her parents went to Canada she had to be left behind in charge of her grandmother Lady Elizabeth Bulteel. There are references to her development, her lessons, and little details such as her writing a letter to her mother with another inside signed " Your affectionate granddaughter Cecilia " which was her doll. But as time passed the relations of father and daughter became much more formal.

There is a consecutive series of letters in 1886 recording several visits in Scotland when his eldest daughter alone accompanied him. After a day's sightseeing in Edinburgh they paid a visit to Lord Rosebery at Dalmeny. In political talks Rosebery, while ready to discuss questions of the day, was unwilling to intervene personally in politics. Betty found him very entertaining and was amused by his telling her that his favourite verse in the Psalms was : " To bind their kings in chains and their nobles with links of iron ". From Dalmeny they went to the Glen where in addition to Sir Charles Tennant

[1] Mrs. Montgomery.

and many of his family were Dick Grosvenor, Reggie Lister, Herbert Gladstone and others. In his letter he expresses admiration for Margot Tennant :

> She in a short black habit with yellow boots, throwing off her coat had a striped jersey — all her hair loose — and galloping at the hurdles, jumped them beautifully over and over again. . . . Miss Margot is all over the place ; drives to the station with some of them before breakfast, picks up the postman and gives him a lift on his way home, draws, sings, plays, dances and wants to be doing something all day long.

He walked with her one day and :

> She asked me whether I thought Gladstone had a heart. I said yes. She clapped her hands and said : " I am so glad you think so — I am sure of it " ; and proceeded to recount how sympathetic he had been about the death of her sister Laura (Mrs. Alfred Lyttelton) ; and she ended " When he spoke to me tears came into his eyes. Now tears must come from the heart, (a pause) unless of course you've got a cold ", and she went off in peals of laughter to some other subject.

Lady Oxford in a recollection of this visit writes :

> I adored him, so did we all. No Queen, Kaiser or King had such a wise, witty and faithful adviser as Sir Henry Ponsonby. I remember my husband saying to me that one of his sorrows (when we went out of office) was that he would no longer hear from Queen Victoria's Secretary. When we sat on the heather at the Glen before we were joined by the shooters we circled round him like plovers and drank in *all* that he could tell us of Balmoral and his other experiences.

The Queen kept her eye on her Private Secretary's movements, although he was on a holiday, and commented on his going only to Gladstonian houses. Wemyss Castle and Gosford completed their round of visits.

Alberta's marriage in 1891 to Colonel William Montgomery of Grey Abbey, Co. Down, an officer in the Scots Guards, her father highly approved of, not only because Montgomery was a Guardsman but because in character and disposition he had the quiet, unobtrusive, gentlemanlike qualities Ponsonby himself possessed and sympathized with. Her regard for Sir Henry Ponsonby made the Queen take the very exceptional step of coming in person to the wedding in the Guards Chapel at Wellington Barracks.

The following year Betty took her mother's place at the Queen's dinner. She has been able to give her vivid recollection of the occasion :

> It was on August 15th, 1892, — a year after I married. I was staying alone at Osborne Cottage, and as my mother wasn't well, I went with my father to dinner with the Queen at Osborne House, wearing my white satin wedding gown.
>
> It proved to be a most interesting, almost historical occasion. It was the day Mr. Gladstone had returned to office as Prime Minister, resolved to bring in his Home Rule Bill. We all waited in the drawing-room till, at 8.30, she swept in. He was most obviously nervous, fumbling over his stick. Not so, the Queen. She hated having to receive him again as the Premier, but with the utmost " *savoir faire* " and " *grâce d'état* " she walked in, shook hands, and added with a smile : " You and I, Mr. Gladstone, are lamer than we used to be ! " Then we all followed her into the dining-room. The Prince and Princess of Wales were also present that night, and other royalties.
>
> I sat next to Mr. Gladstone and he talked to me loudly and eagerly all the time, though guests usually spoke in hushed tones at the Queen's table. Somehow we mentioned Swift at the beginning of dinner and he broke out into " *saeva indignatio* ", worthy of Swift himself, at the iniquity of the " Wood's Halfpence " tax, " all for the King's *Mistress*, the Duchess of Kendal ", he declared angrily. I glanced nervously at the Queen's piercing eye, but she said nothing. He went on openly to a glorification of the policy he advocated for Ireland. I looked at the lovely Belfast linen tablecloth, in which were woven the Rose, Thistle and Shamrock, with the motto " *Quis separabit ?* " just in front of us.
>
> I quite forget who our other two dinner-neighbours were, but they had not much chance of conversation that night. After dinner, the Queen came straight up to me and asked : " What did Mr. Gladstone talk to you about ? " " Home Rule, ma'am ! " She shrugged her shoulders and said : " I know ! . . . he always will ! "

Maggie, his second daughter, also invariably referred to by her full name Magdalen or by an abbreviation of his own, " Mags ", was a special favourite. He delighted in her company and there are frequent messages to her and references, more especially during a visit she paid when he was at Balmoral.

It was a case of the undefinable sympathy which parents feel more for some of their children than for others. Mary Ponsonby was rather exceptional in this respect because she was able to make each child feel that she or he was specially favoured. This was not from any deliberate effort to be fair but from an extraordinarily penetrating capacity to understand the varying points of view of each and to enter into them.

His eldest son John was also, as the letters show, a great favourite. In addition to his father's concern about various examinations he deplores the loss of his companionship when Johnny (as he was called in the family), on entering the Army, was called out to his military duties in Egypt. Johnny took an early interest in public affairs and read the newspapers. His comments and clear-cut opinions were matters of interest and diversion to his father. In a letter dated December 16, 1887, Henry Ponsonby gives an amusing description of his son's argumentative methods :

When I got home to Norman Tower I found Johnny in evening dress, being operated on by Price the corn cutter, Gregson holding the lamp to expedite matters as he was late and Johnny in an excited theological argument with Price, whose feelings it appears he had ruffled by supposing that Plymouth Brethren were the same as the Salvation Army. When I arrived Johnny had reached the practical part of his argument : " Do you cut the corns of the Plymouth Brethren for nothing ? " Price replied that he respected the Elders of his Church. Johnny who always pins his adversary down persisted " Do you cut the corns of your elders for nothing ? " " I am only well acquainted with the elders of the Ealing Connection." " Very well — then do you cut the corns of the elders of the Ealing Connection for nothing ? " This went on and I gathered that there were only two Elders at Ealing who were sufferers but I had to send Johnny off because I wanted Price, who was so exhausted with polemics that he polished me off quickly — and I went to dine with the Queen.

Except for school reports and examinations the two younger sons, Fritz and Arthur, are not often mentioned in the correspondence. Sir Henry was naturally gratified when the elder was appointed in 1891 an Equerry to the Queen after serving as A.D.C. to Lord Elgin in India. The youngest of the family (Arthur) is mentioned when he was five years old. In a letter to Lady Emily on politics Henry Ponsonby says that party spirit will run high and divisions in families may be expected, and he adds : " One such has burst forth in mine. My four eldest children are Whigs. My youngest has announced himself a Tory. I scarcely know how he picked up the word." Arthur was a page of honour to the Queen for five years from 1882.

Ponsonby as already shown did not regard personal religion as a matter for open discussion. He favoured tolerance for all creeds and even lack of creed. He himself went to church regularly. But neither he nor his wife imposed any special religious training on their children at home. When Archbishop Benson who was staying at Norman Tower asked him on the Saturday night at what time family prayers would be on Sunday morning, he must have been slightly embarrassed at having to tell him that no such function would take place. But in church-going there was for the family an interesting variety of opportunities to meet all tastes. At St. George's Chapel at Windsor, where they had friends at the Deanery and among the canons, there was perfect music under the direction of Sir George Elvey and subsequently Sir Walter Parratt. Some of them were occasionally taken by their father to the Domestic chapel within the Castle where there was a clerk who left out his aitches. The Queen was present in the gallery up to which the children were forbidden to look (an injunction which was invariably disobeyed). The preacher, dressed in a Geneva gown, after going up a hidden staircase found himself in the pulpit on a level with the Queen, whose unflagging attention was more often accompanied by a look of disapproval than of appreciation. A mile or so from Windsor, Clewer Church, presided over by the prominent Tractarian Mr. T. T. Carter, provided interesting forms of ritualism. At Osborne there was Whippingham Church, of which Mr. Prothero was vicar. So far as sermons were concerned it was Mr. R. W. Burnaby at East Cowes Parish Church, near Osborne, who by his intellectual discourses attracted the Ponsonby family and furnished them more than any other preacher with food for entertainment and hot dispute.

These passing glimpses into his occasional relaxations and his more intimate family life are introduced to show that the Queen's Private Secretary was not a dry official who regarded

family affairs as trivialities of no consequence as compared with
his important work, but a very human and domestic man who
found special pleasure in the home from which he was constantly separated.

The impression of Henry Ponsonby received by a comparative
stranger may be quoted from an appreciative and discriminating description of him by Arthur C. Benson,[1] at the time a
master at Eton :

> Sir Henry Ponsonby I had met already ; and of him I
> would say that I have always remembered him as being,
> without any exception, the most perfectly and beautifully
> courteous man I have ever seen, so unembarrassed, so
> resourceful, so entirely natural that for a time one hardly
> realised what a triumph of art, in a sense, his manner was,
> how singularly trained, adjusted, and applied to bring
> about the complete ease and security of any circle in which
> he found himself. He was a tall man, as I remember him,
> with a pointed beard, and with a slight stoop, dressed almost
> negligently, but with a quiet self-effacement and appropri-
> ateness that challenged neither attention nor comment.
> His greeting was cordial and reassuring, his talk easy and
> simple, but always with a personal cognisance of his com-
> panion. He listened respectfully and with a genuine interest,
> very flattering to a young and inexperienced man ; and he
> had an ingratiating smile, with a low and appreciative laugh.
> He seemed to me the man of all others formed, both by
> nature and long use, to deprive of its natural terrors and
> awkwardnesses the access of a respectful subject to a much
> reverenced and awe-inspiring sovereign.

To this may be added the comment on him by a colleague and
close friend, the assistant Private Secretary, Colonel Arthur
Bigge (afterwards Lord Stamfordham), who served under him
for fifteen years :

> The longer I live and the more I look back, the more
> remarkable man he seems to me. One of, if not the greatest
> gentlemen I have known : the entire effacement of *self* :
> the absolute non-existence of conceit, side or pose : the
> charming courtesy to strangers old, young, high, low, rich,
> poor. His extraordinary wit and sense of the ridiculous, his
> enormous powers of work — too much — it killed him, but
> I never heard him say he was hard-worked or had too much
> to do, nor did I ever hear him say " Oh, don't bother !

---

[1] *Memories and Friends*, by A. C. Benson.

Come back in five minutes ; I am writing an important
letter to the Queen or Prime Minister or Archbishop of
Canterbury, Cardinal Manning, Mrs. Langtry, etc." The
letter was put down and he listened patiently and considered
whether the Crown Equerry or the Equerry-in-Waiting
should ride on the right of the Queen or whether next
Sunday's preacher should refer to this or that.

So far as knowledge of men was concerned it was with
Henry Ponsonby instinctive rather than critical or analytical.
With his inveterate hatred of humbug whether in writing or
in speech he was never taken in by a charlatan. He seldom
went far wrong in summing up people's qualities or recording
their defects. He seemed to be aware in his dealings with
them that he had formed an estimate of them at the moment
that he could rely on as being safe and true, and he approached
them in a way to invite a disclosure of their natural feelings
and their best side. There is ample evidence that they felt
with him that they could talk without reserve as he was the
soul of discretion. Whether it were a member of the royal
family, a Minister of the Crown, one of the Household or one of
the domestic servants, their reliance on his fairness made him a
recipient of confidences which would have been withheld
from either a sterner or a more openly ingratiating man. He
was neither the strict official nor the over-affable friend. But
he was never aloof. " Don't knock, come in ", which he had
painted on the door of his room, was more than an injunction —
it was his motto.

The entire absence of conceit, mentioned by Lord Stamfordham, and his inability to obtrude himself did not mean that
from laziness or lassitude he let things slide. While he was
aware of his limitations, he was quietly conscious of his capacity
and indeed power within the self-imposed limits and he made
the most of it although he never asserted himself in order to
attract notice. He was not frightened of the Queen. But
early he definitely decided on the best method of handling her.
Had he taken the opposite course of " standing up to her ",
unquestionably some elevated shelf outside the Court would
have been found for him. It certainly required conscientious
industry and decision not to succumb to the enervating atmosphere of the mid-Victorian Court. The turmoil, controversy
and competition of military or political life would be stimulat-

ing and energetic action needed. As it was, study, preparation and careful choice of opportunity were his weapons and patience and imperturbability his shield.

He never spoke about his health. But there are occasional references to his feeling tired as his years were drawing to a close. As late as January 1894 however, in a letter to Spencer Ponsonby-Fane, he wrote in his most jocose vein : " I hear there are paragraphs about you and me in *The World* — that you are all right which I am glad to learn and that I am 69 and causing great anxiety by my health. I immediately sent to enquire after myself and the answer was Never was better." The Queen however was beginning to notice the change in his manner and in his handwriting.[1]

On the morning of January 6, 1895, just one year later, at Osborne Cottage before his day's work began he was seized by a paralytic stroke and fell. The serious nature of the illness was at once realized, depriving him as it did of his powers of speech.

Randall Davidson, then Bishop of Rochester, wrote at once direct to the Queen :

Edinburgh, 8 January, 1895

Madam,

I venture, with my humble duty, to convey to Your Majesty an assurance of the loyal and profound sympathy which, in company with thousands of others today, I feel for Your Majesty, on this sudden illness of Sir Henry Ponsonby, of which the newspapers inform us. I trust the newspaper report may be an exaggerated one, and that the illness may be less severe than the account would lead one to suppose, but in any case I know how much anxiety must be caused to Your Majesty by the illness of so close and trusted a friend and servant. No Sovereign has ever been more loyally, capably and diligently served than has Your Majesty by Sir Henry Ponsonby, and I trust he may yet be spared for much active work with the same devotion as he has ever shown. Many of us have, of course, for some time been feeling anxious about him, and I know that these anxieties have been shared also by Your Majesty, and that thus the shock of the sudden news of this illness may have been lessened. God grant he may speedily and completely recover, for the sake of those who hold him dear, which indeed means all who have learned to know him. To me,

---

[1] *Letters of Queen Victoria*, 3rd Series, vol. ii, p. 464.

he has ever been the most kindly and helpful of friends,
and I can scarcely tell Your Majesty how deeply I grieve to
think of him as lying ill. Your Majesty will, I trust, graciously
pardon this letter, which is due merely to my earnest desire
that Your Majesty should know our appreciation and care
for the anxiety which must at such a time be pressing on
Your Majesty. . . .
    I have the honour to be,
      Your Majesty's obedient humble servant,
                    RANDALL T. ROFFEN

A few days later Lady Ponsonby received the following letter :

From *Mr. Gladstone*

                  Château de Thorenc, Cannes
                        Jan. 14, 1895

MY DEAR LADY PONSONBY,
    I must perforce have written to you sooner but for
my unwillingness in your great trial to make such an addition
to your cares even as the perusal of these few lines. But I
really feel so much that I cannot be quite silent, feeling as I
do quite assured that — unless indeed all your anxieties
have already given place to a bright recovery — you will
believe in the request I make that you will on no account
dream of acknowledging this letter.
    I ask myself why I write, the answer is not because you
would doubt our deep and lively interest in your husband.
No one could have known him so long as I and seen him
continually and for such long periods together in each
passage of life and business, without being compelled to
feel and care about him. No, it is simply that I cannot
help again recording the impression that all along he has
made upon me. How easy to make a long catalogue of his
qualities, his unrivalled tact, his wise reserve, which never
degenerated into stiff and artificial caution, his admirable
judgment, his unsparing loyal self-devotion, most remarkable
in this of all other points that it all appeared to be totally
unconscious, one might have supposed him to be possessed
of some kind of sinecure.
    But of course I cannot say that the sad news of the illness
was in any way a surprise. I may almost say that for a
long time, I had waited almost from day to day for the news
that oppressed nature had at last rebelled. It will indeed
be a joy to me and I am sure to all who knew him if that
rebellion in securing relief for the future shall be found to
have secured it in such time as to appropriate to him a serene

and bright autumn of life, and to you and his family a larger share of united domestic life. In the meantime I can only wish for you, for him and for you all that Almighty God may minister abundantly to all your needs. Certainly, so far as human relations are concerned, I can hardly conceive a case where the retrospect of noble and unselfish living could contribute a larger share of consolation. God be with you all now and for evermore.

The Queen will be a profound sympathiser and though she has been and will doubtless continue to be most wise and happy in choosing her servants, can hardly hope not to be when *his* service ends, a heavy loser.

Believe me and my wife to be in strong sympathy,

Sincerely yours,

W. E. GLADSTONE

Mercifully the protracted interval of ten months before the end was not accompanied by any distressing or painful symptoms. There were moments even of alleviation from discomfort. The devoted and watchful care of his wife, day in day out, helped by his daughter Magdalen, seemed to be noticed by glances of recognition.

He died on Nobember 21, 1895, within three weeks of his seventieth birthday. The formal Court Circular announcement need not be quoted. But the Queen's letter to Mary Ponsonby on the day may be given :

Windsor Castle, November 21, 1895

DEAREST MARY,

It is very difficult for me to find words to express how deeply grieved I am at the sad termination of dear Sir Henry's long & trying tho' I think & believe painless illness. Prepared to a great extent as we were lately — one never is really prepared & the blow is not the less severe when it comes. You have been the most devoted of wives & have nursed him with the most touching & unremitting love & care, & this must be satisfaction to you & I fear however that now that the strain is over the blank will be terrible & I can only pray that you & dear unselfish devoted Maggie may be supported in the loss of dear kind Sir Henry, who was so universally beloved by all, high & low — is very great. He was always so kind & so fair & just that I miss him terribly — his memory will ever be gratefully remembered by me & mine.

It is a comfort to have one of his sons with me & keep

up a tie with you & your children. Begging you to say
everything kind to your children,
      Believe me always,
                              Yours very aff^{ly},
                                          V. R. I.

The funeral with full military honours took place at Whippingham Church near Osborne, all his family being present. The
Duke of Connaught represented the Queen, and Count von
Eulenstein represented the Emperor William. There were
officers from the various units quartered at Portsmouth and
bluejackets from the royal yacht. A contingent of Grenadiers
from the 1st Battalion he had once commanded bore the coffin
from the gun-carriage into the church.

It would be impossible to enumerate or note the letters
and messages of condolence received by Lady Ponsonby from
friends, acquaintances and admirers at home and abroad.
But a notable tribute may be added from a book written in
later years by Herbert, Viscount Gladstone, who had access to
all his father's papers.

Extract from *After Thirty Years*, by Viscount Gladstone
(1928) : [1]

Behind the scenes Sir H. Ponsonby worked quietly and
continuously until his death in 1895. Sagacious, of keen
insight, patient, understanding, and with a great range of
knowledge, the Queen possessed in him not only a secretary
but a counsellor of the highest worth. Of this admirable
man Mr. Gladstone had the highest opinion. The Queen's
knowledge of leading politicians was often very slight.
Excepting Disraeli, and of course Lord Melbourne, the
formalism of her manner in personal relations kept her
ministers at a distance. Granville tried hard to get through
it, but after 1880 he completely failed. Ponsonby had a
close, often an intimate, knowledge of all these men. He
knew the political currents and the bearings of the questions
of the day as well as anybody. He was a mine of information. Courteously impartial, he held the confidence of all
politicians, Liberal or Conservative. In discretion he never
failed : he was intensely loyal to the Queen. . . .

When the career even of a prominent public man comes to
its close, it is telescoped up with some finality and a short

[1] Part III, chap. i, pp. 349-351.

general verdict is pronounced on his achievements. There the matter ends. After an interval, often brief in these days, some biographer may step in and elaborate from collected papers a full story.

In this case the writers of eulogistic paragraphs in the press on Sir Henry Ponsonby's death were obliged to admit that " so very little was known about him " ; and that details describing his work and " the exact position he held must await the pen of a writer in the next generation ".

After an interval of nearly fifty years this has been done from the ample material that has been found. The endeavour may be justified from the very fact that the full light of publicity never shone on the labours of a man who was content to be regarded in his day just as one courtier amongst many.

The temptation to over-praise and stress by exaggeration Henry Ponsonby's work and services, which in the case of a son writing of his father might be natural, it may be hoped has been avoided. By no extravagant eulogy has any claim been made that Queen Victoria's Private Secretary was what is superficially called " a great man ". He had no outstanding or spectacular talents. Whatever his career might have been as a soldier — and we get some idea of his proficiency when his successor wrote on his retirement from the Guards,[1] " You made us the best battalion in the service " — in all probability as an administrator or as a politician he would not have made any particular mark. There is no record of his ever having made a public speech. Discriminating service rather than creative initiative was the line he cultivated to a degree of unsurpassed excellence. Some men rise, court popular applause and establish their position by judicious blasts from their own trumpet, others insinuate by discreetly indiscreet hints the important influence they exercise behind the scenes. As already said, Ponsonby had not got a trumpet, and the idea of hinting that he had done anything of consequence never entered his head. His silences seemed to denote ignorance, indeed they were intended to do so. When a settlement was reached or a ticklish corner rounded, he often was not to be found. Little did he care for being given credit or receiving recognition, except perhaps by a word of commendation from the Queen herself which he valued but which was imparted to

[1] See p. 313.

no one but his wife. His governing characteristic should not
be described as modesty, which is generally self-conscious and
sometimes not quite sincere. But considering the temptations
of his position, natural self-effacement can never have reached
such a high level.

A soldier who could never join in the activities of a profession he infinitely preferred but could only watch from afar
— a domestic man who could be so little at home — an ardently
devoted husband whose separation from his wife can be
measured by the thousands of letters — a father who snatched
only occasional views of his children as they grew up — Henry
Ponsonby worked day in day out to fit himself for a post for
which there were no rules or set regulations. His one object
was not only to serve but to guard, protect, guide and when
possible to encourage or console his sovereign, who partly from
circumstances but chiefly from her specially original personality
had created for herself one of the strangest positions any monarch
has held.

Incessant toil became a habit. He was in the highest sense
of the word a Servant, a servant of tested reliability and perfect
integrity who in a position he himself had created worked
unremittingly with loyalty, faithfulness and sagacity, accommodating himself to men of sharply divergent opinions.
Ever watchful, he never spared himself ; and as the years
advanced the burden pressed too heavily on him. That he
was killed by his work, far from being a fancy, was a fact.

HENRY FREDERICK PONSONBY

Born in Corfu	Dec. 10, 1825
In Malta	1826–1836
Educated at Coombe Wood, Kingston, and Sandhurst	1836–1841
Ensign in 49th Regiment	Dec. 27, 1842
Transferred to Grenadier Guards. Lieutenant .	Feb. 16, 1844
Captain .	July 18, 1848
Major .	Oct. 19, 1849
A.D.C. or Private Secretary to a succession of Lords Lieutenant of Ireland : Lord Bessborough, Lord Clarendon, Lord Eglinton, Lord St. Germans and Lord Carlisle . .	1846–1857
Served in Crimean War	1855–1856
Lt.-Colonel .	Aug. 31, 1855
Equerry to Prince Consort	1857
Colonel .	Aug. 2, 1860
Extra Equerry to the Queen on Prince Consort's death	1861
Married Mary Elizabeth Bulteel . . .	April 30, 1861
In Canada with a battalion of Grenadier Guards which was stationed in the colony during the American Civil War	1862–1863
In Command of 1st Battalion of Grenadier Guards	1864–1870
Major-General	March 6, 1872
Appointed Private Secretary to the Queen and retired from the Army . . .	April 8, 1870
Keeper of the Privy Purse	1878
K.C.B. .	1879
P.C. . .	1880
G.C.B. .	1887
Died at Osborne	Nov. 21, 1895

INDEX

THE END

Printed in Great Britain by R. & R. CLARK, LIMITED, *Edinburgh*